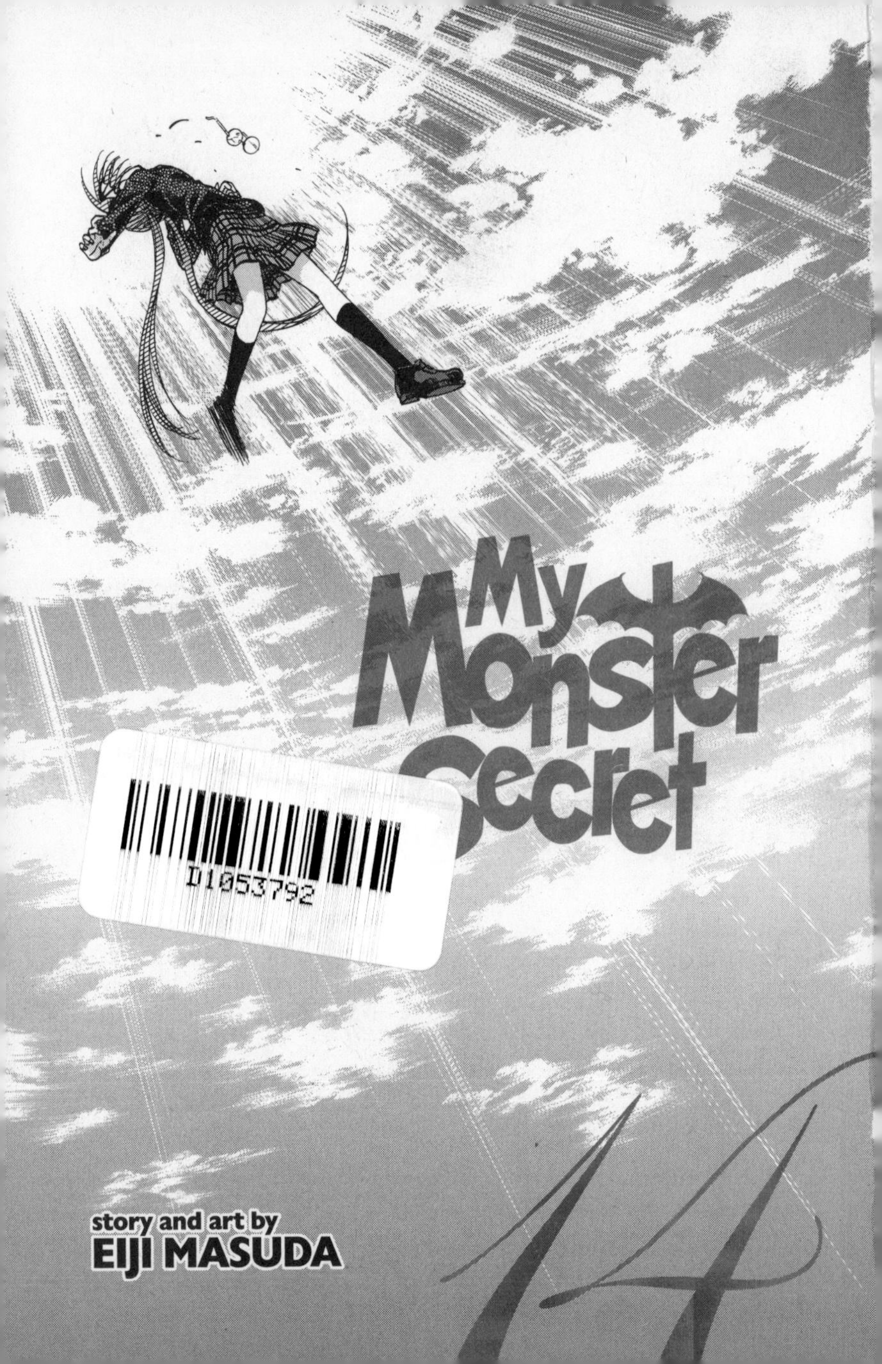
My Monster Secret
14
story and art by
EIJI MASUDA

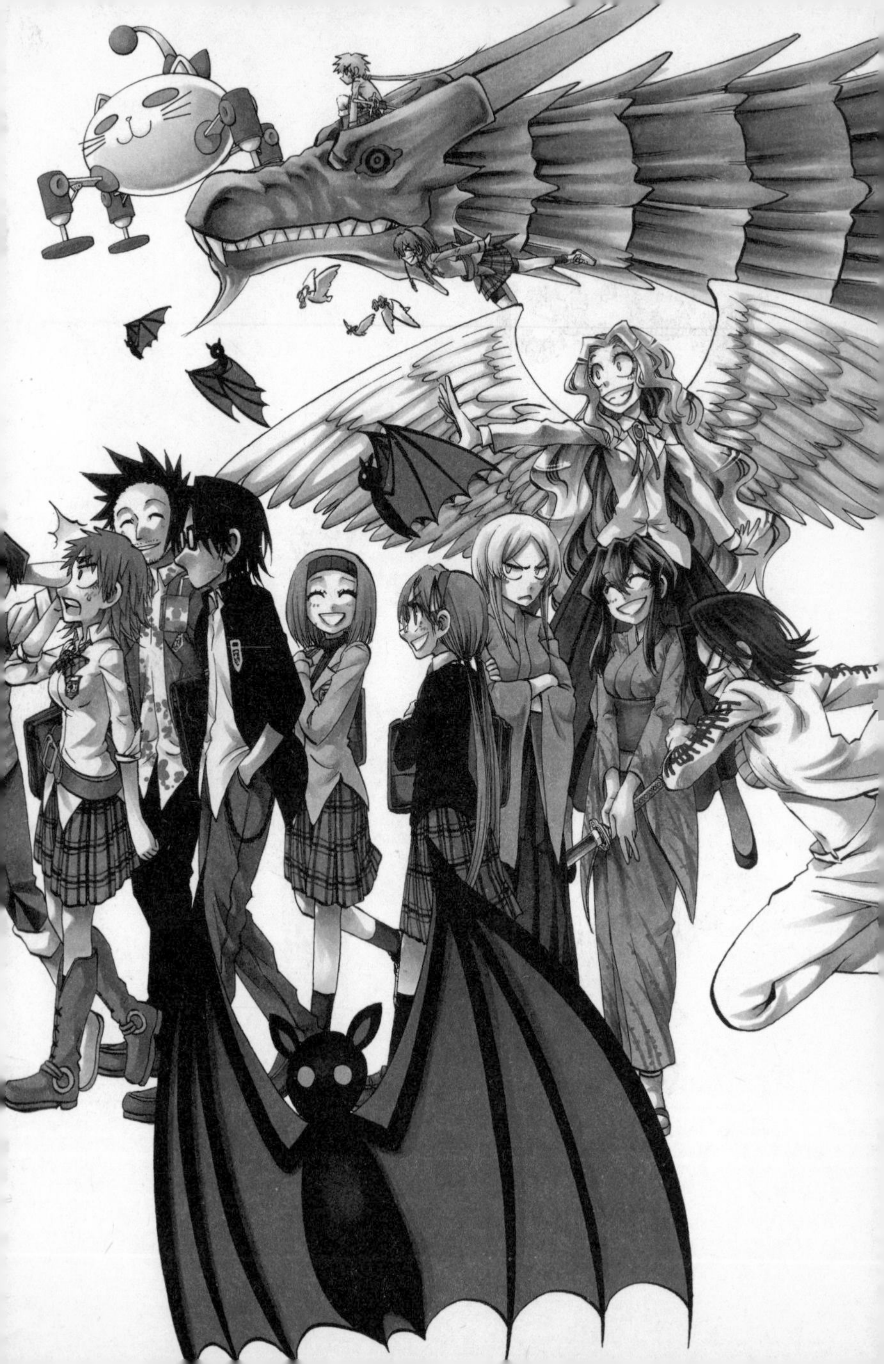

My Monster Secret

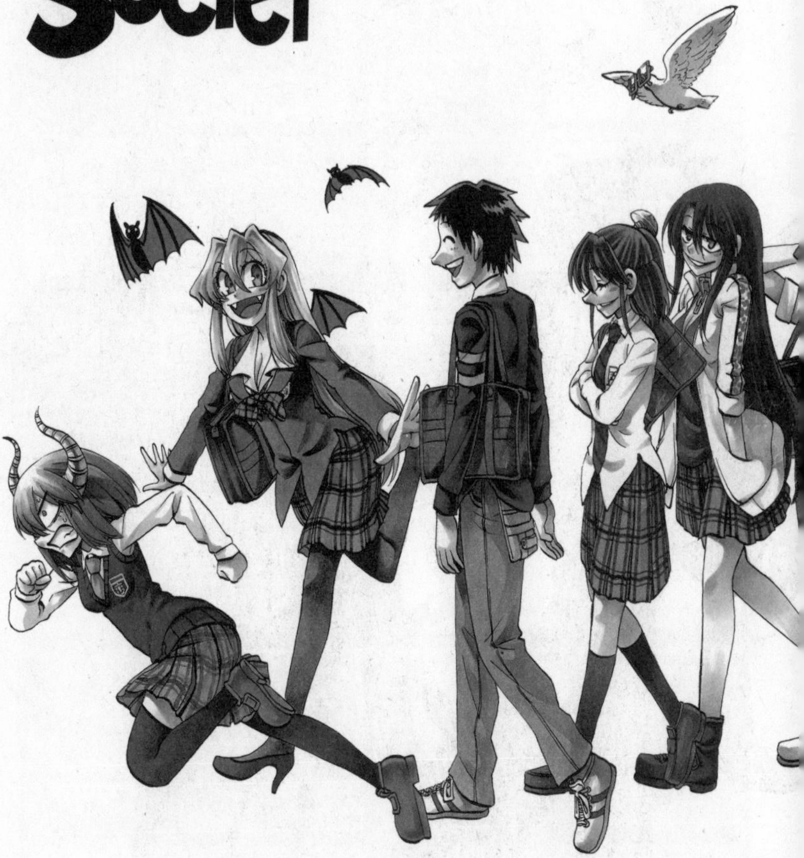

My Monster Secret
"Actually, I am..."

Story & Characters

Kuromine Asahi fell in love with Shiragami Youko, a vampire who will have to quit school if anyone finds out what she really is. They've managed to keep her secret safe, and even started dating...but can Asahi keep Youko's secret long enough to graduate?!

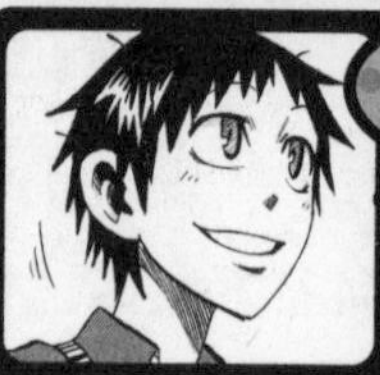

THE HOLEY SIEVE

KUROMINE ASAHI

The man with the worst poker face in the world, he's known as ***The Sieve with a Hole in It...*** because secrets slide right out of him. Now he has to hide the fact that Shiragami-san--the girl he's in love with--is a vampire.

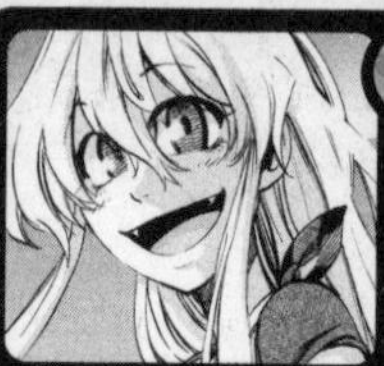

ACTUALLY A VAMPIRE

SHIRAGAMI YOUKO

She's attending a human high school under the condition that she'll ***stop going immediately*** if her true identity is discovered. Asahi found out (whoops), but she believes him when he says he'll keep her secret, and the two are now dating.

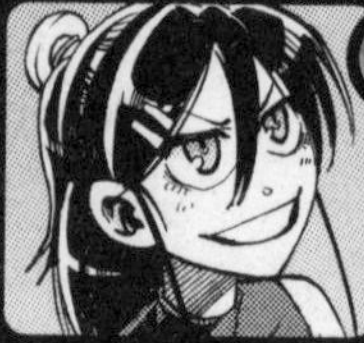

ACTUALLY AN ALIEN

AIZAWA NAGISA

Currently investigating Earth as a class representative, she once mercilessly tore Asahi to shreds before he could confess his love, but she now harbors an unrequited crush on him. Her true (tiny) form emerges from the screw-shaped cockpit on her head. Her brother **Aizawa Ryo** is also staying on Earth.

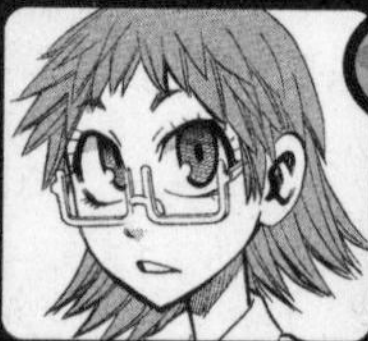

THE QUEEN OF PURE EVIL

AKEMI MIKAN

Editor-in-chief of the school newspaper and a childhood friend of Asahi's. Currently straying from the path of villainy since her favorite pair of glasses became the **Goddess of Fortune, Fuku-chan.**

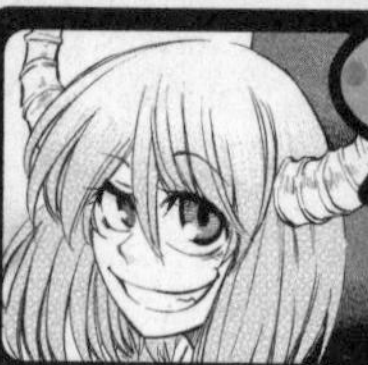

HORNED DEVIL

KOUMOTO AKANE

The principal of Asahi's high school looks adorable, but she's actually a **millennia-old devil.** The great-great-grandmother of Asahi's homeroom teacher, Koumoto-sensei. Her true weakness is junk food.

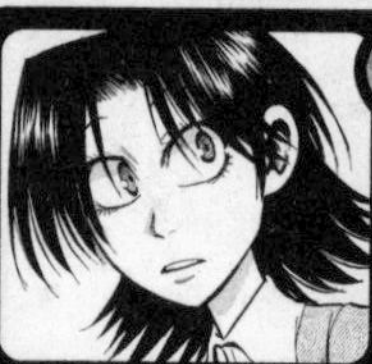

FORMER GANGSTER

KOUMOTO AKARI

The teacher in charge of Asahi's class. Although she's a descendant of Principal Akane, she has no demon powers of her own. Formerly a gangster, currently single.

ACTUALLY A VAMPIRE

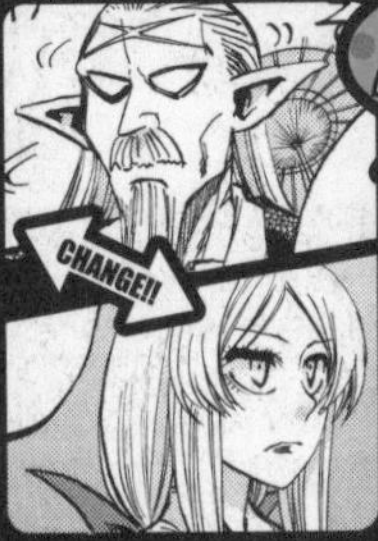
CHANGE!!

SHIRAGAMI GENJIROU ♂

RYOKUENZAKA YUMI ♀

A full-blooded vampire and Shiragami-san's **father.** Worried about Shiragami-san, he has transformed into Ryokuenzaka-sensei and infiltrated the school as the **assistant teacher** of Asahi's class.

ACTUALLY A WOLFMAN

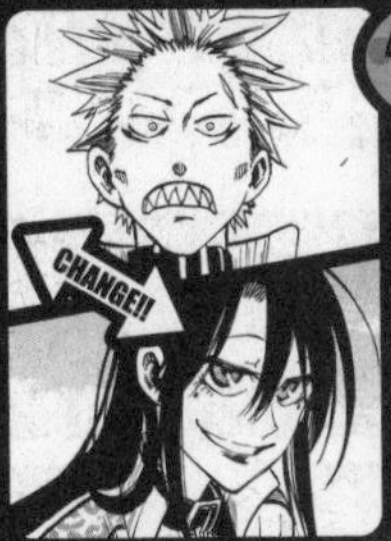
CHANGE!!

SHISHIDO SHIROU ♂

SHISHIDO SHIHO ♀

This childhood friend of Youko's is a nympho. When she sees the moon, she transforms into the wolfman Shishido Shirou (male body and all), and that dude is in love with Youko. Her mother is a nympho icon.

ACTUALLY AN ANGEL

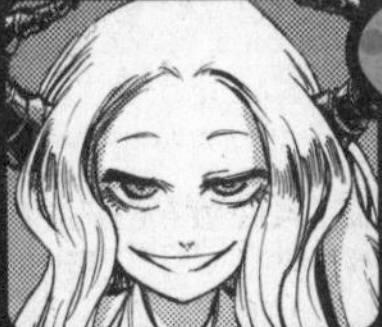

SHIROGANE KAREN

The student council president of Asahi's school. She lost her halo to one of the principal's practical jokes and thus became a (self-proclaimed) **fallen angel.** Was a classmate of Shiragami-san's parents.

ACTUALLY FROM THE FUTURE

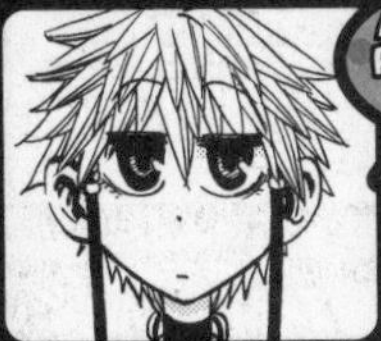

KIRYUIN RIN

Came from fifty years in the future to save the world from the clutches of a nympho tyrant. Now she's a refugee who can't return home because she told Asahi (among others) about the future. Asahi's granddaughter.

ACTUALLY A SUCCUBUS

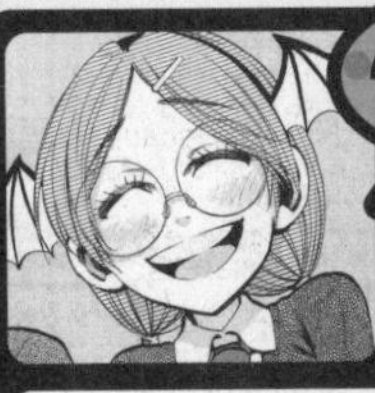

MINAGAWA SAKI

A first-year at Asahi's school. Currently fighting to reclaim the honor of the **succubus clan** from the Nympho Icon who stole it.

ACTUALLY A NINJA

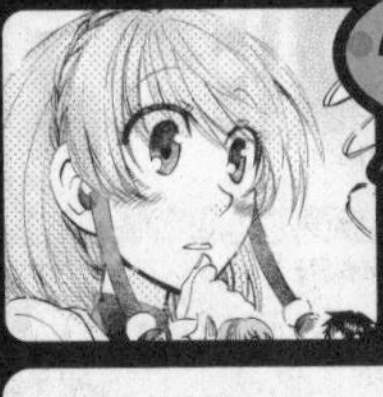

MOMOCHI YUKA

A first-year at Asahi's school. **Falls in love** ridiculously quickly. She seems to know something about the future.....?!

THEM

ASAHI'S WORTHLESS FRIENDS

OKADA

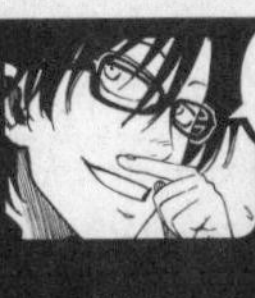

SAKURADA

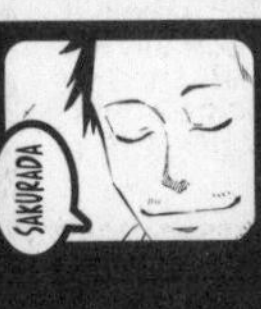

SHIMADA

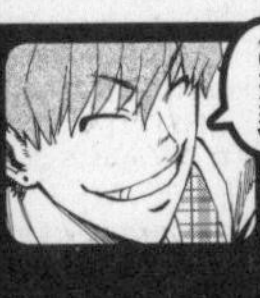

SEVEN SEAS ENTERTAINMENT PRESENTS

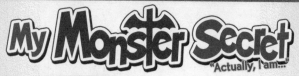

My Monster Secret

"Actually, I am..."

story and art by **Eiji Masuda**

VOLUME 14

TRANSLATION
Alethea and Athena Nibley

ADAPTATION
Rebecca Scoble

LETTERING AND RETOUCH
Annaliese Christman

LOGO DESIGN
Karis Page

COVER DESIGN
Nicky Lim

PROOFREADER
Shanti Whitesides
Danielle King

EDITOR
Jenn Grunigen

PRODUCTION ASSISTANT
CK Russell

PRODUCTION MANAGER
Lissa Pattillo

EDITOR IN CHIEF
Adam Arnold

PUBLISHER
Jason DeAngelis

ISBN: 978-1-626929-71-5

Printed in Canada

First Printing: December 2018

10 9 8 7 6 5 4 3 2 1

FOLLOW US ONLINE: ***www.sevenseasentertainment.com***

READING DIRECTIONS

This book reads from ***right to left***, Japanese style. If this is your first time reading manga, you start reading from the top right panel on each page and take it from there. If you get lost, just follow the numbered diagram here. It may seem backwards at first, but you'll get the hang of it! Have fun!!

1
2
3
4
5
6
7
8
9

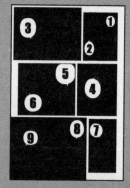

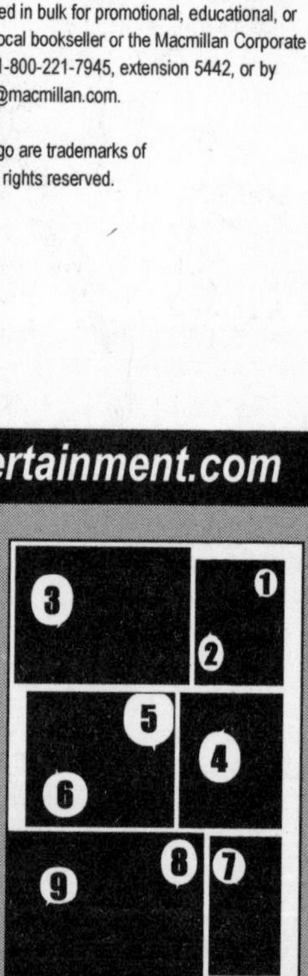

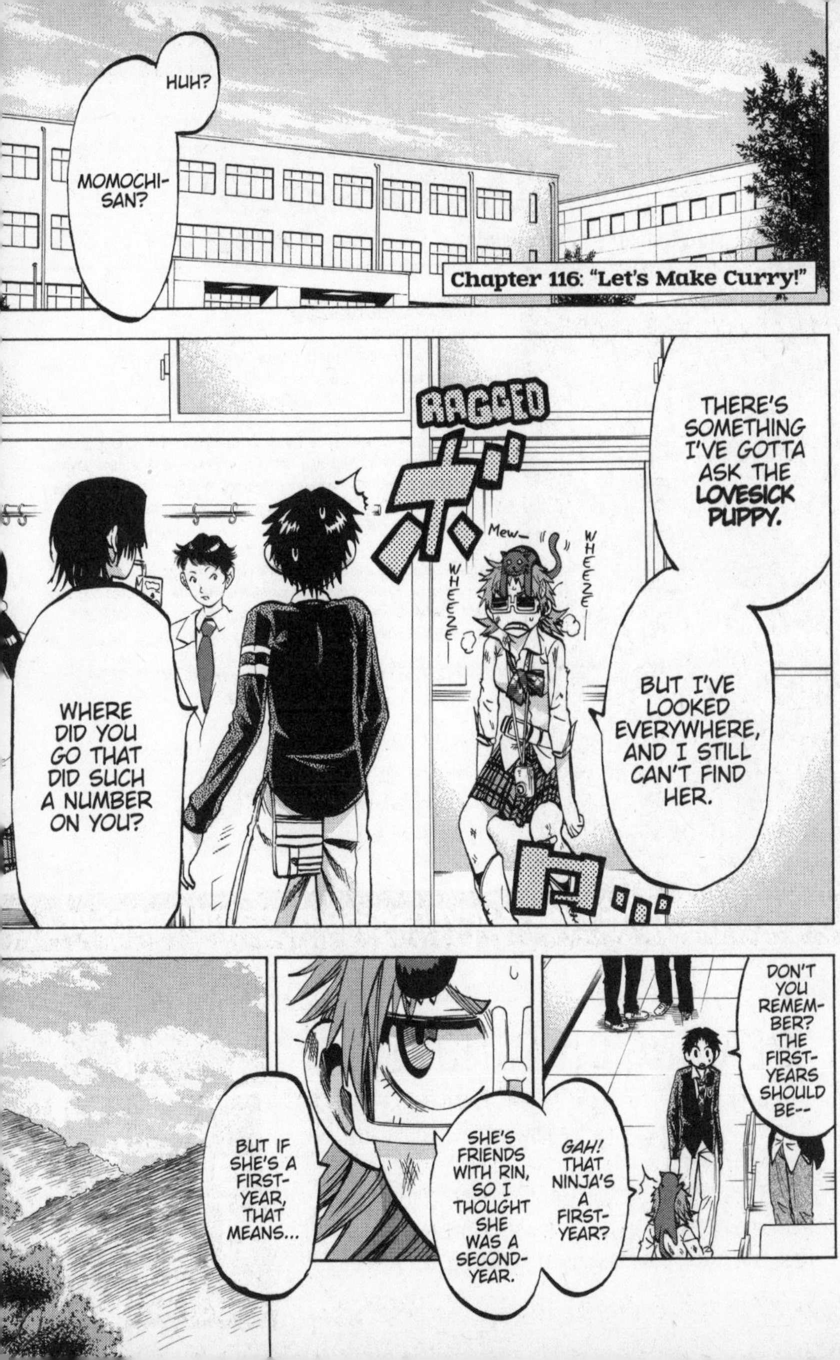
HUH?
MOMOCHI-SAN?
Chapter 116: "Let's Make Curry!"
THERE'S SOMETHING I'VE GOTTA ASK THE LOVESICK PUPPY.
RAGGED
Mew
WHEEZE
WHEEZE
BUT I'VE LOOKED EVERYWHERE, AND I STILL CAN'T FIND HER.
WHERE DID YOU GO THAT DID SUCH A NUMBER ON YOU?
DON'T YOU REMEMBER? THE FIRST-YEARS SHOULD BE--
GAH! THAT NINJA'S A FIRST-YEAR?
SHE'S FRIENDS WITH RIN, SO I THOUGHT SHE WAS A SECOND-YEAR.
BUT IF SHE'S A FIRST-YEAR, THAT MEANS...

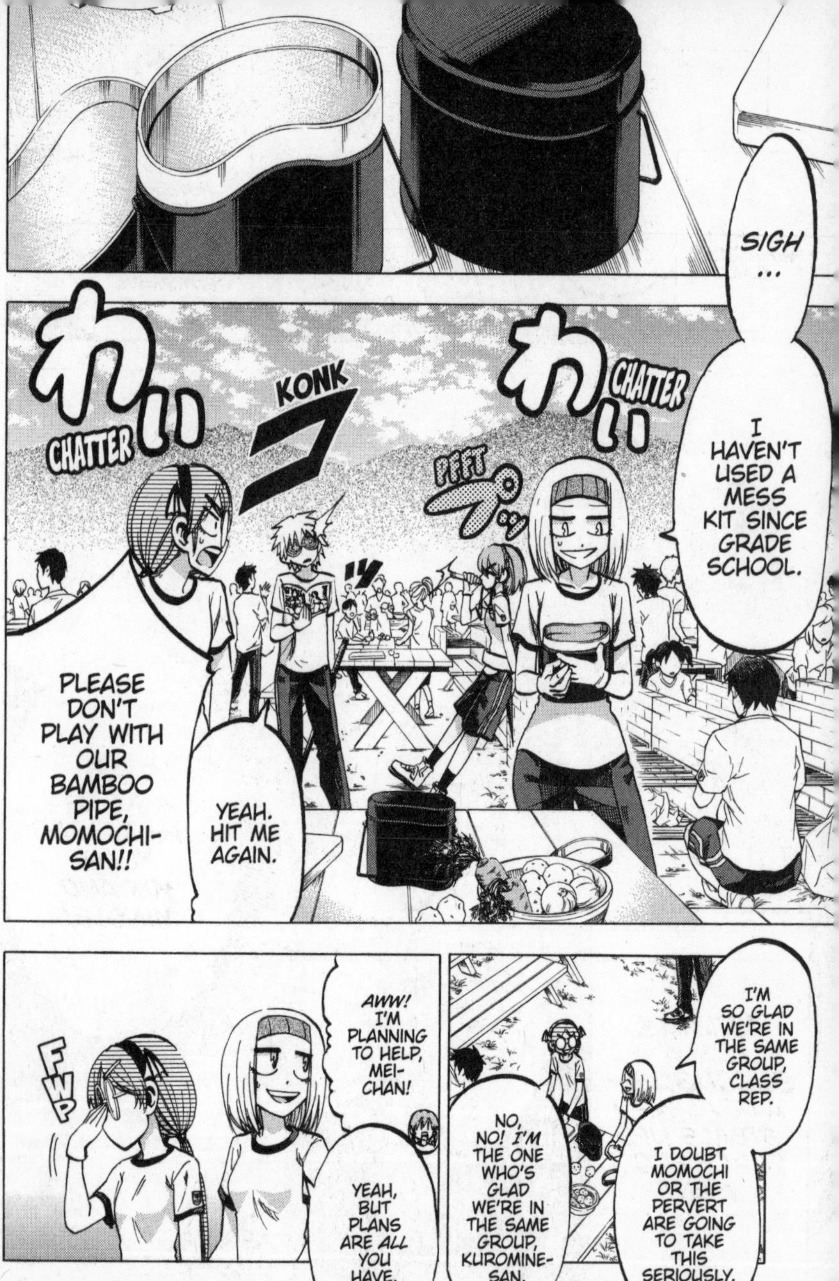
SIGH ...
I HAVEN'T USED A MESS KIT SINCE GRADE SCHOOL.
わい CHATTER
ぷッ PFFT
コ KONK
わい CHATTER
PLEASE DON'T PLAY WITH OUR BAMBOO PIPE, MOMOCHI-SAN!!
YEAH. HIT ME AGAIN.
I'M SO GLAD WE'RE IN THE SAME GROUP, CLASS REP.
NO, NO! I'M THE ONE WHO'S GLAD WE'RE IN THE SAME GROUP, KUROMINE-SAN.
I DOUBT MOMOCHI OR THE PERVERT ARE GOING TO TAKE THIS SERIOUSLY.
AWW! I'M PLANNING TO HELP, MEI-CHAN!
YEAH, BUT PLANS ARE ALL YOU HAVE.
FWP

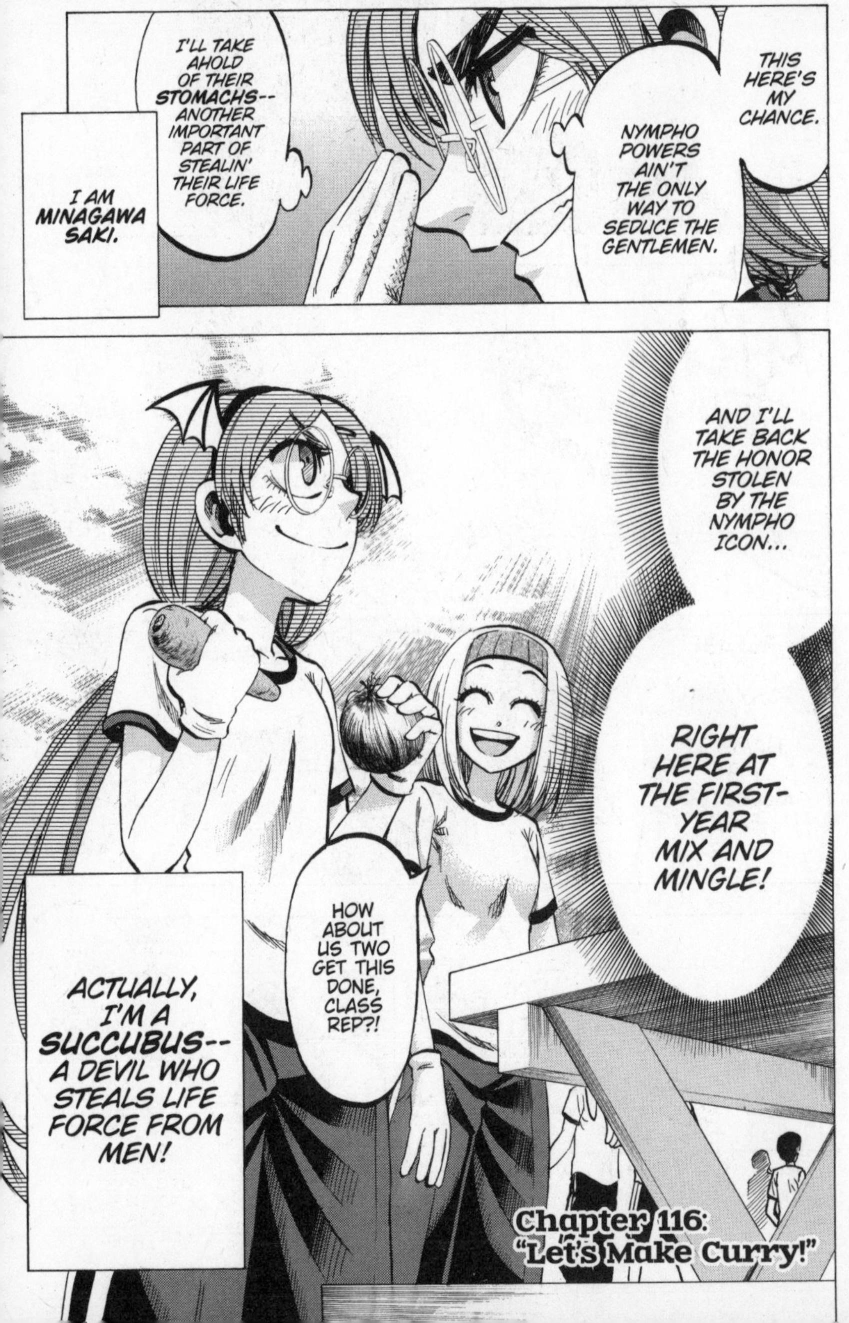
THIS HERE'S MY CHANCE.
NYMPHO POWERS AIN'T THE ONLY WAY TO SEDUCE THE GENTLEMEN.
I'LL TAKE AHOLD OF THEIR STOMACHS-- ANOTHER IMPORTANT PART OF STEALIN' THEIR LIFE FORCE.
I AM MINAGAWA SAKI.
AND I'LL TAKE BACK THE HONOR STOLEN BY THE NYMPHO ICON...
RIGHT HERE AT THE FIRST-YEAR MIX AND MINGLE!
HOW ABOUT US TWO GET THIS DONE, CLASS REP?!
ACTUALLY, I'M A SUCCUBUS-- A DEVIL WHO STEALS LIFE FORCE FROM MEN!
Chapter 116: "Let's Make Curry!"

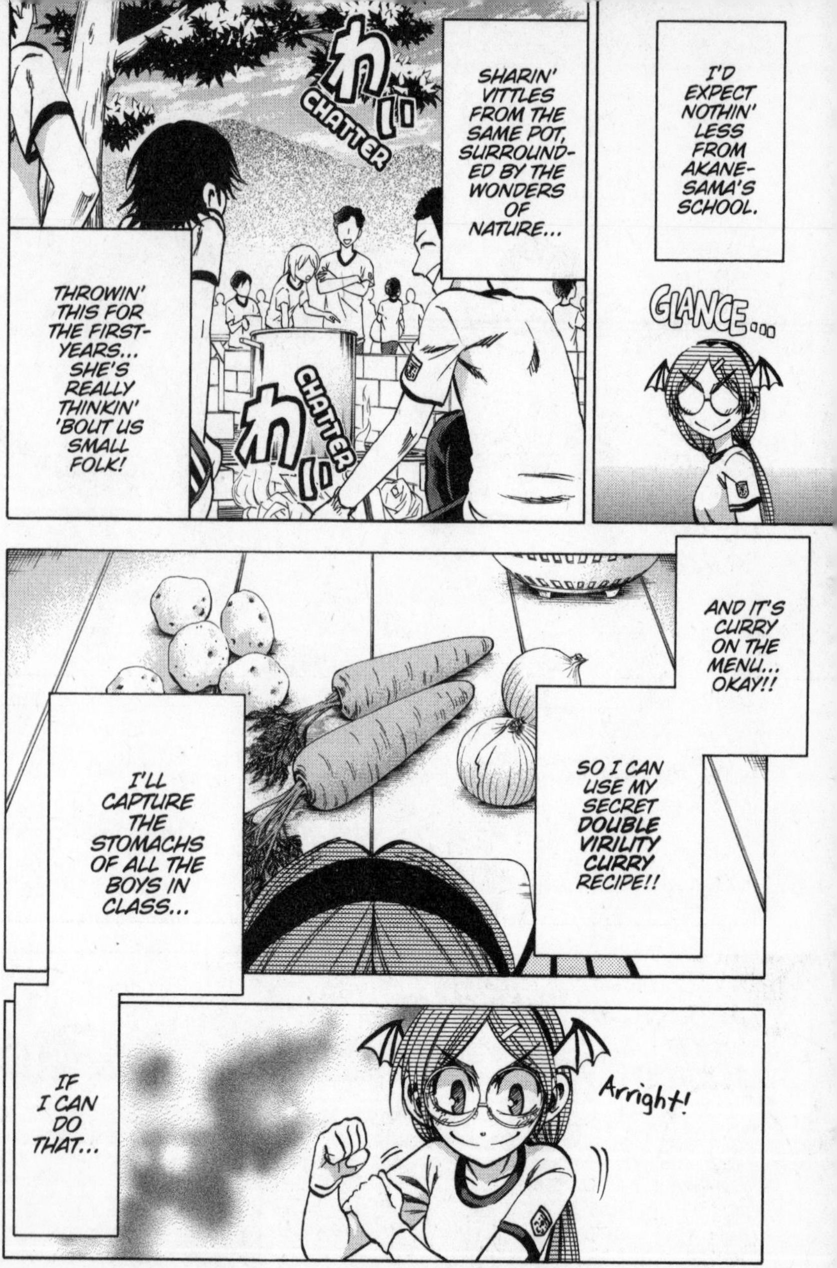

I'D EXPECT NOTHIN' LESS FROM AKANE-SAMA'S SCHOOL.
GLANCE...
SHARIN' VITTLES FROM THE SAME POT, SURROUNDED BY THE WONDERS OF NATURE...
わい
CHATTER
THROWIN' THIS FOR THE FIRST-YEARS... SHE'S REALLY THINKIN' 'BOUT US SMALL FOLK!
わい
CHATTER
AND IT'S CURRY ON THE MENU... OKAY!!
SO I CAN USE MY SECRET DOUBLE VIRILITY CURRY RECIPE!!
I'LL CAPTURE THE STOMACHS OF ALL THE BOYS IN CLASS...
Arright!
IF I CAN DO THAT...

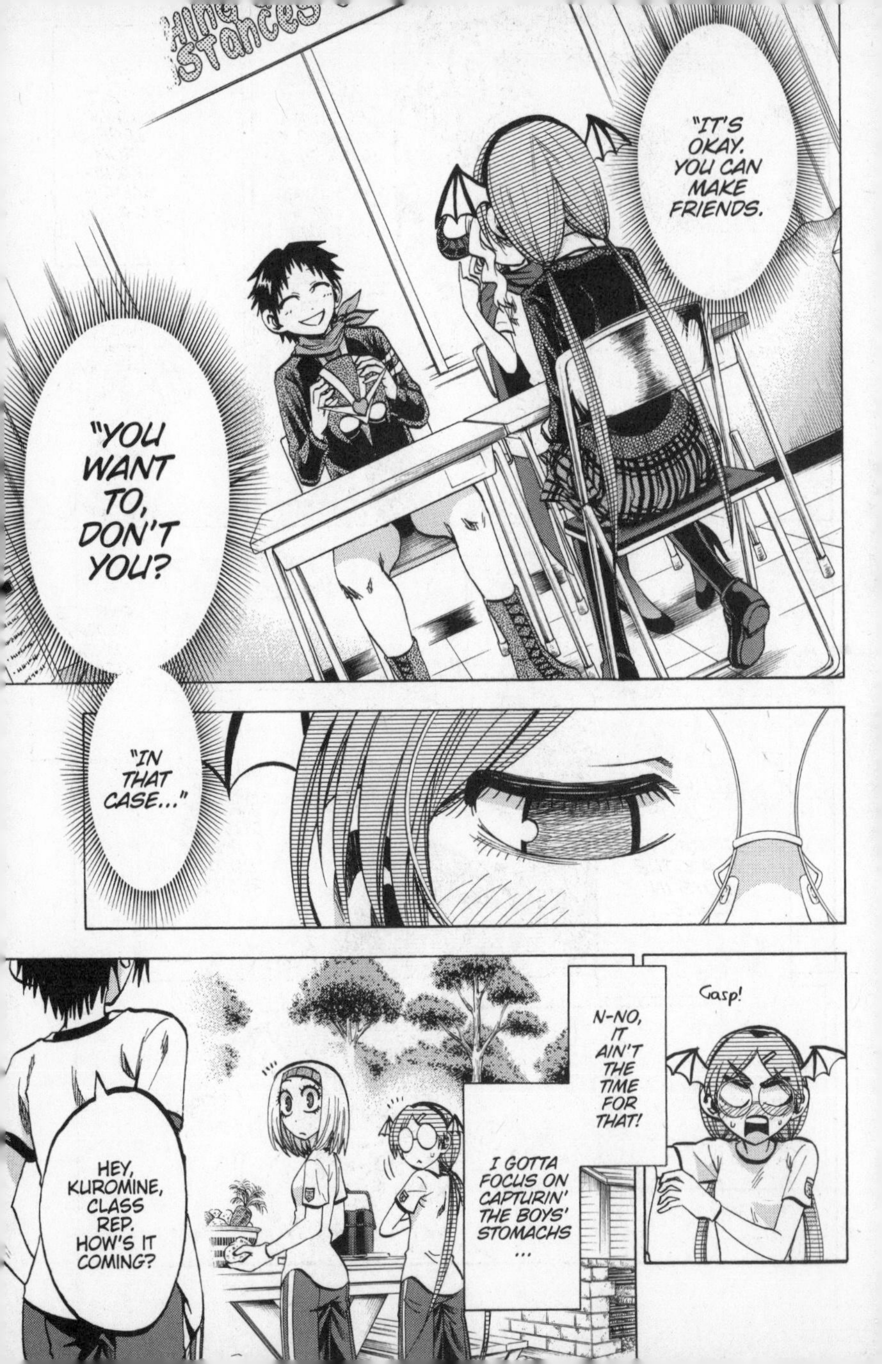
"IT'S OKAY. YOU CAN MAKE FRIENDS.
"YOU WANT TO, DON'T YOU?
"IN THAT CASE..."
Gasp!
N-NO, IT AIN'T THE TIME FOR THAT!
I GOTTA FOCUS ON CAPTURIN' THE BOYS' STOMACHS ...
HEY, KUROMINE, CLASS REP. HOW'S IT COMING?

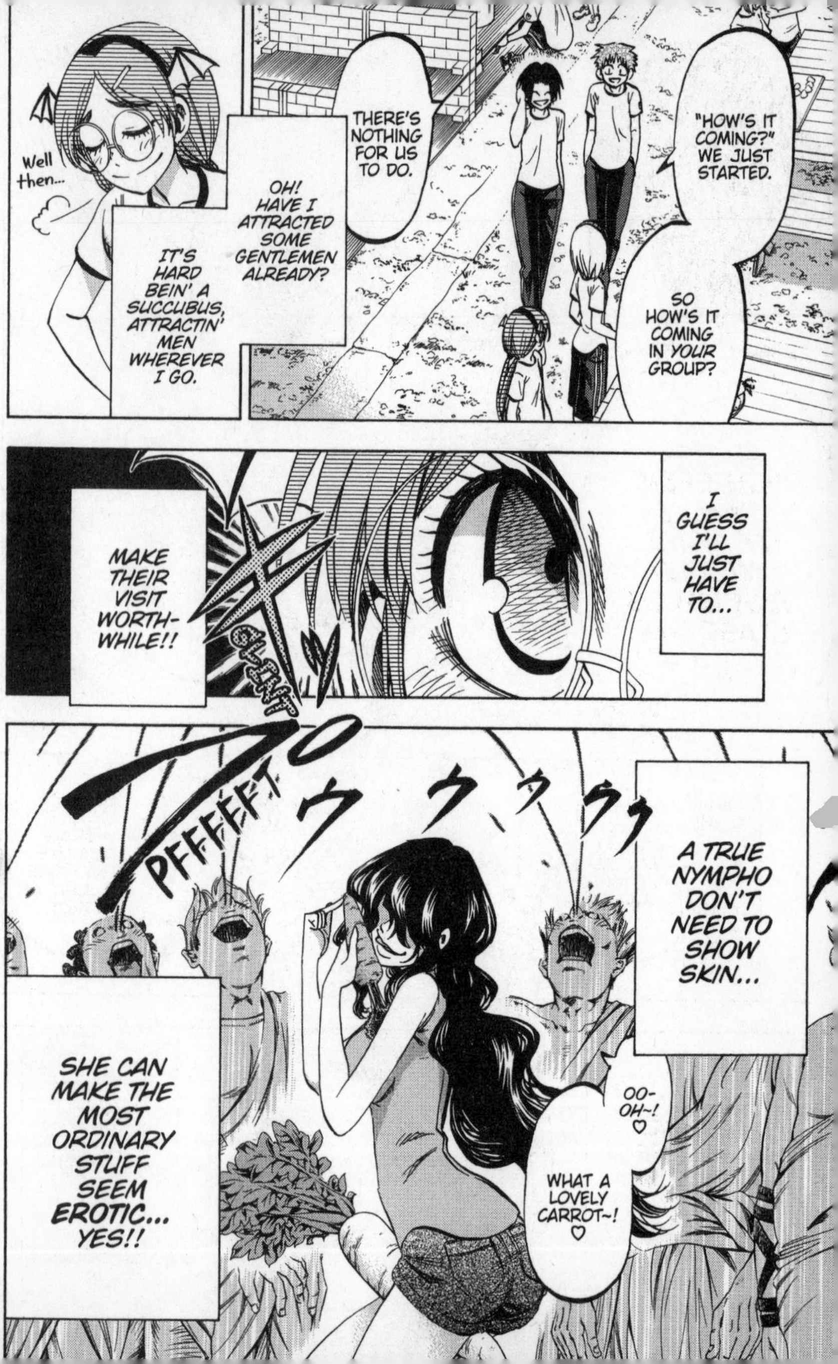
SO HOW'S IT COMING IN YOUR GROUP?
"HOW'S IT COMING?" WE JUST STARTED.
THERE'S NOTHING FOR US TO DO.
OH! HAVE I ATTRACTED SOME GENTLEMEN ALREADY?
Well then...
IT'S HARD BEIN' A SUCCUBUS, ATTRACTIN' MEN WHEREVER I GO.
I GUESS I'LL JUST HAVE TO...
MAKE THEIR VISIT WORTH-WHILE!!
A TRUE NYMPHO DON'T NEED TO SHOW SKIN...
PFFFFFT
OO-OH~! ♡
WHAT A LOVELY CARROT~! ♡
SHE CAN MAKE THE MOST ORDINARY STUFF SEEM EROTIC... YES!!

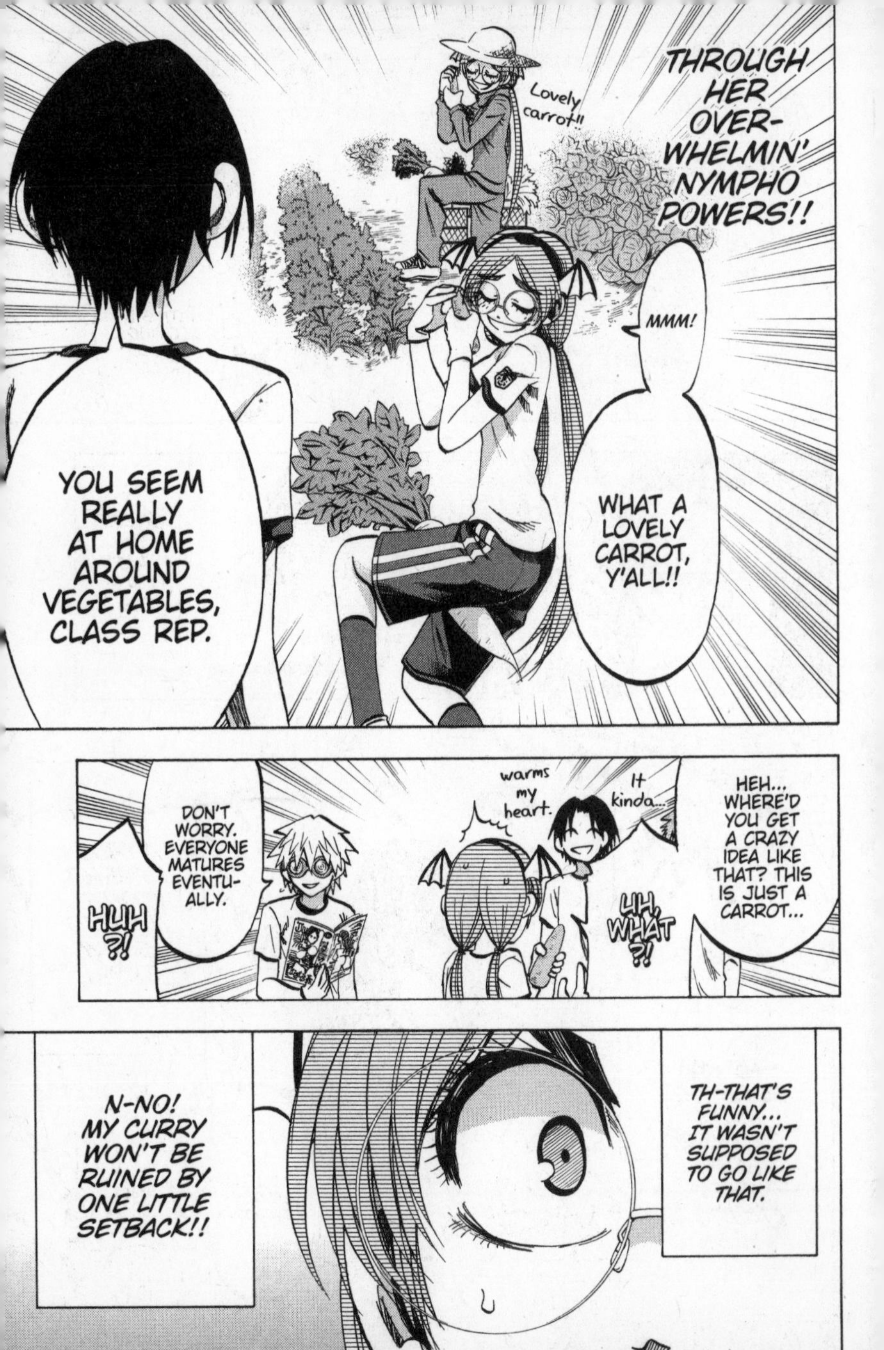
THROUGH HER OVER-WHELMIN' NYMPHO POWERS!!
Lovely carrot!!
MMM!
WHAT A LOVELY CARROT, Y'ALL!!
YOU SEEM REALLY AT HOME AROUND VEGETABLES, CLASS REP.
HEH... WHERE'D YOU GET A CRAZY IDEA LIKE THAT? THIS IS JUST A CARROT...
It kinda...
warms my heart.
UH, WHAT ?!
DON'T WORRY. EVERYONE MATURES EVENTU-ALLY.
HUH ?!
TH-THAT'S FUNNY... IT WASN'T SUPPOSED TO GO LIKE THAT.
N-NO! MY CURRY WON'T BE RUINED BY ONE LITTLE SETBACK!!

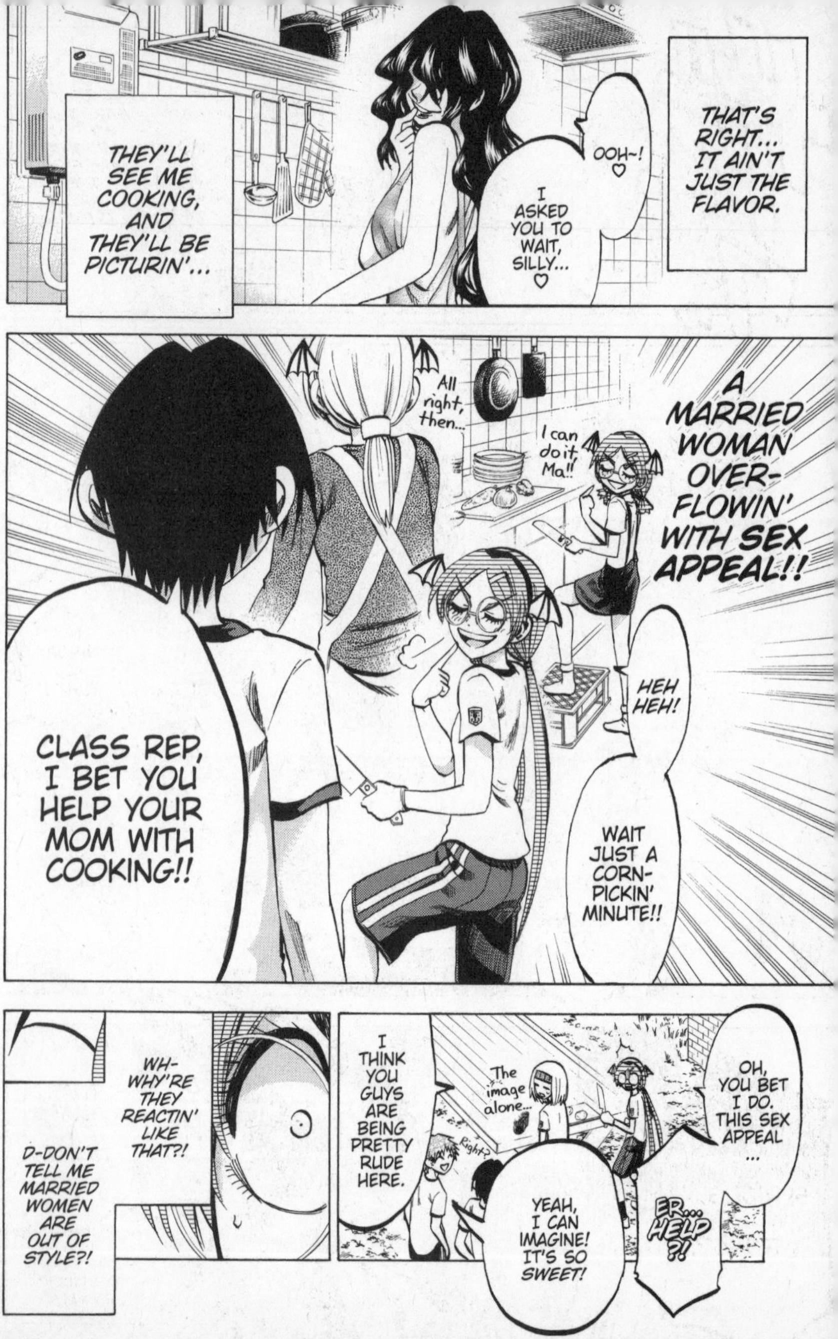
THAT'S RIGHT... IT AIN'T JUST THE FLAVOR.
OOH~! ♡
I ASKED YOU TO WAIT, SILLY... ♡
THEY'LL SEE ME COOKING, AND THEY'LL BE PICTURIN'...
A MARRIED WOMAN OVER-FLOWIN' WITH SEX APPEAL!!
I can do it, Ma!!
All right, then...
HEH HEH!
WAIT JUST A CORN-PICKIN' MINUTE!!
CLASS REP, I BET YOU HELP YOUR MOM WITH COOKING!!
OH, YOU BET I DO. THIS SEX APPEAL ...
The image alone...
Right?
I THINK YOU GUYS ARE BEING PRETTY RUDE HERE.
YEAH, I CAN IMAGINE! IT'S SO SWEET!
ER... HELP?!
WH-WHY'RE THEY REACTIN' LIKE THAT?!
D-DON'T TELL ME MARRIED WOMEN ARE OUT OF STYLE?!

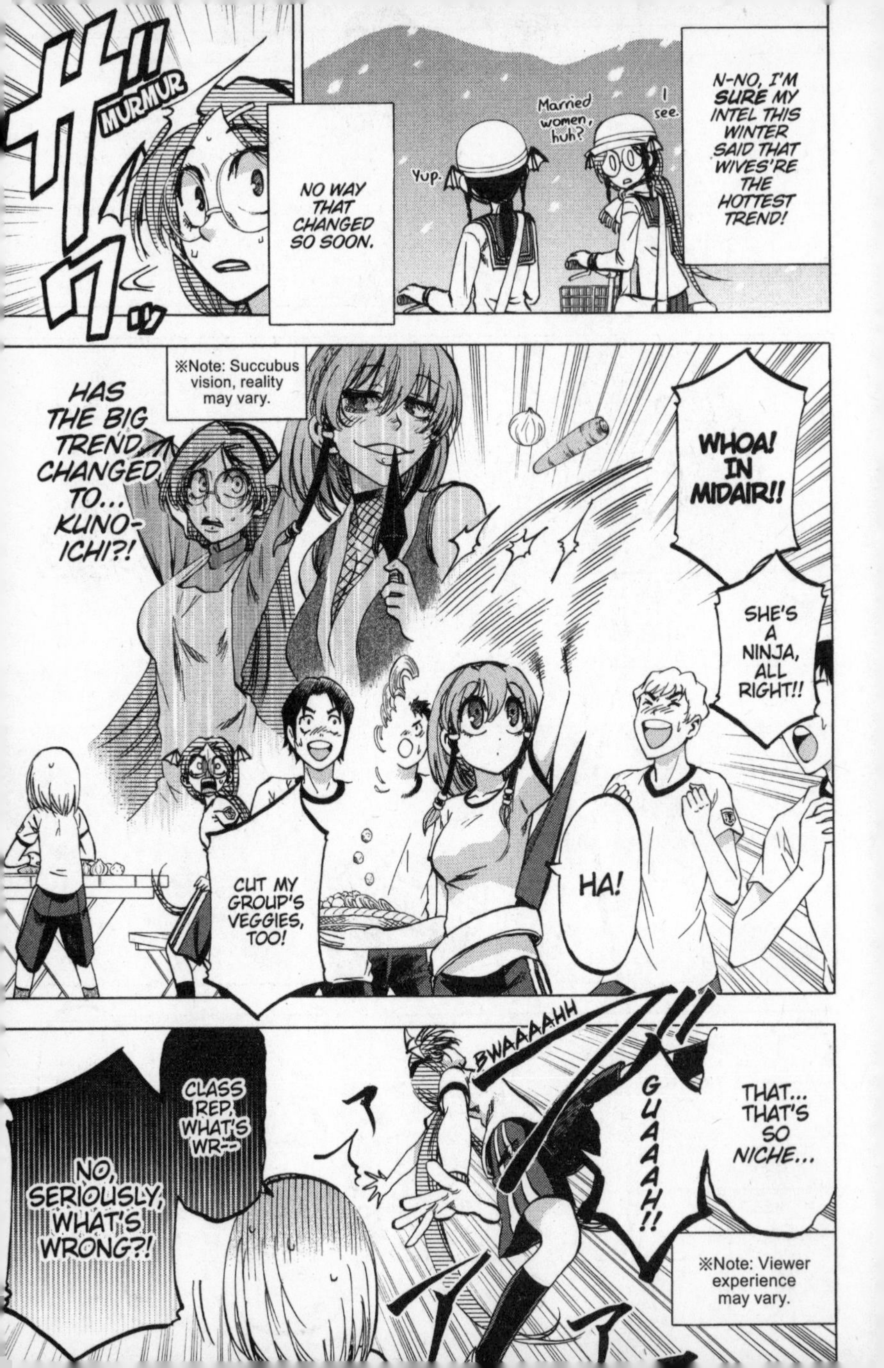
N-NO, I'M SURE MY INTEL THIS WINTER SAID THAT WIVES'RE THE HOTTEST TREND!
I see.
Married women, huh?
Yup.
NO WAY THAT CHANGED SO SOON.
MURMUR
WHOA! IN MIDAIR!!
SHE'S A NINJA, ALL RIGHT!!
HA!
※Note: Succubus vision, reality may vary.
HAS THE BIG TREND CHANGED TO... KUNOICHI?!
CUT MY GROUP'S VEGGIES, TOO!
THAT... THAT'S SO NICHE...
GUAAAAH!!
BWAAAAHH
CLASS REP, WHAT'S WR--
NO, SERIOUSLY, WHAT'S WRONG?!
※Note: Viewer experience may vary.

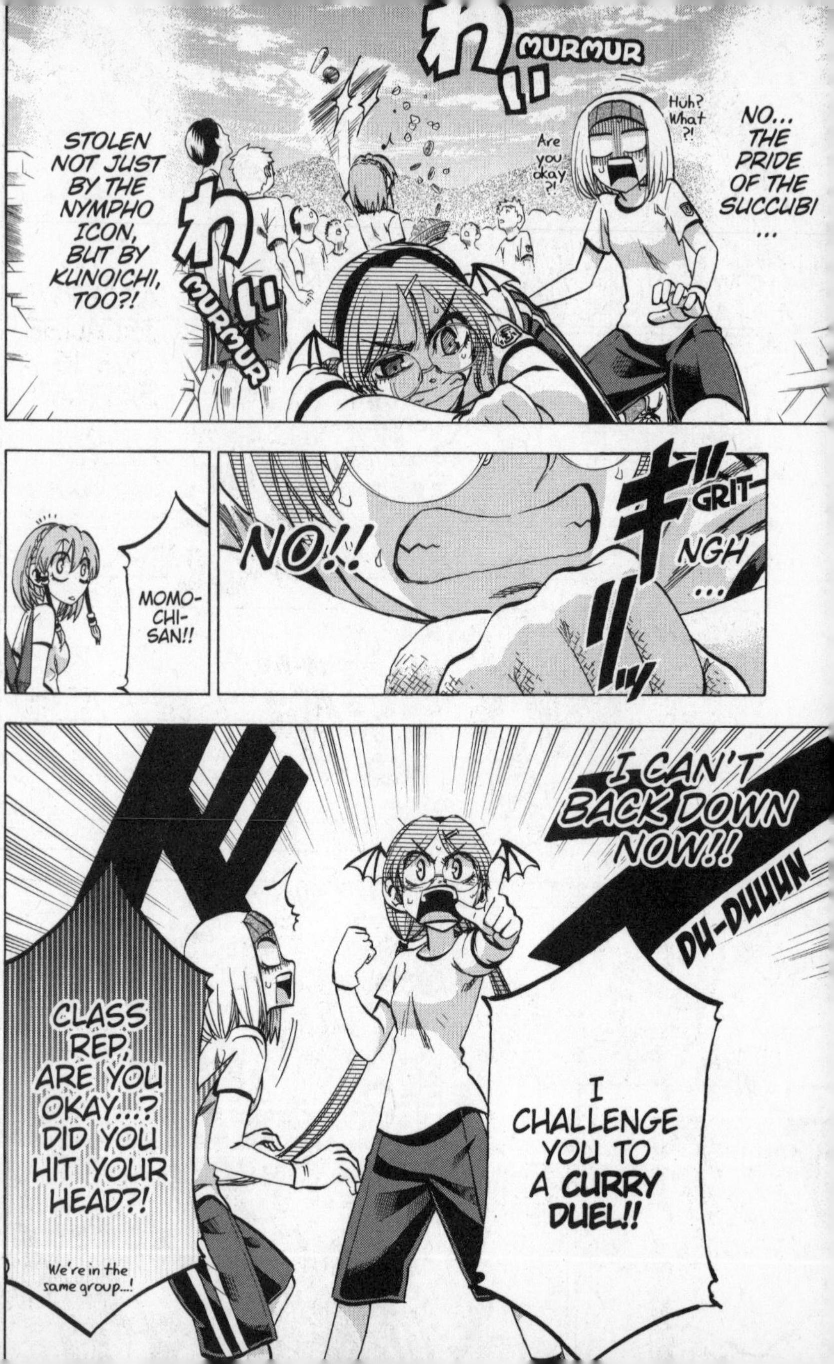

MURMUR
NO... THE PRIDE OF THE SUCCUBI...
Huh? What?!
Are you okay?!
STOLEN NOT JUST BY THE NYMPHO ICON, BUT BY KUNOICHI, TOO?!
MURMUR
GRIT-
NGH...
NO!!
MOMO-CHI-SAN!!
I CAN'T BACK DOWN NOW!!
DU-DUUUN
I CHALLENGE YOU TO A CURRY DUEL!!
CLASS REP, ARE YOU OKAY...? DID YOU HIT YOUR HEAD?!
We're in the same group...!

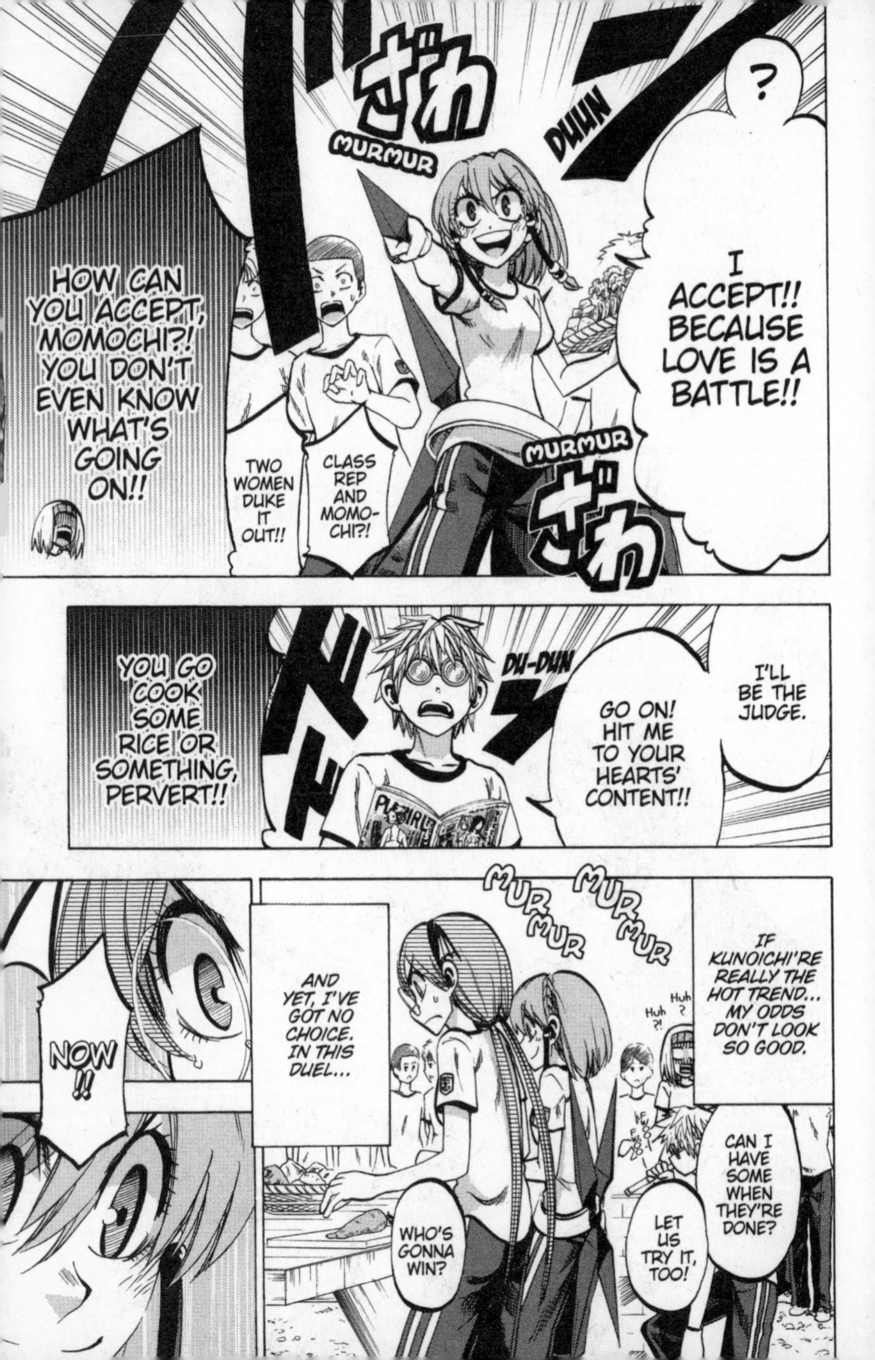
?
DUUN
ざわ
MURMUR
I ACCEPT!! BECAUSE LOVE IS A BATTLE!!
MURMUR
ざわ
CLASS REP AND MOMOCHI?!
TWO WOMEN DUKE IT OUT!!
HOW CAN YOU ACCEPT, MOMOCHI?! YOU DON'T EVEN KNOW WHAT'S GOING ON!!
I'LL BE THE JUDGE.
GO ON! HIT ME TO YOUR HEARTS' CONTENT!!
DU-DUN
YOU GO COOK SOME RICE OR SOMETHING, PERVERT!!
IF KUNOICHI'RE REALLY THE HOT TREND... MY ODDS DON'T LOOK SO GOOD.
Huh ?
Huh ?!
MURMUR
MURMUR
CAN I HAVE SOME WHEN THEY'RE DONE?
LET US TRY IT, TOO!
WHO'S GONNA WIN?
AND YET, I'VE GOT NO CHOICE. IN THIS DUEL...
NOW !!

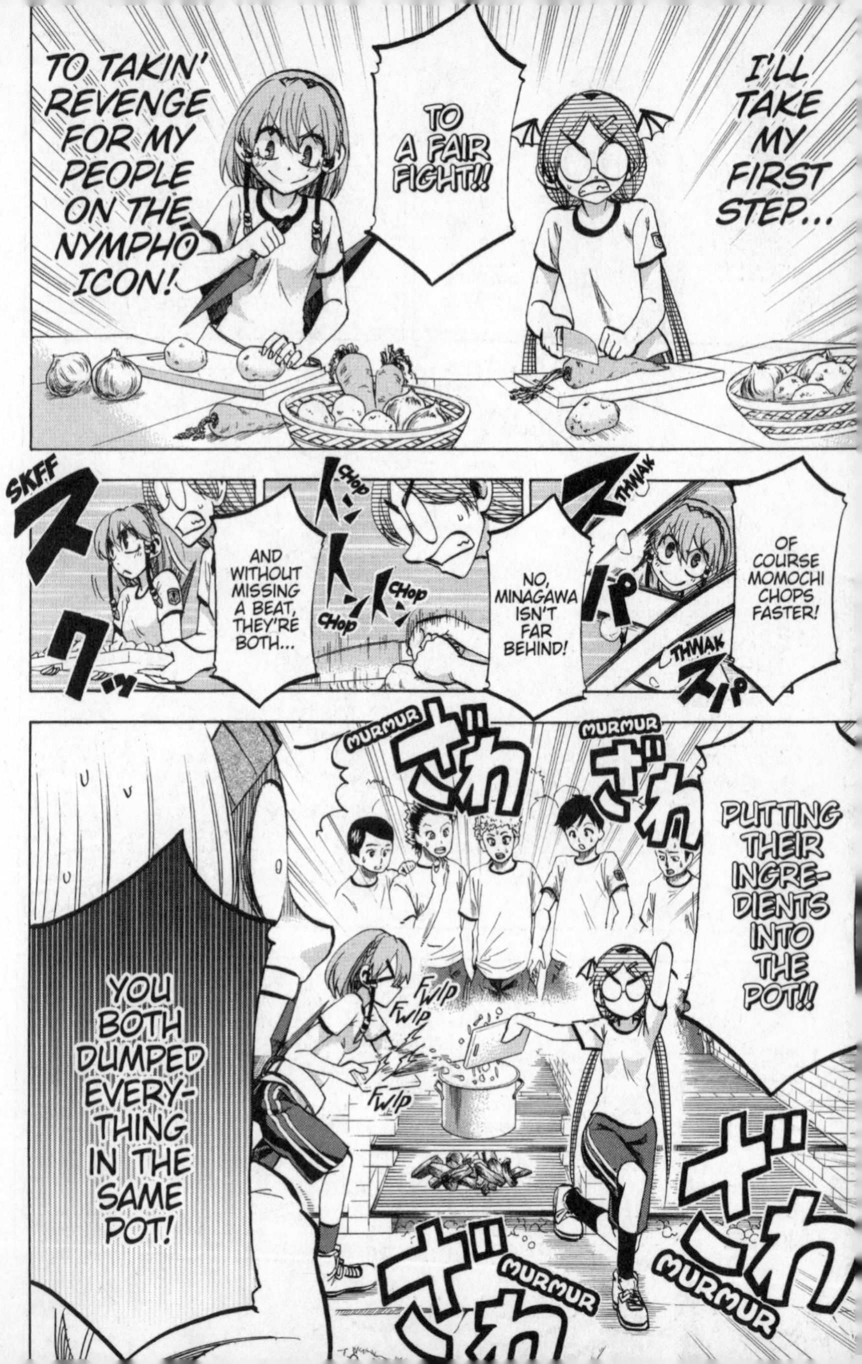
I'LL TAKE MY FIRST STEP...
TO A FAIR FIGHT!!
TO TAKIN' REVENGE FOR MY PEOPLE ON THE NYMPHO ICON!
THWAK
OF COURSE MOMOCHI CHOPS FASTER!
THWAK
NO, MINAGAWA ISN'T FAR BEHIND!
CHOP
CHOP
CHOP
AND WITHOUT MISSING A BEAT, THEY'RE BOTH...
SKFF
MURMUR
MURMUR
PUTTING THEIR INGREDIENTS INTO THE POT!!
FWIP
FWIP
FWIP
YOU BOTH DUMPED EVERYTHING IN THE SAME POT!
MURMUR
MURMUR

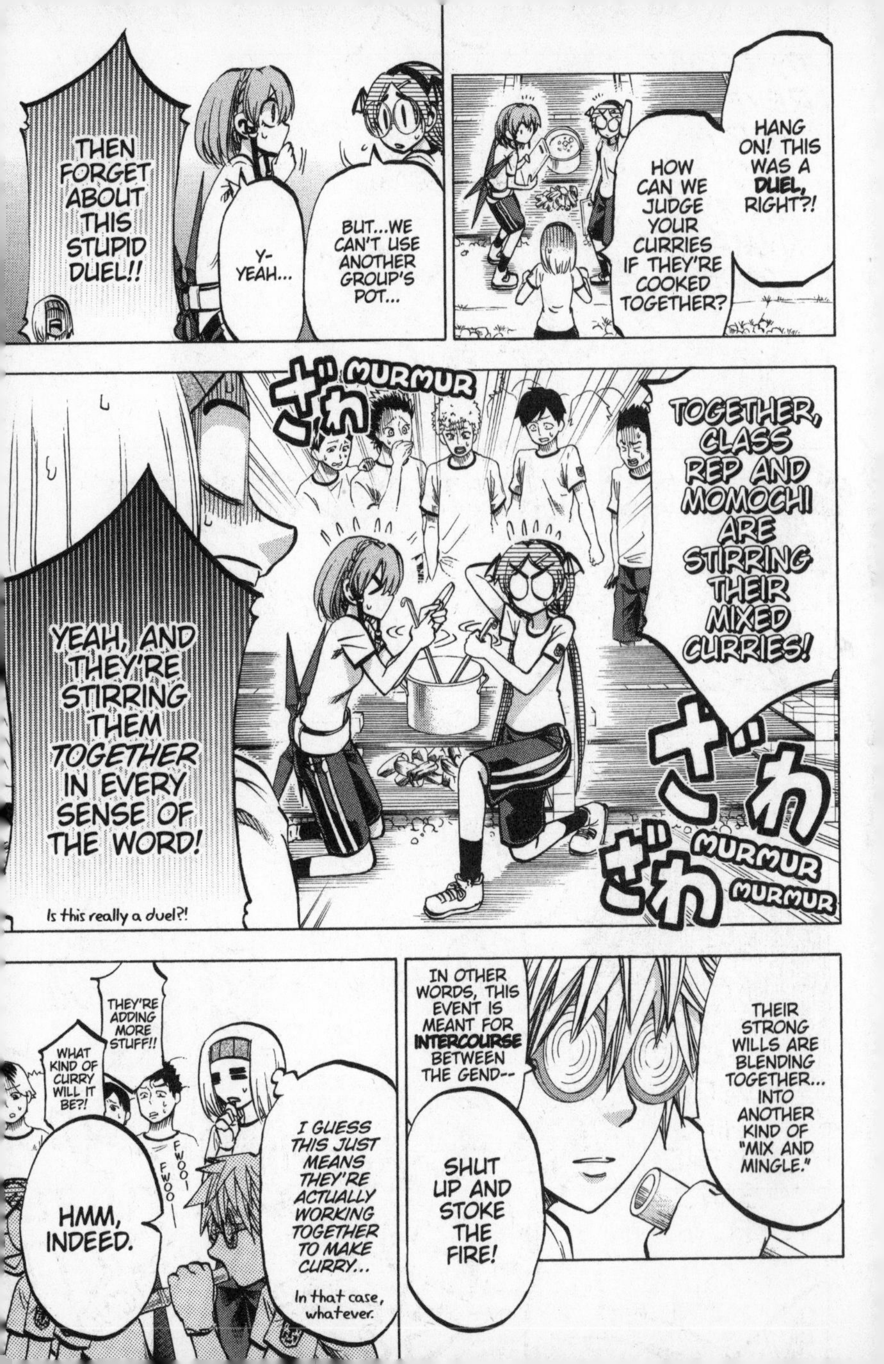
HANG ON! THIS WAS A DUEL, RIGHT?!
HOW CAN WE JUDGE YOUR CURRIES IF THEY'RE COOKED TOGETHER?
BUT...WE CAN'T USE ANOTHER GROUP'S POT...
Y-YEAH...
THEN FORGET ABOUT THIS STUPID DUEL!!
TOGETHER, CLASS REP AND MOMOCHI ARE STIRRING THEIR MIXED CURRIES!
ざわ MURMUR
ざわ MURMUR
ざわ MURMUR
YEAH, AND THEY'RE STIRRING THEM TOGETHER IN EVERY SENSE OF THE WORD!
Is this really a duel?!
THEIR STRONG WILLS ARE BLENDING TOGETHER... INTO ANOTHER KIND OF "MIX AND MINGLE."
IN OTHER WORDS, THIS EVENT IS MEANT FOR INTERCOURSE BETWEEN THE GEND--
SHUT UP AND STOKE THE FIRE!
THEY'RE ADDING MORE STUFF!!
WHAT KIND OF CURRY WILL IT BE?!
I GUESS THIS JUST MEANS THEY'RE ACTUALLY WORKING TOGETHER TO MAKE CURRY...
In that case, whatever.
FWOO FWOO
HMM, INDEED.

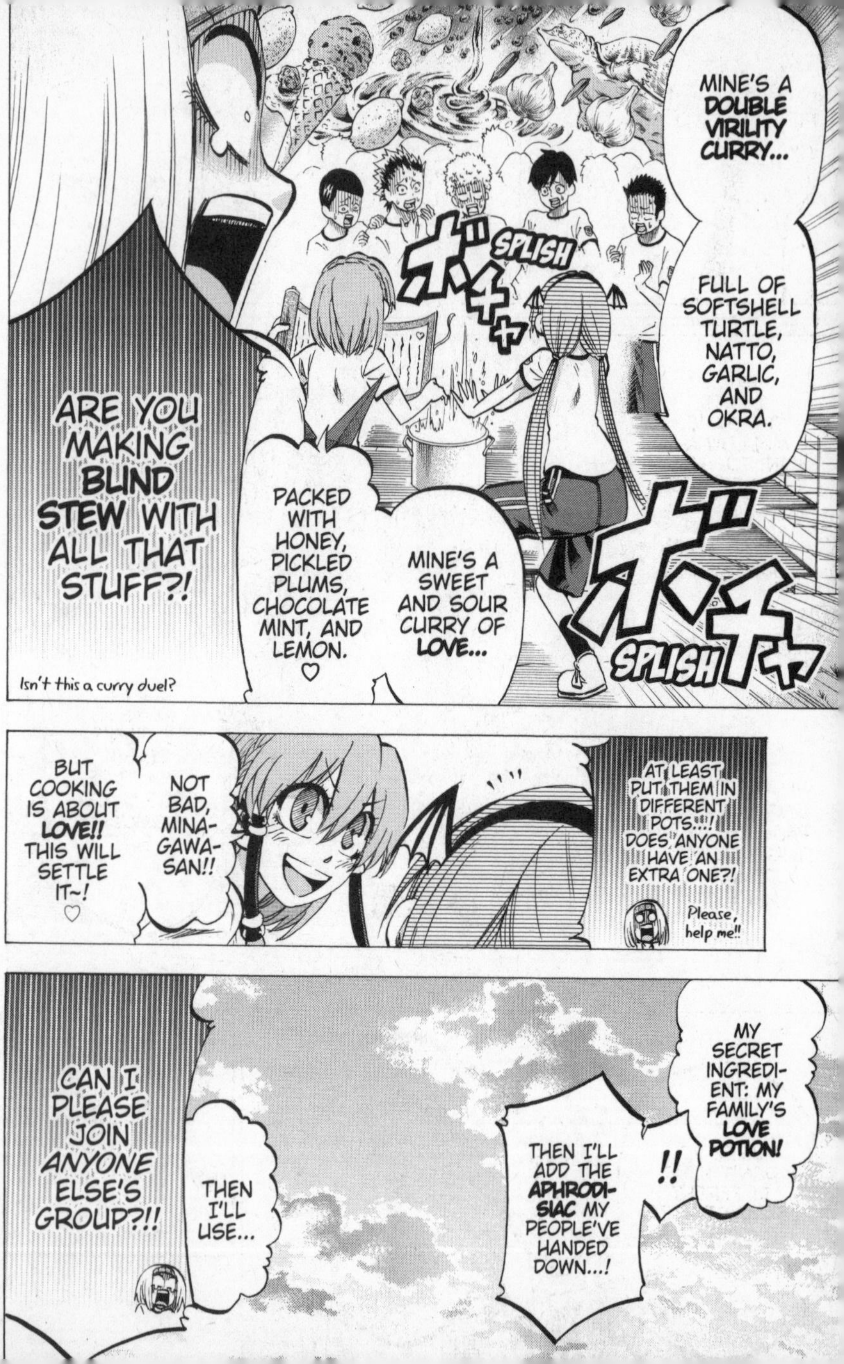
MINE'S A DOUBLE VIRILITY CURRY...
FULL OF SOFTSHELL TURTLE, NATTO, GARLIC, AND OKRA.
SPLISH
SPLISH
MINE'S A SWEET AND SOUR CURRY OF LOVE...
PACKED WITH HONEY, PICKLED PLUMS, CHOCOLATE MINT, AND LEMON. ♡
ARE YOU MAKING BLIND STEW WITH ALL THAT STUFF?!
Isn't this a curry duel?
AT LEAST PUT THEM IN DIFFERENT POTS...! DOES ANYONE HAVE AN EXTRA ONE?!
Please, help me!!
NOT BAD, MINAGAWA-SAN!!
BUT COOKING IS ABOUT LOVE!! THIS WILL SETTLE IT~! ♡
MY SECRET INGREDIENT: MY FAMILY'S LOVE POTION!
!!
THEN I'LL ADD THE APHRODISIAC MY PEOPLE'VE HANDED DOWN...!
THEN I'LL USE...
CAN I PLEASE JOIN ANYONE ELSE'S GROUP?!!

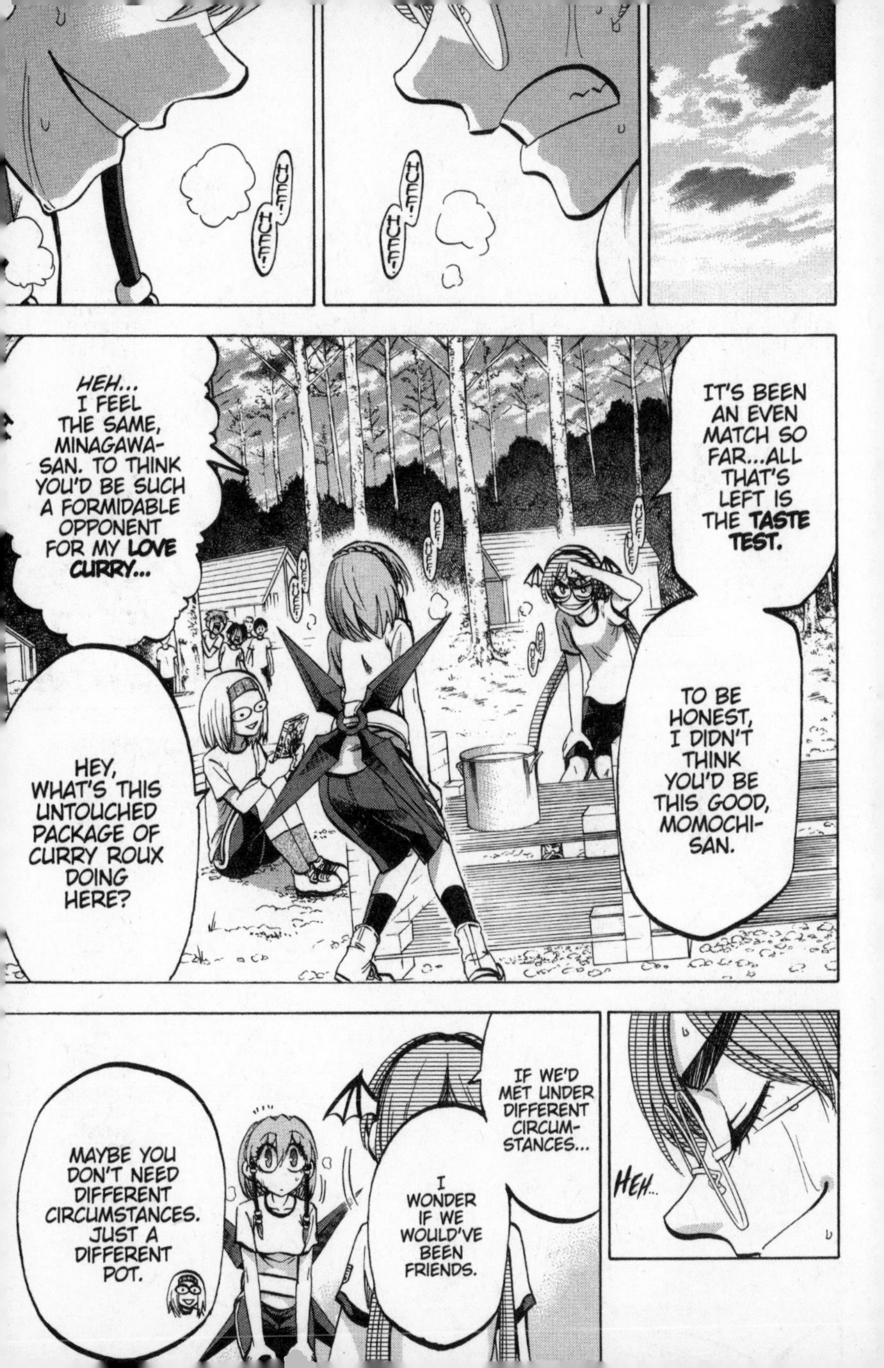
HUFF! HUFF!
HUFF! HUFF!
IT'S BEEN AN EVEN MATCH SO FAR...ALL THAT'S LEFT IS THE **TASTE TEST.**
TO BE HONEST, I DIDN'T THINK YOU'D BE THIS GOOD, MOMOCHI-SAN.
HUFF! HUFF!
HUFF! HUFF!
HUFF! HUFF!
HEH... I FEEL THE SAME, MINAGAWA-SAN. TO THINK YOU'D BE SUCH A FORMIDABLE OPPONENT FOR MY **LOVE CURRY...**
HEY, WHAT'S THIS UNTOUCHED PACKAGE OF CURRY ROUX DOING HERE?
HEH...
IF WE'D MET UNDER DIFFERENT CIRCUM-STANCES...
I WONDER IF WE WOULD'VE BEEN FRIENDS.
MAYBE YOU DON'T NEED DIFFERENT CIRCUMSTANCES. JUST A DIFFERENT POT.

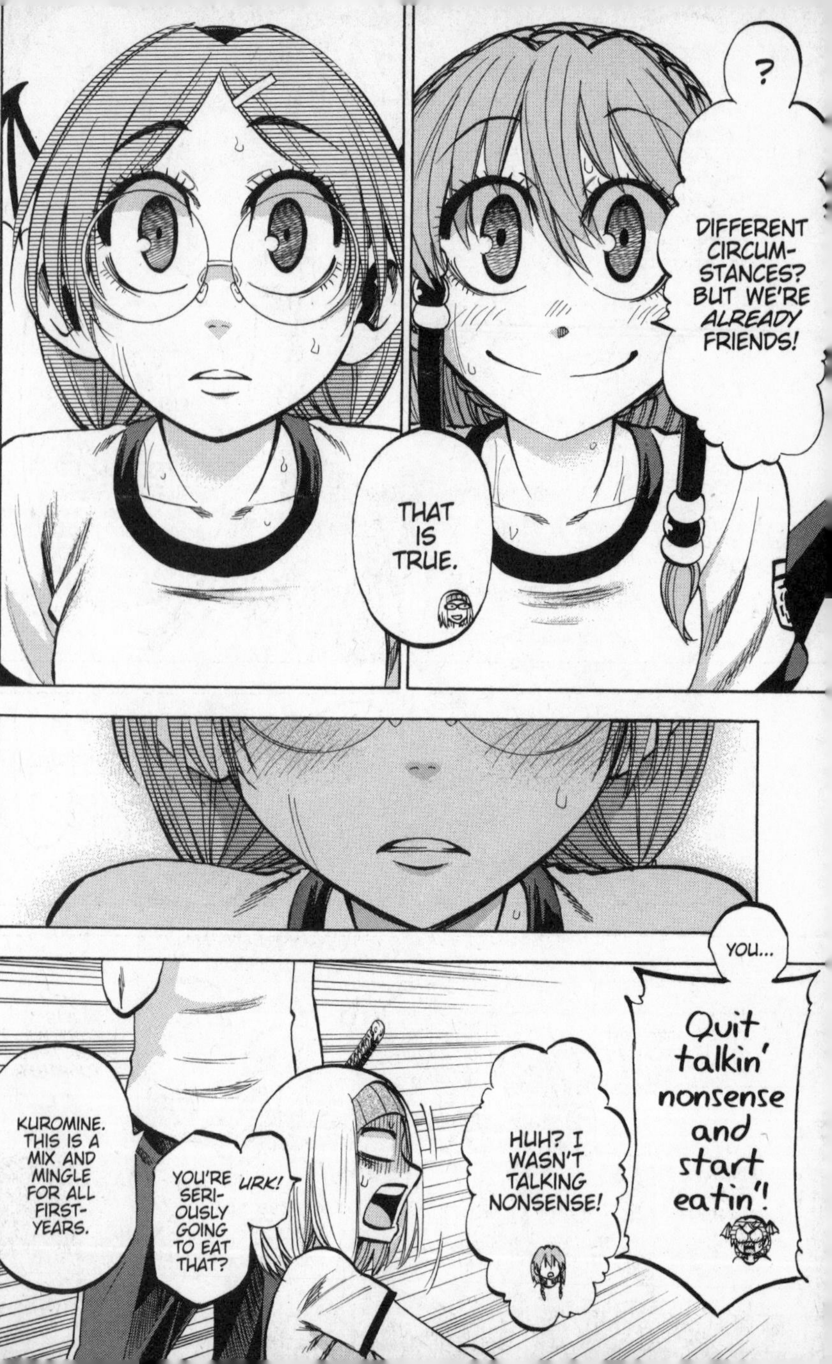
?
DIFFERENT CIRCUM-STANCES? BUT WE'RE ALREADY FRIENDS!
THAT IS TRUE.
YOU...
Quit talkin' nonsense and start eatin'!
HUH? I WASN'T TALKING NONSENSE!
URK!
YOU'RE SERI-OUSLY GOING TO EAT THAT?
KUROMINE. THIS IS A MIX AND MINGLE FOR ALL FIRST-YEARS.

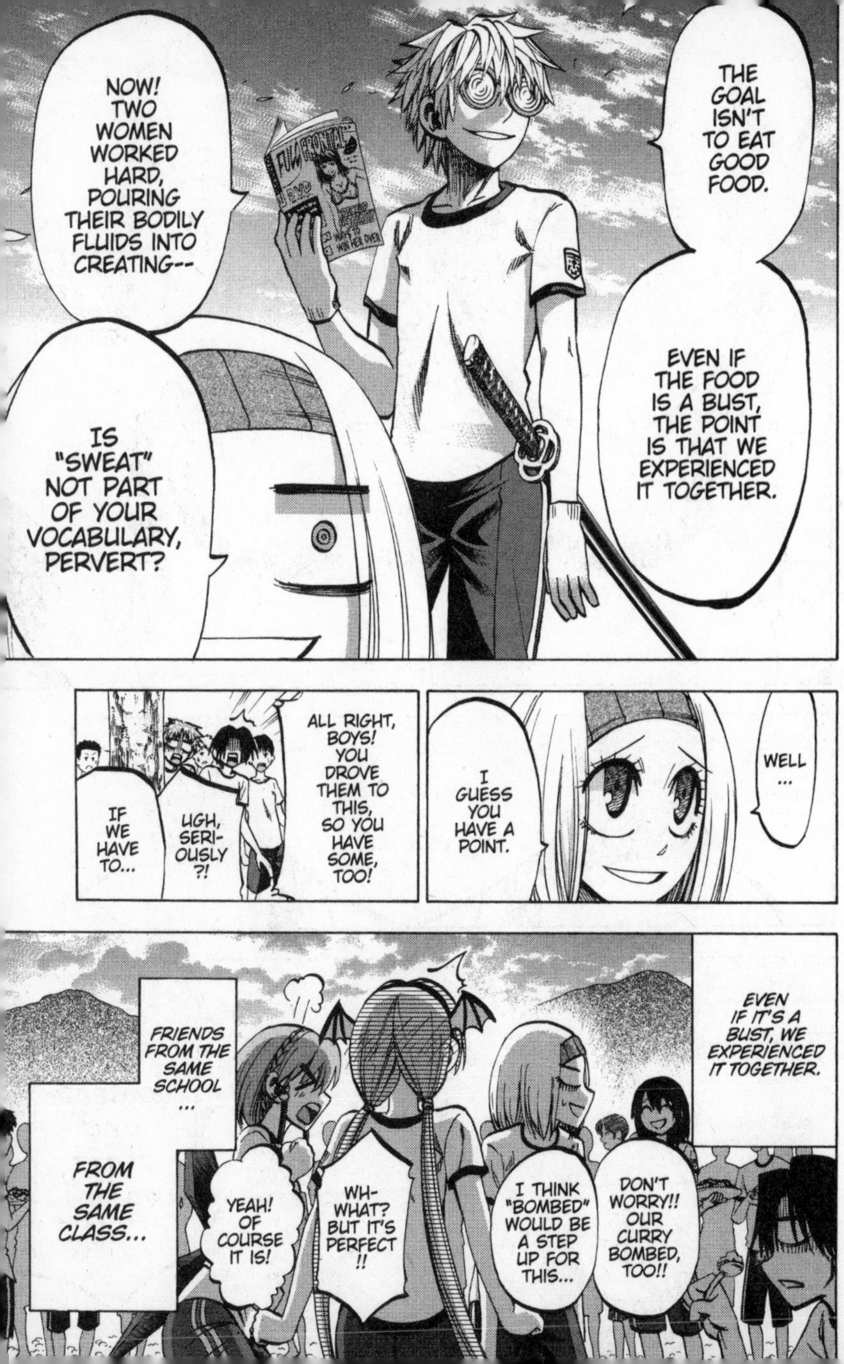
THE GOAL ISN'T TO EAT GOOD FOOD.
EVEN IF THE FOOD IS A BUST, THE POINT IS THAT WE EXPERIENCED IT TOGETHER.
NOW! TWO WOMEN WORKED HARD, POURING THEIR BODILY FLUIDS INTO CREATING--
IS "SWEAT" NOT PART OF YOUR VOCABULARY, PERVERT?
WELL ...
I GUESS YOU HAVE A POINT.
ALL RIGHT, BOYS! YOU DROVE THEM TO THIS, SO YOU HAVE SOME, TOO!
UGH, SERIOUSLY?!
IF WE HAVE TO...
EVEN IF IT'S A BUST, WE EXPERIENCED IT TOGETHER.
DON'T WORRY!! OUR CURRY BOMBED, TOO!!
I THINK "BOMBED" WOULD BE A STEP UP FOR THIS...
WH-WHAT? BUT IT'S PERFECT!!
YEAH! OF COURSE IT IS!
FRIENDS FROM THE SAME SCHOOL ...
FROM THE SAME CLASS...

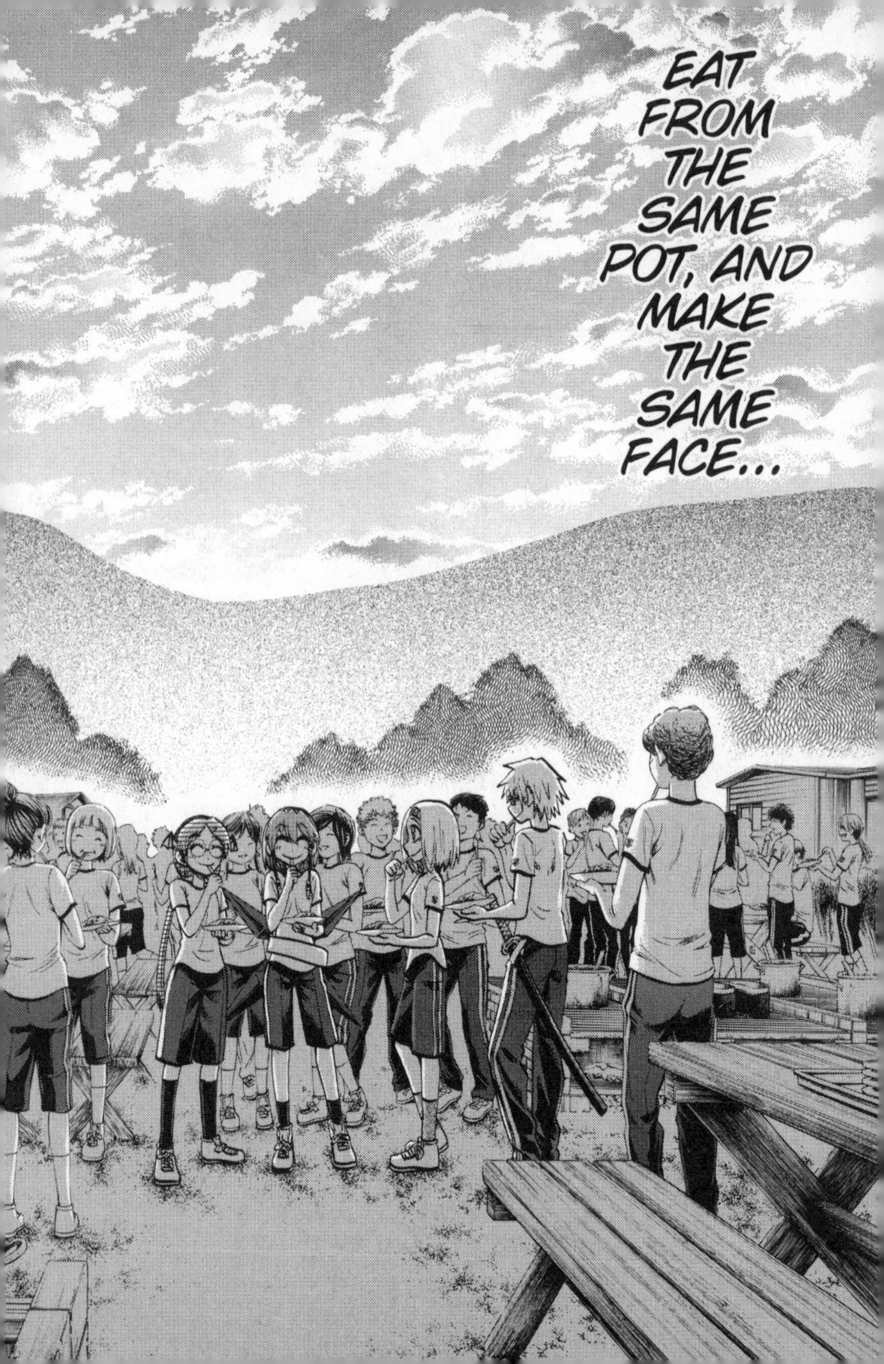
EAT FROM THE SAME POT, AND MAKE THE SAME FACE...

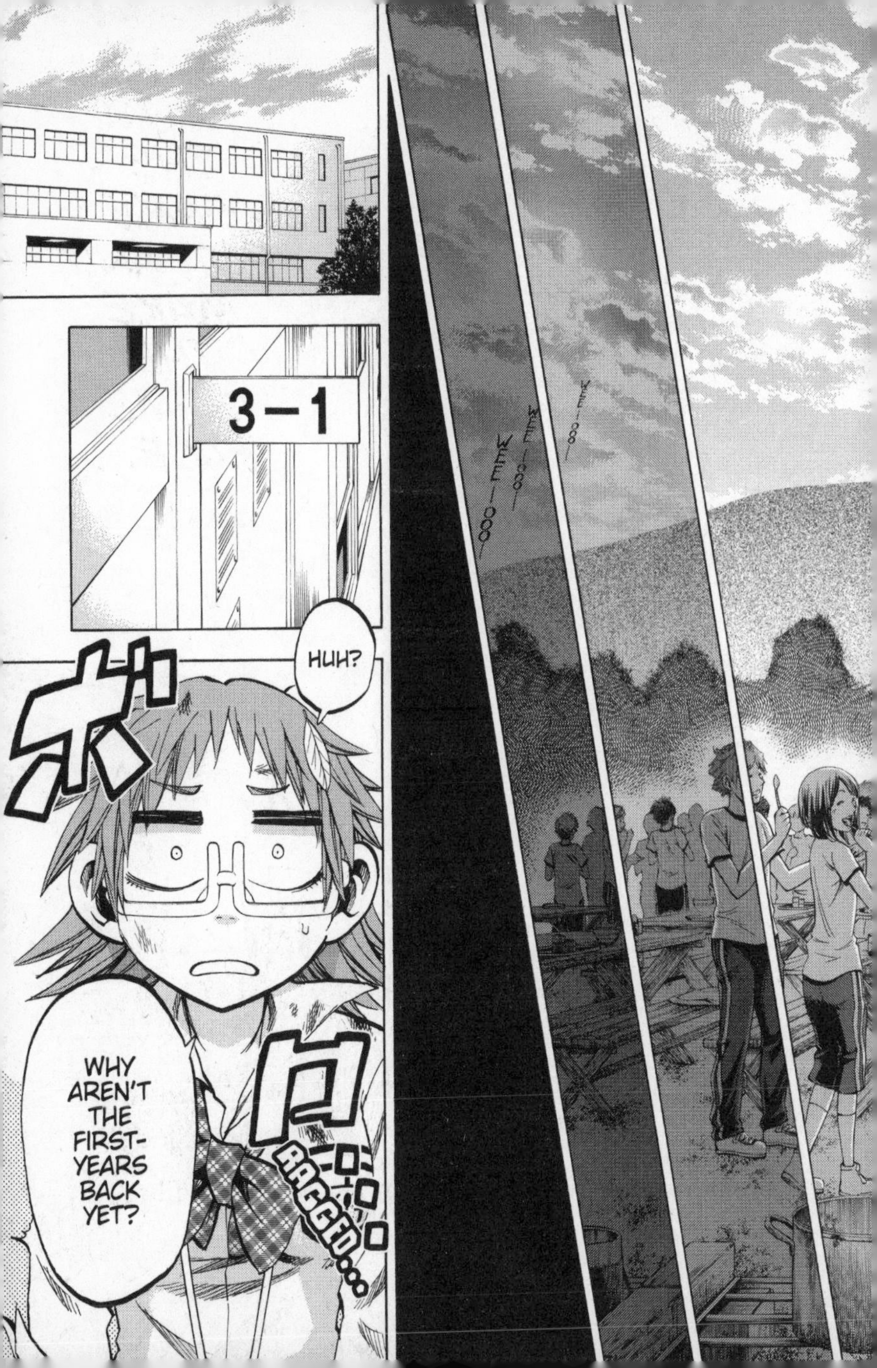

WEE-OOO
WEE-OOO
WEEE-OOO
3-1
HUH?
WHY AREN'T THE FIRST-YEARS BACK YET?
RAGGED...

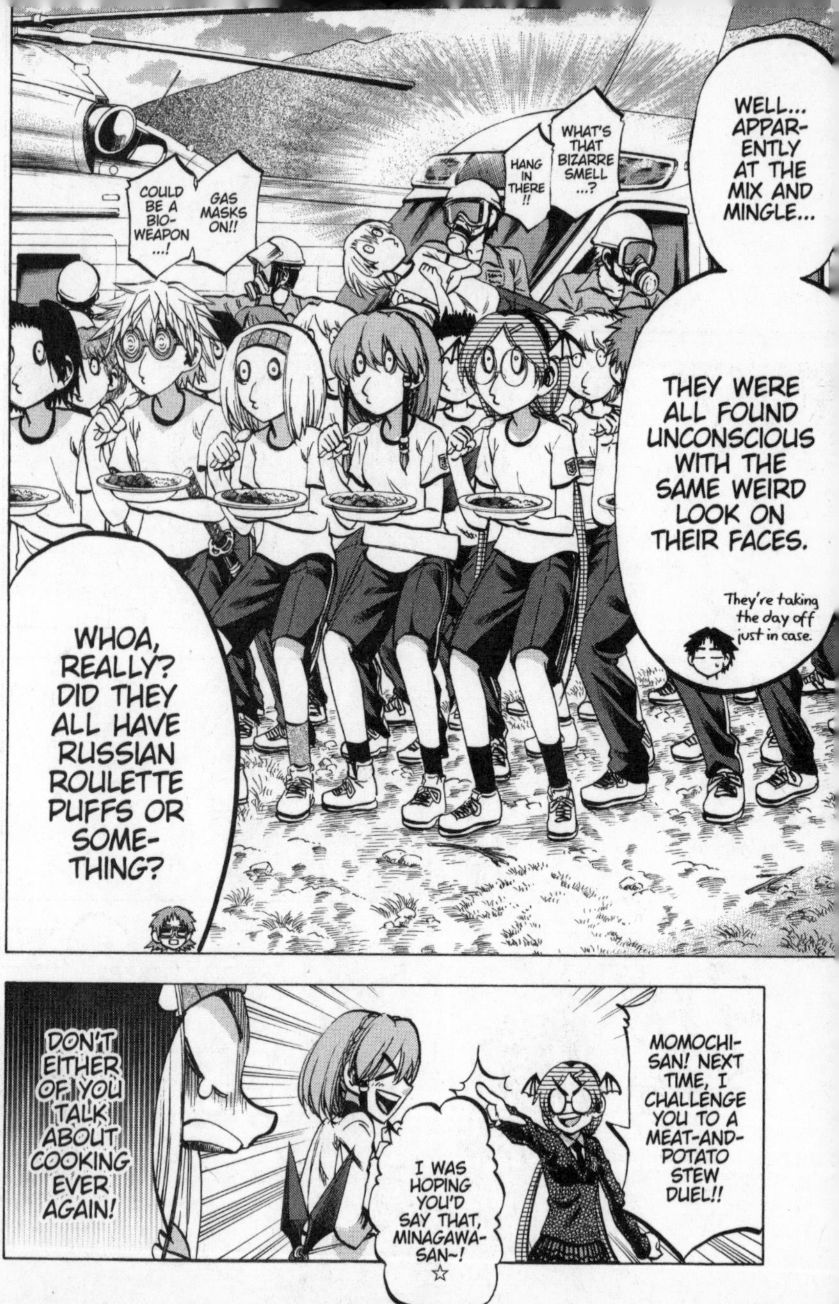
WELL... APPARENTLY AT THE MIX AND MINGLE...
THEY WERE ALL FOUND UNCONSCIOUS WITH THE SAME WEIRD LOOK ON THEIR FACES.
They're taking the day off just in case.
WHAT'S THAT BIZARRE SMELL ...?
HANG IN THERE !!
GAS MASKS ON!!
COULD BE A BIO-WEAPON ...!
WHOA, REALLY? DID THEY ALL HAVE RUSSIAN ROULETTE PUFFS OR SOME-THING?
MOMOCHI-SAN! NEXT TIME, I CHALLENGE YOU TO A MEAT-AND-POTATO STEW DUEL!!
I WAS HOPING YOU'D SAY THAT, MINAGAWA-SAN~! ☆
DON'T EITHER OF YOU TALK ABOUT COOKING EVER AGAIN!

Chapter 117: "Let's Be a Teacher!"

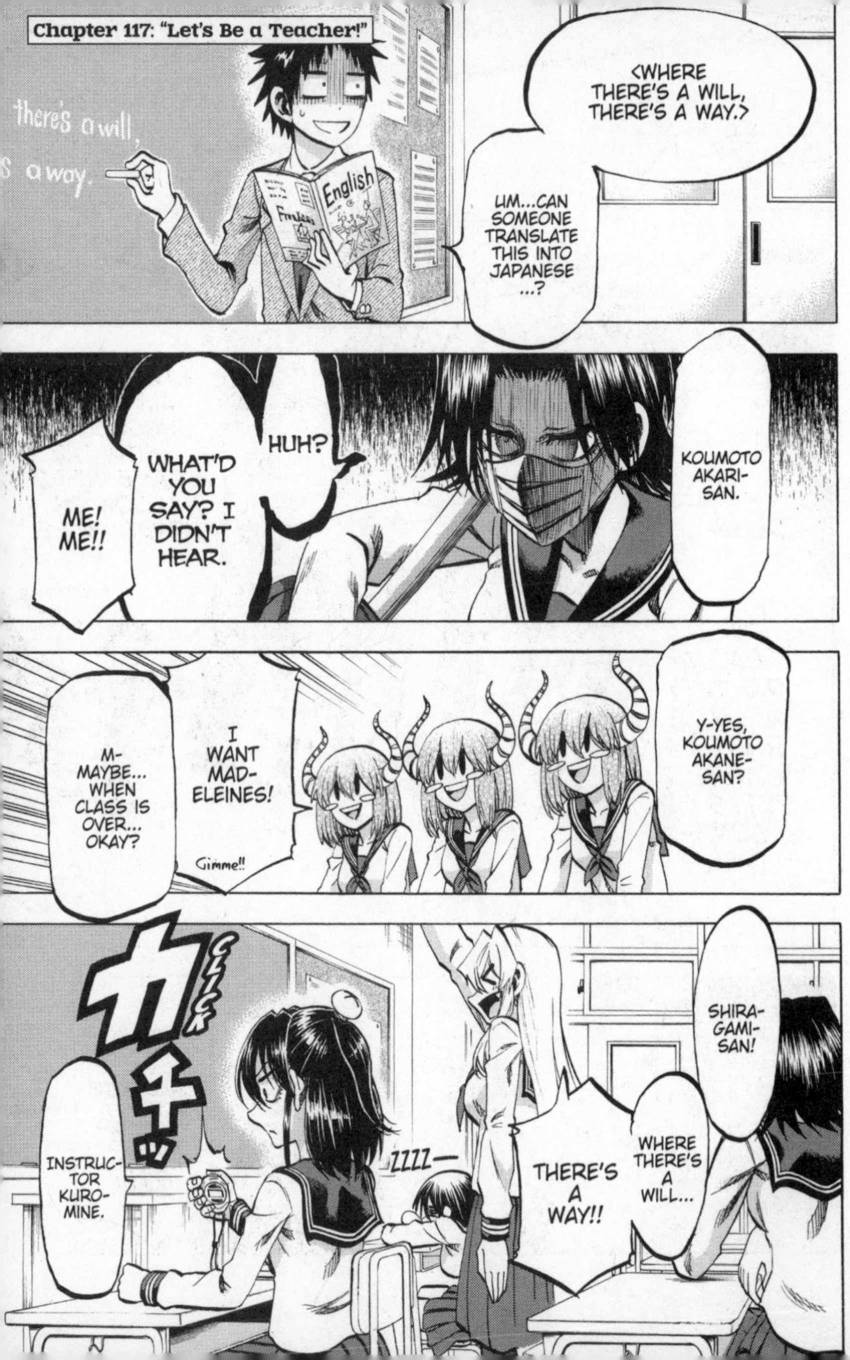

<WHERE THERE'S A WILL, THERE'S A WAY.>
UM...CAN SOMEONE TRANSLATE THIS INTO JAPANESE ...?
English
there's a will, s a way.
KOUMOTO AKARI-SAN.
HUH?
WHAT'D YOU SAY? I DIDN'T HEAR.
ME! ME!!
Y-YES, KOUMOTO AKANE-SAN?
I WANT MAD-ELEINES!
Gimme!!
M-MAYBE... WHEN CLASS IS OVER... OKAY?
SHIRAGAMI-SAN!
WHERE THERE'S A WILL...
THERE'S A WAY!!
ZZZZ—
カチッ
CLICK
INSTRUCTOR KURO-MINE.

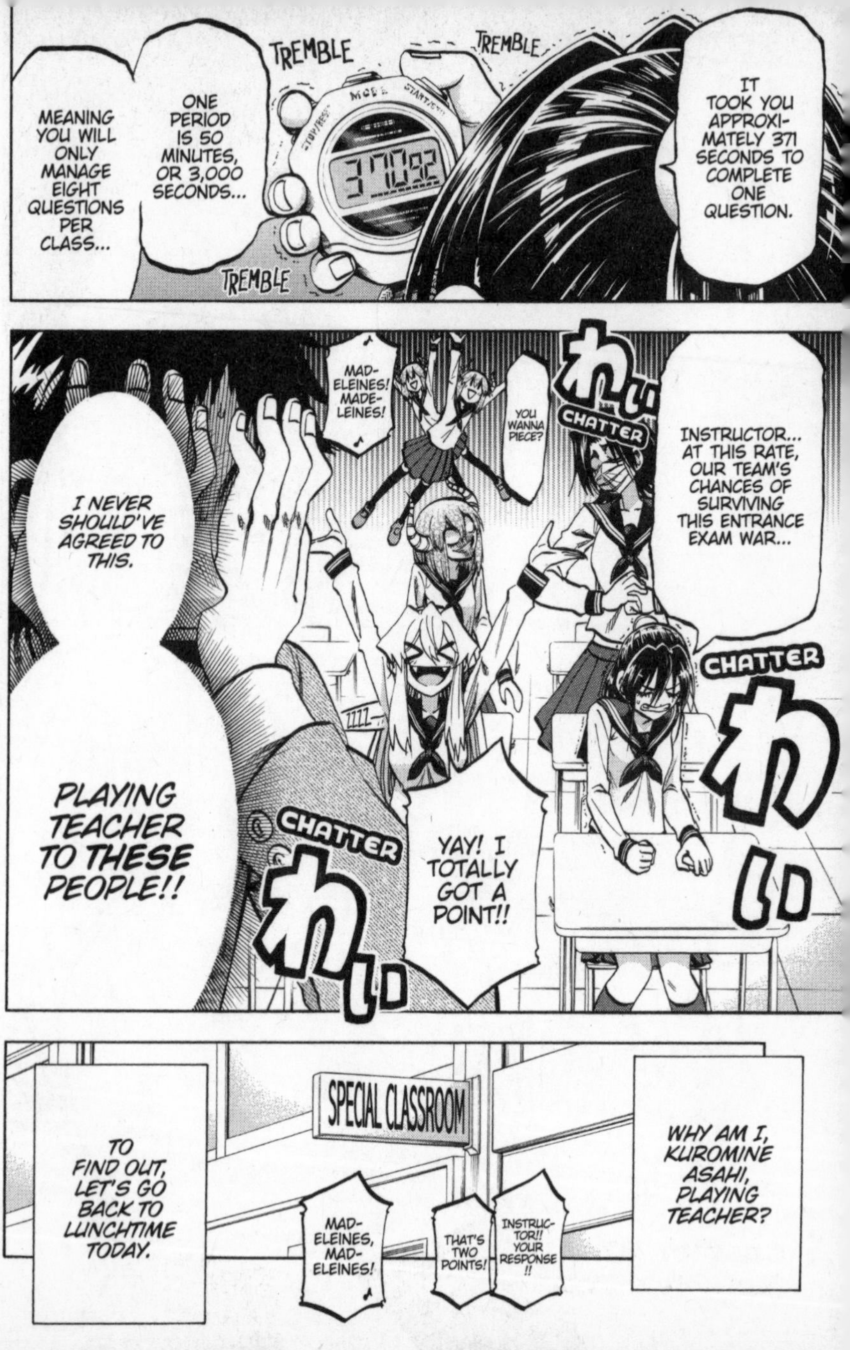
IT TOOK YOU APPROXIMATELY 371 SECONDS TO COMPLETE ONE QUESTION.
TREMBLE
TREMBLE
TREMBLE
ONE PERIOD IS 50 MINUTES, OR 3,000 SECONDS...
MEANING YOU WILL ONLY MANAGE EIGHT QUESTIONS PER CLASS...
INSTRUCTOR... AT THIS RATE, OUR TEAM'S CHANCES OF SURVIVING THIS ENTRANCE EXAM WAR...
CHATTER
CHATTER
YOU WANNA PIECE?
MADELEINES! MADELEINES!
YAY! I TOTALLY GOT A POINT!!
CHATTER
I NEVER SHOULD'VE AGREED TO THIS.
PLAYING TEACHER TO THESE PEOPLE!!
WHY AM I, KUROMINE ASAHI, PLAYING TEACHER?
INSTRUCTOR!! YOUR RESPONSE!!
THAT'S TWO POINTS!
MADELEINES, MADELEINES!
SPECIAL CLASSROOM
TO FIND OUT, LET'S GO BACK TO LUNCHTIME TODAY.

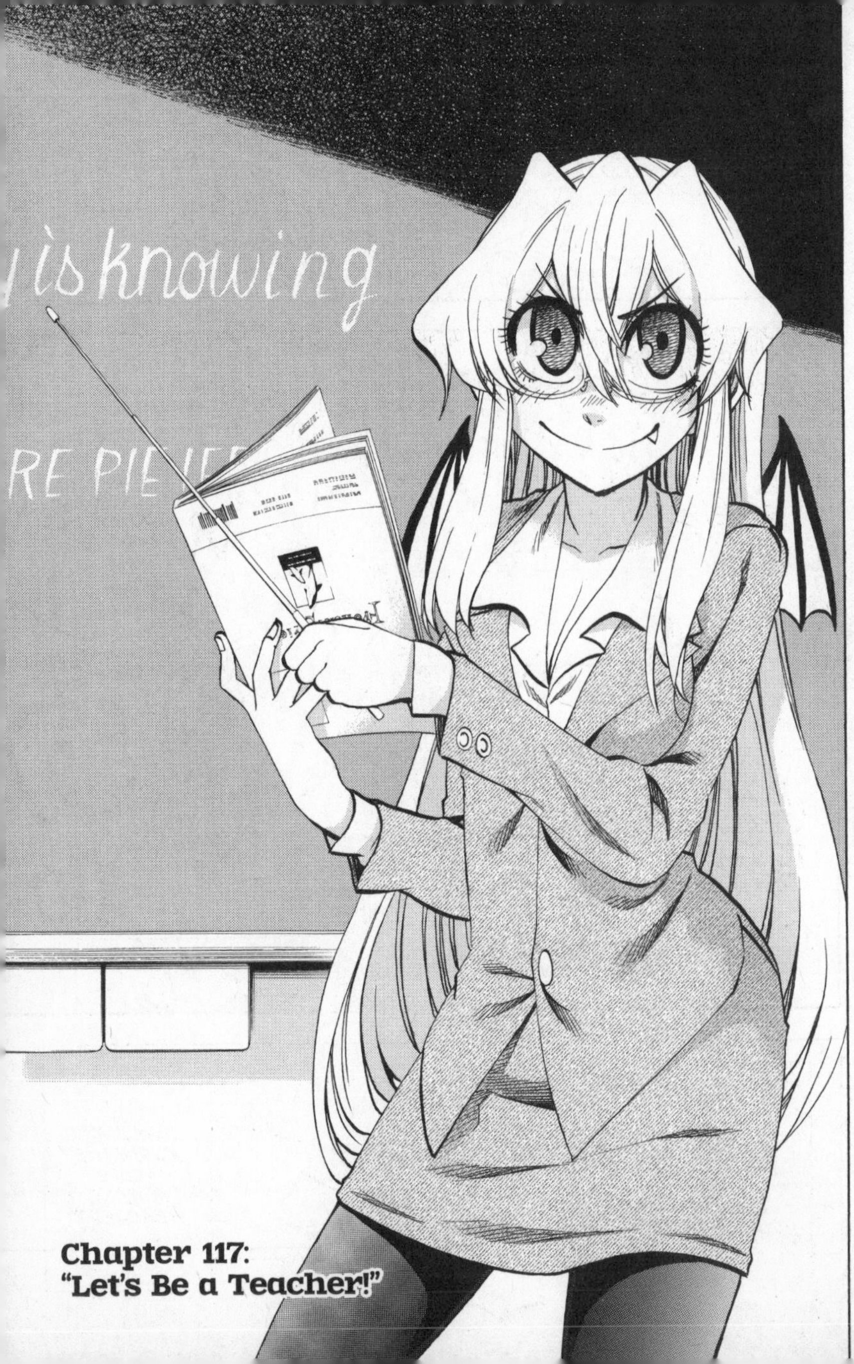
is knowing
RE PIE IE

Chapter 117:
"Let's Be a Teacher!"

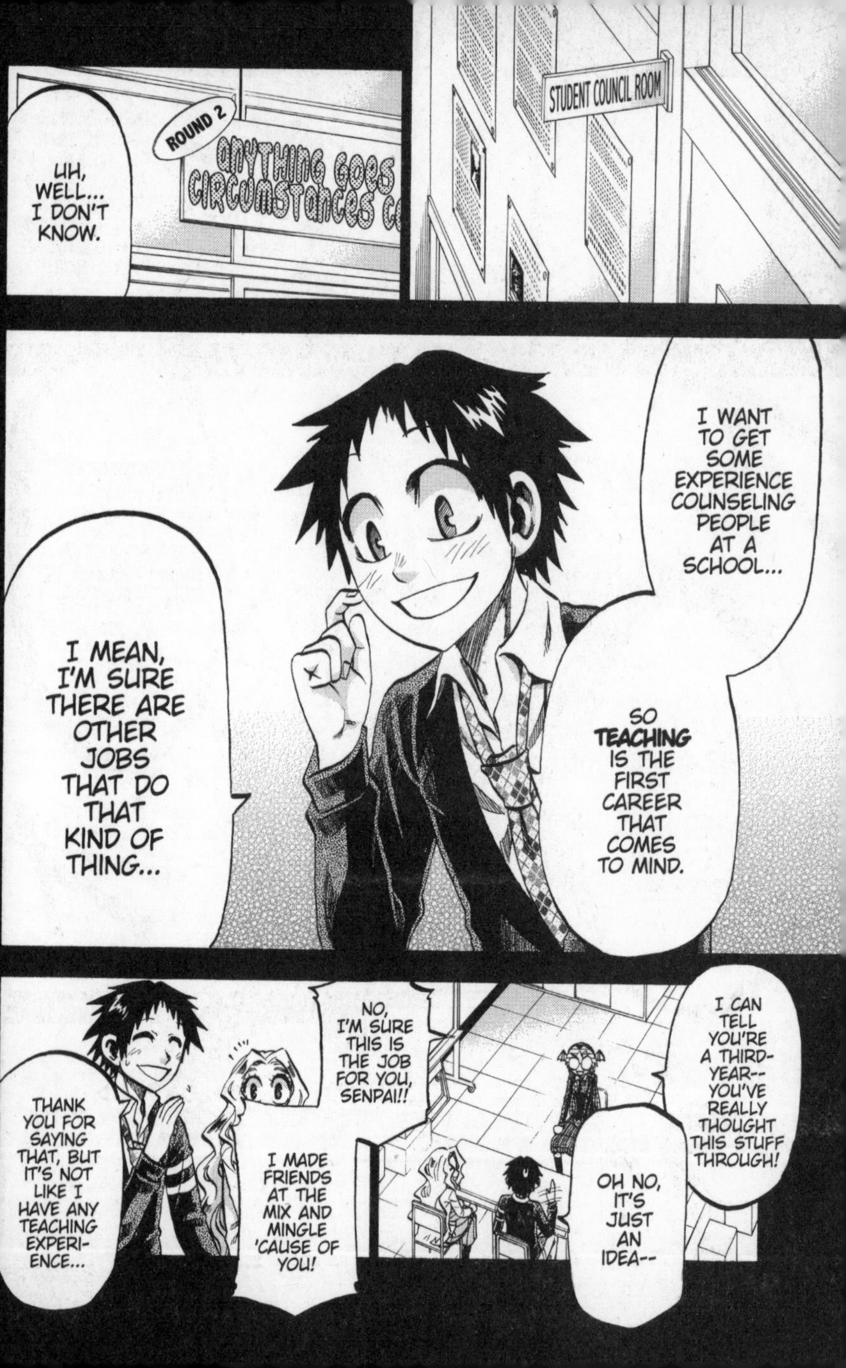
STUDENT COUNCIL ROOM
ROUND 2
ANYTHING GOES CIRCUMSTANCES
UH, WELL... I DON'T KNOW.
I WANT TO GET SOME EXPERIENCE COUNSELING PEOPLE AT A SCHOOL...
SO **TEACHING** IS THE FIRST CAREER THAT COMES TO MIND.
I MEAN, I'M SURE THERE ARE OTHER JOBS THAT DO THAT KIND OF THING...
I CAN TELL YOU'RE A THIRD-YEAR-- YOU'VE REALLY THOUGHT THIS STUFF THROUGH!
OH NO, IT'S JUST AN IDEA--
NO, I'M SURE THIS IS THE JOB FOR YOU, SENPAI!!
I MADE FRIENDS AT THE MIX AND MINGLE 'CAUSE OF YOU!
THANK YOU FOR SAYING THAT, BUT IT'S NOT LIKE I HAVE ANY TEACHING EXPERI-ENCE...

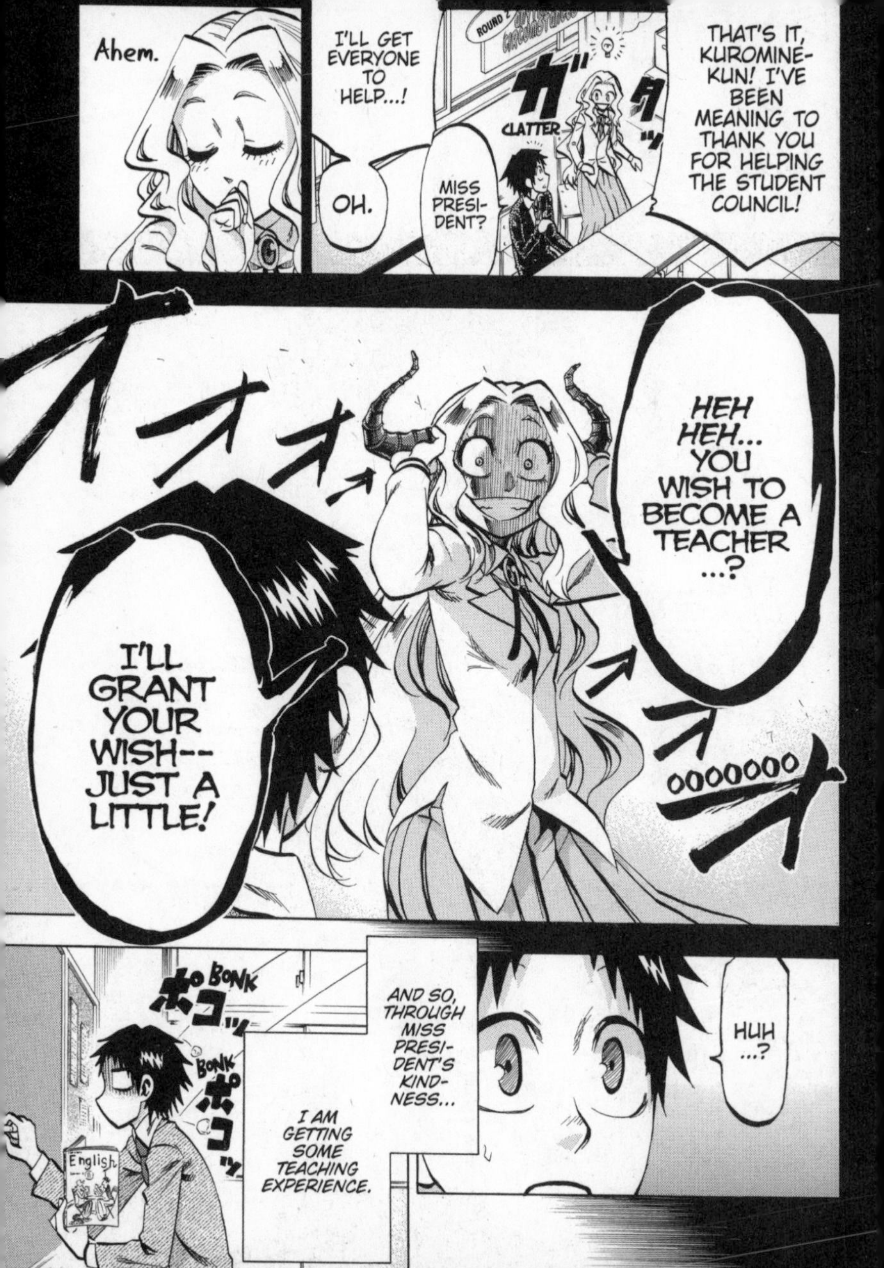

ROUND 2
THAT'S IT, KUROMINE-KUN! I'VE BEEN MEANING TO THANK YOU FOR HELPING THE STUDENT COUNCIL!
CLATTER
MISS PRESIDENT?
I'LL GET EVERYONE TO HELP...!
OH.
Ahem.
HEH HEH... YOU WISH TO BECOME A TEACHER ...?
OOOOOOO
I'LL GRANT YOUR WISH-- JUST A LITTLE!
HUH ...?
AND SO, THROUGH MISS PRESIDENT'S KINDNESS...
I AM GETTING SOME TEACHING EXPERIENCE.
BONK
BONK
English

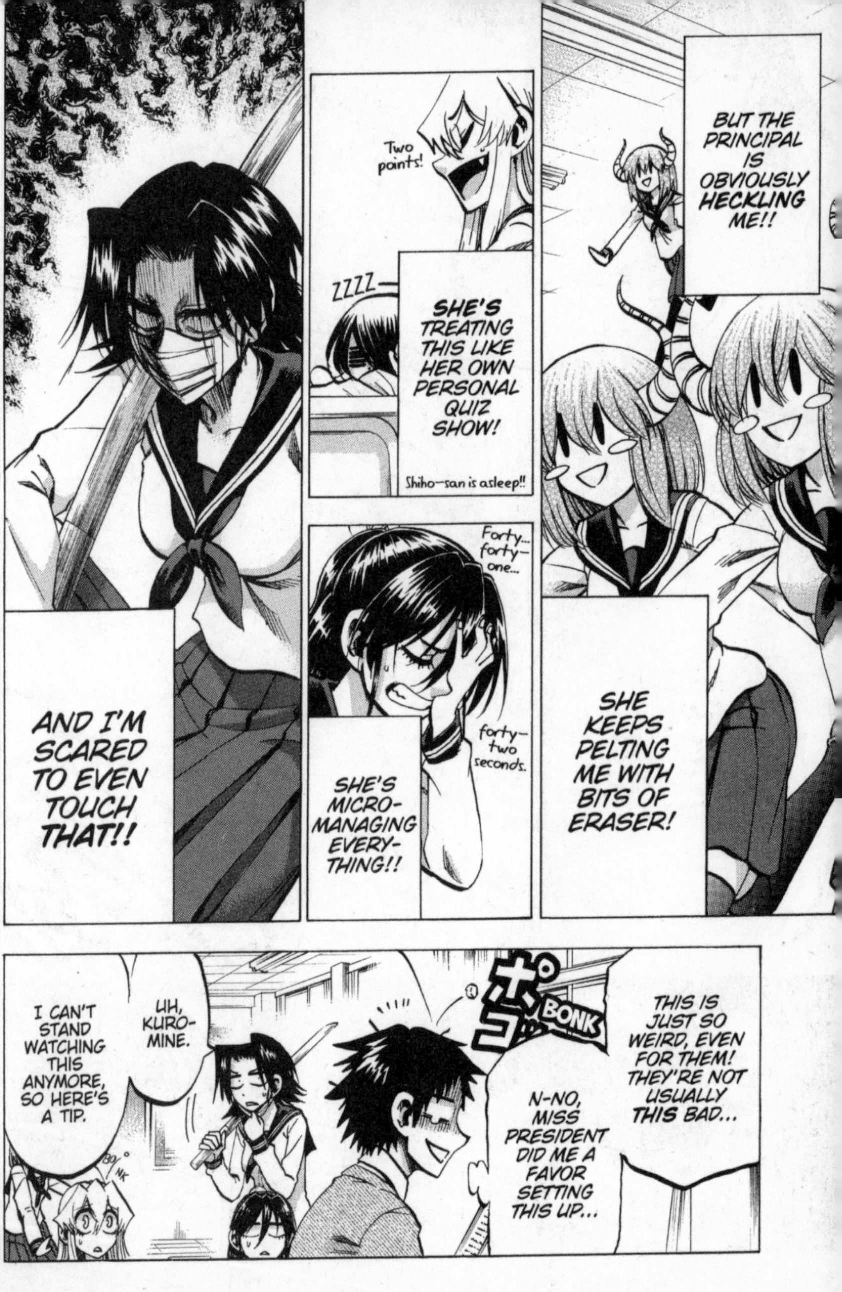

BUT THE PRINCIPAL IS OBVIOUSLY HECKLING ME!!
SHE KEEPS PELTING ME WITH BITS OF ERASER!
Two points!
ZZZZ
SHE'S TREATING THIS LIKE HER OWN PERSONAL QUIZ SHOW!
Shiho-san is asleep!!
Forty... forty-one...
forty-two seconds.
SHE'S MICRO-MANAGING EVERY-THING!!
AND I'M SCARED TO EVEN TOUCH THAT!!
THIS IS JUST SO WEIRD, EVEN FOR THEM! THEY'RE NOT USUALLY THIS BAD...
BONK
N-NO, MISS PRESIDENT DID ME A FAVOR SETTING THIS UP...
UH, KURO-MINE.
I CAN'T STAND WATCHING THIS ANYMORE, SO HERE'S A TIP.

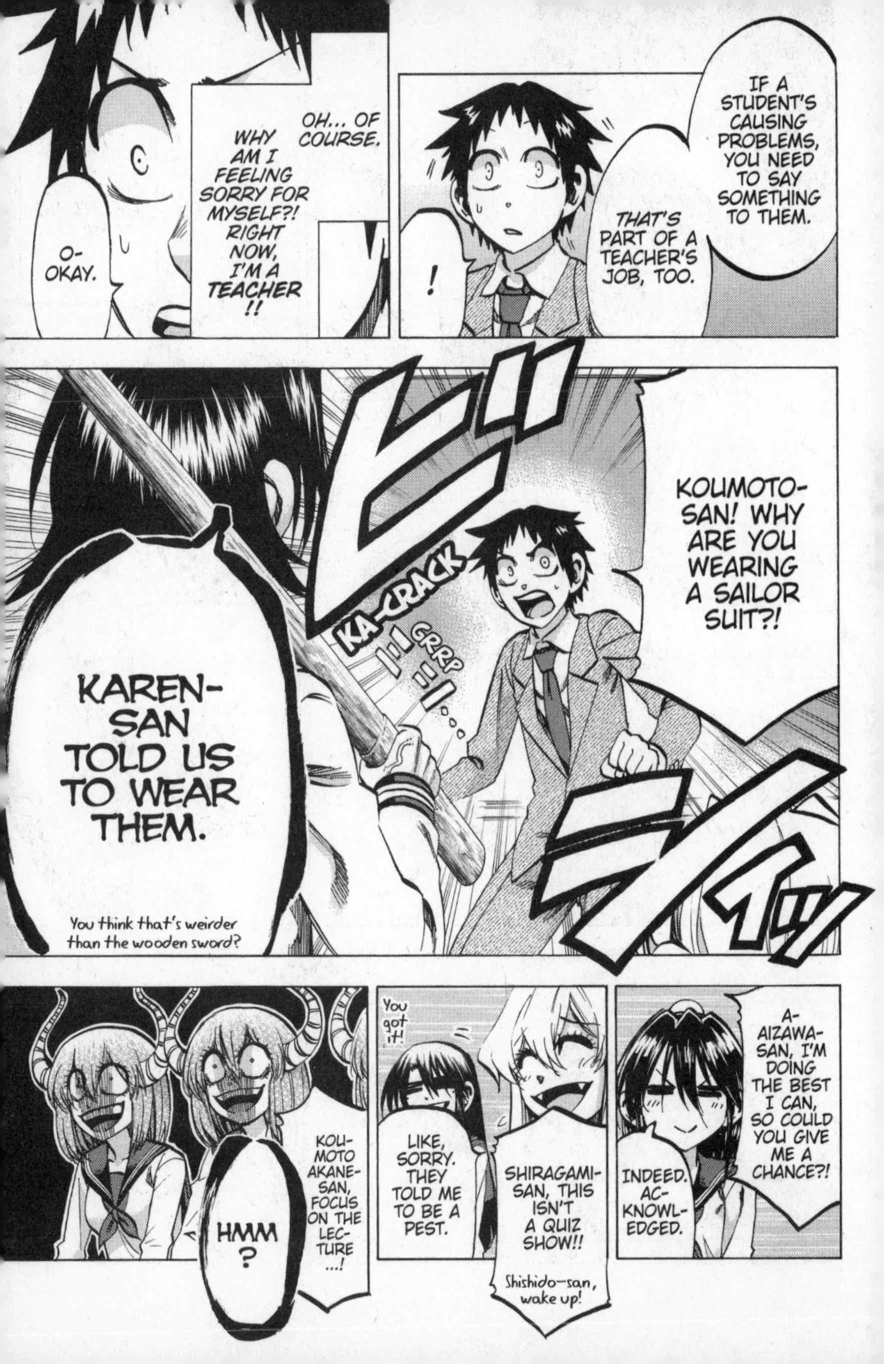
IF A STUDENT'S CAUSING PROBLEMS, YOU NEED TO SAY SOMETHING TO THEM.
THAT'S PART OF A TEACHER'S JOB, TOO.
!
OH... OF COURSE.
WHY AM I FEELING SORRY FOR MYSELF?! RIGHT NOW, I'M A TEACHER!!
O-OKAY.
KOUMOTO-SAN! WHY ARE YOU WEARING A SAILOR SUIT?!
KA-CRACK
GRRP
KAREN-SAN TOLD US TO WEAR THEM.
You think that's weirder than the wooden sword?
A-AIZAWA-SAN, I'M DOING THE BEST I CAN, SO COULD YOU GIVE ME A CHANCE?!
INDEED. ACKNOWLEDGED.
SHIRAGAMI-SAN, THIS ISN'T A QUIZ SHOW!!
LIKE, SORRY. THEY TOLD ME TO BE A PEST.
You got it!
Shishido-san, wake up!
KOUMOTO AKANE-SAN, FOCUS ON THE LECTURE...!
HMM?

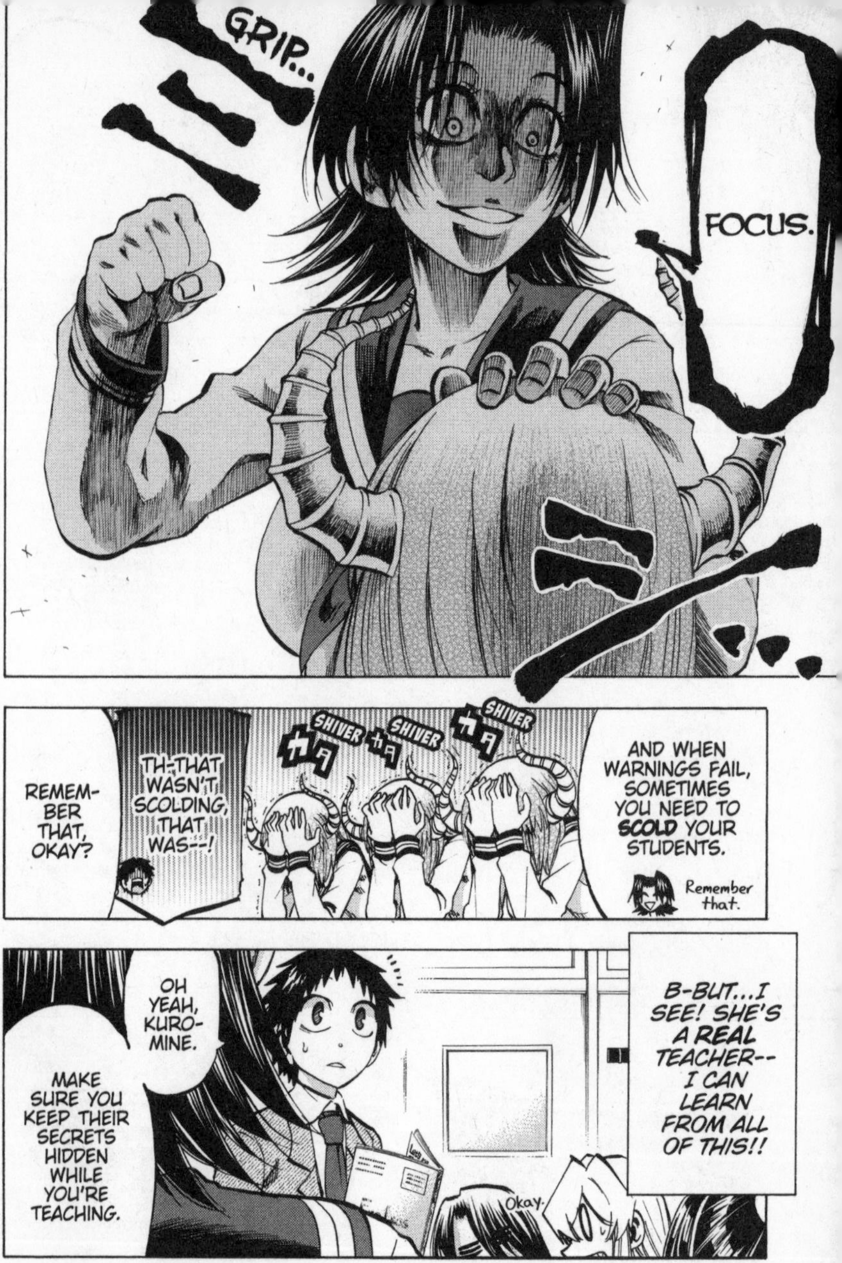
FOCUS.
GRIP...
AND WHEN WARNINGS FAIL, SOMETIMES YOU NEED TO **SCOLD** YOUR STUDENTS.
Remember that.
SHIVER カタ
SHIVER カタ
SHIVER カタ
TH-THAT WASN'T SCOLDING, THAT WAS--!
REMEM-BER THAT, OKAY?
B-BUT...I SEE! SHE'S A REAL TEACHER-- I CAN LEARN FROM ALL OF THIS!!
Okay.
OH YEAH, KURO-MINE.
MAKE SURE YOU KEEP THEIR SECRETS HIDDEN WHILE YOU'RE TEACHING.

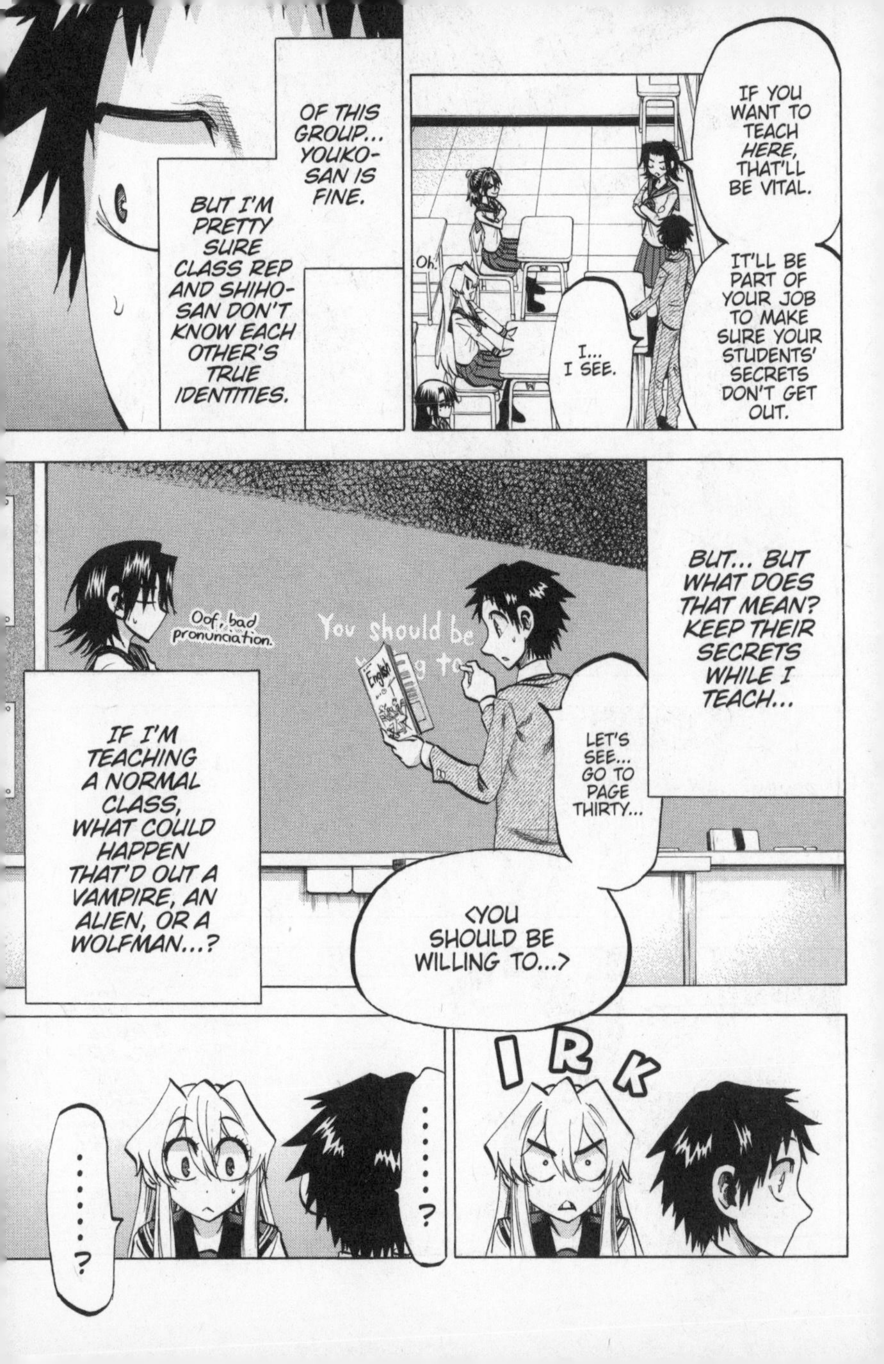
IF YOU WANT TO TEACH HERE, THAT'LL BE VITAL.
IT'LL BE PART OF YOUR JOB TO MAKE SURE YOUR STUDENTS' SECRETS DON'T GET OUT.
Oh.
I... I SEE.
OF THIS GROUP... YOUKO-SAN IS FINE.
BUT I'M PRETTY SURE CLASS REP AND SHIHO-SAN DON'T KNOW EACH OTHER'S TRUE IDENTITIES.
BUT... BUT WHAT DOES THAT MEAN? KEEP THEIR SECRETS WHILE I TEACH...
LET'S SEE... GO TO PAGE THIRTY...
You should be
English
Oof, bad pronunciation.
<YOU SHOULD BE WILLING TO...>
IF I'M TEACHING A NORMAL CLASS, WHAT COULD HAPPEN THAT'D OUT A VAMPIRE, AN ALIEN, OR A WOLFMAN...?
IRK
......?
......?

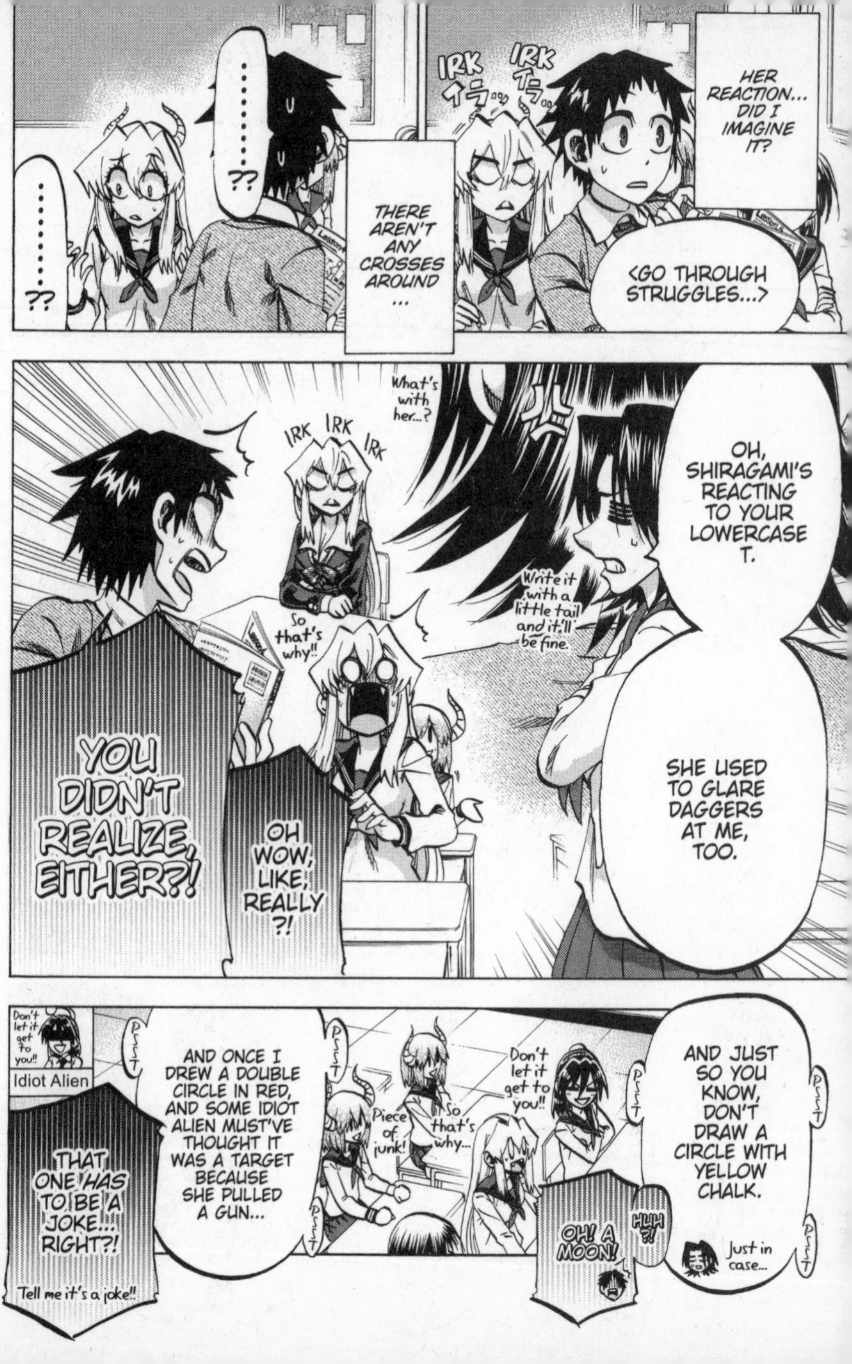
HER REACTION... DID I IMAGINE IT?
IRK IRK
<GO THROUGH STRUGGLES...>
THERE AREN'T ANY CROSSES AROUND...
......??
......??
OH, SHIRAGAMI'S REACTING TO YOUR LOWERCASE T.
SHE USED TO GLARE DAGGERS AT ME, TOO.
What's with her...?
IRK IRK IRK
Write it with a little tail and it'll be fine.
So that's why!!
OH WOW, LIKE, REALLY?!
YOU DIDN'T REALIZE, EITHER?!
AND JUST SO YOU KNOW, DON'T DRAW A CIRCLE WITH YELLOW CHALK.
PSST
PSST
Just in case...
HUH?!
OH! A MOON!
Don't let it get to you!!
So that's why...
Piece of junk!
PSST
PSST
AND ONCE I DREW A DOUBLE CIRCLE IN RED, AND SOME IDIOT ALIEN MUST'VE THOUGHT IT WAS A TARGET BECAUSE SHE PULLED A GUN...
PSST
THAT ONE HAS TO BE A JOKE... RIGHT?!
Tell me it's a joke!!
Don't let it get to you!!
Idiot Alien

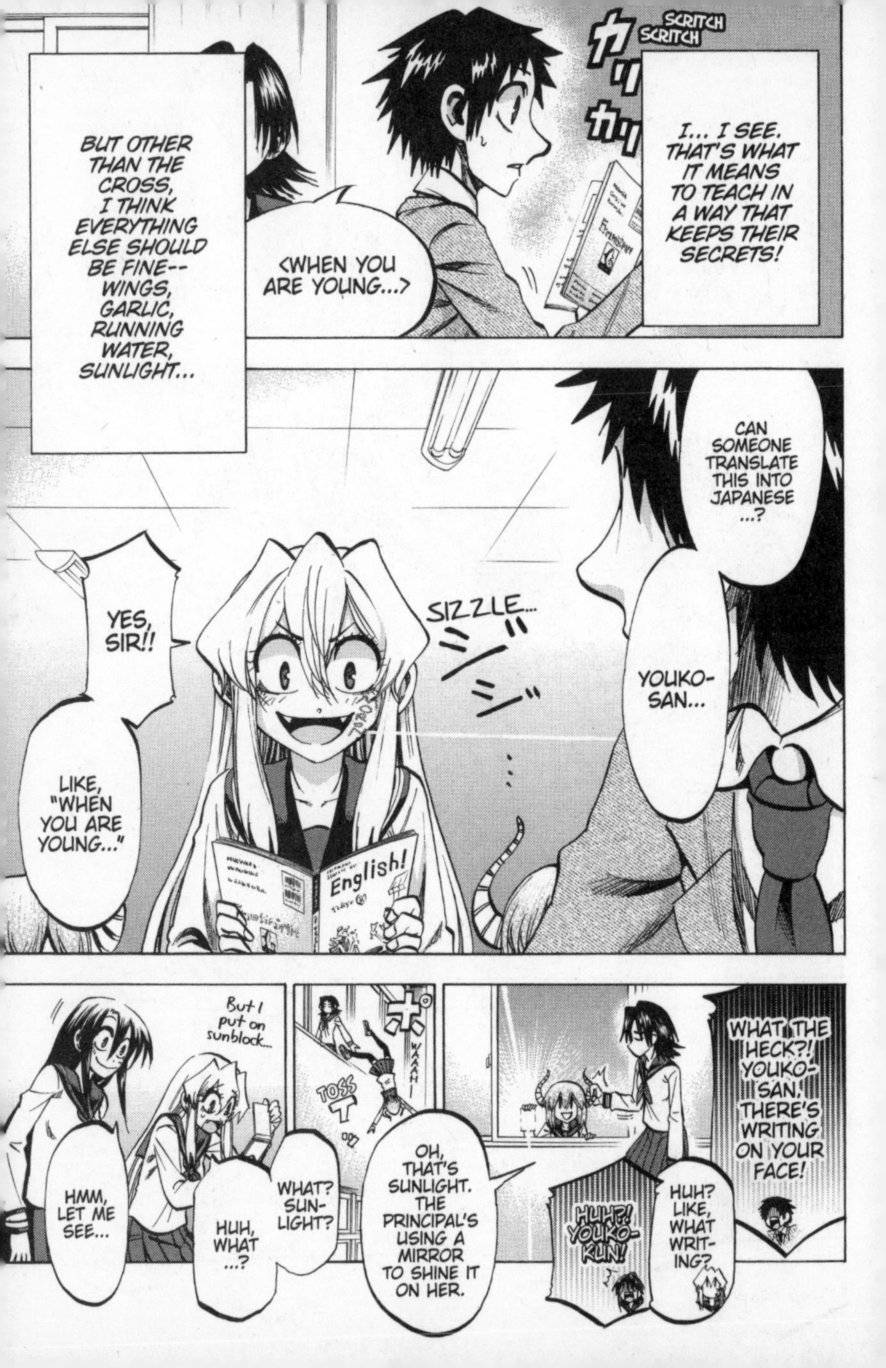
SCRITCH SCRITCH
I... I SEE. THAT'S WHAT IT MEANS TO TEACH IN A WAY THAT KEEPS THEIR SECRETS!
<WHEN YOU ARE YOUNG...>
BUT OTHER THAN THE CROSS, I THINK EVERYTHING ELSE SHOULD BE FINE-- WINGS, GARLIC, RUNNING WATER, SUNLIGHT...
CAN SOMEONE TRANSLATE THIS INTO JAPANESE ...?
YOUKO-SAN...
SIZZLE...
YES, SIR!!
LIKE, "WHEN YOU ARE YOUNG..."
English!
WHAT THE HECK?! YOUKO-SAN. THERE'S WRITING ON YOUR FACE!
HUH? LIKE, WHAT WRIT-ING?
HUH?! YOUKO-KUN!
WAAAH!
TOSS
OH, THAT'S SUNLIGHT. THE PRINCIPAL'S USING A MIRROR TO SHINE IT ON HER.
But I put on sunblock...
WHAT? SUN-LIGHT?
HUH, WHAT ...?
HMM, LET ME SEE...

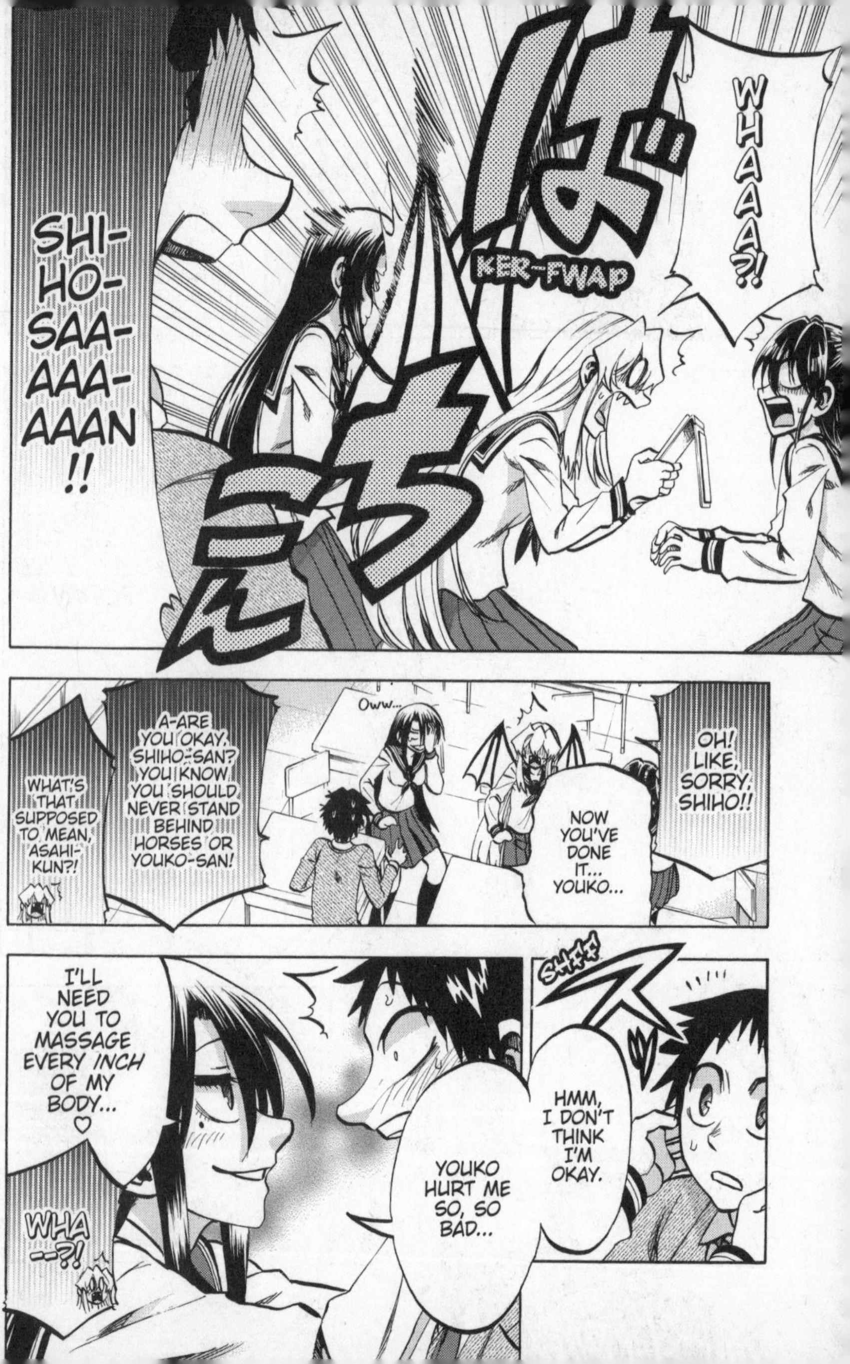
WHAAAA?!
KER-FWAP
SHI-HO-SAAA-AAAA-AAAN!!
OH! LIKE, SORRY, SHIHO!!
NOW YOU'VE DONE IT... YOUKO...
Oww...
A-ARE YOU OKAY, SHIHO-SAN? YOU KNOW YOU SHOULD NEVER STAND BEHIND HORSES OR YOUKO-SAN!
WHAT'S THAT SUPPOSED TO MEAN, ASAHI-KUN?!
SHFF!
HMM, I DON'T THINK I'M OKAY.
YOUKO HURT ME SO, SO BAD...
I'LL NEED YOU TO MASSAGE EVERY *INCH* OF MY BODY... ♡
WHA--?!

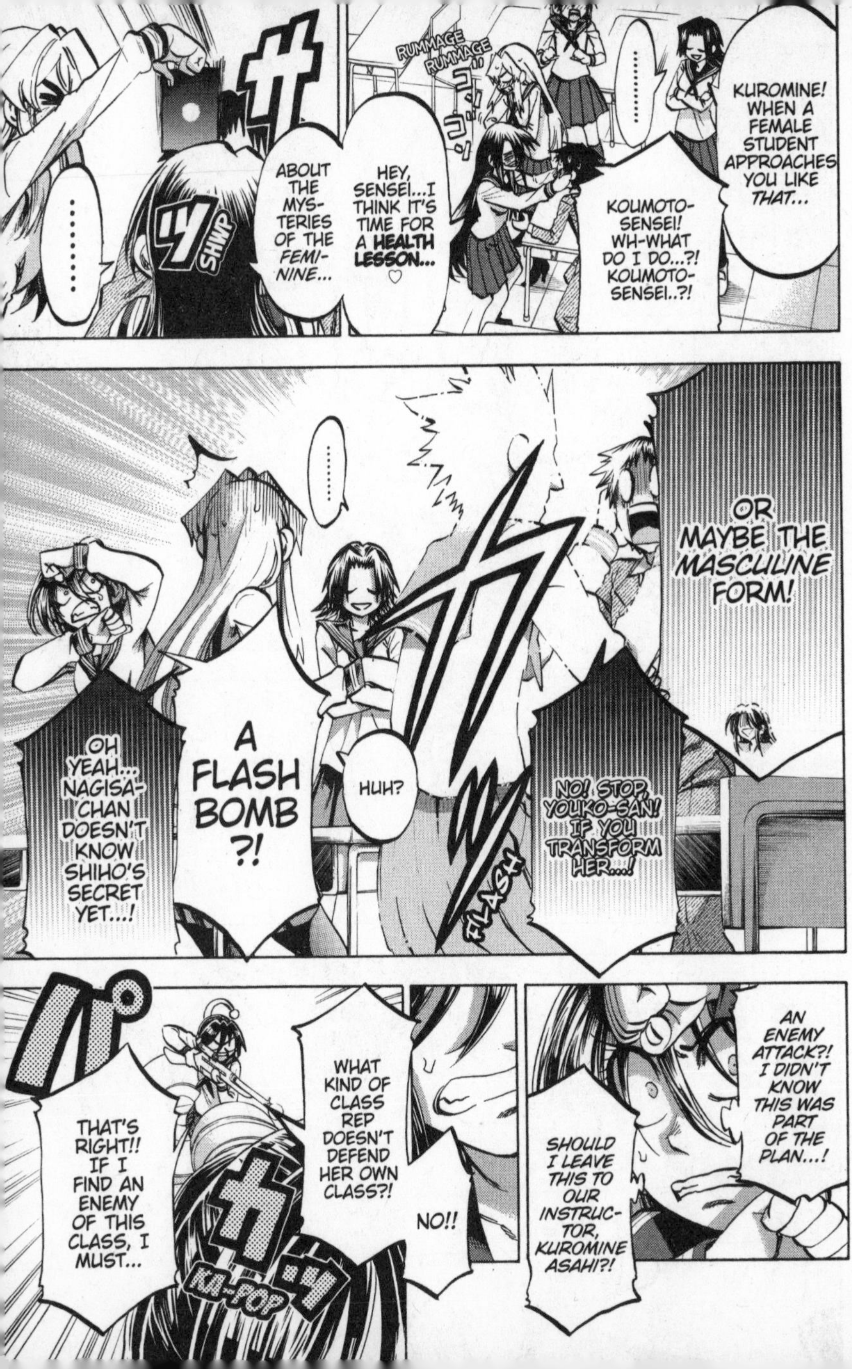
KUROMINE! WHEN A FEMALE STUDENT APPROACHES YOU LIKE *THAT*...
......
KOUMOTO-SENSEI! WH-WHAT DO I DO...?! KOUMOTO-SENSEI..?!
RUMMAGE RUMMAGE
HEY, SENSEI...I THINK IT'S TIME FOR A **HEALTH LESSON...** ♡
ABOUT THE MYSTERIES OF THE *FEMININE*...
SHWP
......
OR MAYBE THE *MASCULINE* FORM!
NO! STOP, YOUKO-SAN! IF YOU TRANSFORM HER...!
FLASH
......
HUH?
A FLASH BOMB?!
OH YEAH... NAGISA-CHAN DOESN'T KNOW SHIHO'S SECRET YET...!
AN ENEMY ATTACK?! I DIDN'T KNOW THIS WAS PART OF THE PLAN...!
SHOULD I LEAVE THIS TO OUR INSTRUCTOR, KUROMINE ASAHI?!
NO!!
WHAT KIND OF CLASS REP DOESN'T DEFEND HER OWN CLASS?!
THAT'S RIGHT!! IF I FIND AN ENEMY OF THIS CLASS, I MUST...
KA-POP

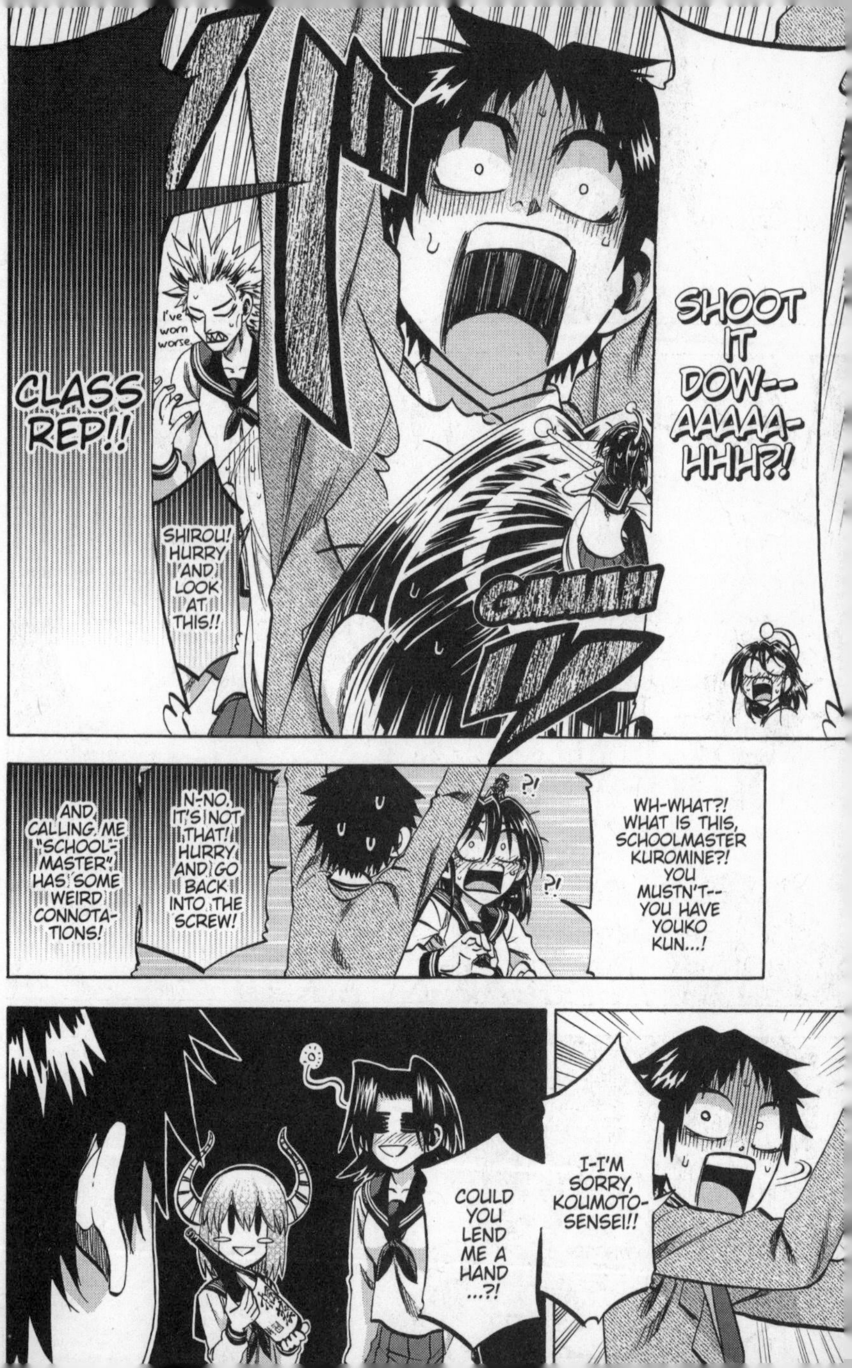
SHOOT IT DOW--AAAAA-HHH?!
CLASS REP!!
SHIROU! HURRY AND LOOK AT THIS!!
I've worn worse.
WH-WHAT?! WHAT IS THIS, SCHOOLMASTER KUROMINE?! YOU MUSTN'T-- YOU HAVE YOUKO KUN...!
?!
?!
N-NO, IT'S NOT THAT! HURRY AND GO BACK INTO THE SCREW!
AND CALLING ME "SCHOOL-MASTER" HAS SOME WEIRD CONNOTA-TIONS!
I-I'M SORRY, KOUMOTO-SENSEI!!
COULD YOU LEND ME A HAND ...?!

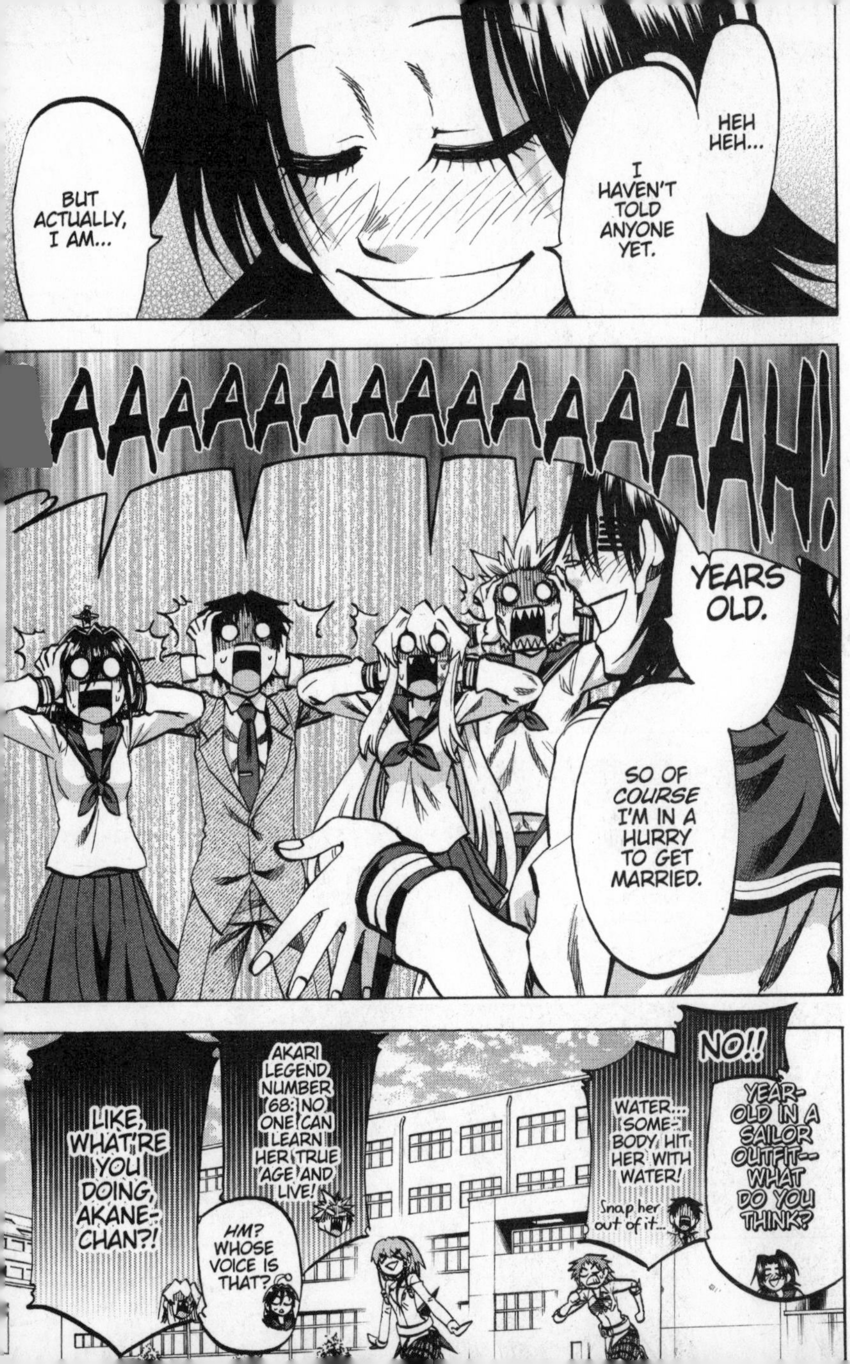
HEH HEH...
I HAVEN'T TOLD ANYONE YET.
BUT ACTUALLY, I AM...
YEARS OLD.
AAAAAAAAAAAAAAAH!
SO OF COURSE I'M IN A HURRY TO GET MARRIED.
NO!!
YEAR-OLD IN A SAILOR OUTFIT-- WHAT DO YOU THINK?
WATER... SOMEBODY, HIT HER WITH WATER!
Snap her out of it...
AKARI LEGEND NUMBER 68: NO ONE CAN LEARN HER TRUE AGE AND LIVE!
HM? WHOSE VOICE IS THAT?
LIKE, WHAT'RE YOU DOING, AKANE-CHAN?!

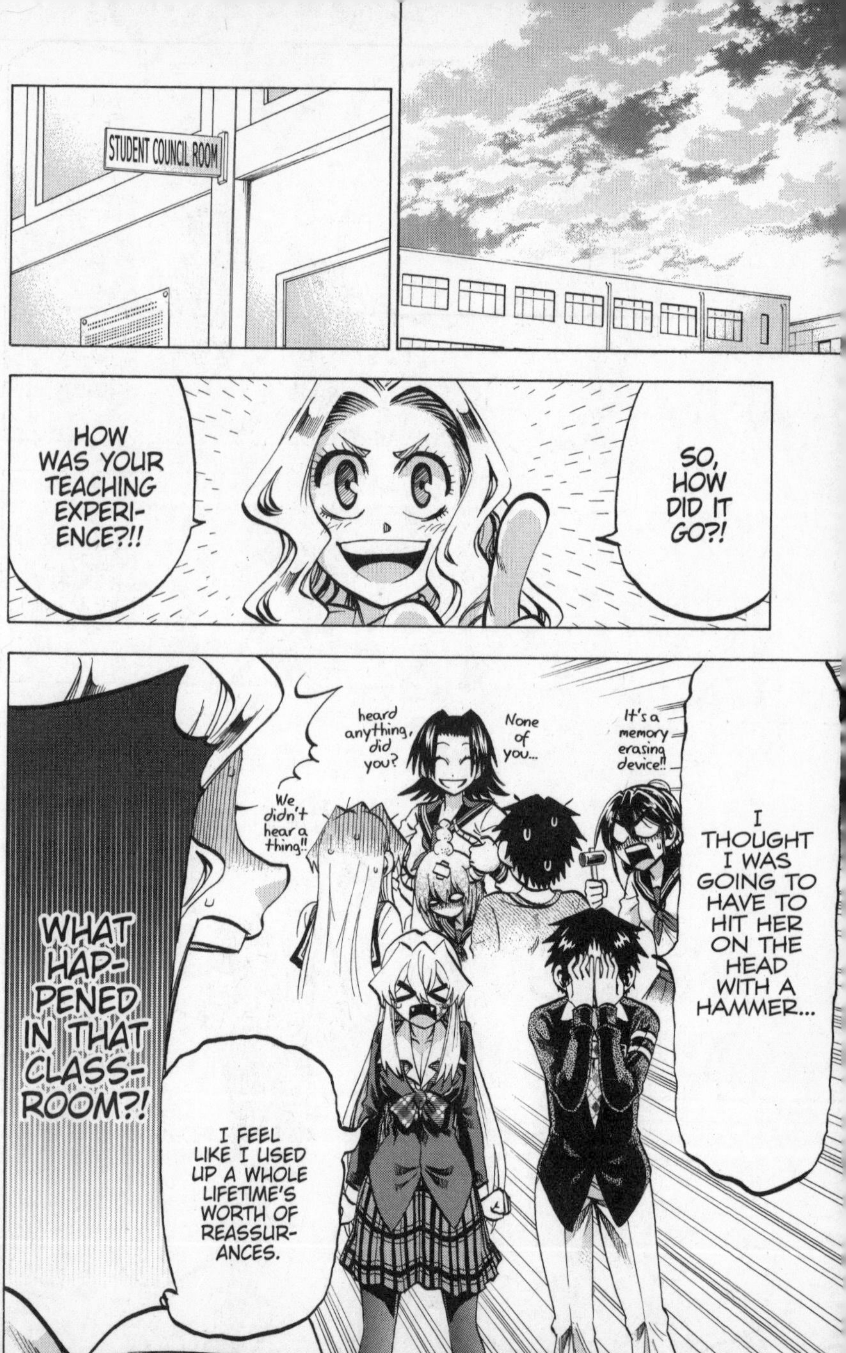
STUDENT COUNCIL ROOM
SO, HOW DID IT GO?!
HOW WAS YOUR TEACHING EXPERIENCE?!!
I THOUGHT I WAS GOING TO HAVE TO HIT HER ON THE HEAD WITH A HAMMER...
It's a memory erasing device!!
None of you...
heard anything, did you?
We, didn't hear a thing!!
I FEEL LIKE I USED UP A WHOLE LIFETIME'S WORTH OF REASSURANCES.
WHAT HAPPENED IN THAT CLASSROOM?!

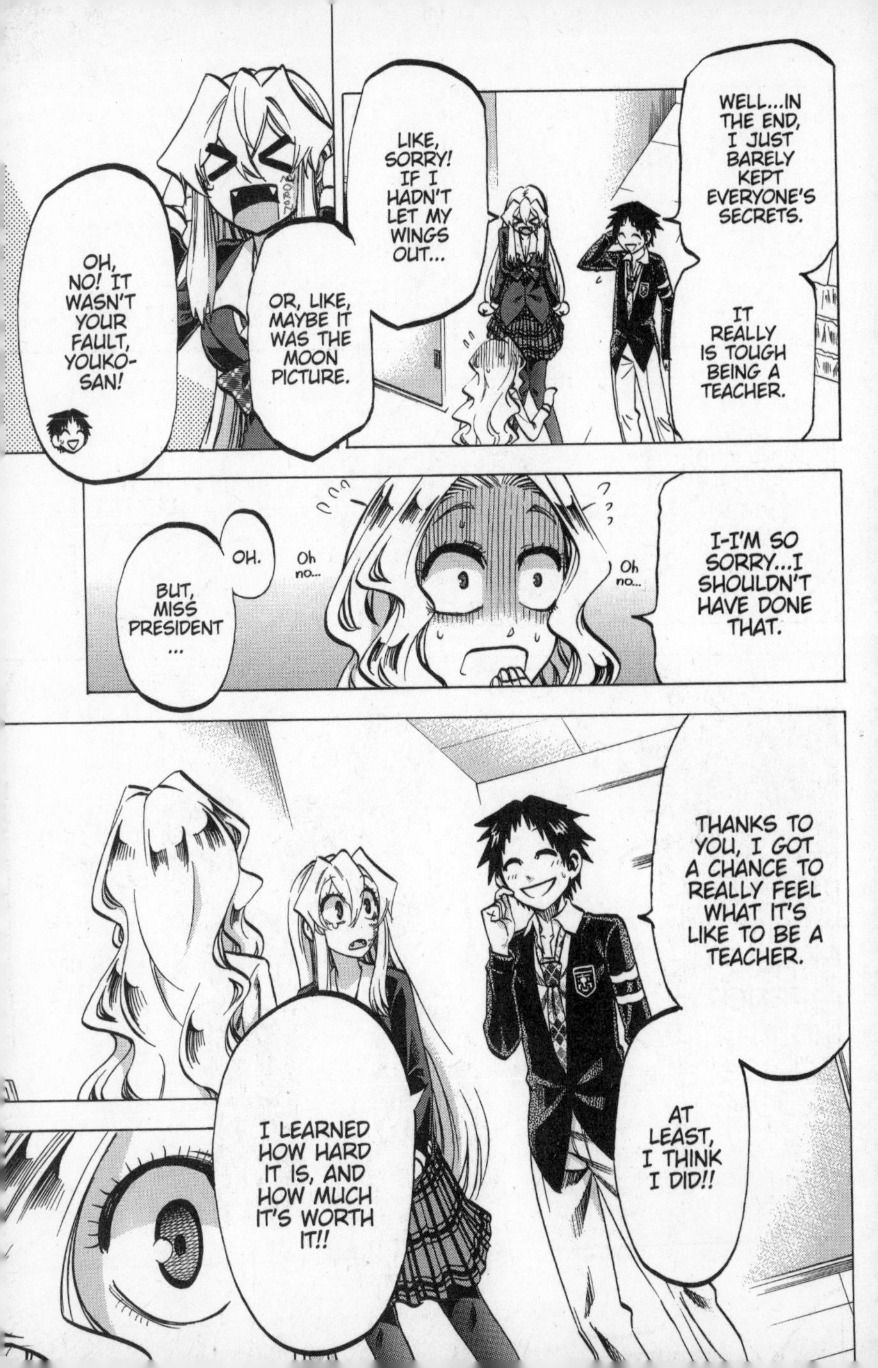
WELL...IN THE END, I JUST BARELY KEPT EVERYONE'S SECRETS.
IT REALLY IS TOUGH BEING A TEACHER.
LIKE, SORRY! IF I HADN'T LET MY WINGS OUT...
OR, LIKE, MAYBE IT WAS THE MOON PICTURE.
OH, NO! IT WASN'T YOUR FAULT, YOUKO-SAN!
I-I'M SO SORRY...I SHOULDN'T HAVE DONE THAT.
Oh no...
Oh no...
OH.
BUT, MISS PRESIDENT...
THANKS TO YOU, I GOT A CHANCE TO REALLY FEEL WHAT IT'S LIKE TO BE A TEACHER.
AT LEAST, I THINK I DID!!
I LEARNED HOW HARD IT IS, AND HOW MUCH IT'S WORTH IT!!

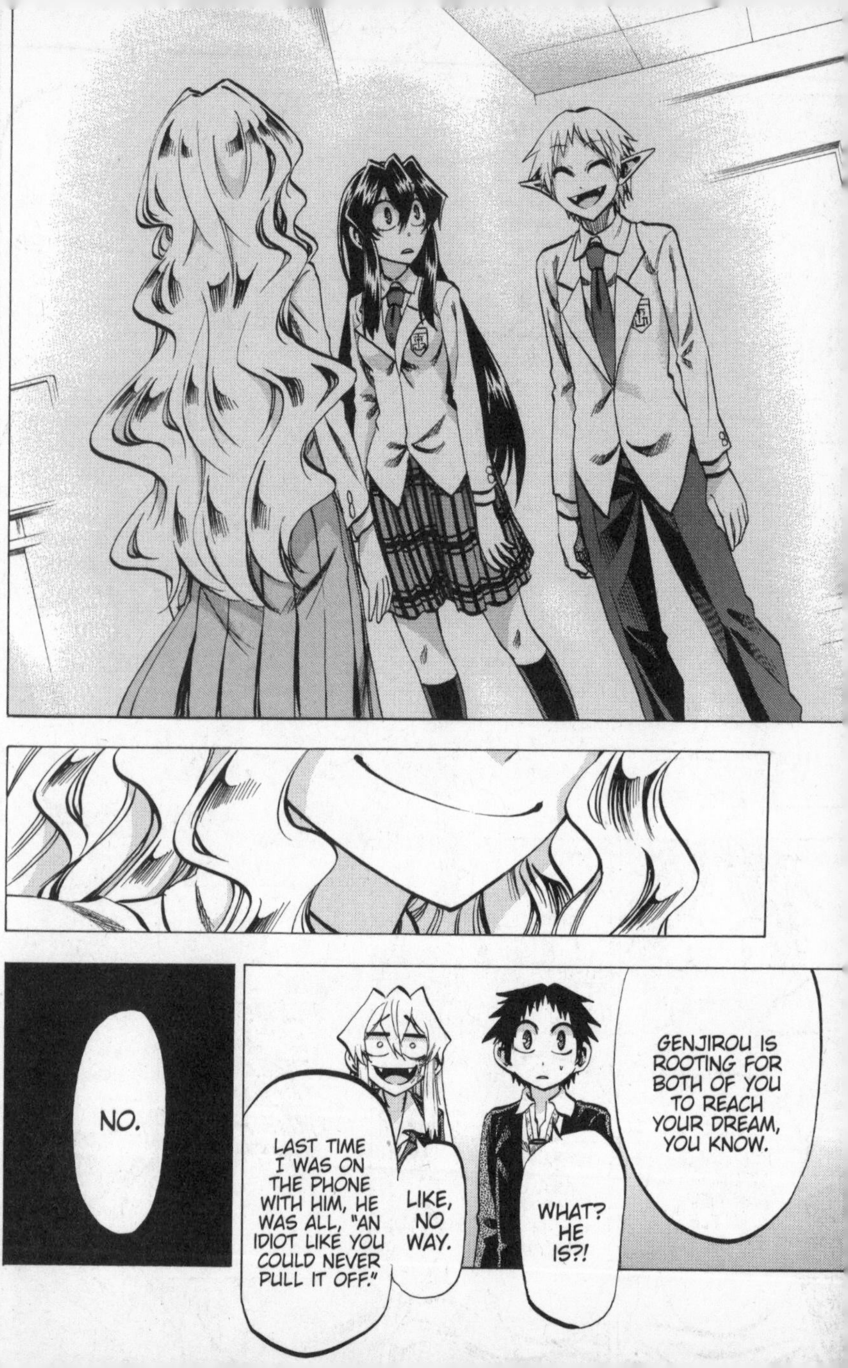
GENJIROU IS ROOTING FOR BOTH OF YOU TO REACH YOUR DREAM, YOU KNOW.
WHAT? HE IS?!
LIKE, NO WAY.
LAST TIME I WAS ON THE PHONE WITH HIM, HE WAS ALL, "AN IDIOT LIKE YOU COULD NEVER PULL IT OFF."
NO.

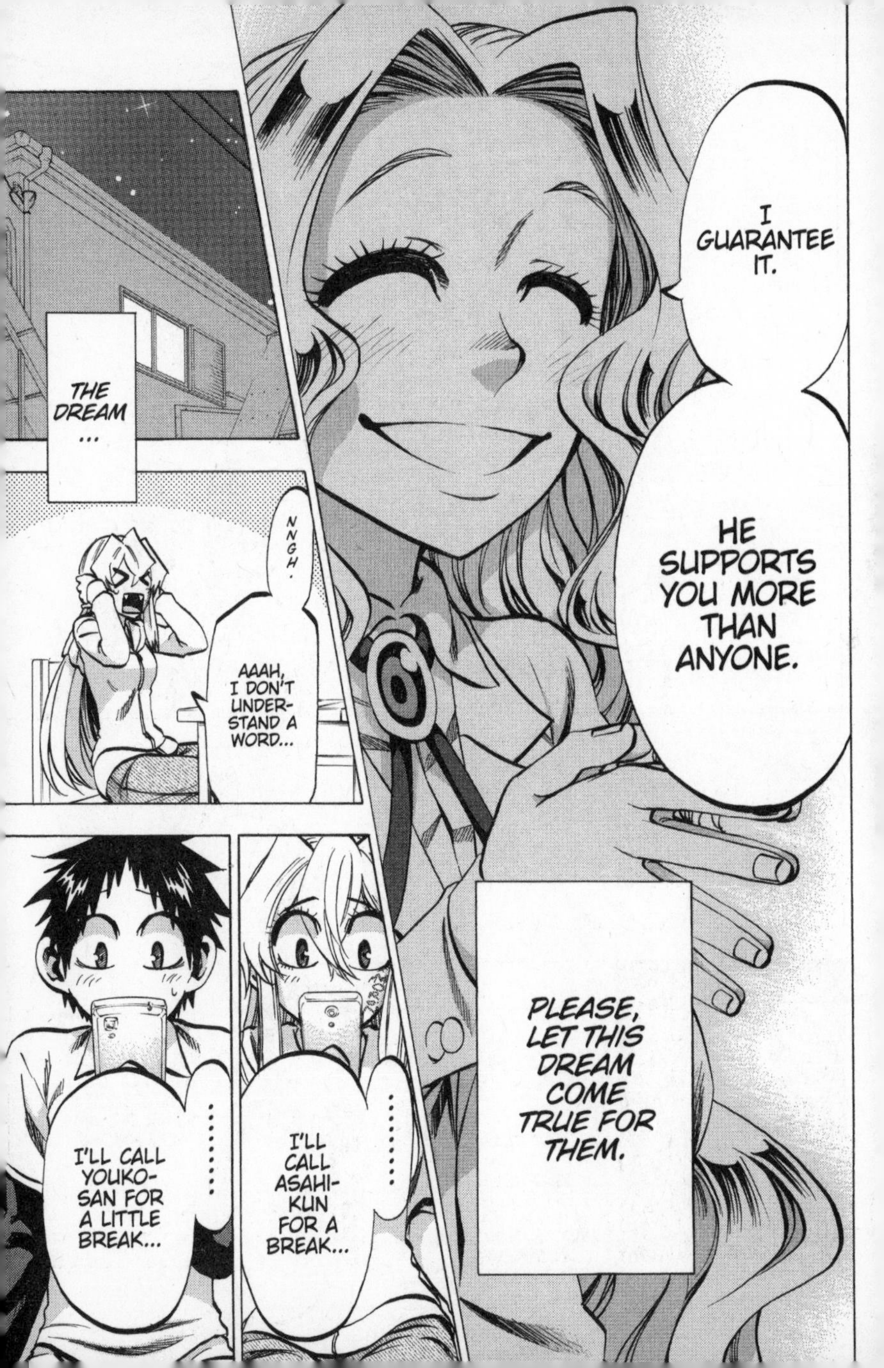
I GUARANTEE IT.
HE SUPPORTS YOU MORE THAN ANYONE.
PLEASE, LET THIS DREAM COME TRUE FOR THEM.
THE DREAM...
NNGH.
AAAH, I DON'T UNDER-STAND A WORD...
......
I'LL CALL ASAHI-KUN FOR A BREAK...
......
I'LL CALL YOUKO-SAN FOR A LITTLE BREAK...

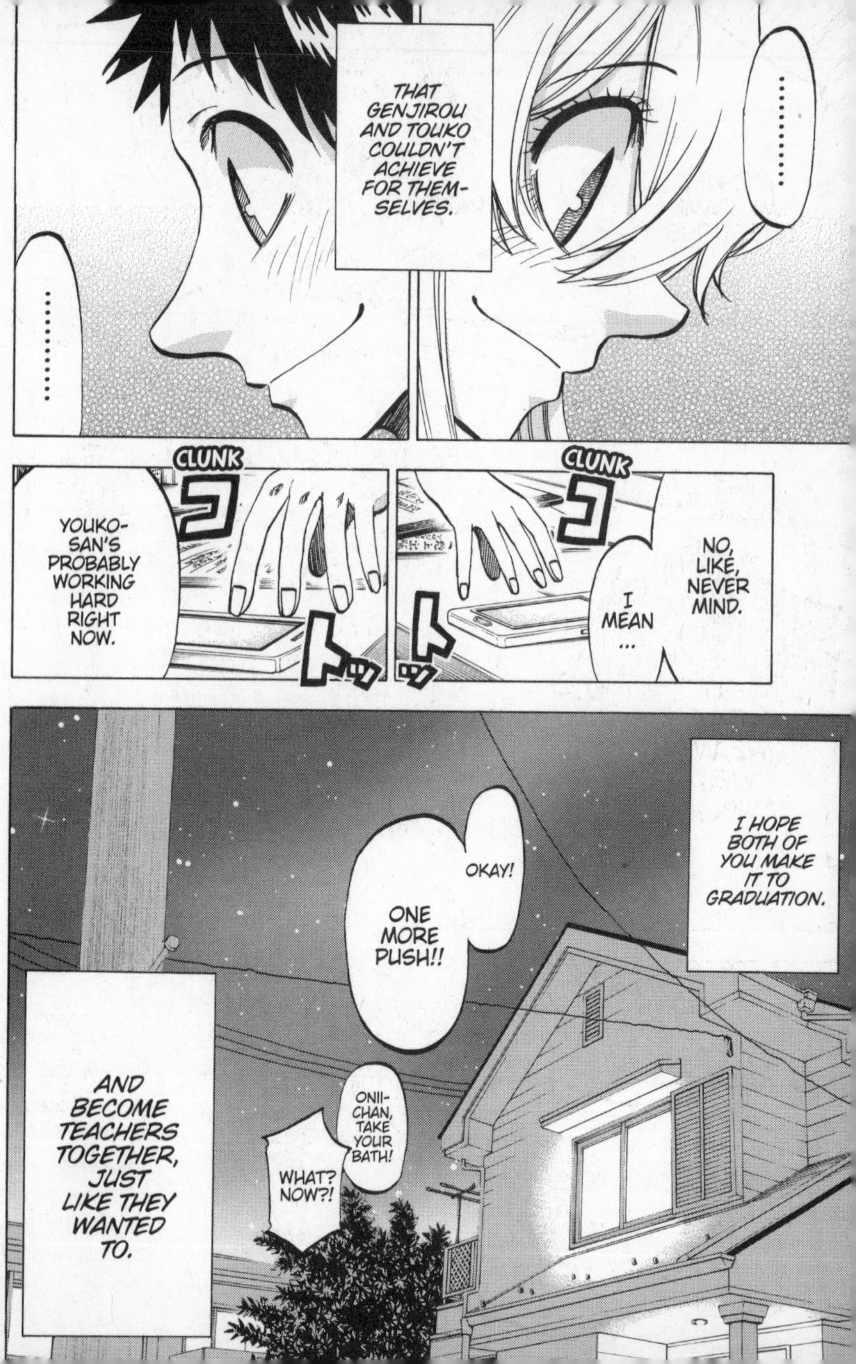
……
THAT GENJIROU AND TOUKO COULDN'T ACHIEVE FOR THEMSELVES.
……
CLUNK
コ
ドッ
NO, LIKE, NEVER MIND.
I MEAN ...
CLUNK
コ
ドッ
YOUKO-SAN'S PROBABLY WORKING HARD RIGHT NOW.
I HOPE BOTH OF YOU MAKE IT TO GRADUATION.
OKAY!
ONE MORE PUSH!!
ONII-CHAN, TAKE YOUR BATH!
WHAT? NOW?!
AND BECOME TEACHERS TOGETHER, JUST LIKE THEY WANTED TO.

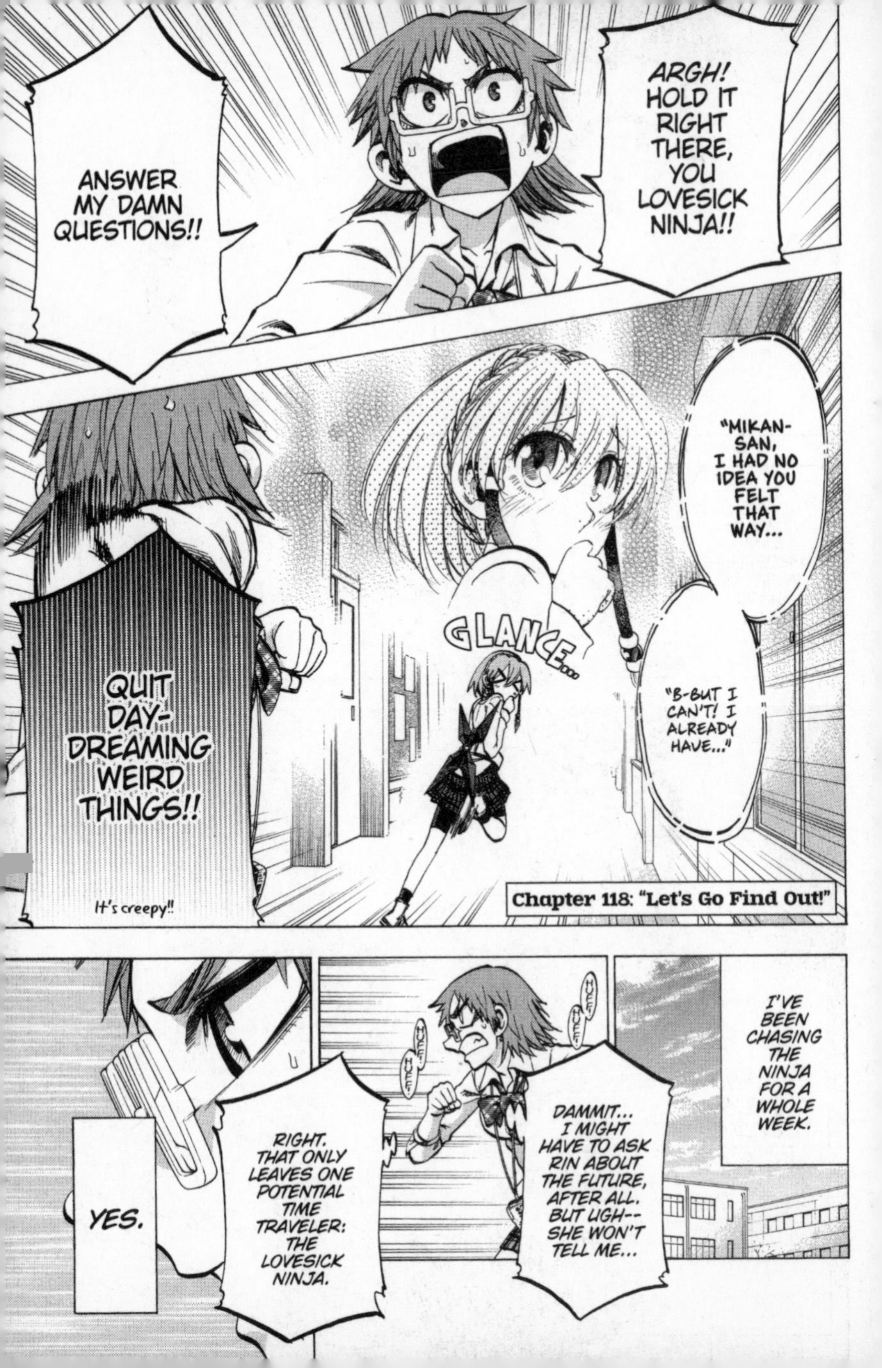
ARGH! HOLD IT RIGHT THERE, YOU LOVESICK NINJA!!
ANSWER MY DAMN QUESTIONS!!
"MIKAN-SAN, I HAD NO IDEA YOU FELT THAT WAY...
"B-BUT I CAN'T! I ALREADY HAVE..."
GLANCE...
QUIT DAY-DREAMING WEIRD THINGS!!
It's creepy!!
Chapter 118: "Let's Go Find Out!"
I'VE BEEN CHASING THE NINJA FOR A WHOLE WEEK.
HUFF HUFF
HUFF HUFF
DAMMIT... I MIGHT HAVE TO ASK RIN ABOUT THE FUTURE, AFTER ALL. BUT UGH-- SHE WON'T TELL ME...
RIGHT. THAT ONLY LEAVES ONE POTENTIAL TIME TRAVELER: THE LOVESICK NINJA.
YES.

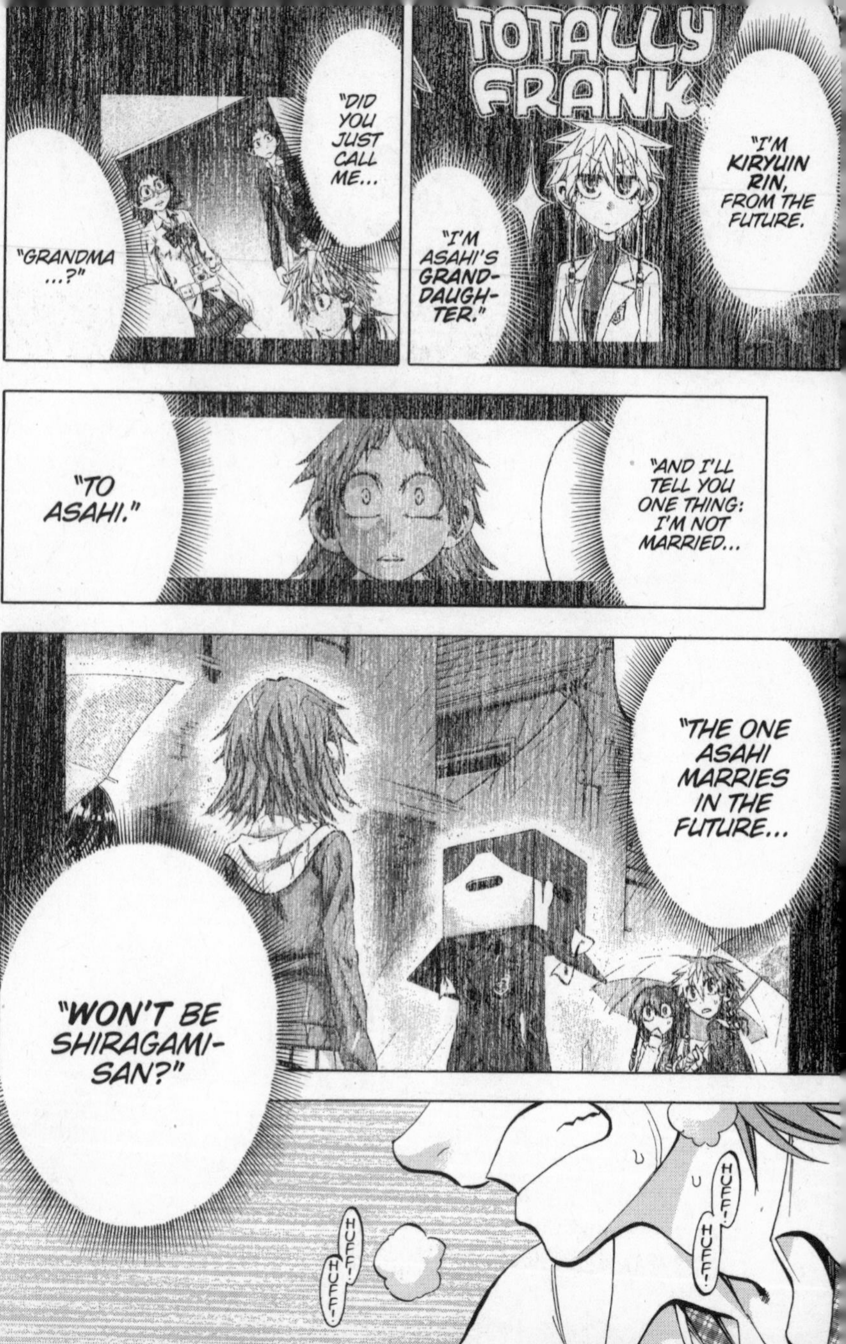
TOTALLY FRANK
"I'M KIRYUIN RIN, FROM THE FUTURE.
"I'M ASAHI'S GRAND-DAUGH-TER."
"DID YOU JUST CALL ME...
"GRANDMA ...?"
"AND I'LL TELL YOU ONE THING: I'M NOT MARRIED...
"TO ASAHI."
"THE ONE ASAHI MARRIES IN THE FUTURE...
"WON'T BE SHIRAGAMI-SAN?"
HUFF! HUFF!
HUFF! HUFF!

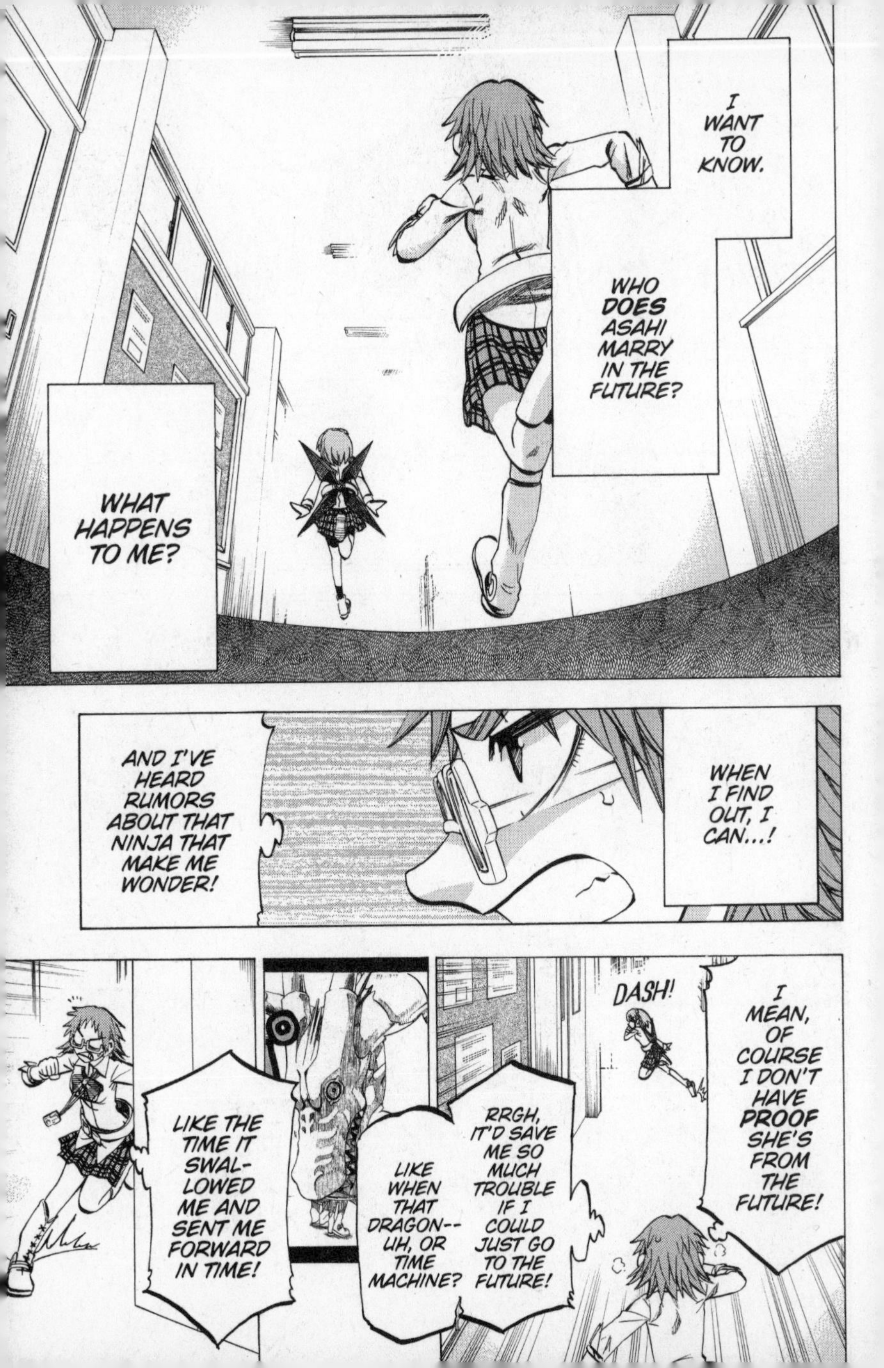
I WANT TO KNOW.
WHO DOES ASAHI MARRY IN THE FUTURE?
WHAT HAPPENS TO ME?
WHEN I FIND OUT, I CAN...!
AND I'VE HEARD RUMORS ABOUT THAT NINJA THAT MAKE ME WONDER!
I MEAN, OF COURSE I DON'T HAVE PROOF SHE'S FROM THE FUTURE!
DASH!
RRGH, IT'D SAVE ME SO MUCH TROUBLE IF I COULD JUST GO TO THE FUTURE!
LIKE WHEN THAT DRAGON-- UH, OR TIME MACHINE?
LIKE THE TIME IT SWAL-LOWED ME AND SENT ME FORWARD IN TIME!

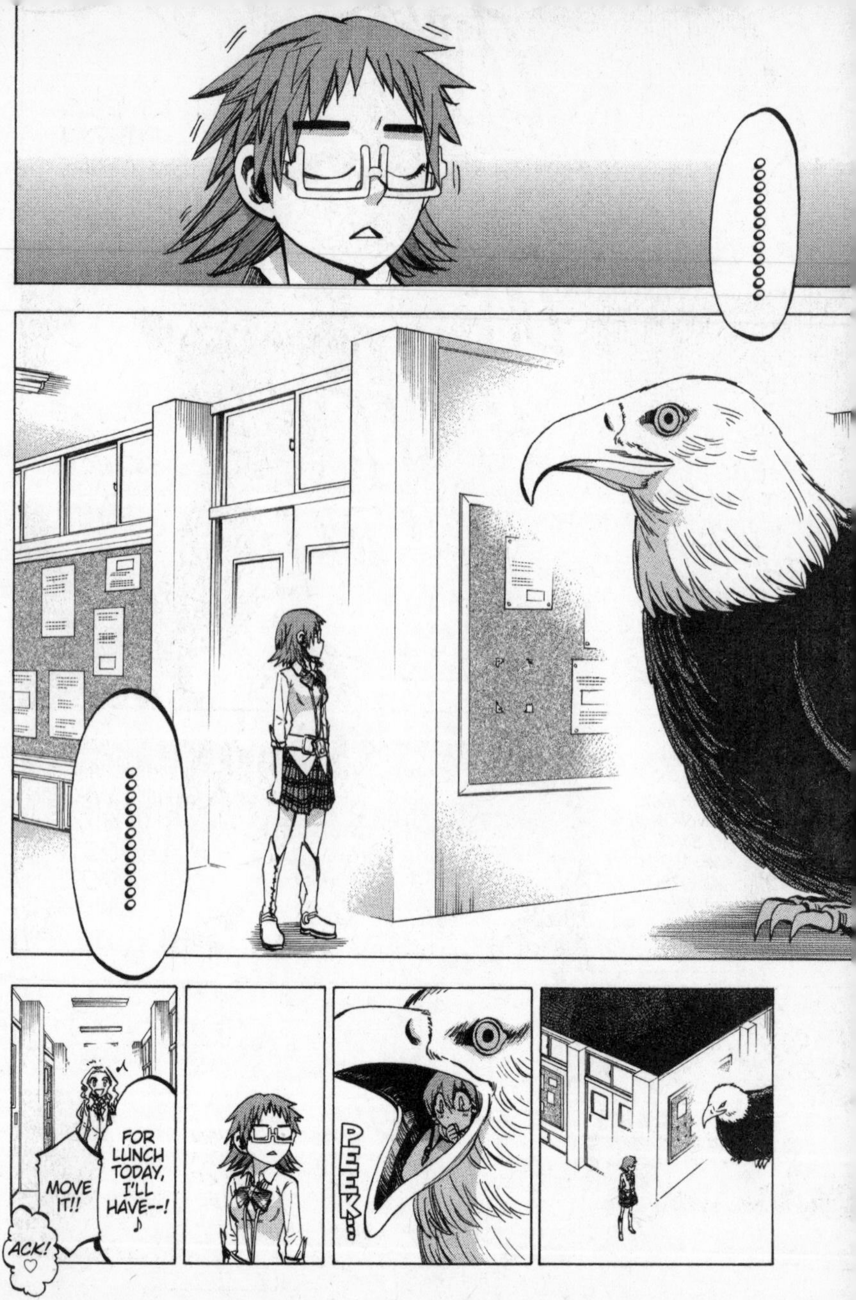

...
...
PEEK...
FOR LUNCH TODAY, I'LL HAVE--! ♪
MOVE IT!!
ACK! ♡

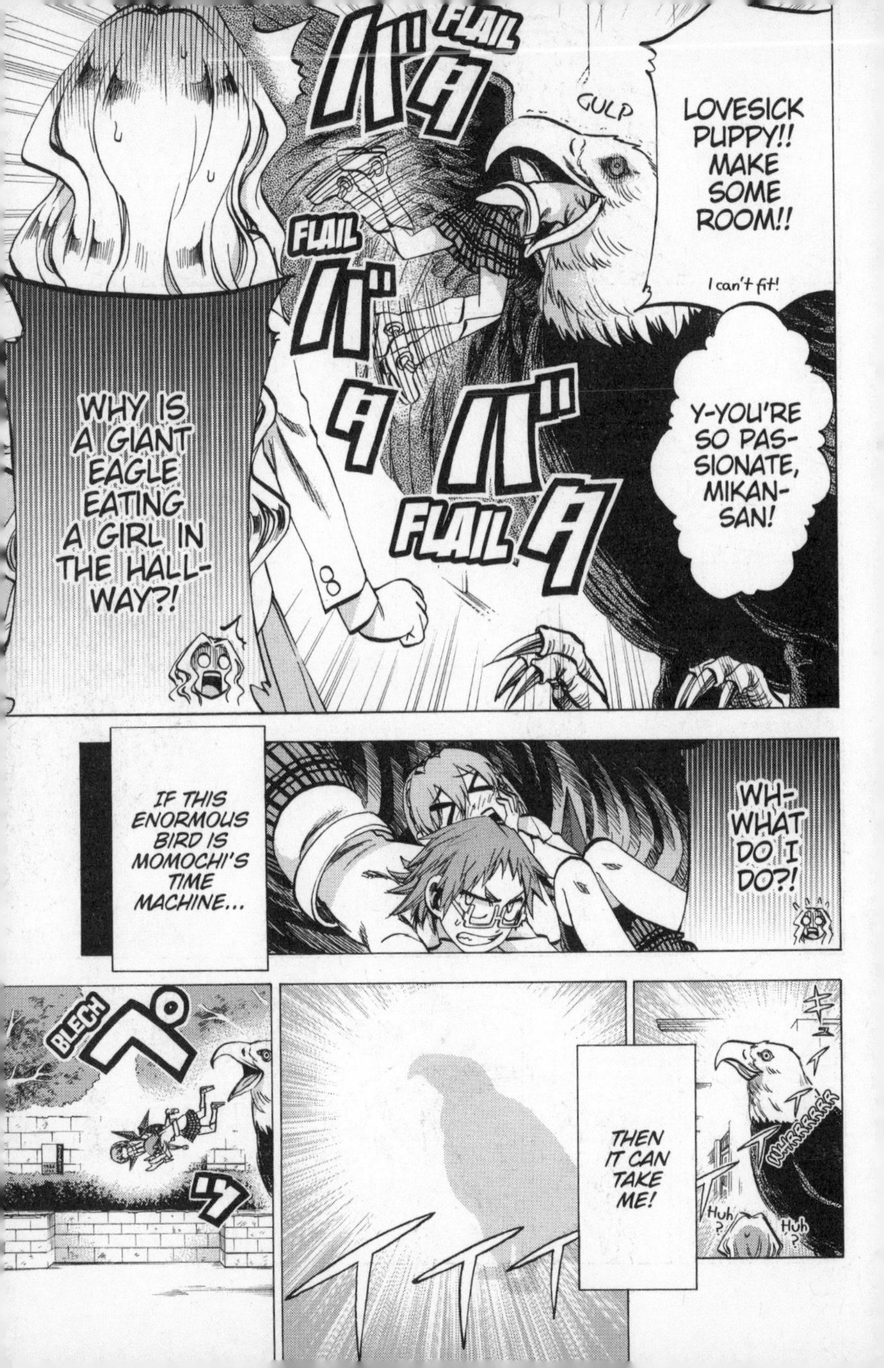

LOVESICK PUPPY!! MAKE SOME ROOM!!
GULP
I can't fit!
FLAIL
FLAIL
Y-YOU'RE SO PAS-SIONATE, MIKAN-SAN!
FLAIL
WHY IS A GIANT EAGLE EATING A GIRL IN THE HALL-WAY?!
WH-WHAT DO I DO?!
IF THIS ENORMOUS BIRD IS MOMOCHI'S TIME MACHINE...
Huh?
Huh?
WHRRRRRR
THEN IT CAN TAKE ME!
BLECH

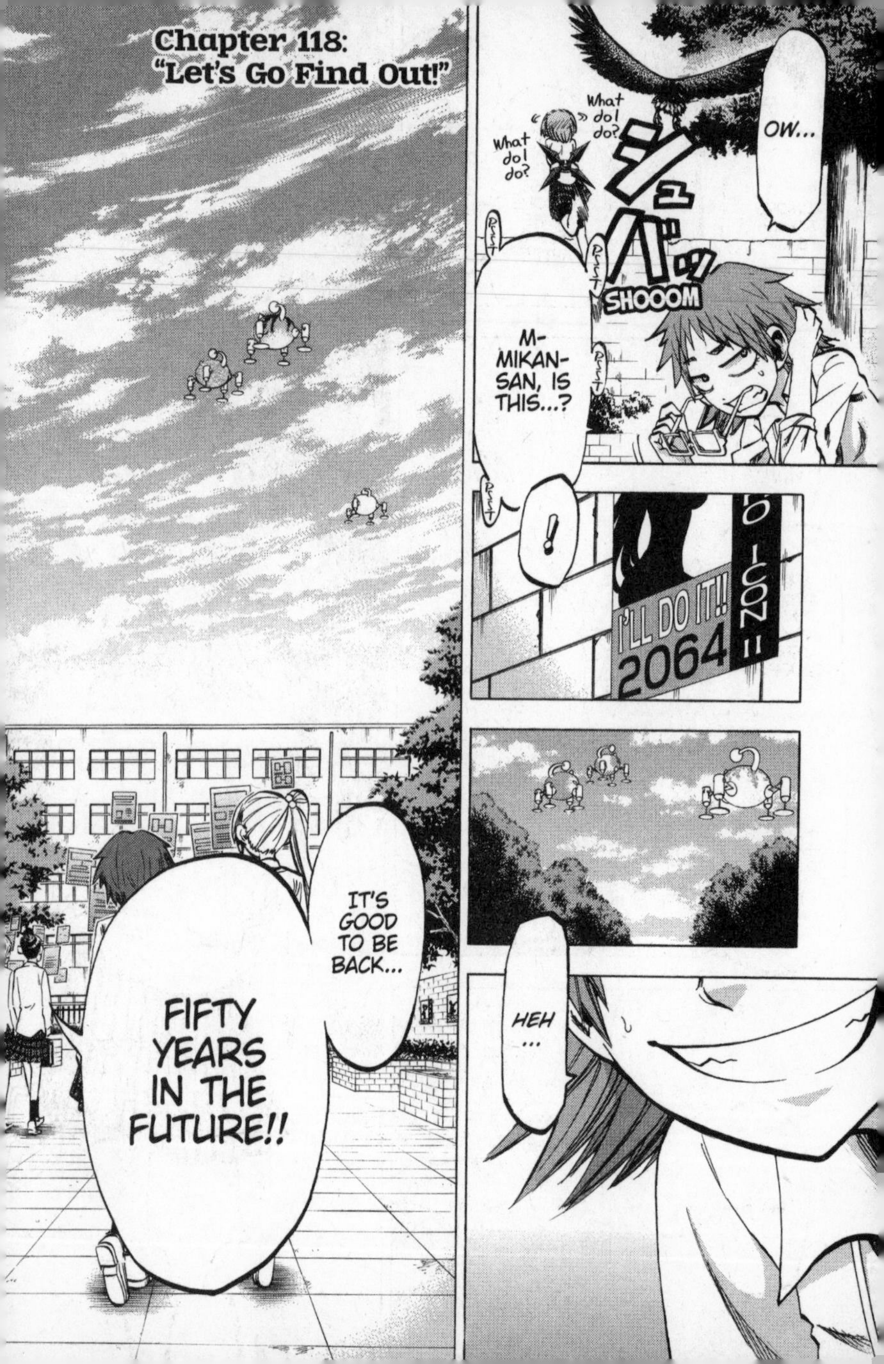
OW...
What do I do? What do I do?
シュバッ
SHOOOM
PSST PSST PSST
M-MIKAN-SAN, IS THIS...?
PSST
!
I'LL DO IT!! 2064
ICON
HEH ...
Chapter 118: "Let's Go Find Out!"
IT'S GOOD TO BE BACK...
FIFTY YEARS IN THE FUTURE!!

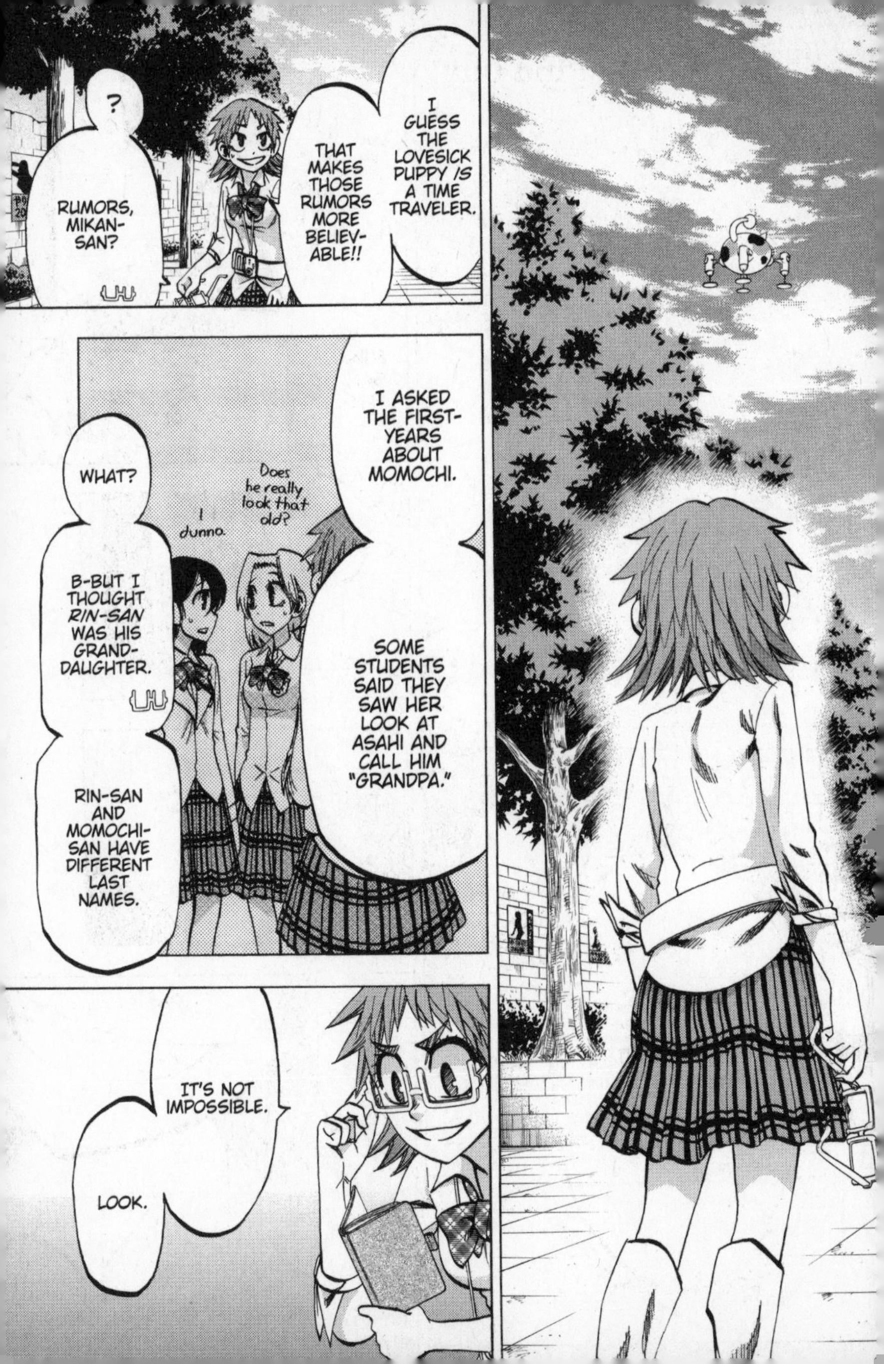
I GUESS THE LOVESICK PUPPY *IS* A TIME TRAVELER.
THAT MAKES THOSE RUMORS MORE BELIEVABLE!!
?
RUMORS, MIKAN-SAN?
I ASKED THE FIRST-YEARS ABOUT MOMOCHI.
SOME STUDENTS SAID THEY SAW HER LOOK AT ASAHI AND CALL HIM "GRANDPA."
Does he really look that old?
I dunno.
WHAT?
B-BUT I THOUGHT *RIN-SAN* WAS HIS GRANDDAUGHTER.
RIN-SAN AND MOMOCHI-SAN HAVE DIFFERENT LAST NAMES.
IT'S NOT IMPOSSIBLE.
LOOK.

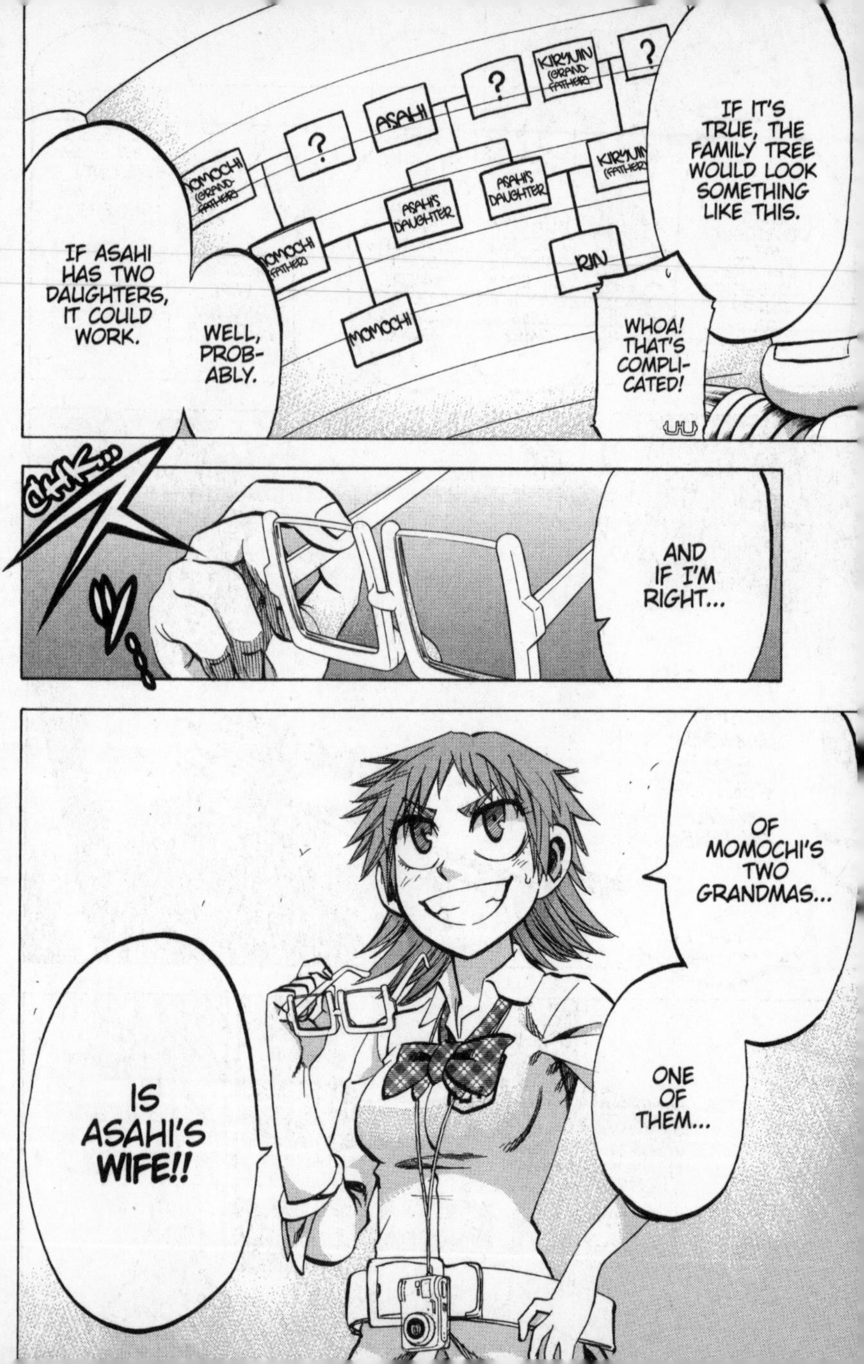
IF IT'S TRUE, THE FAMILY TREE WOULD LOOK SOMETHING LIKE THIS.
?
KIRYUIN (GRANDFATHER)
?
ASAHI
?
MOMOCHI (GRANDFATHER)
KIRYUIN (FATHER)
ASAHI'S DAUGHTER
ASAHI'S DAUGHTER
MOMOCHI (FATHER)
RIN
MOMOCHI
WHOA! THAT'S COMPLICATED!
WELL, PROBABLY.
IF ASAHI HAS TWO DAUGHTERS, IT COULD WORK.
AND IF I'M RIGHT...
OF MOMOCHI'S TWO GRANDMAS...
ONE OF THEM...
IS ASAHI'S WIFE!!

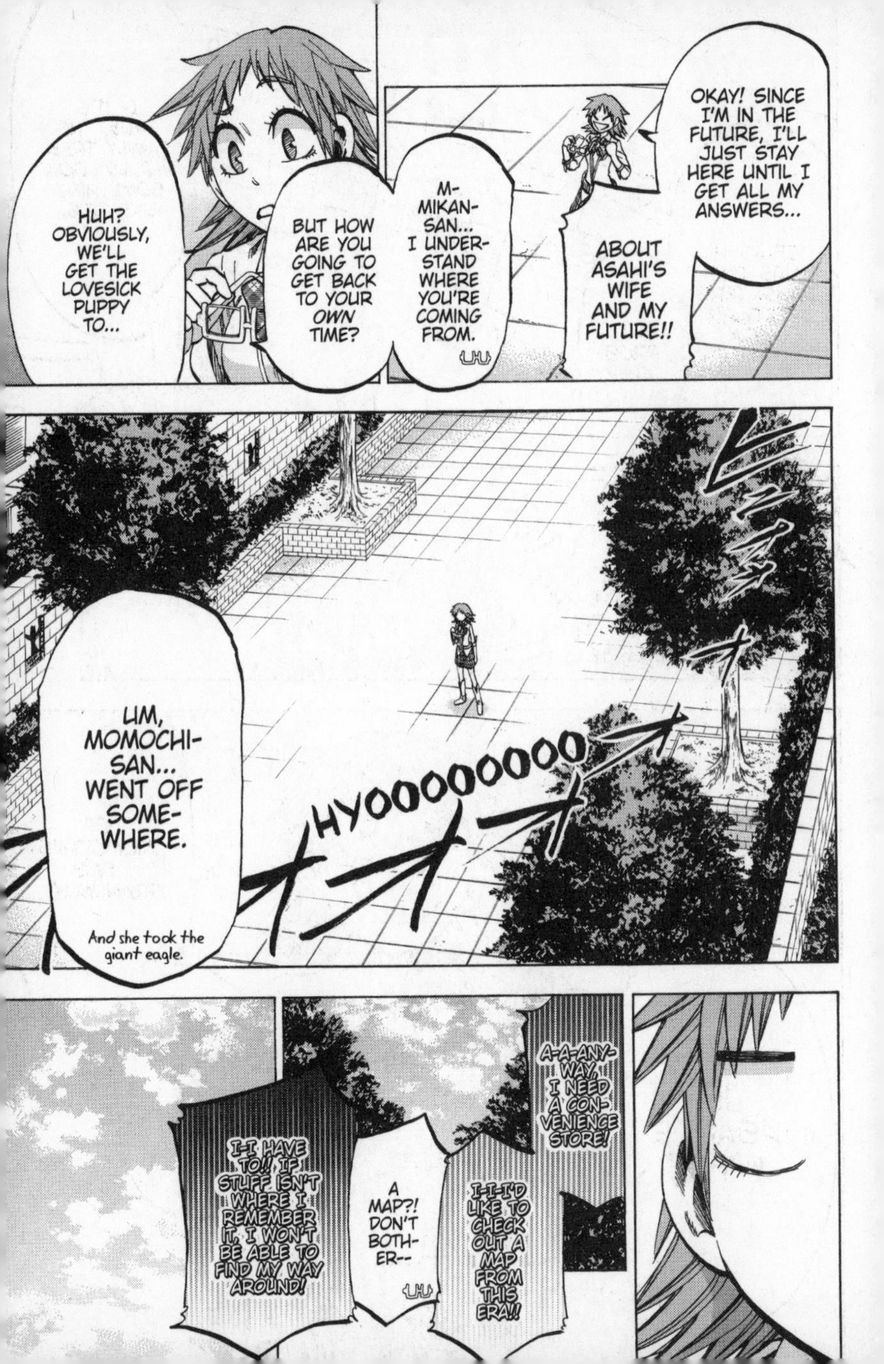
OKAY! SINCE I'M IN THE FUTURE, I'LL JUST STAY HERE UNTIL I GET ALL MY ANSWERS...
ABOUT ASAHI'S WIFE AND MY FUTURE!!
M-MIKAN-SAN... I UNDERSTAND WHERE YOU'RE COMING FROM.
BUT HOW ARE YOU GOING TO GET BACK TO YOUR *OWN* TIME?
HUH? OBVIOUSLY, WE'LL GET THE LOVESICK PUPPY TO...
HYOOOOOOOOO
UM, MOMOCHI-SAN... WENT OFF SOMEWHERE.
And she took the giant eagle.
A-A-ANYWAY, I NEED A CONVENIENCE STORE!
I-I-I'D LIKE TO CHECK OUT A MAP FROM THIS ERA!!
A MAP?! DON'T BOTHER--
I-I HAVE TO!! IF STUFF ISN'T WHERE I REMEMBER IT, I WON'T BE ABLE TO FIND MY WAY AROUND!

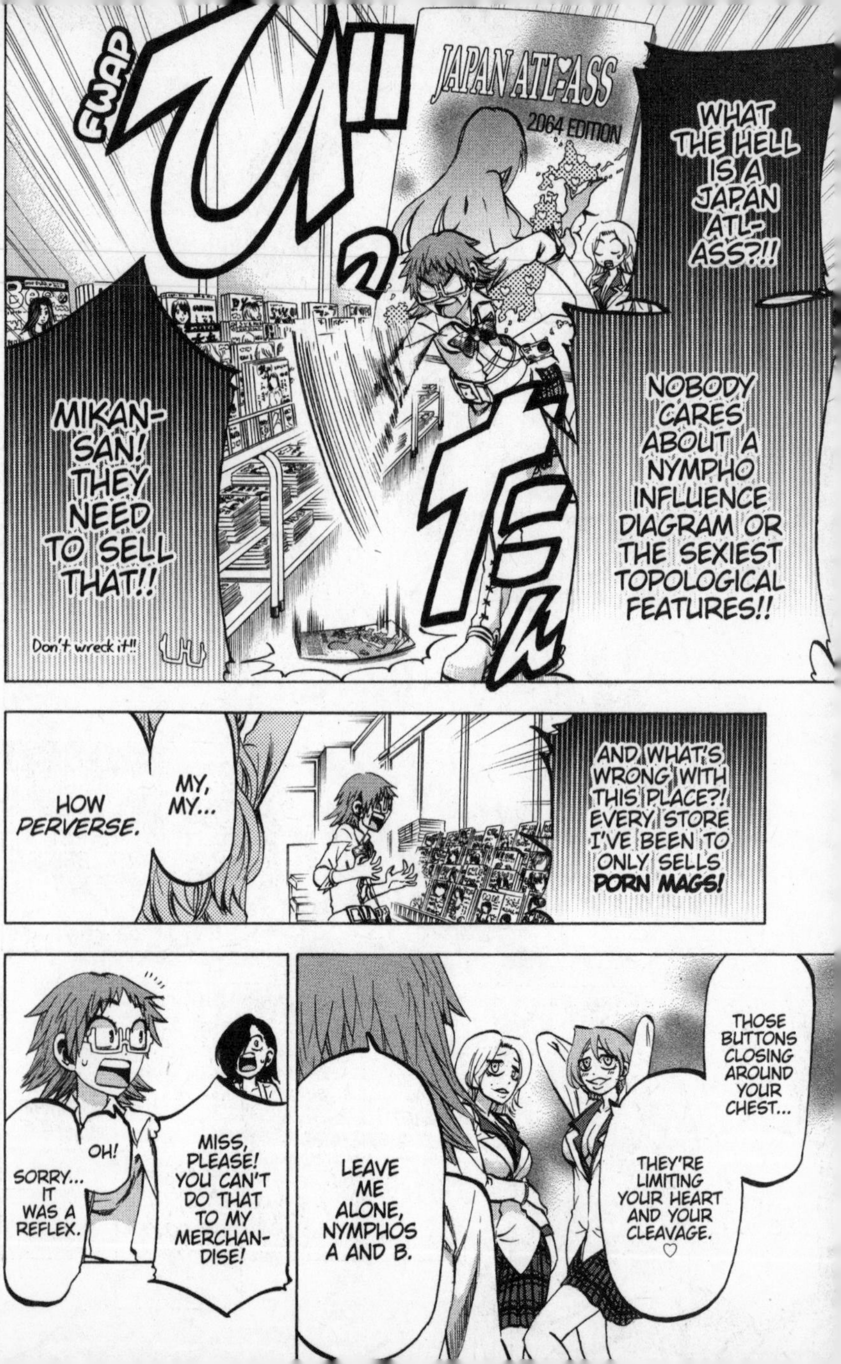
JAPAN ATL-ASS
2064 EDITION
WHAT THE HELL IS A JAPAN ATL-ASS?!!
FWAP
NOBODY CARES ABOUT A NYMPHO INFLUENCE DIAGRAM OR THE SEXIEST TOPOLOGICAL FEATURES!!
MIKAN-SAN! THEY NEED TO SELL THAT!!
Don't wreck it!!
AND WHAT'S WRONG WITH THIS PLACE?! EVERY STORE I'VE BEEN TO ONLY SELLS **PORN MAGS!**
MY, MY...
HOW *PERVERSE.*
THOSE BUTTONS CLOSING AROUND YOUR CHEST...
THEY'RE LIMITING YOUR HEART AND YOUR CLEAVAGE. ♡
LEAVE ME ALONE, NYMPHOS A AND B.
MISS, PLEASE! YOU CAN'T DO THAT TO MY MERCHANDISE!
OH!
SORRY... IT WAS A REFLEX.

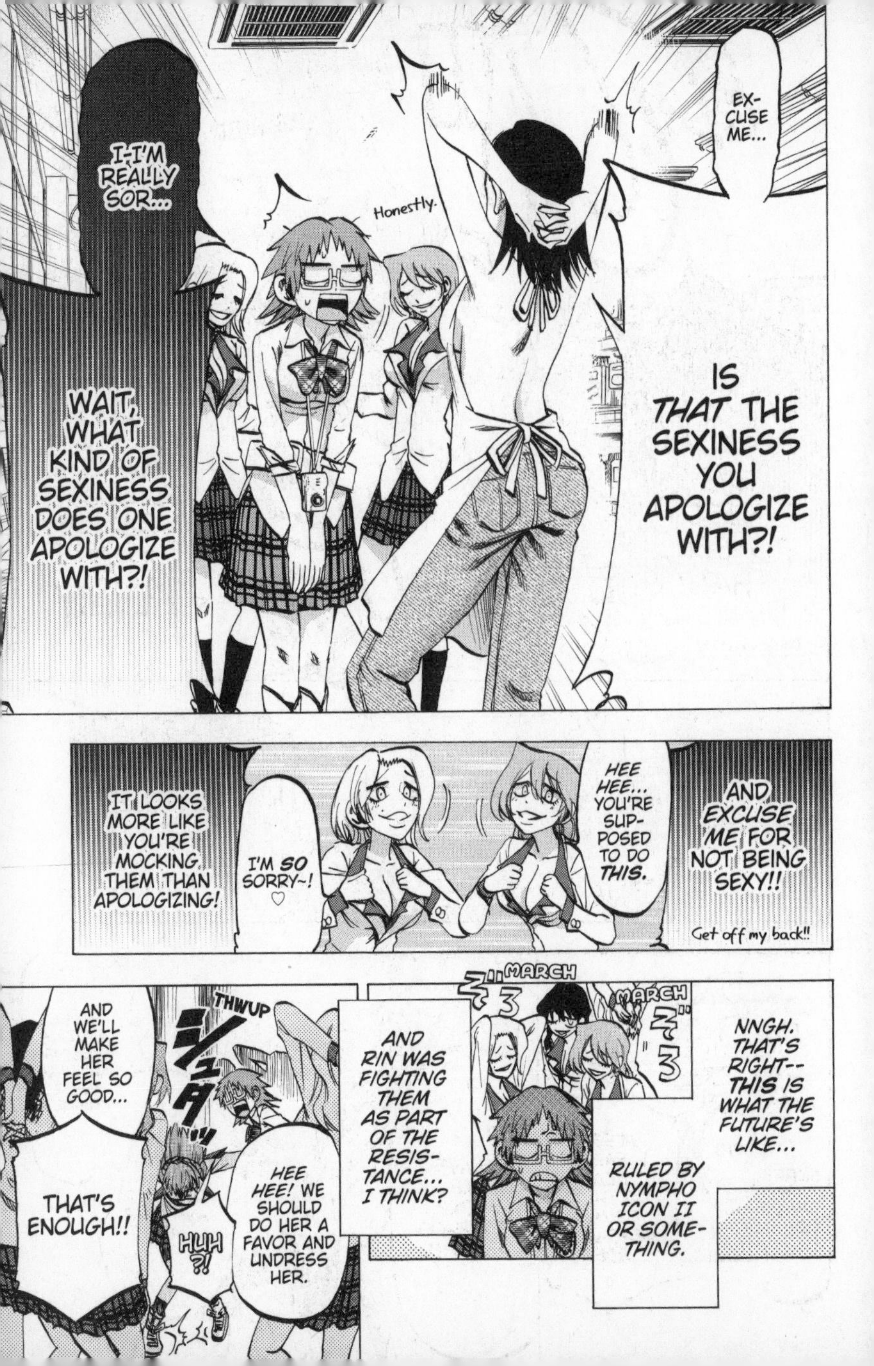
EX-CUSE ME...
IS THAT THE SEXINESS YOU APOLOGIZE WITH?!
Honestly.
I-I'M REALLY SOR...
WAIT, WHAT KIND OF SEXINESS DOES ONE APOLOGIZE WITH?!
AND EXCUSE ME FOR NOT BEING SEXY!!
Get off my back!!
HEE HEE... YOU'RE SUP-POSED TO DO THIS.
I'M SO SORRY~! ♡
IT LOOKS MORE LIKE YOU'RE MOCKING THEM THAN APOLOGIZING!
NNGH. THAT'S RIGHT-- THIS IS WHAT THE FUTURE'S LIKE...
MARCH
MARCH
RULED BY NYMPHO ICON II OR SOME-THING.
AND RIN WAS FIGHTING THEM AS PART OF THE RESIS-TANCE... I THINK?
HEE HEE! WE SHOULD DO HER A FAVOR AND UNDRESS HER.
AND WE'LL MAKE HER FEEL SO GOOD...
THWUP
THAT'S ENOUGH!!
HUH ?!

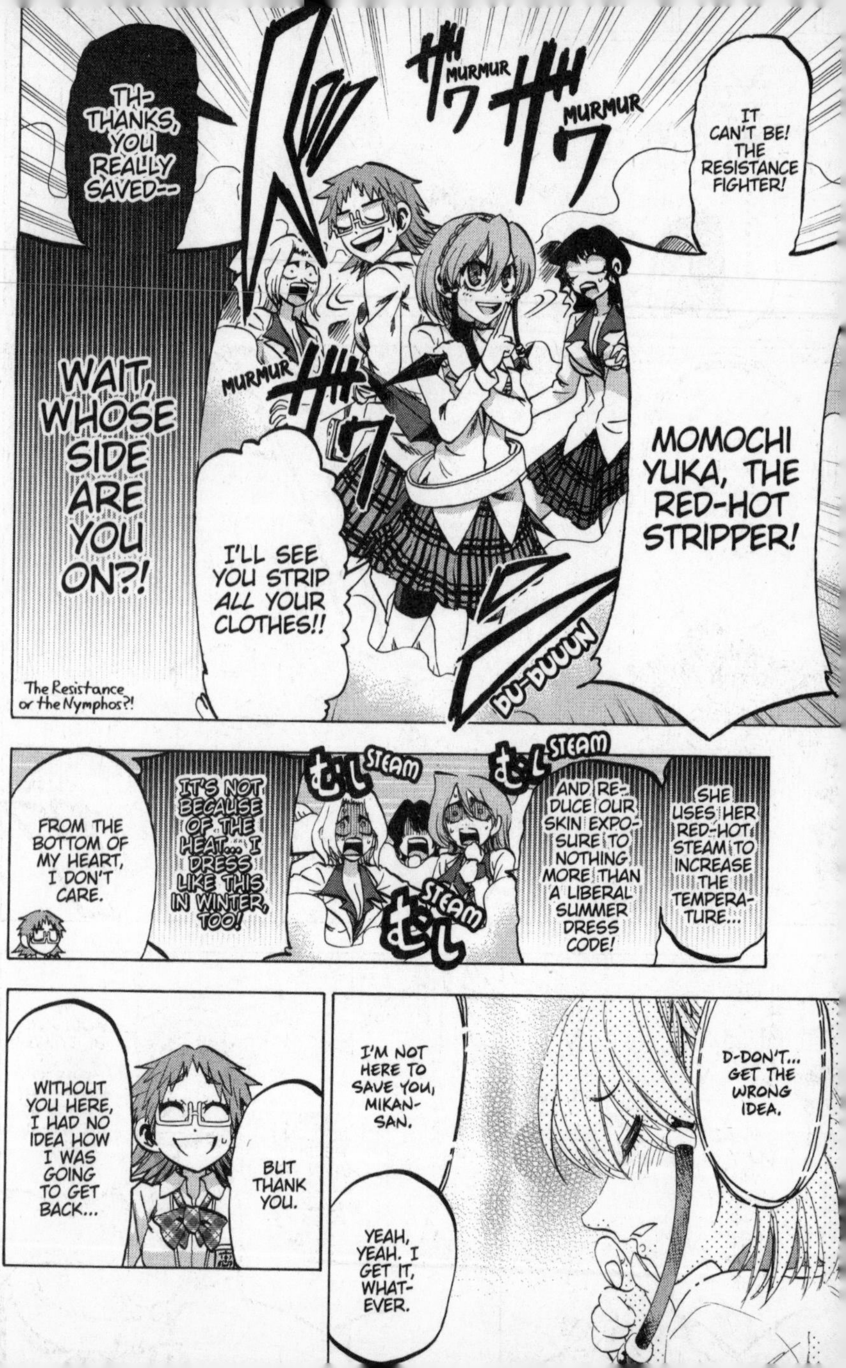
IT CAN'T BE! THE RESISTANCE FIGHTER!
ザワ MURMUR
ザワ MURMUR
TH-THANKS, YOU REALLY SAVED--
MOMOCHI YUKA, THE RED-HOT STRIPPER!
ザワ MURMUR
DU-DUUUN
I'LL SEE YOU STRIP ALL YOUR CLOTHES!!
WAIT, WHOSE SIDE ARE YOU ON?!
The Resistance or the Nymphos?!
SHE USES HER RED-HOT STEAM TO INCREASE THE TEMPERA-TURE...
AND RE-DUCE OUR SKIN EXPO-SURE TO NOTHING MORE THAN A LIBERAL SUMMER DRESS CODE!
むし STEAM
むし STEAM
むし STEAM
IT'S NOT BECAUSE OF THE HEAT... I DRESS LIKE THIS IN WINTER, TOO!
FROM THE BOTTOM OF MY HEART, I DON'T CARE.
D-DON'T... GET THE WRONG IDEA.
I'M NOT HERE TO SAVE YOU, MIKAN-SAN.
BUT THANK YOU.
YEAH, YEAH. I GET IT, WHATEVER.
WITHOUT YOU HERE, I HAD NO IDEA HOW I WAS GOING TO GET BACK...

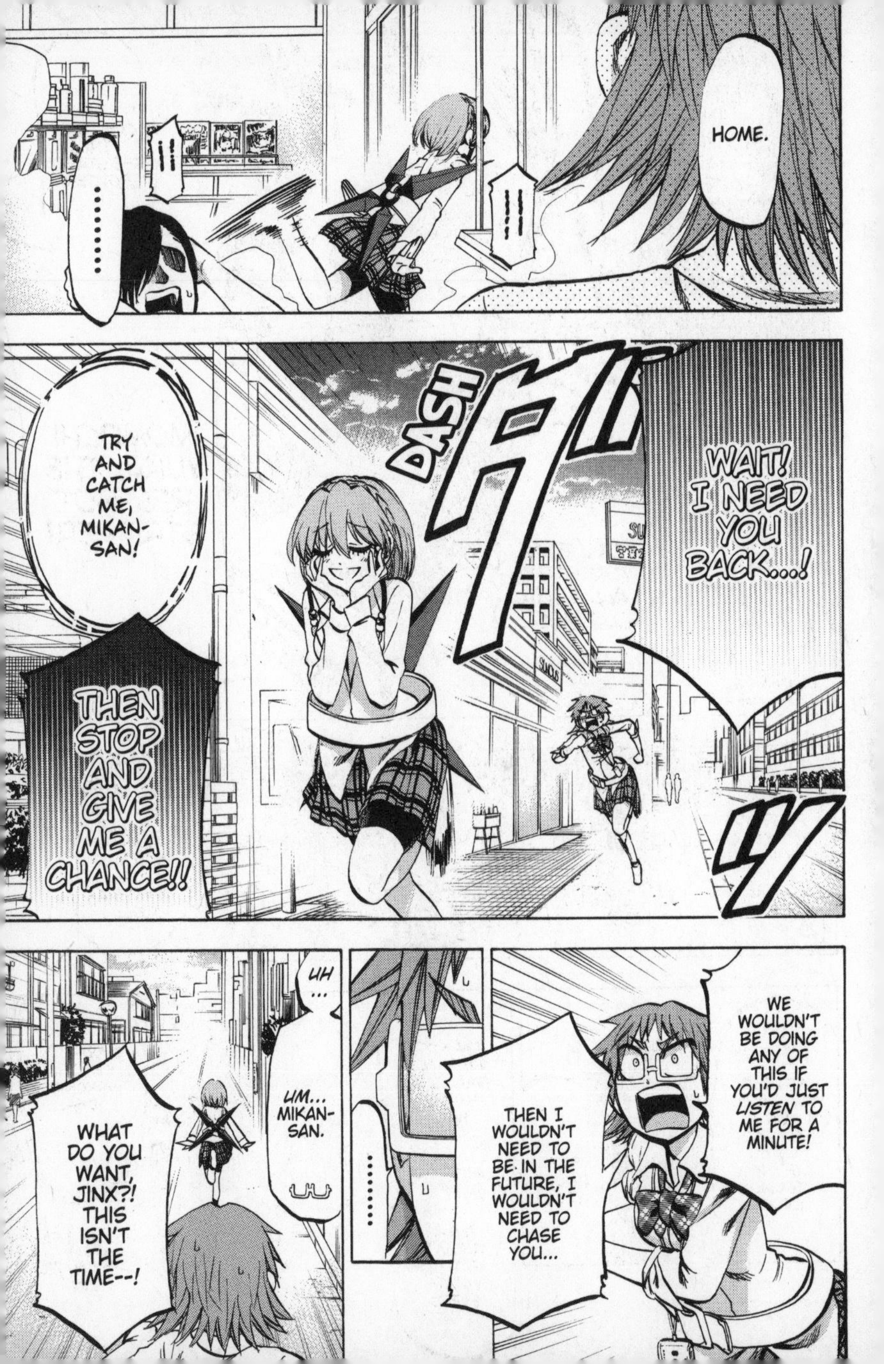
HOME.
!!!
!!!
....
WAIT! I NEED YOU BACK...!
DASH
TRY AND CATCH ME, MIKAN-SAN!
THEN STOP AND GIVE ME A CHANCE!!
WE WOULDN'T BE DOING ANY OF THIS IF YOU'D JUST *LISTEN* TO ME FOR A MINUTE!
THEN I WOULDN'T NEED TO BE IN THE FUTURE, I WOULDN'T NEED TO CHASE YOU...
UH...
UM... MIKAN-SAN.
....
WHAT DO YOU WANT, JINX?! THIS ISN'T THE TIME--!

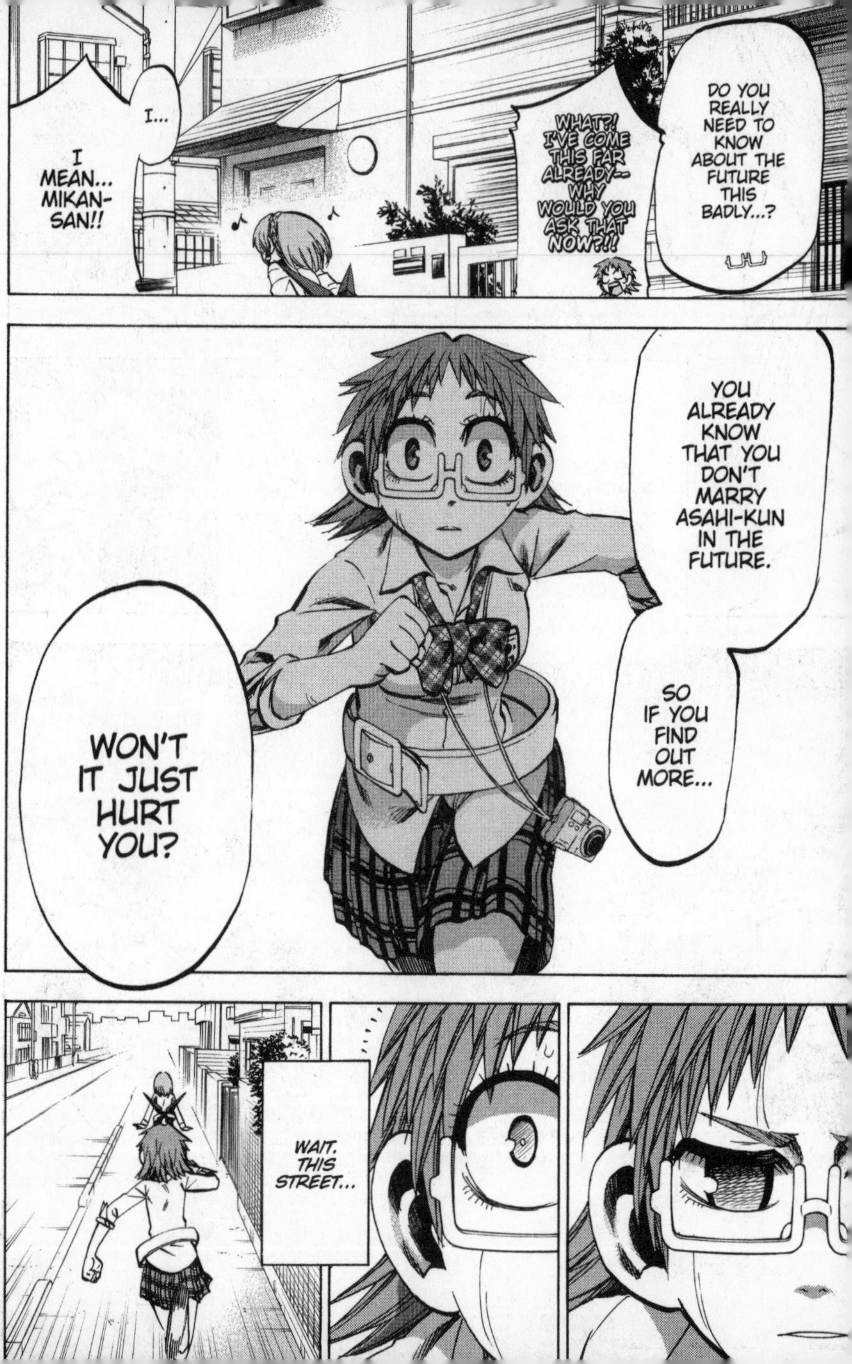
DO YOU REALLY NEED TO KNOW ABOUT THE FUTURE THIS BADLY...?
WHAT?! I'VE COME THIS FAR ALREADY-- WHY WOULD YOU ASK THAT NOW?!!
I...
I MEAN... MIKAN-SAN!!
YOU ALREADY KNOW THAT YOU DON'T MARRY ASAHI-KUN IN THE FUTURE.
SO IF YOU FIND OUT MORE...
WON'T IT JUST HURT YOU?
WAIT. THIS STREET...

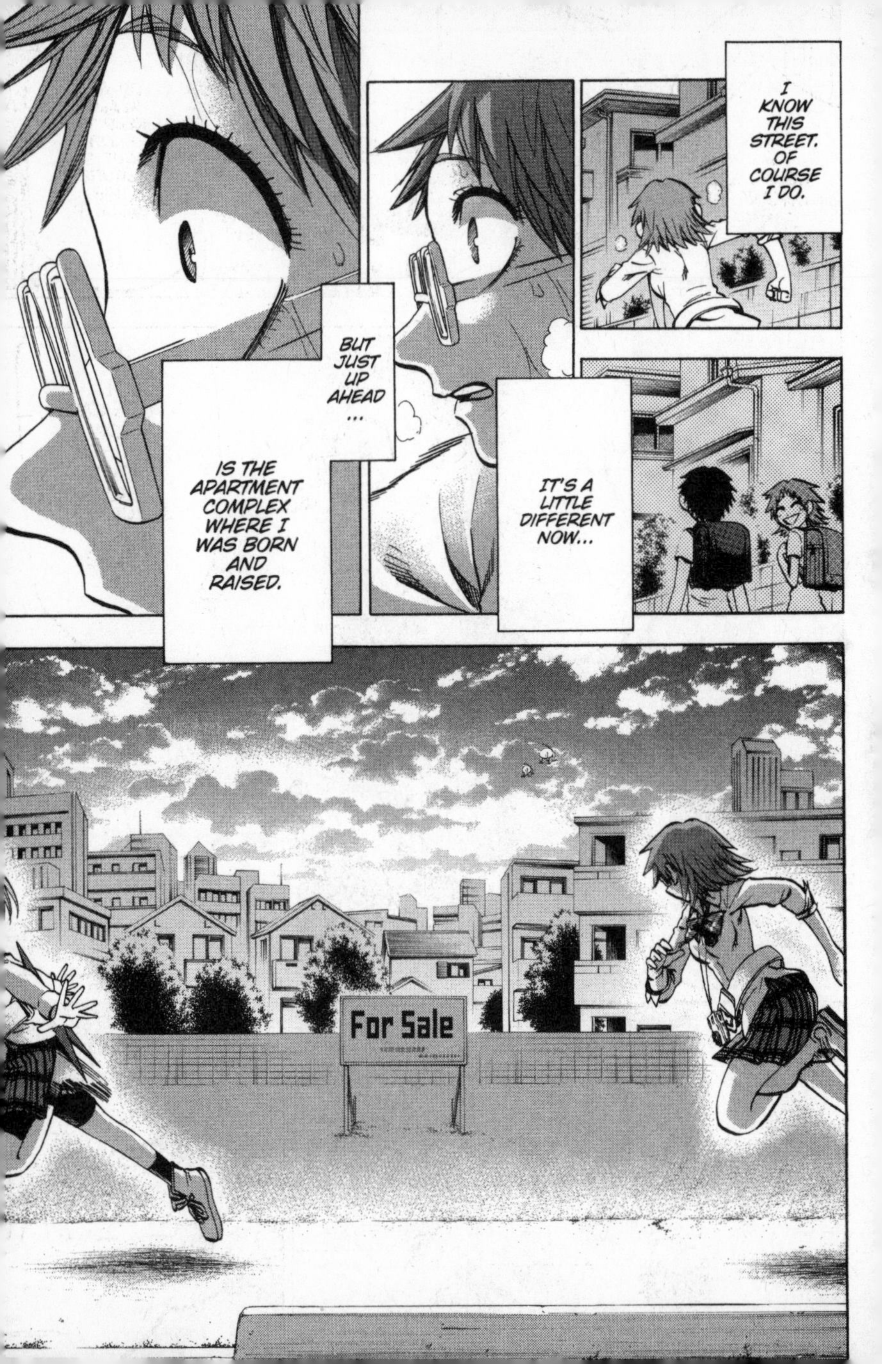
I KNOW THIS STREET. OF COURSE I DO.
IT'S A LITTLE DIFFERENT NOW...
BUT JUST UP AHEAD...
IS THE APARTMENT COMPLEX WHERE I WAS BORN AND RAISED.
For Sale

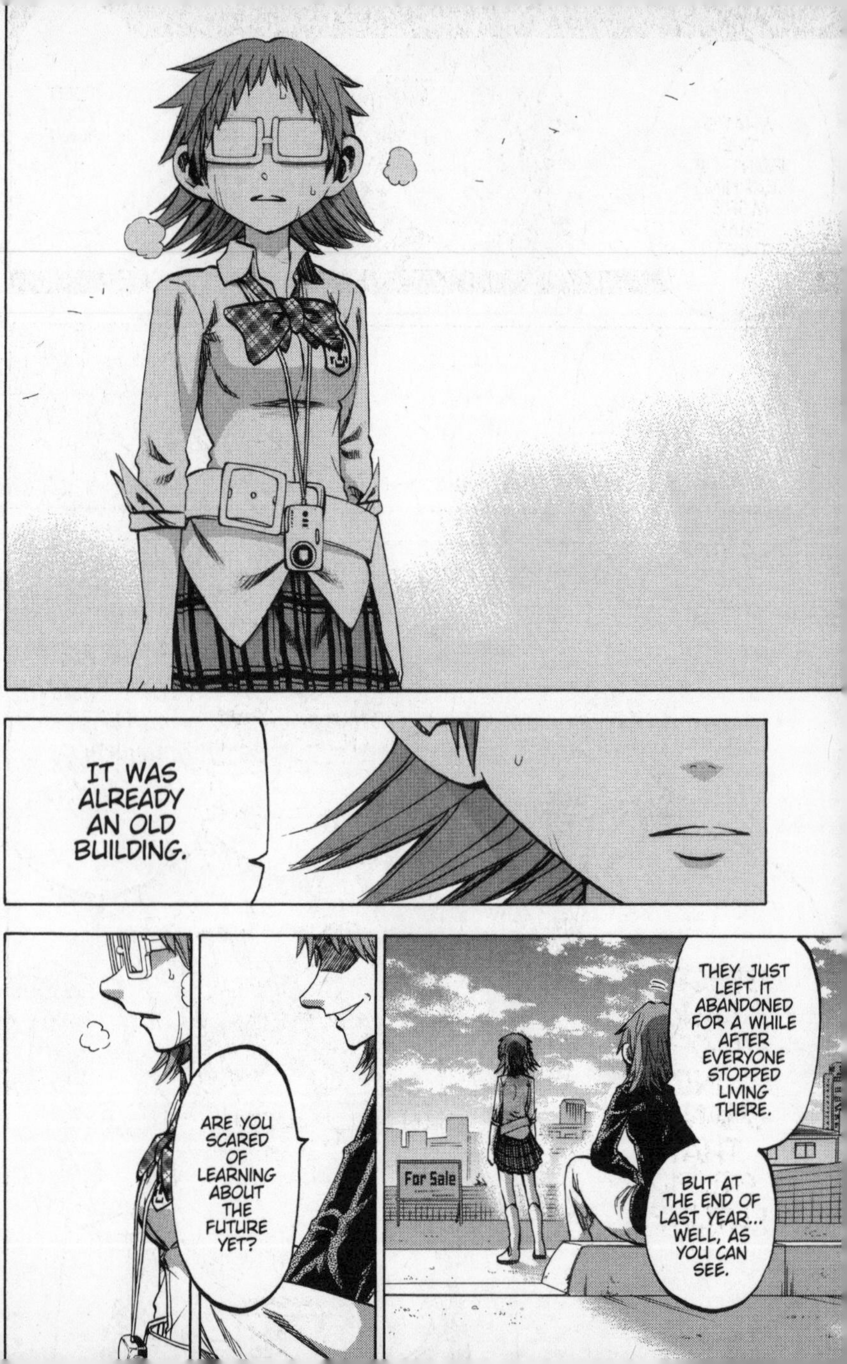
IT WAS ALREADY AN OLD BUILDING.
THEY JUST LEFT IT ABANDONED FOR A WHILE AFTER EVERYONE STOPPED LIVING THERE.
BUT AT THE END OF LAST YEAR... WELL, AS YOU CAN SEE.
For Sale
ARE YOU SCARED OF LEARNING ABOUT THE FUTURE YET?

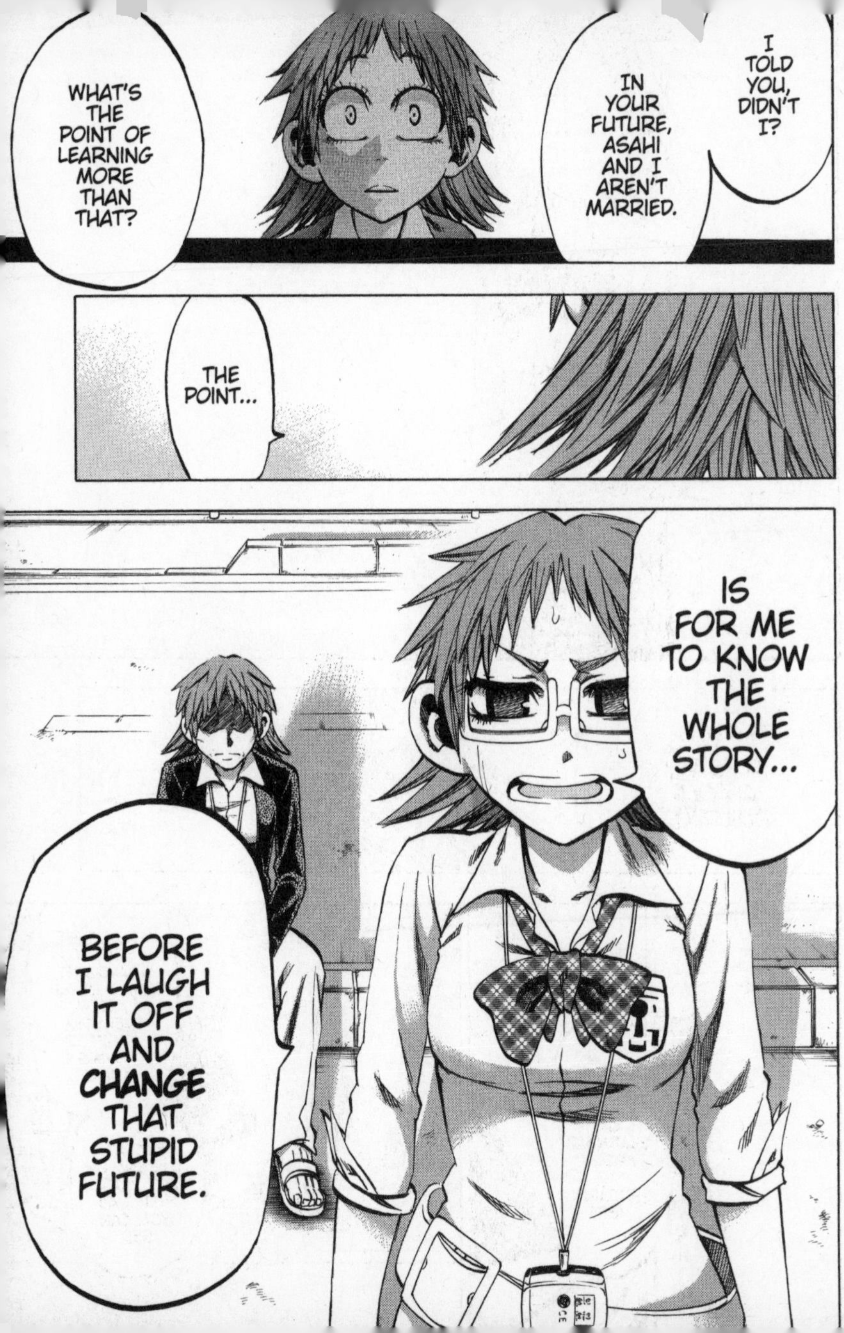
I TOLD YOU, DIDN'T I?
IN YOUR FUTURE, ASAHI AND I AREN'T MARRIED.
WHAT'S THE POINT OF LEARNING MORE THAN THAT?
THE POINT...
IS FOR ME TO KNOW THE WHOLE STORY...
BEFORE I LAUGH IT OFF AND CHANGE THAT STUPID FUTURE.

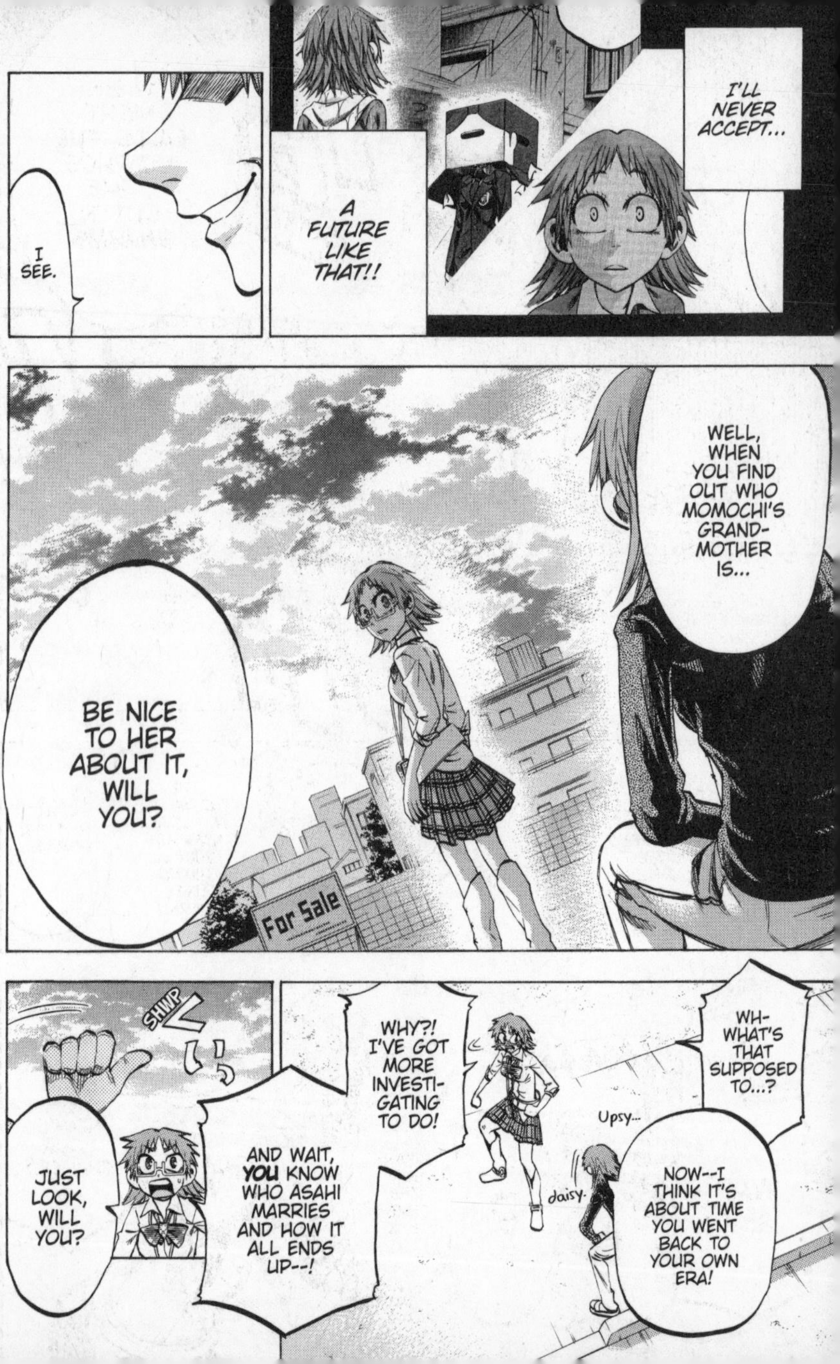
I'LL NEVER ACCEPT...
A FUTURE LIKE THAT!!
I SEE.
WELL, WHEN YOU FIND OUT WHO MOMOCHI'S GRANDMOTHER IS...
BE NICE TO HER ABOUT IT, WILL YOU?
For Sale
WH-WHAT'S THAT SUPPOSED TO...?
Upsy...
daisy.
NOW--I THINK IT'S ABOUT TIME YOU WENT BACK TO YOUR OWN ERA!
WHY?! I'VE GOT MORE INVESTIGATING TO DO!
AND WAIT, YOU KNOW WHO ASAHI MARRIES AND HOW IT ALL ENDS UP--!
SHWP
JUST LOOK, WILL YOU?

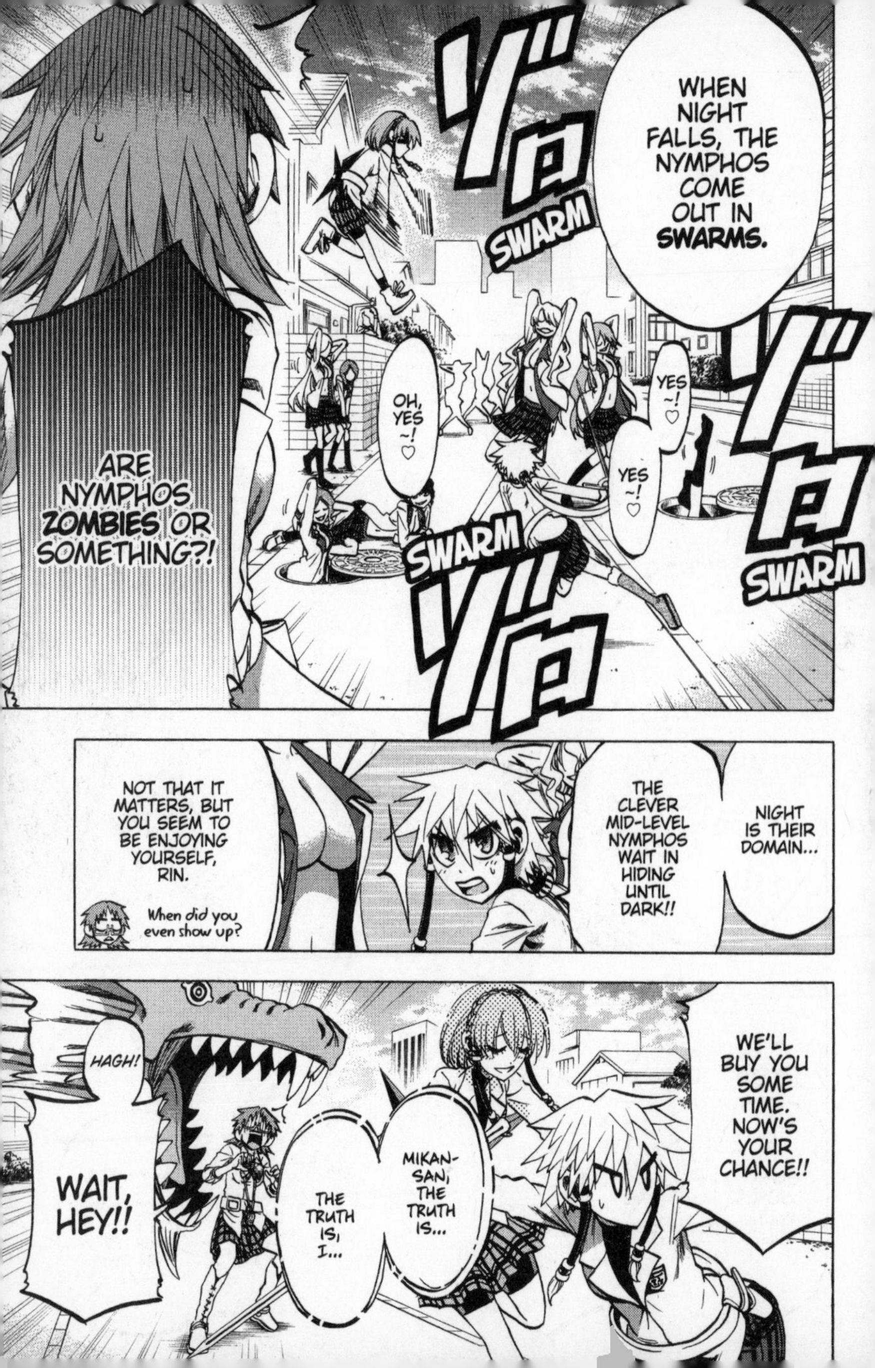
WHEN NIGHT FALLS, THE NYMPHOS COME OUT IN SWARMS.
ゾロ
SWARM
ゾロ
SWARM
YES ~! ♡
YES ~! ♡
OH, YES ~! ♡
SWARM
ゾロ
ARE NYMPHOS ZOMBIES OR SOMETHING?!
NIGHT IS THEIR DOMAIN...
THE CLEVER MID-LEVEL NYMPHOS WAIT IN HIDING UNTIL DARK!!
NOT THAT IT MATTERS, BUT YOU SEEM TO BE ENJOYING YOURSELF, RIN.
When did you even show up?
WE'LL BUY YOU SOME TIME. NOW'S YOUR CHANCE!!
MIKAN-SAN, THE TRUTH IS...
THE TRUTH IS, I...
HAGH!
WAIT, HEY!!

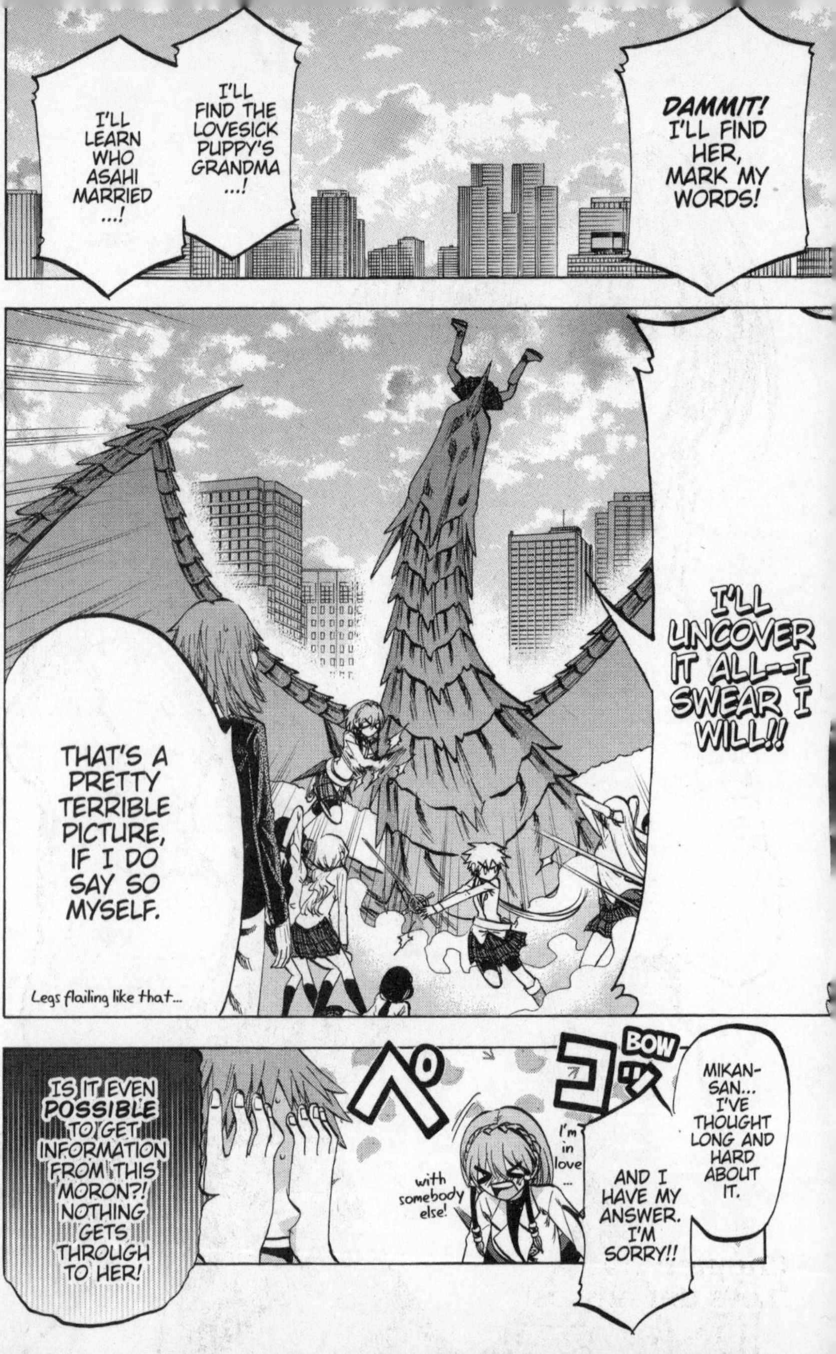
DAMMIT! I'LL FIND HER, MARK MY WORDS!
I'LL FIND THE LOVESICK PUPPY'S GRANDMA ...!
I'LL LEARN WHO ASAHI MARRIED ...!
I'LL UNCOVER IT ALL--I SWEAR I WILL!!
THAT'S A PRETTY TERRIBLE PICTURE, IF I DO SAY SO MYSELF.
Legs flailing like that...
ペコッ
BOW
MIKAN-SAN... I'VE THOUGHT LONG AND HARD ABOUT IT.
AND I HAVE MY ANSWER. I'M SORRY!!
I'm in love ...
with somebody else!
IS IT EVEN POSSIBLE TO GET INFORMATION FROM THIS MORON?! NOTHING GETS THROUGH TO HER!

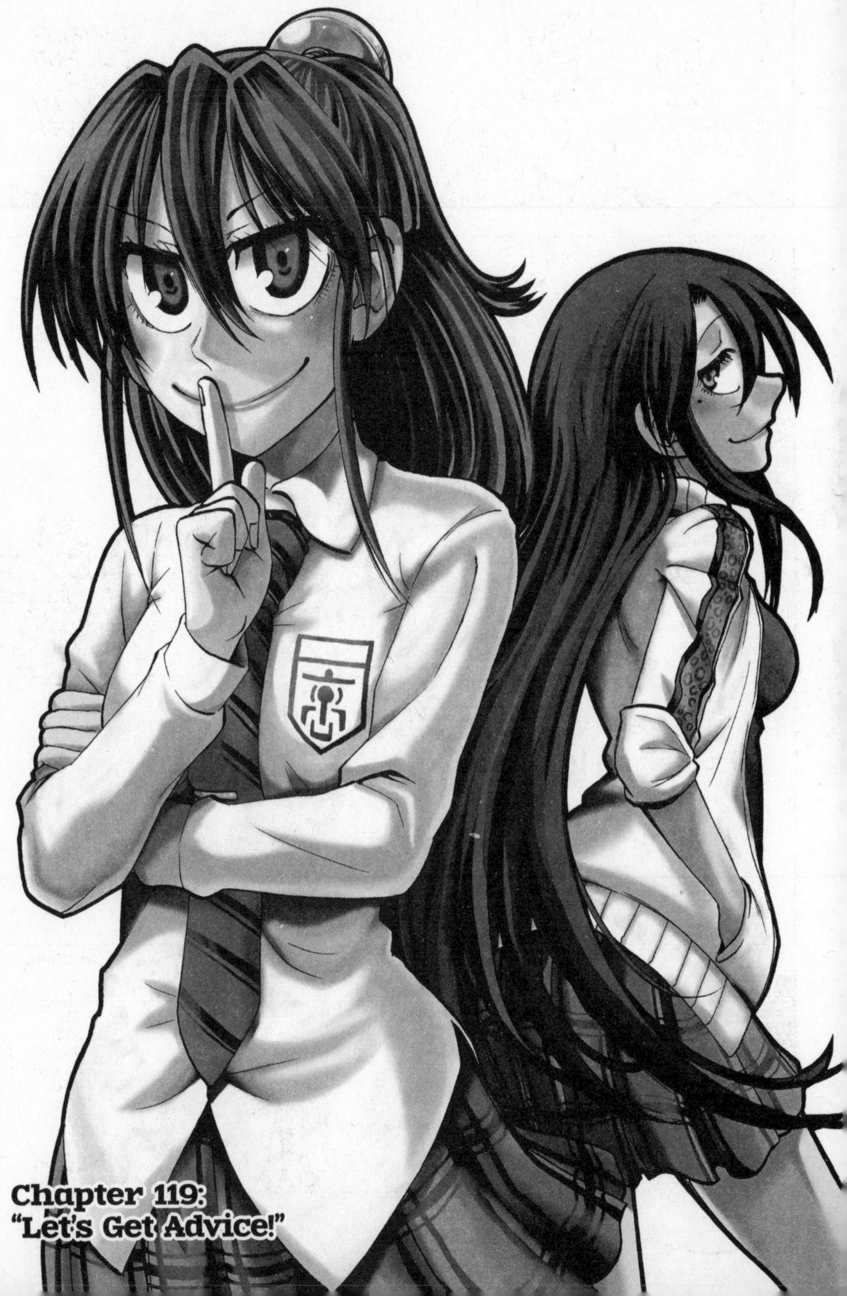

Chapter 119: "Let's Get Advice!"

TOP SECRET

My Monster Secret 14

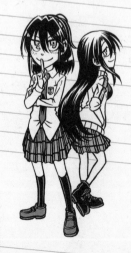

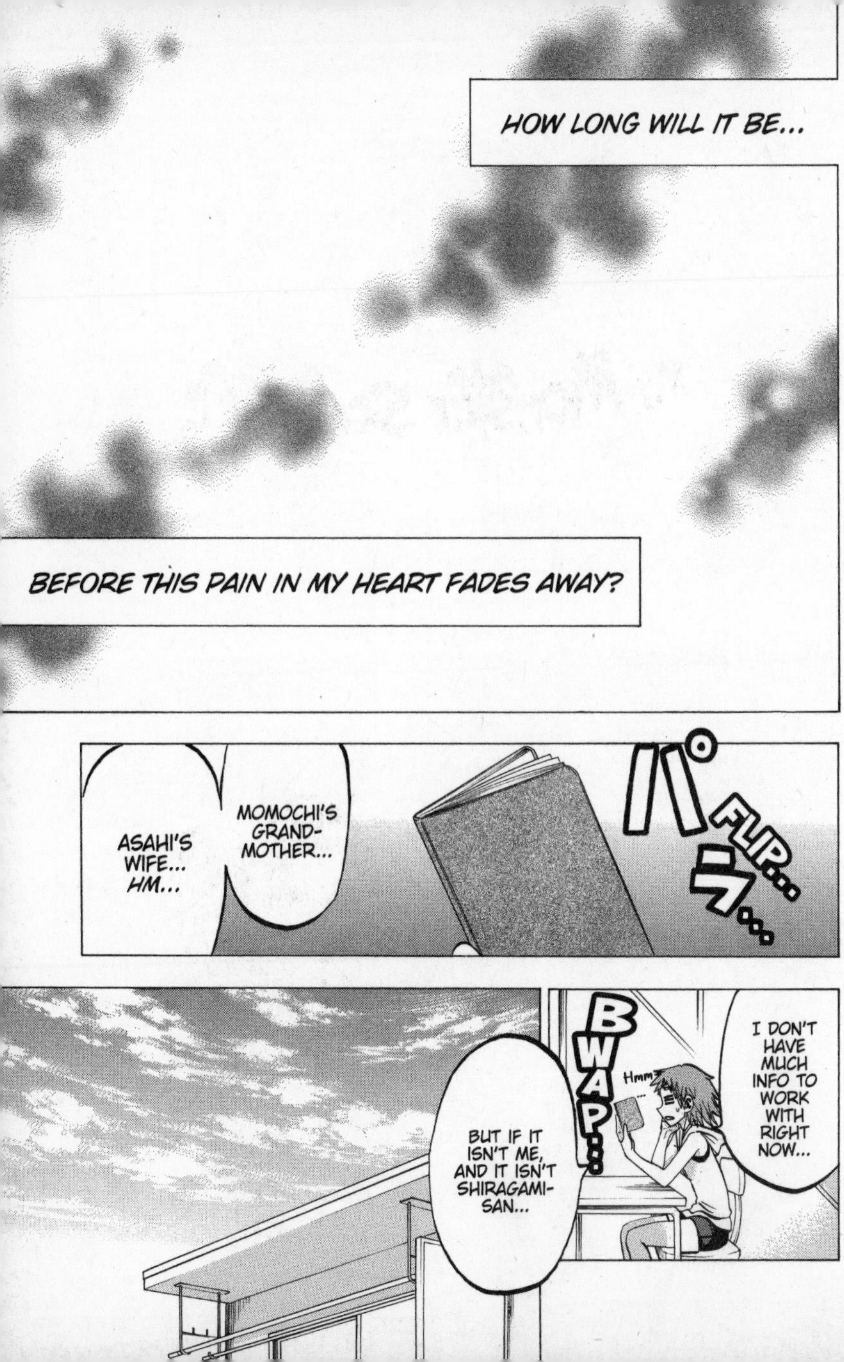
HOW LONG WILL IT BE...
BEFORE THIS PAIN IN MY HEART FADES AWAY?
パ FLIP...
ラ...
MOMOCHI'S GRAND-MOTHER...
ASAHI'S WIFE... HM...
I DON'T HAVE MUCH INFO TO WORK WITH RIGHT NOW...
BWAP...
Hmm...
BUT IF IT ISN'T ME, AND IT ISN'T SHIRAGAMI-SAN...

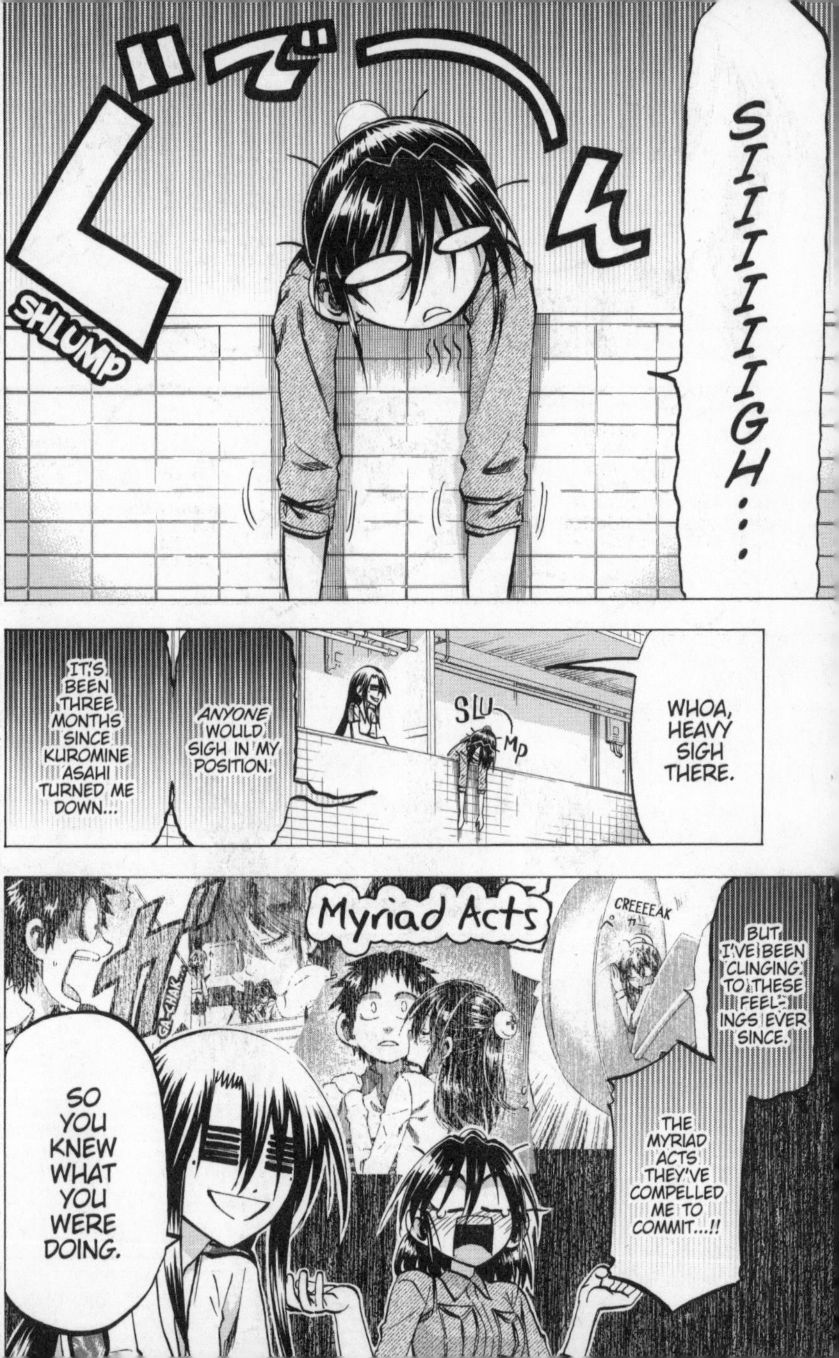
SIIIIIIIGH...
SHLUMP
WHOA, HEAVY SIGH THERE.
SLUMP
ANYONE WOULD SIGH IN MY POSITION.
IT'S BEEN THREE MONTHS SINCE KUROMINE ASAHI TURNED ME DOWN...
BUT I'VE BEEN CLINGING TO THESE FEEL-INGS EVER SINCE.
CREEEEAK
Myriad Acts
THE MYRIAD ACTS THEY'VE COMPELLED ME TO COMMIT...!!
SO YOU KNEW WHAT YOU WERE DOING.

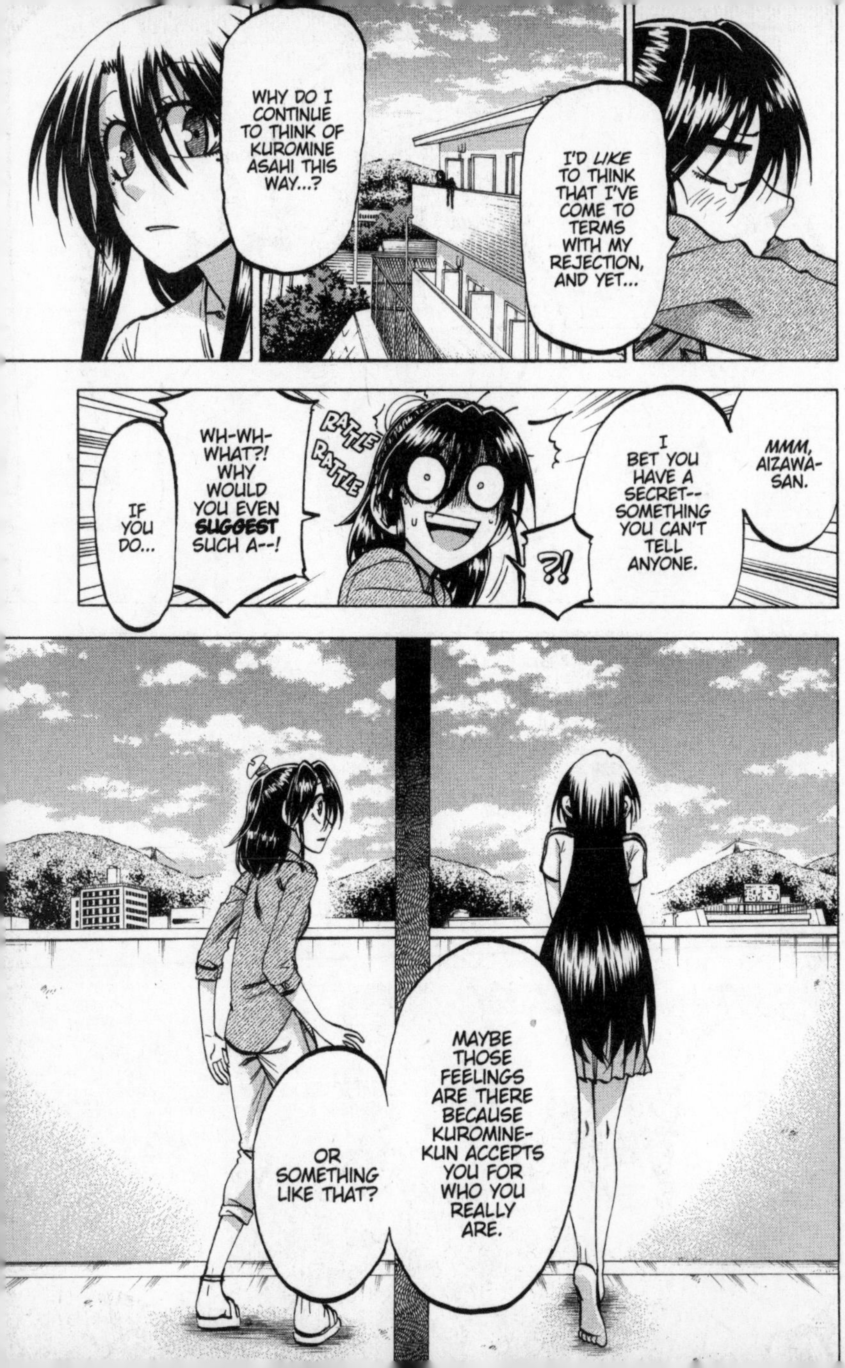
I'D LIKE TO THINK THAT I'VE COME TO TERMS WITH MY REJECTION, AND YET...
WHY DO I CONTINUE TO THINK OF KUROMINE ASAHI THIS WAY...?
MMM, AIZAWA-SAN.
I BET YOU HAVE A SECRET--SOMETHING YOU CAN'T TELL ANYONE.
?!
RATTLE RATTLE
WH-WH-WHAT?! WHY WOULD YOU EVEN SUGGEST SUCH A--!
IF YOU DO...
MAYBE THOSE FEELINGS ARE THERE BECAUSE KUROMINE-KUN ACCEPTS YOU FOR WHO YOU REALLY ARE.
OR SOMETHING LIKE THAT?

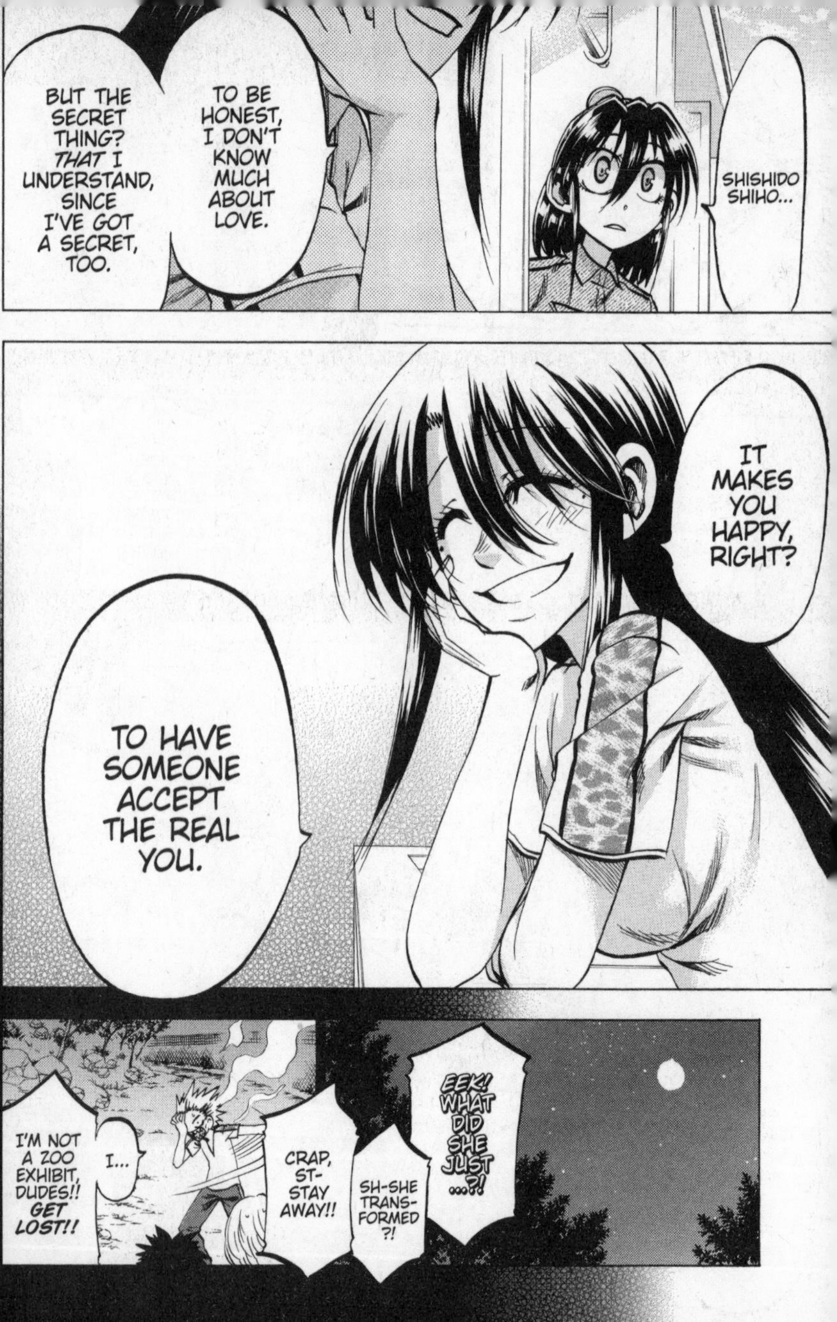
SHISHIDO SHIHO...
TO BE HONEST, I DON'T KNOW MUCH ABOUT LOVE.
BUT THE SECRET THING? *THAT* I UNDERSTAND, SINCE I'VE GOT A SECRET, TOO.
IT MAKES YOU HAPPY, RIGHT?
TO HAVE SOMEONE ACCEPT THE REAL YOU.
EEK! WHAT DID SHE JUST ...?!
SH-SHE TRANS-FORMED ?!
CRAP, ST-STAY AWAY!!
I...
I'M NOT A ZOO EXHIBIT, DUDES!! GET LOST!!

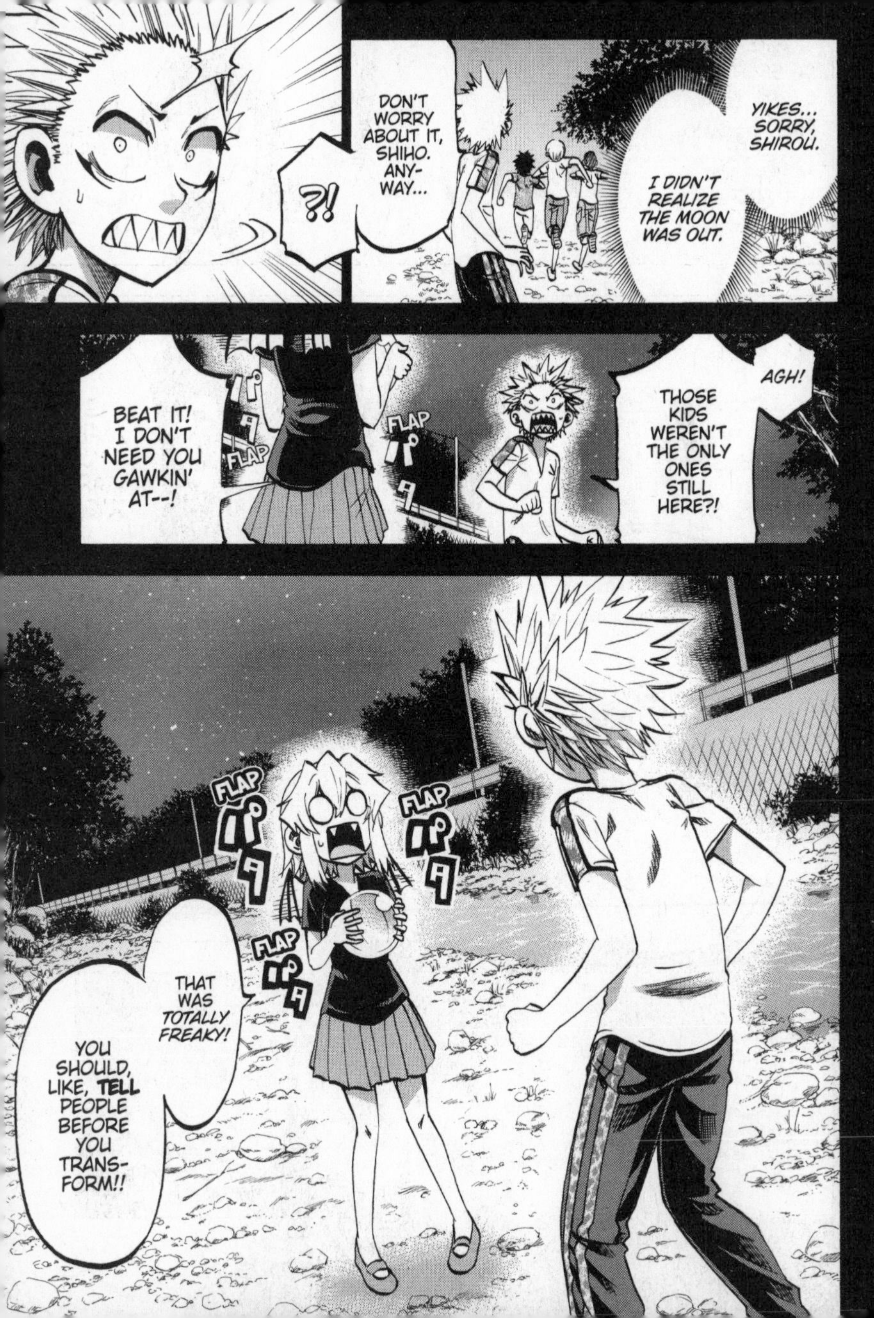
YIKES... SORRY, SHIROU.
I DIDN'T REALIZE THE MOON WAS OUT.
DON'T WORRY ABOUT IT, SHIHO. ANYWAY...
?!
AGH!
THOSE KIDS WEREN'T THE ONLY ONES STILL HERE?!
FLAP
FLAP
BEAT IT! I DON'T NEED YOU GAWKIN' AT--!
FLAP
FLAP
FLAP
THAT WAS *TOTALLY* FREAKY!
YOU SHOULD, LIKE, **TELL** PEOPLE BEFORE YOU TRANSFORM!!

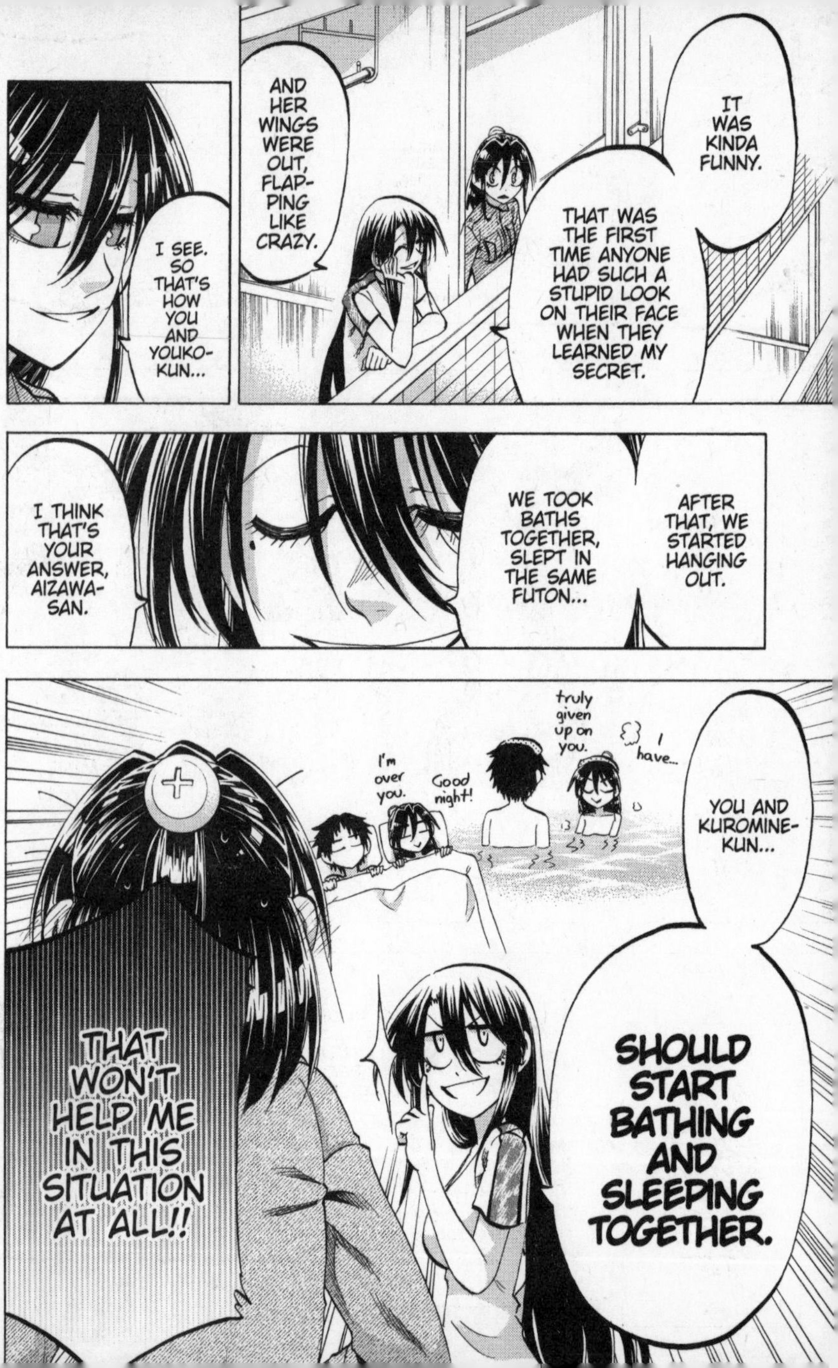
IT WAS KINDA FUNNY.
THAT WAS THE FIRST TIME ANYONE HAD SUCH A STUPID LOOK ON THEIR FACE WHEN THEY LEARNED MY SECRET.
AND HER WINGS WERE OUT, FLAP-PING LIKE CRAZY.
I SEE. SO THAT'S HOW YOU AND YOUKO-KUN...
AFTER THAT, WE STARTED HANGING OUT.
WE TOOK BATHS TOGETHER, SLEPT IN THE SAME FUTON...
I THINK THAT'S YOUR ANSWER, AIZAWA-SAN.
YOU AND KUROMINE-KUN...
I have... truly given up on you.
Good night!
I'm over you.
SHOULD START BATHING AND SLEEPING TOGETHER.
THAT WON'T HELP ME IN THIS SITUATION AT ALL!!

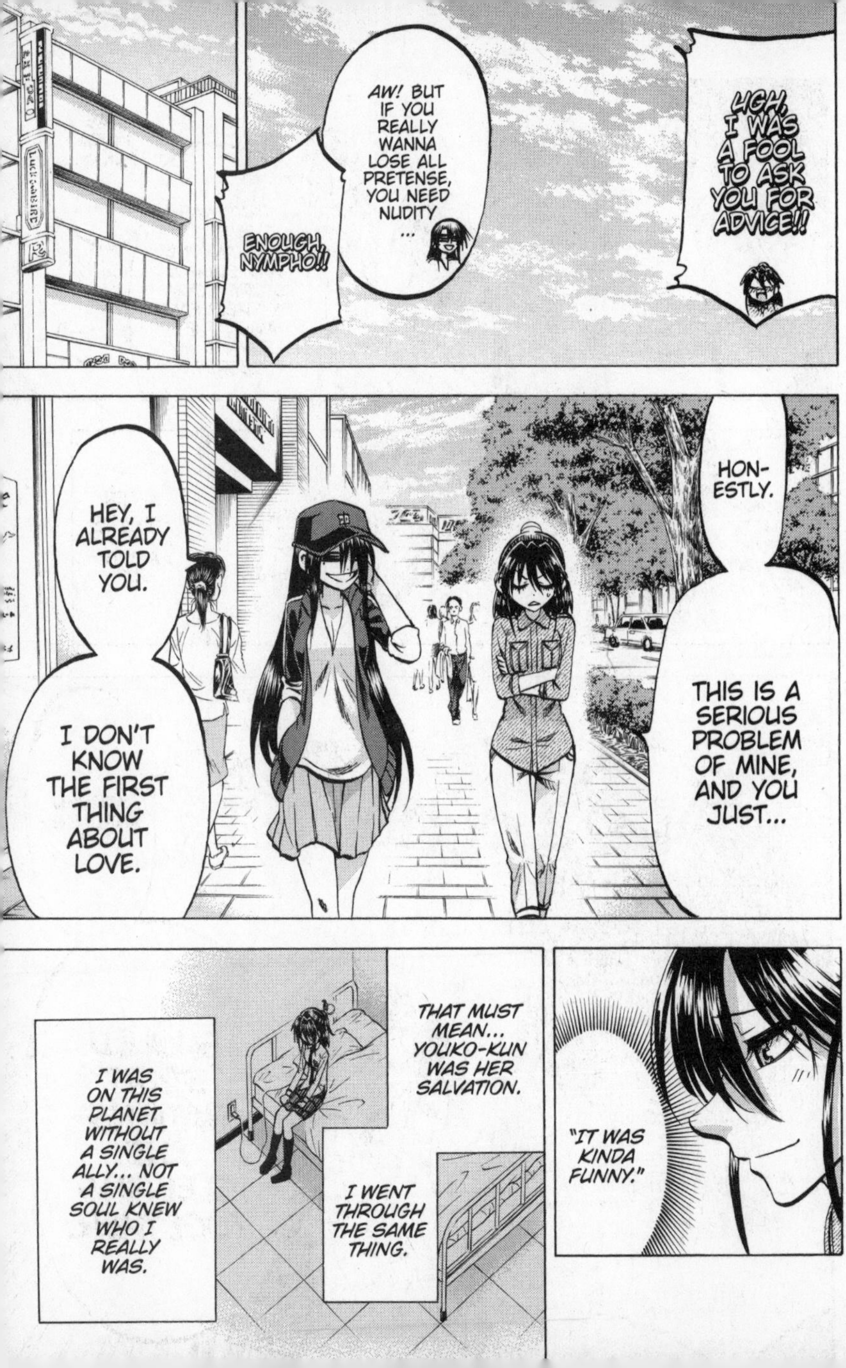
UGH, I WAS A FOOL TO ASK YOU FOR ADVICE!!
AW! BUT IF YOU REALLY WANNA LOSE ALL PRETENSE, YOU NEED NUDITY ...
ENOUGH, NYMPHO!!
HON-ESTLY.
THIS IS A SERIOUS PROBLEM OF MINE, AND YOU JUST...
HEY, I ALREADY TOLD YOU.
I DON'T KNOW THE FIRST THING ABOUT LOVE.
"IT WAS KINDA FUNNY."
THAT MUST MEAN... YOUKO-KUN WAS HER SALVATION.
I WAS ON THIS PLANET WITHOUT A SINGLE ALLY... NOT A SINGLE SOUL KNEW WHO I REALLY WAS.
I WENT THROUGH THE SAME THING.

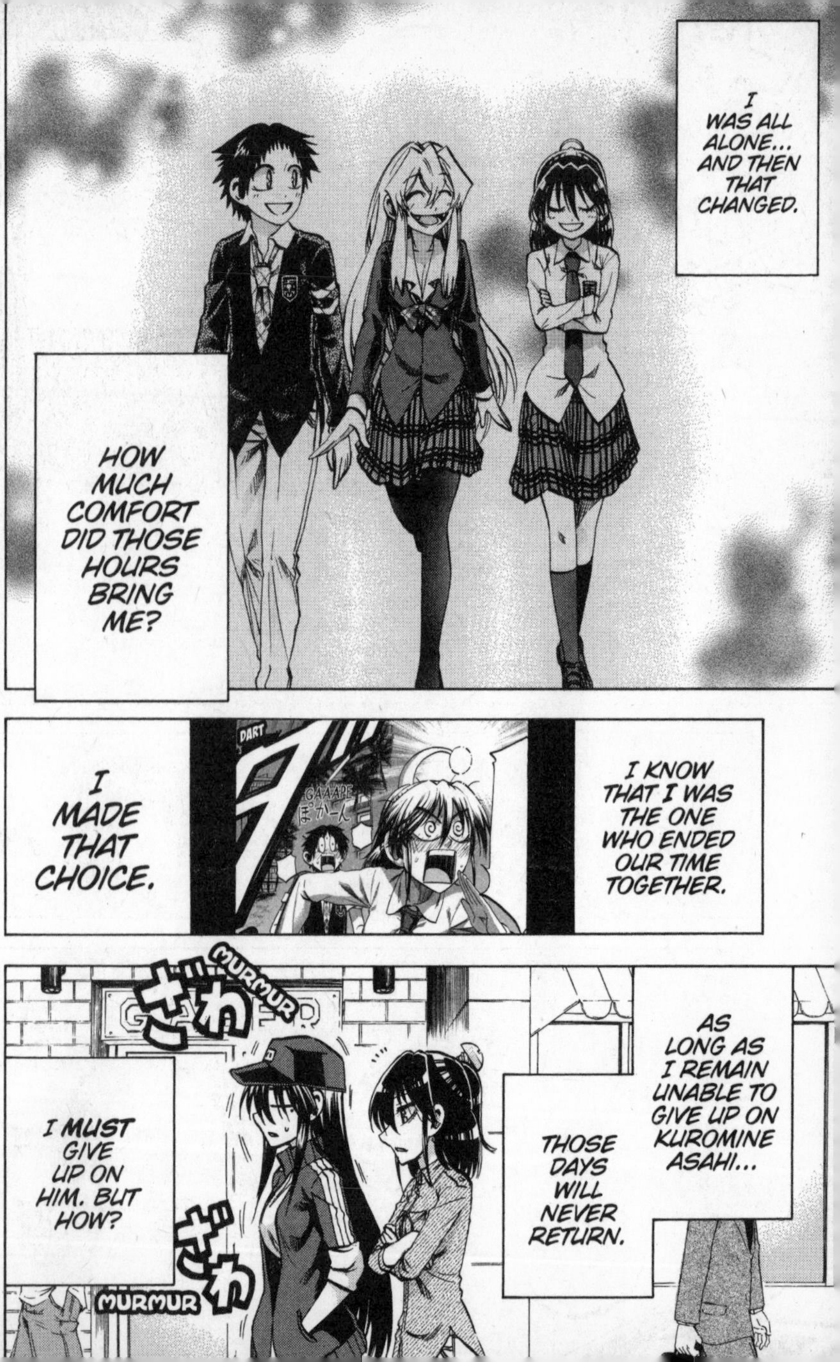
I WAS ALL ALONE... AND THEN THAT CHANGED.
HOW MUCH COMFORT DID THOSE HOURS BRING ME?
I KNOW THAT I WAS THE ONE WHO ENDED OUR TIME TOGETHER.
DART
GAAAPE
ぽかーん
I MADE THAT CHOICE.
AS LONG AS I REMAIN UNABLE TO GIVE UP ON KUROMINE ASAHI...
THOSE DAYS WILL NEVER RETURN.
ざわ
MURMUR
I MUST GIVE UP ON HIM. BUT HOW?
ざわ
MURMUR

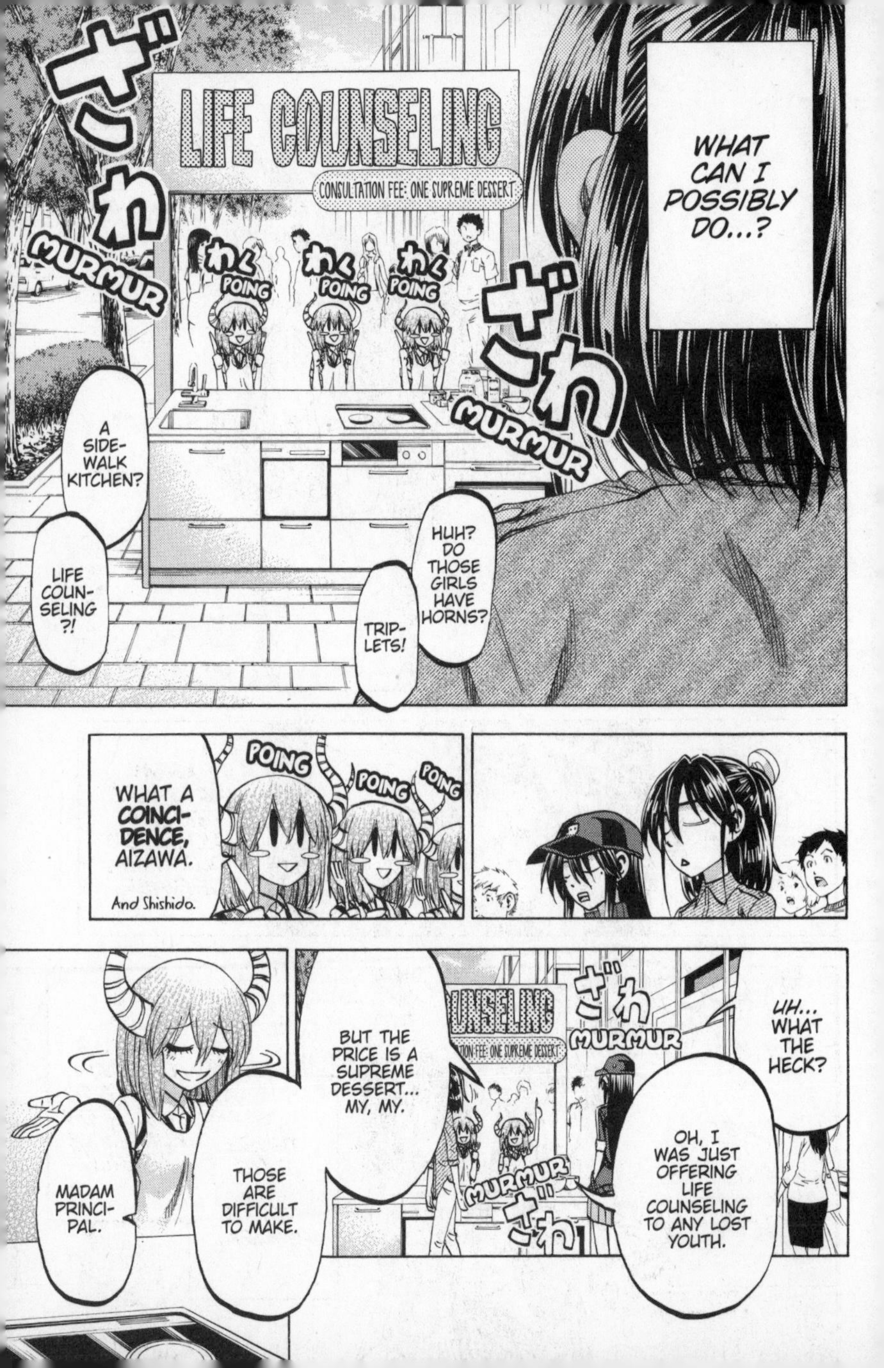
WHAT CAN I POSSIBLY DO...?
ざわ
MURMUR
HUH? DO THOSE GIRLS HAVE HORNS?
TRIPLETS!
わく POING
わく POING
わく POING
LIFE COUNSELING
CONSULTATION FEE: ONE SUPREME DESSERT
ざわ
MURMUR
A SIDE-WALK KITCHEN?
LIFE COUN-SELING?!
POING POING POING
WHAT A COINCI-DENCE, AIZAWA.
And Shishido.
UH... WHAT THE HECK?
ざわ
MURMUR
OH, I WAS JUST OFFERING LIFE COUNSELING TO ANY LOST YOUTH.
BUT THE PRICE IS A SUPREME DESSERT... MY, MY.
MURMUR
ざわ
THOSE ARE DIFFICULT TO MAKE.
MADAM PRINCI-PAL.

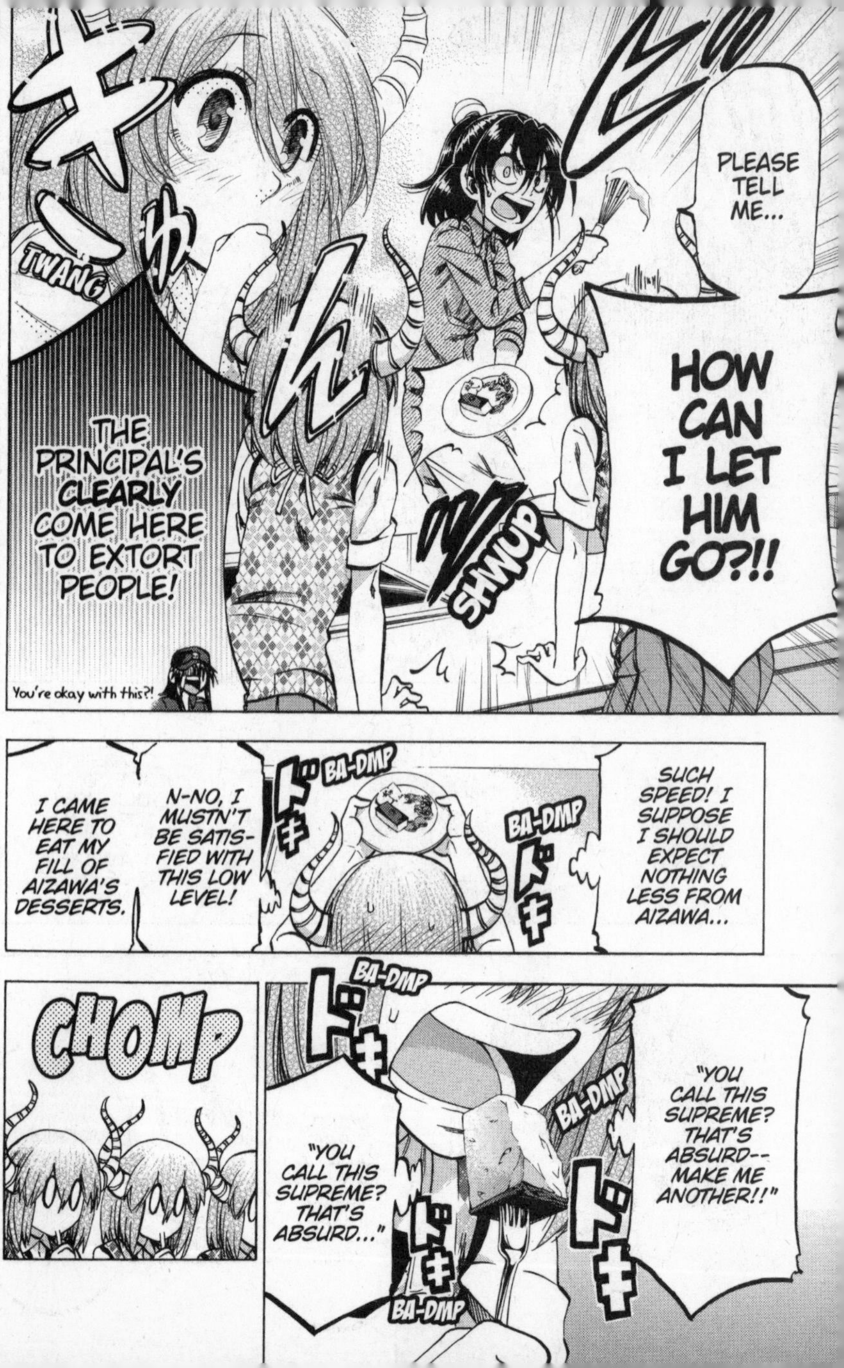
PLEASE TELL ME...
HOW CAN I LET HIM GO?!!
SHWUP
TWANG
THE PRINCIPAL'S CLEARLY COME HERE TO EXTORT PEOPLE!
You're okay with this?!
SUCH SPEED! I SUPPOSE I SHOULD EXPECT NOTHING LESS FROM AIZAWA...
BA-DMP
ドキ
BA-DMP
ドキ
N-NO, I MUSTN'T BE SATIS-FIED WITH THIS LOW LEVEL!
I CAME HERE TO EAT MY FILL OF AIZAWA'S DESSERTS.
"YOU CALL THIS SUPREME? THAT'S ABSURD--MAKE ME ANOTHER!!"
BA-DMP
ドキ
BA-DMP
ドキ
"YOU CALL THIS SUPREME? THAT'S ABSURD..."
BA-DMP
ドキ
CHOMP

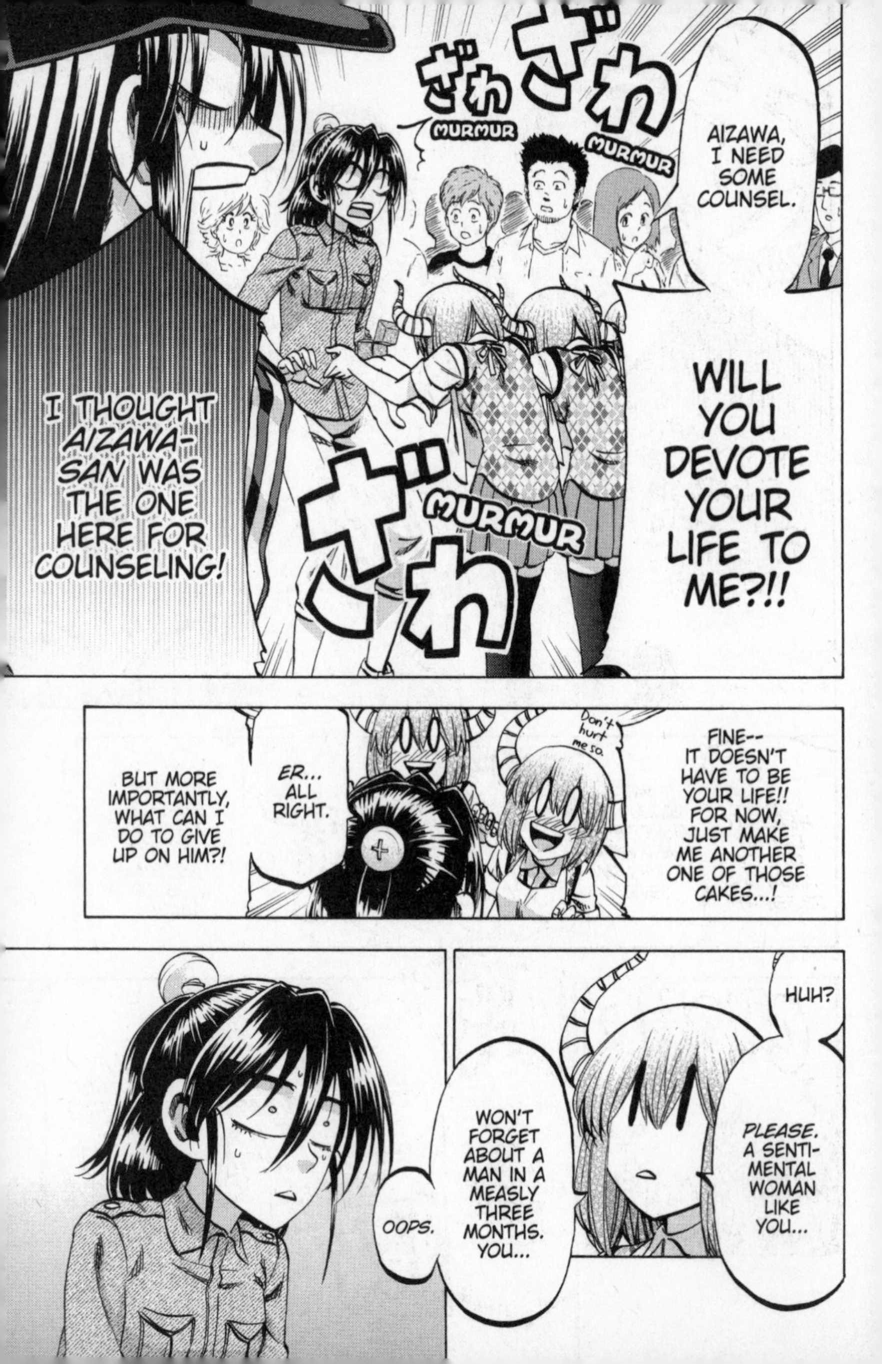
AIZAWA, I NEED SOME COUNSEL.
ざわざわ
MURMUR
MURMUR
WILL YOU DEVOTE YOUR LIFE TO ME?!!
ざわ
MURMUR
I THOUGHT AIZAWA-SAN WAS THE ONE HERE FOR COUNSELING!
FINE-- IT DOESN'T HAVE TO BE YOUR LIFE!! FOR NOW, JUST MAKE ME ANOTHER ONE OF THOSE CAKES...!
Don't hurt me so.
ER... ALL RIGHT.
BUT MORE IMPORTANTLY, WHAT CAN I DO TO GIVE UP ON HIM?!
HUH?
PLEASE. A SENTIMENTAL WOMAN LIKE YOU...
WON'T FORGET ABOUT A MAN IN A MEASLY THREE MONTHS. YOU...
OOPS.

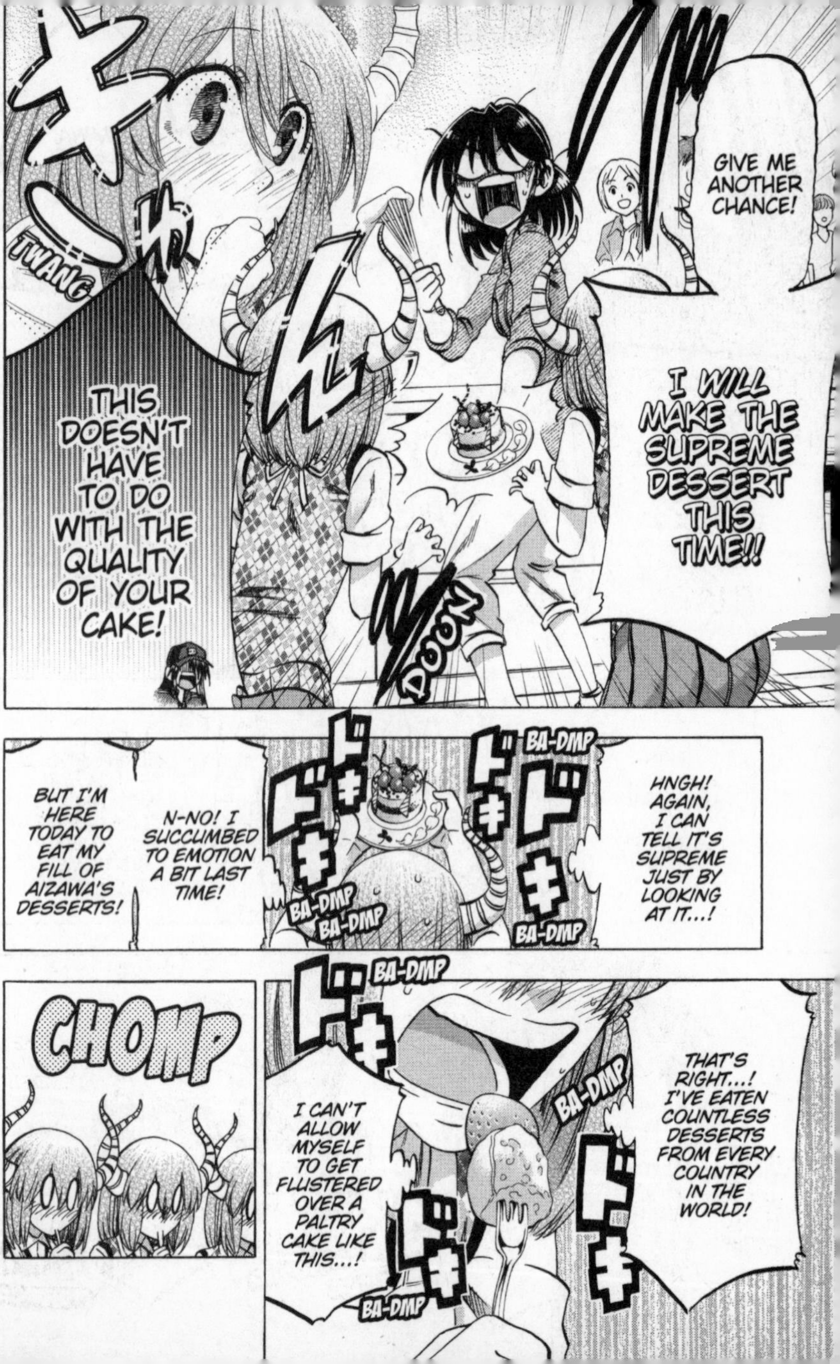
GIVE ME ANOTHER CHANCE!
I WILL MAKE THE SUPREME DESSERT THIS TIME!!
DOOON
TWANG
THIS DOESN'T HAVE TO DO WITH THE QUALITY OF YOUR CAKE!
BA-DMP
HNGH! AGAIN, I CAN TELL IT'S SUPREME JUST BY LOOKING AT IT...!
BA-DMP
BA-DMP
BA-DMP
N-NO! I SUCCUMBED TO EMOTION A BIT LAST TIME!
BUT I'M HERE TODAY TO EAT MY FILL OF AIZAWA'S DESSERTS!
BA-DMP
THAT'S RIGHT...! I'VE EATEN COUNTLESS DESSERTS FROM EVERY COUNTRY IN THE WORLD!
BA-DMP
I CAN'T ALLOW MYSELF TO GET FLUSTERED OVER A PALTRY CAKE LIKE THIS...!
BA-DMP
CHOMP

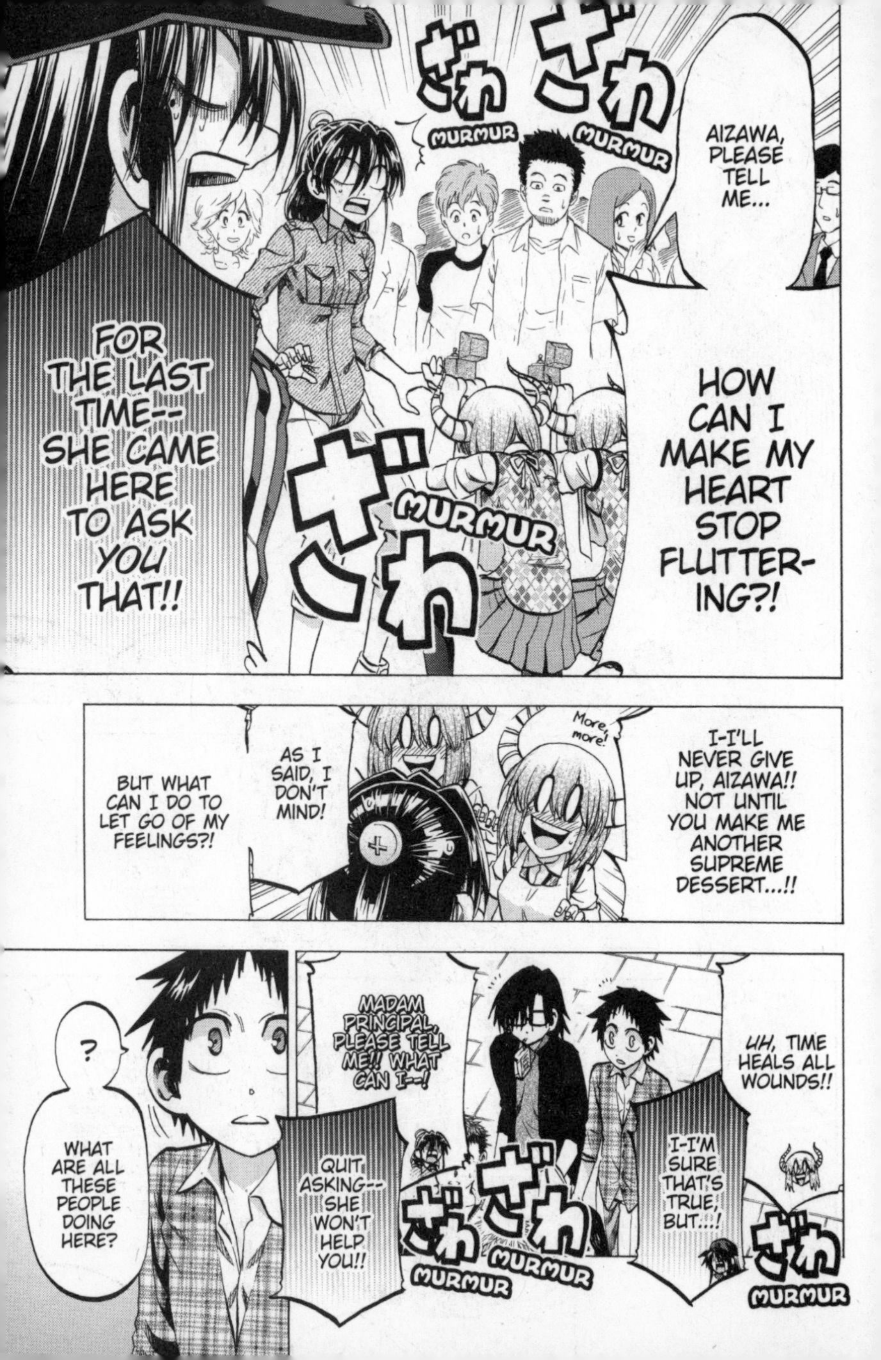
ざわ ざわ
MURMUR
MURMUR
AIZAWA, PLEASE TELL ME...
HOW CAN I MAKE MY HEART STOP FLUTTERING?!
ざわ
MURMUR
FOR THE LAST TIME-- SHE CAME HERE TO ASK YOU THAT!!
I-I'LL NEVER GIVE UP, AIZAWA!! NOT UNTIL YOU MAKE ME ANOTHER SUPREME DESSERT...!!
More, more!
AS I SAID, I DON'T MIND!
BUT WHAT CAN I DO TO LET GO OF MY FEELINGS?!
UH, TIME HEALS ALL WOUNDS!!
I-I'M SURE THAT'S TRUE, BUT...!
ざわ
MURMUR
MADAM PRINCIPAL, PLEASE TELL ME!! WHAT CAN I--!
QUIT ASKING-- SHE WON'T HELP YOU!!
ざわ ざわ
MURMUR
MURMUR
?
WHAT ARE ALL THESE PEOPLE DOING HERE?

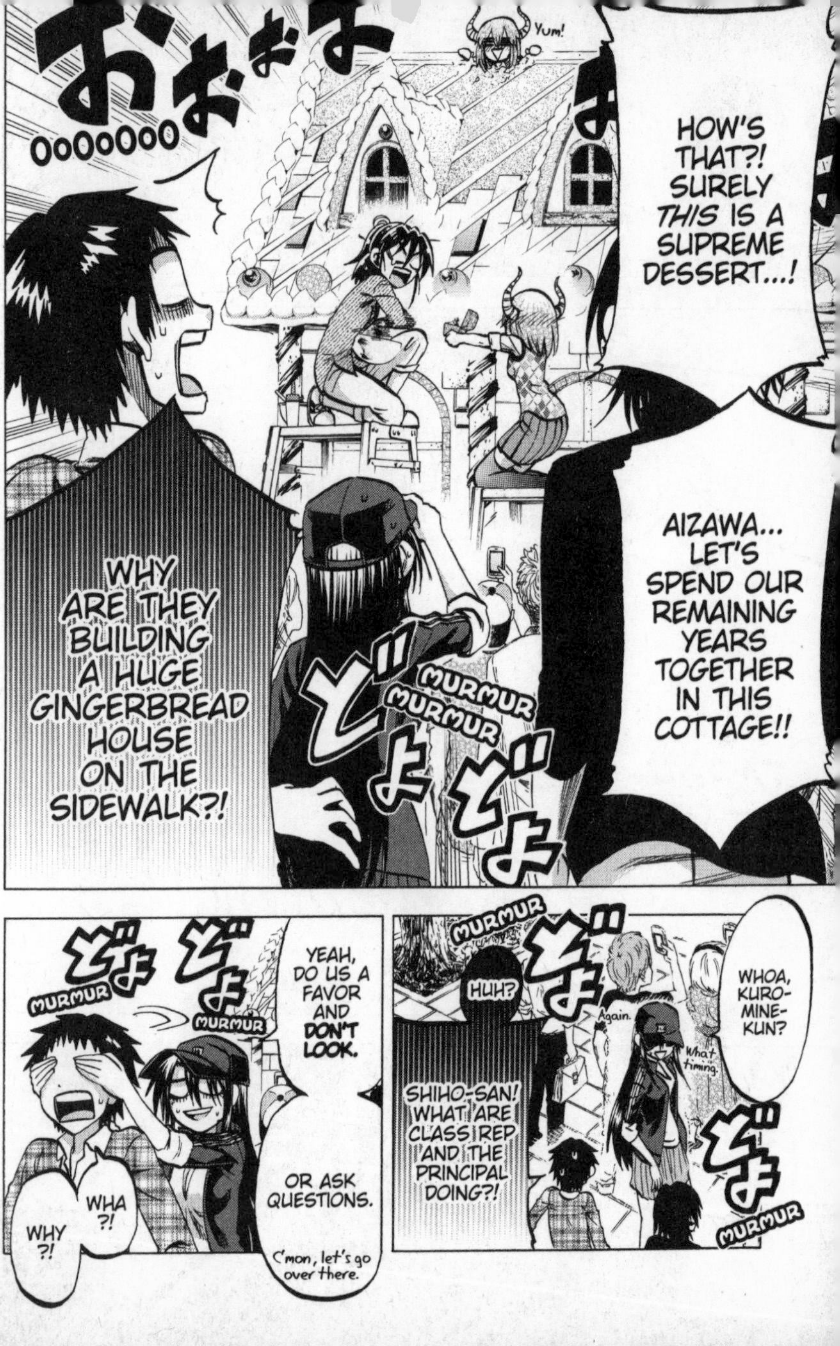
Yum!
HOW'S THAT?! SURELY *THIS* IS A SUPREME DESSERT...!
OOOOOOO
AIZAWA... LET'S SPEND OUR REMAINING YEARS TOGETHER IN THIS COTTAGE!!
WHY ARE THEY BUILDING A HUGE GINGERBREAD HOUSE ON THE SIDEWALK?!
MURMUR
MURMUR
WHOA, KURO-MINE-KUN?
MURMUR
Again.
What timing.
HUH?
SHIHO-SAN! WHAT ARE CLASS REP AND THE PRINCIPAL DOING?!
MURMUR
YEAH, DO US A FAVOR AND **DON'T LOOK.**
MURMUR
MURMUR
OR ASK QUESTIONS.
C'mon, let's go over there.
WHA?!
WHY?!

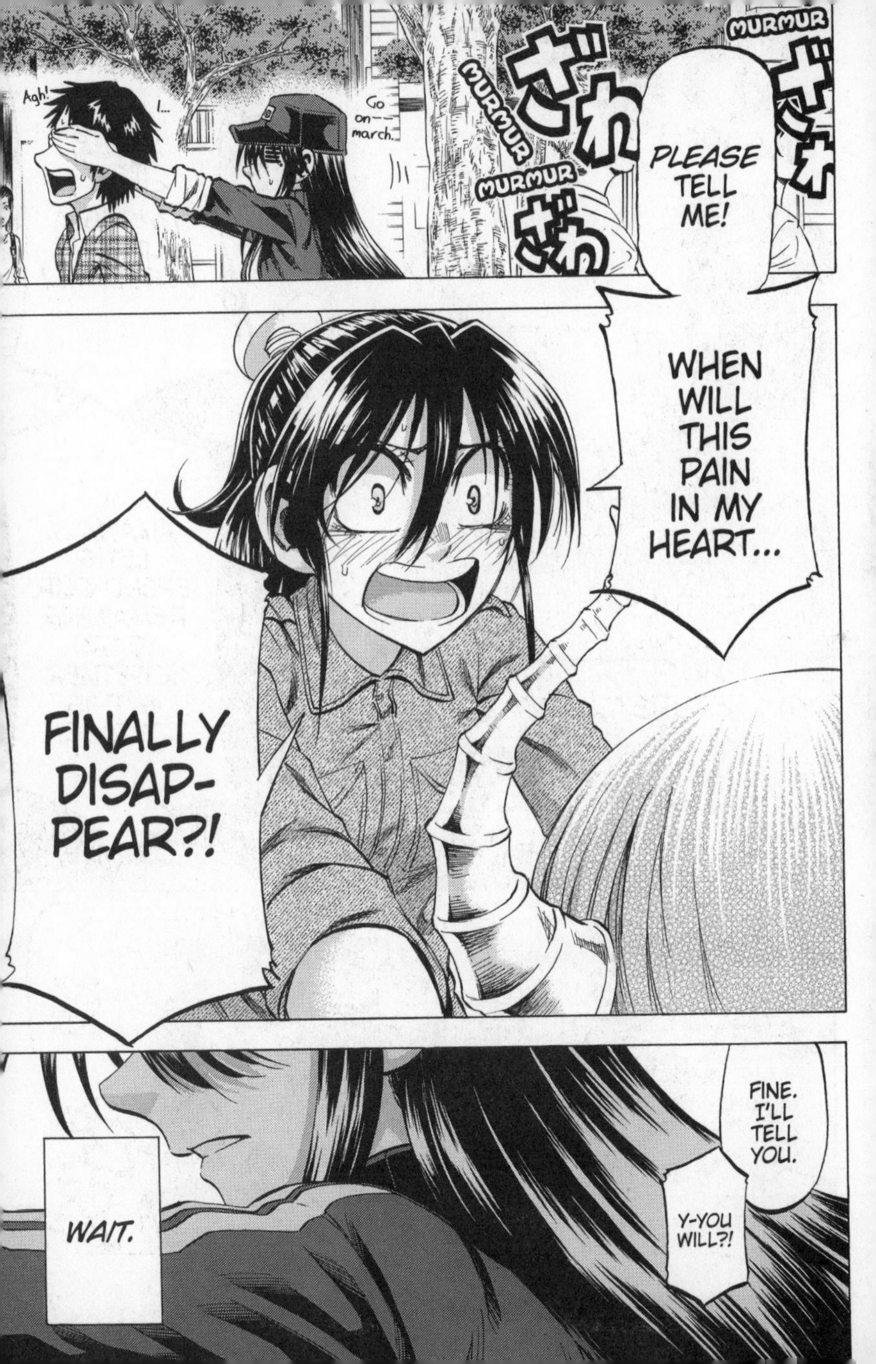
MURMUR
PLEASE TELL ME!
MURMUR
ざわ
MURMUR
ざわ
Go on-- march.
I...
Agh!
WHEN WILL THIS PAIN IN MY HEART...
FINALLY DISAP-PEAR?!
FINE. I'LL TELL YOU.
Y-YOU WILL?!
WAIT.

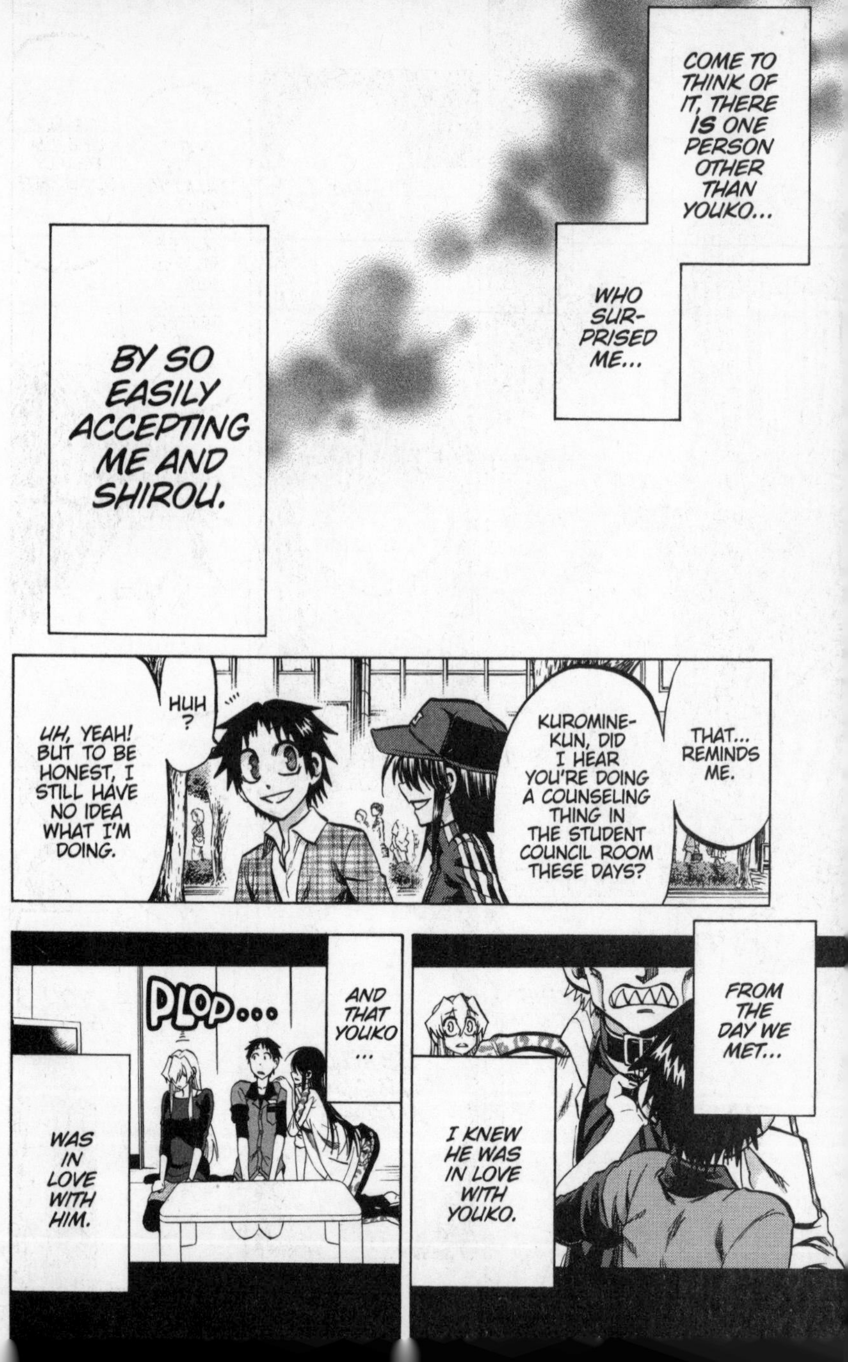
COME TO THINK OF IT, THERE **IS** ONE PERSON OTHER THAN YOUKO...
WHO SUR-PRISED ME...
BY SO EASILY ACCEPTING ME AND SHIROU.
THAT... REMINDS ME.
KUROMINE-KUN, DID I HEAR YOU'RE DOING A COUNSELING THING IN THE STUDENT COUNCIL ROOM THESE DAYS?
HUH?
UH, YEAH! BUT TO BE HONEST, I STILL HAVE NO IDEA WHAT I'M DOING.
FROM THE DAY WE MET...
I KNEW HE WAS IN LOVE WITH YOUKO.
AND THAT YOUKO...
PLOP...
WAS IN LOVE WITH HIM.

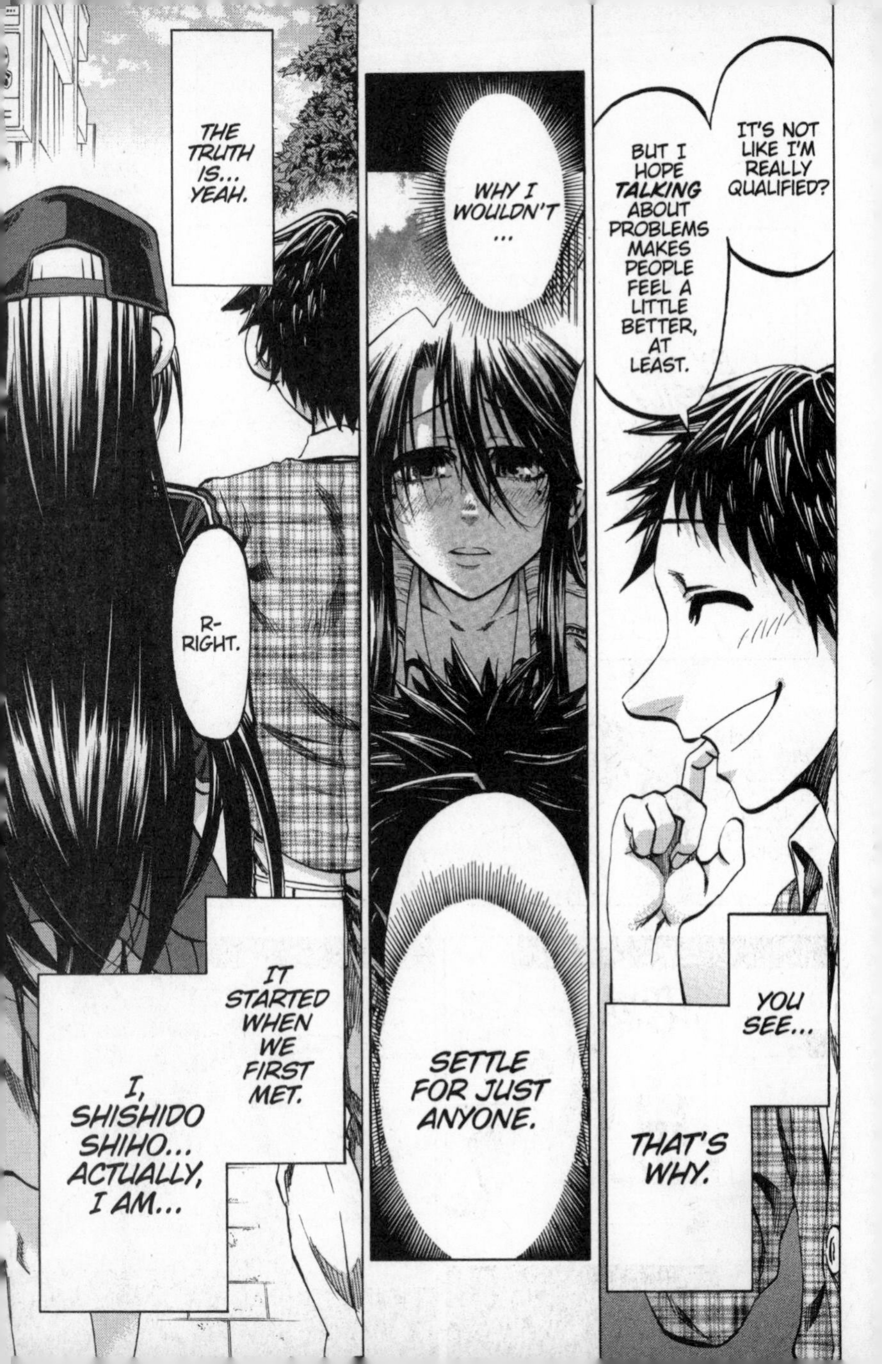
IT'S NOT LIKE I'M REALLY QUALIFIED?
BUT I HOPE TALKING ABOUT PROBLEMS MAKES PEOPLE FEEL A LITTLE BETTER, AT LEAST.
YOU SEE...
THAT'S WHY.
WHY I WOULDN'T ...
SETTLE FOR JUST ANYONE.
THE TRUTH IS... YEAH.
R-RIGHT.
IT STARTED WHEN WE FIRST MET.
I, SHISHIDO SHIHO... ACTUALLY, I AM...

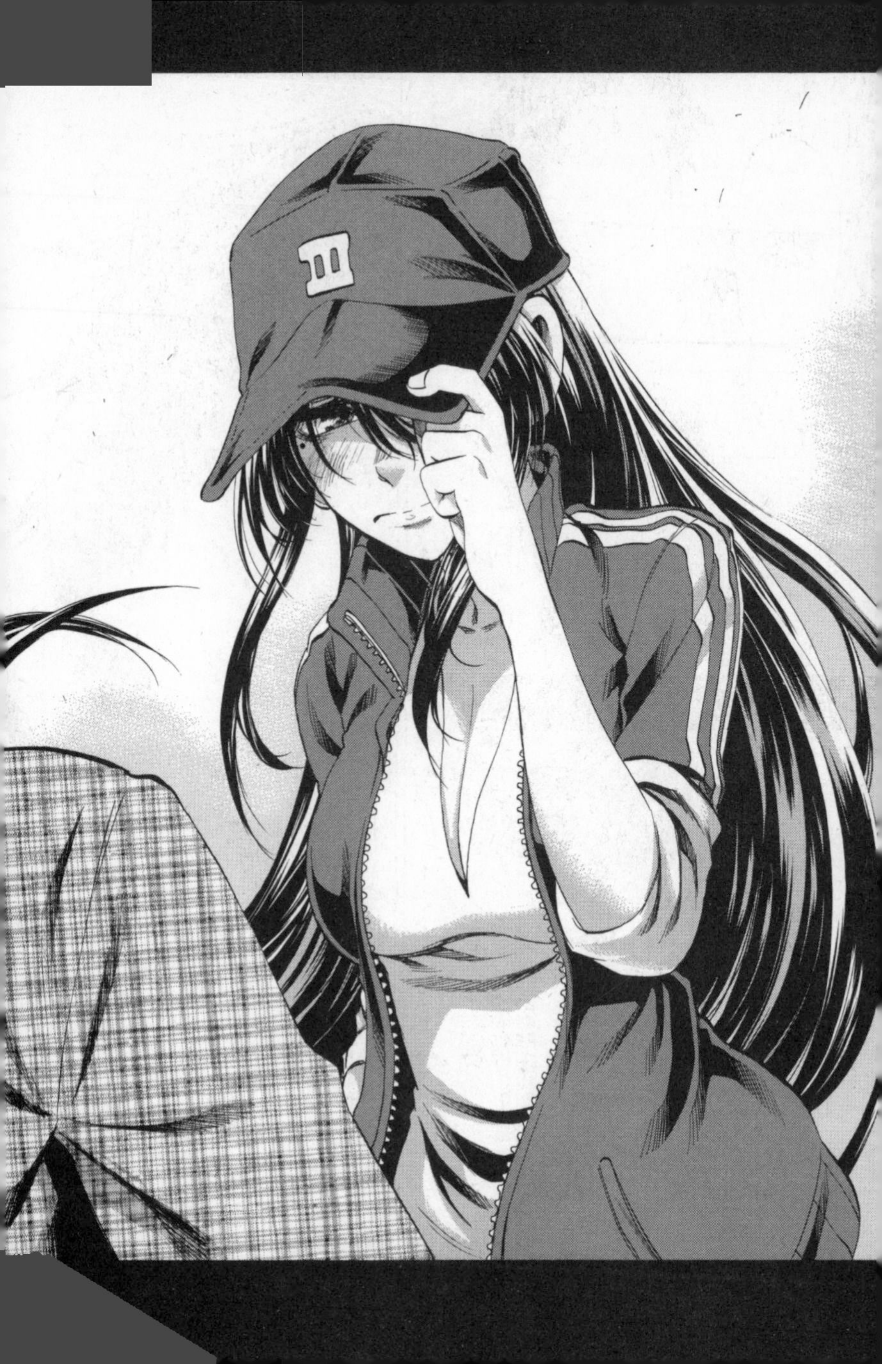

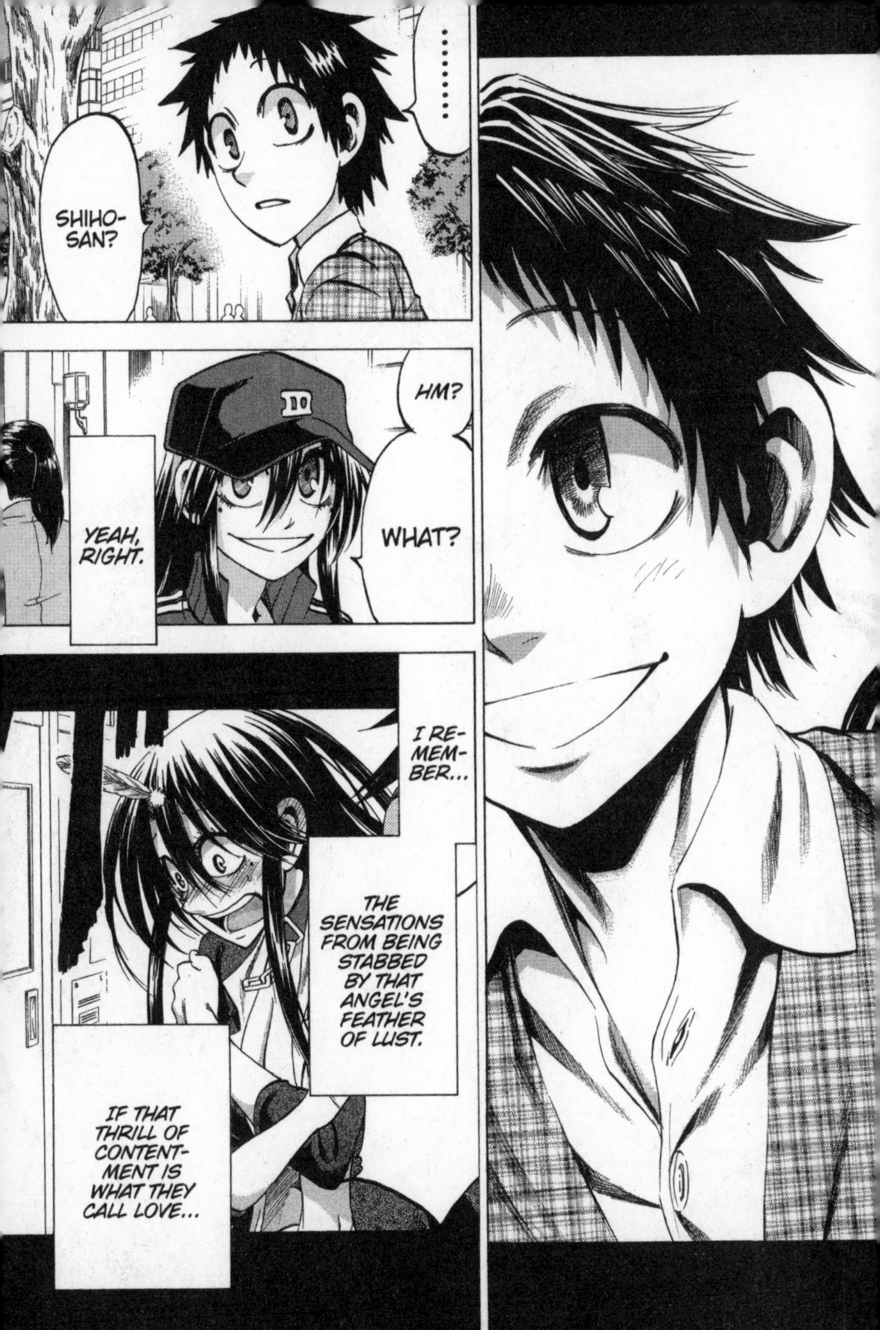
......
SHIHO-SAN?
HM?
WHAT?
YEAH, RIGHT.
I RE-MEM-BER...
THE SENSATIONS FROM BEING STABBED BY THAT ANGEL'S FEATHER OF LUST.
IF THAT THRILL OF CONTENT-MENT IS WHAT THEY CALL LOVE...

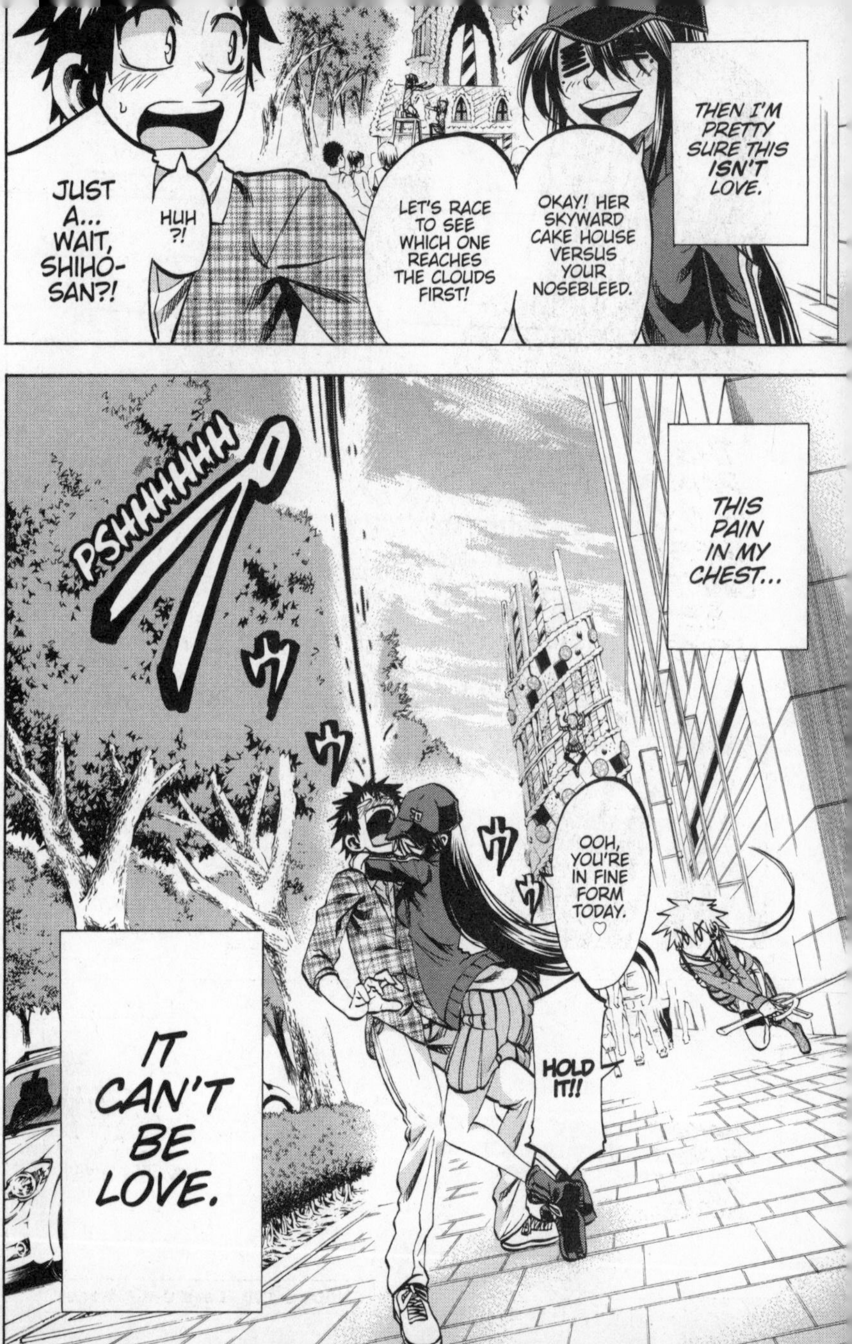
THEN I'M PRETTY SURE THIS ISN'T LOVE.
OKAY! HER SKYWARD CAKE HOUSE VERSUS YOUR NOSEBLEED.
LET'S RACE TO SEE WHICH ONE REACHES THE CLOUDS FIRST!
HUH?!
JUST A... WAIT, SHIHO-SAN?!
THIS PAIN IN MY CHEST...
OOH, YOU'RE IN FINE FORM TODAY. ♡
PSHHHHHH
HOLD IT!!
IT CAN'T BE LOVE.

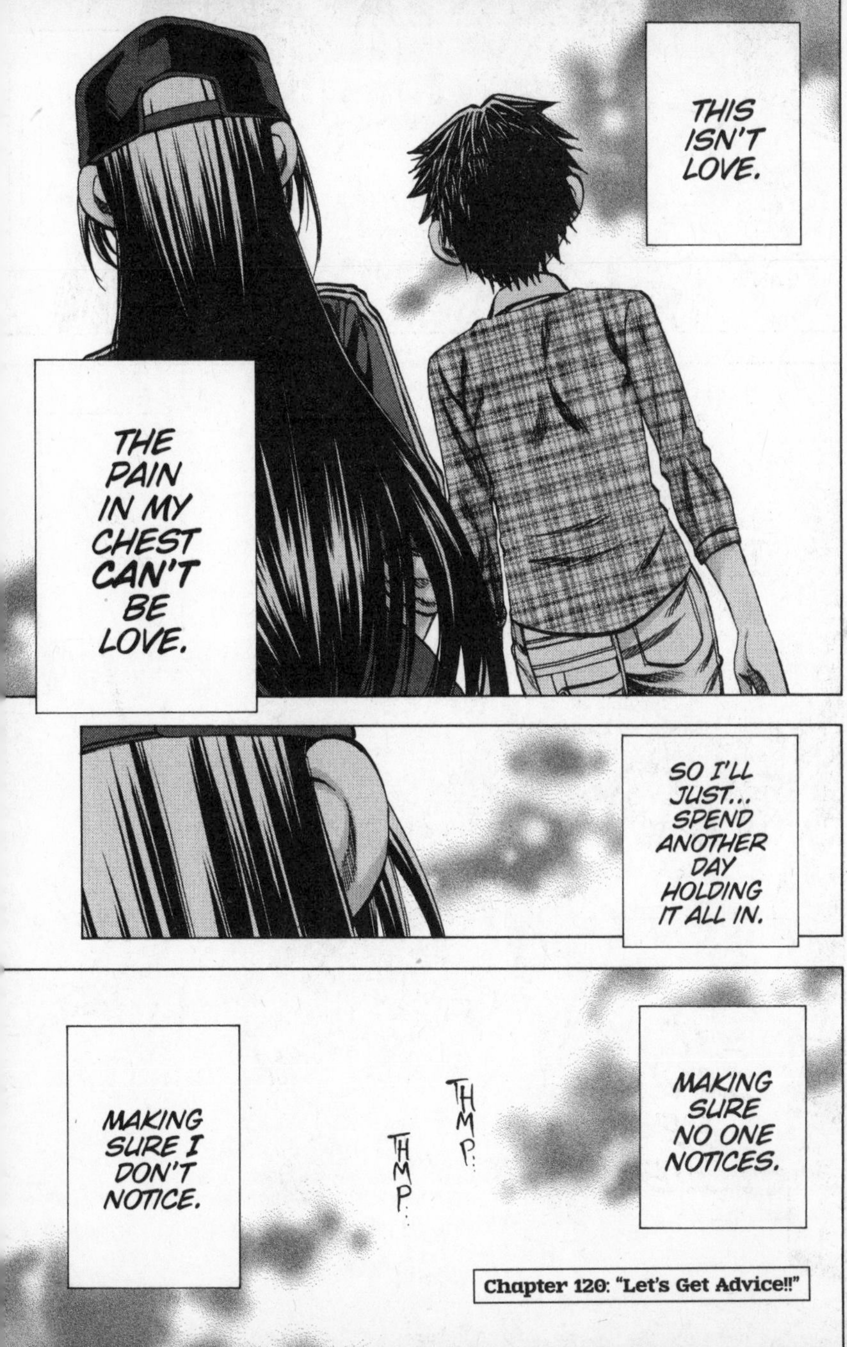
THIS ISN'T LOVE.
THE PAIN IN MY CHEST CAN'T BE LOVE.
SO I'LL JUST... SPEND ANOTHER DAY HOLDING IT ALL IN.
MAKING SURE NO ONE NOTICES.
THMP...
THMP...
MAKING SURE I DON'T NOTICE.

Chapter 120: "Let's Get Advice!!"

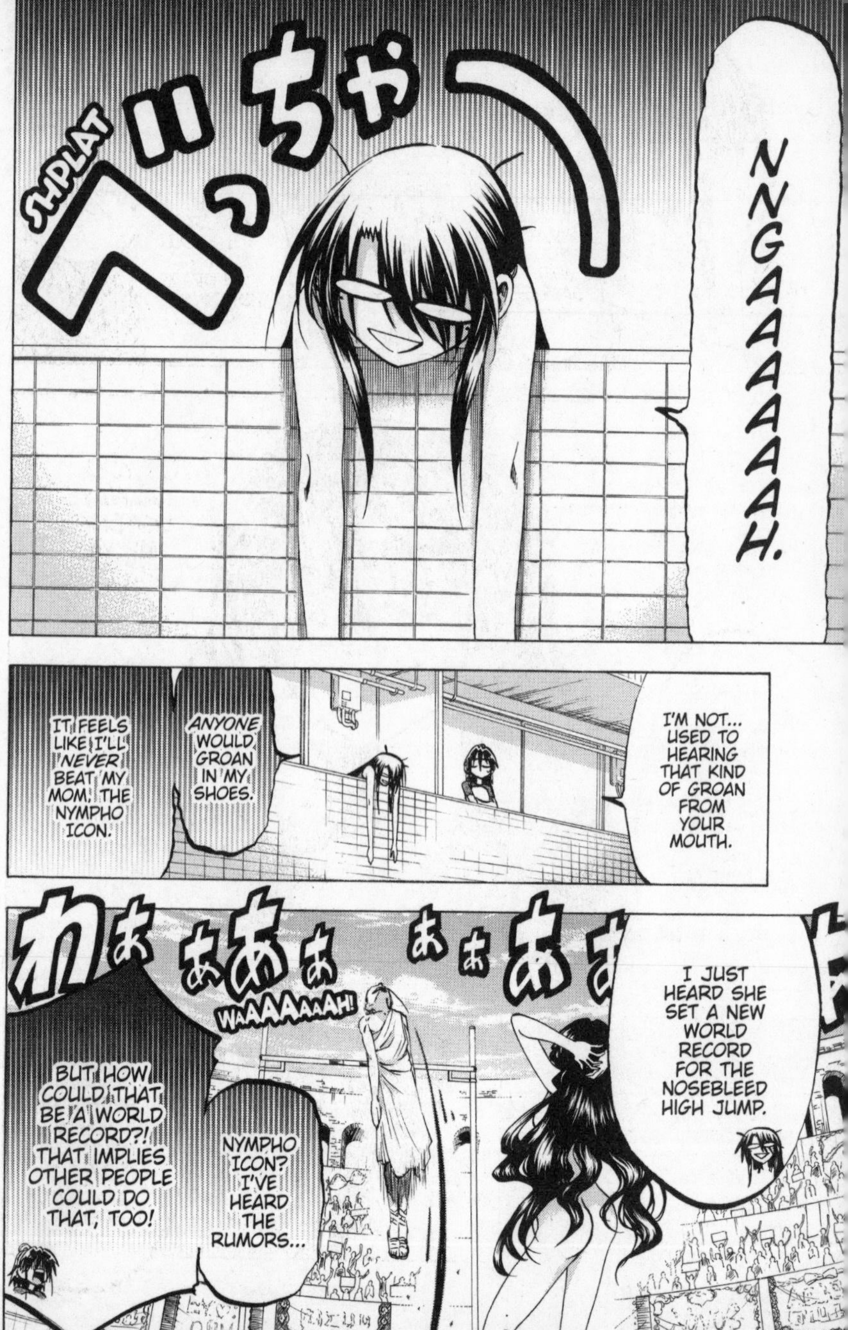
NNGAAAAAAH.
べっちゃ〜
SHPLAT
I'M NOT... USED TO HEARING THAT KIND OF GROAN FROM YOUR MOUTH.
ANYONE WOULD GROAN IN MY SHOES.
IT FEELS LIKE I'LL *NEVER* BEAT MY MOM, THE NYMPHO ICON.
I JUST HEARD SHE SET A NEW WORLD RECORD FOR THE NOSEBLEED HIGH JUMP.
WAAAAAAAH!
NYMPHO ICON? I'VE HEARD THE RUMORS...
BUT HOW COULD THAT BE A WORLD RECORD?! THAT IMPLIES OTHER PEOPLE COULD DO THAT, TOO!

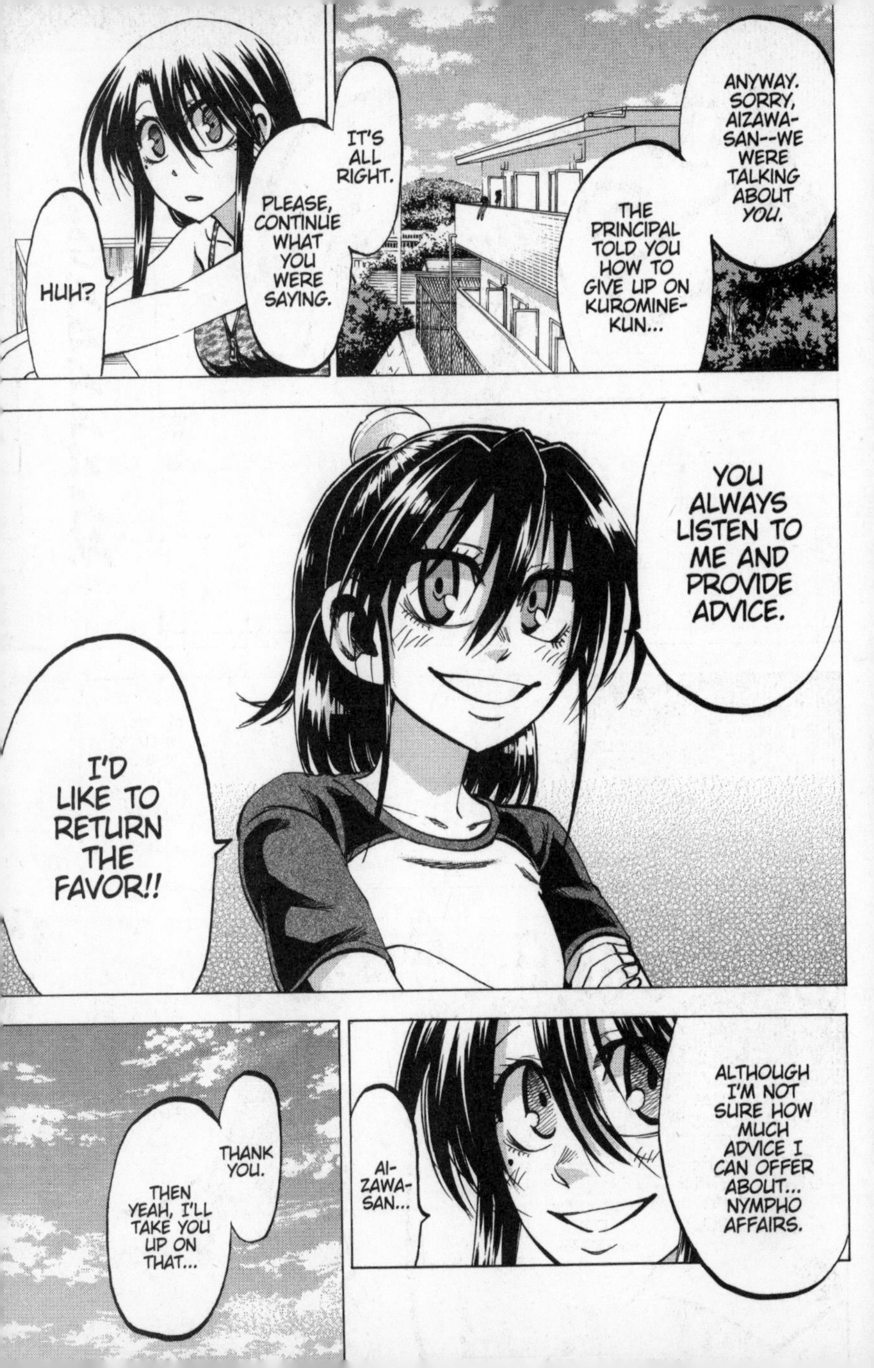
ANYWAY. SORRY, AIZAWA-SAN--WE WERE TALKING ABOUT YOU.
THE PRINCIPAL TOLD YOU HOW TO GIVE UP ON KUROMINE-KUN...
IT'S ALL RIGHT.
PLEASE, CONTINUE WHAT YOU WERE SAYING.
HUH?
YOU ALWAYS LISTEN TO ME AND PROVIDE ADVICE.
I'D LIKE TO RETURN THE FAVOR!!
ALTHOUGH I'M NOT SURE HOW MUCH ADVICE I CAN OFFER ABOUT... NYMPHO AFFAIRS.
AI-ZAWA-SAN...
THANK YOU.
THEN YEAH, I'LL TAKE YOU UP ON THAT...

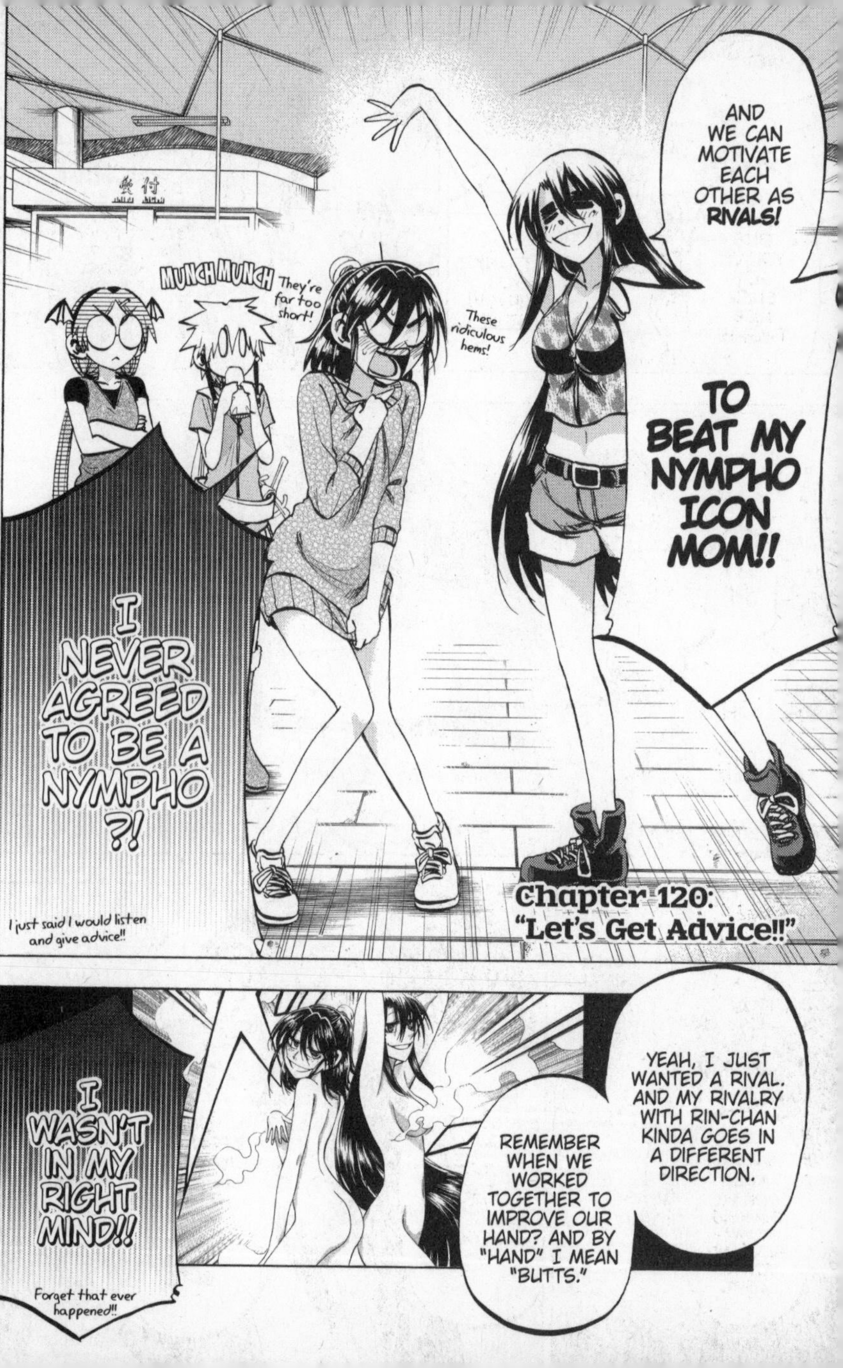
AND WE CAN MOTIVATE EACH OTHER AS RIVALS!
TO BEAT MY NYMPHO ICON MOM!!
These ridiculous hems!
They're far too short!
MUNCH MUNCH
I NEVER AGREED TO BE A NYMPHO?!
I just said I would listen and give advice!!
Chapter 120: "Let's Get Advice!!"
YEAH, I JUST WANTED A RIVAL. AND MY RIVALRY WITH RIN-CHAN KINDA GOES IN A DIFFERENT DIRECTION.
REMEMBER WHEN WE WORKED TOGETHER TO IMPROVE OUR HAND? AND BY "HAND" I MEAN "BUTTS."
I WASN'T IN MY RIGHT MIND!!
Forget that ever happened!!

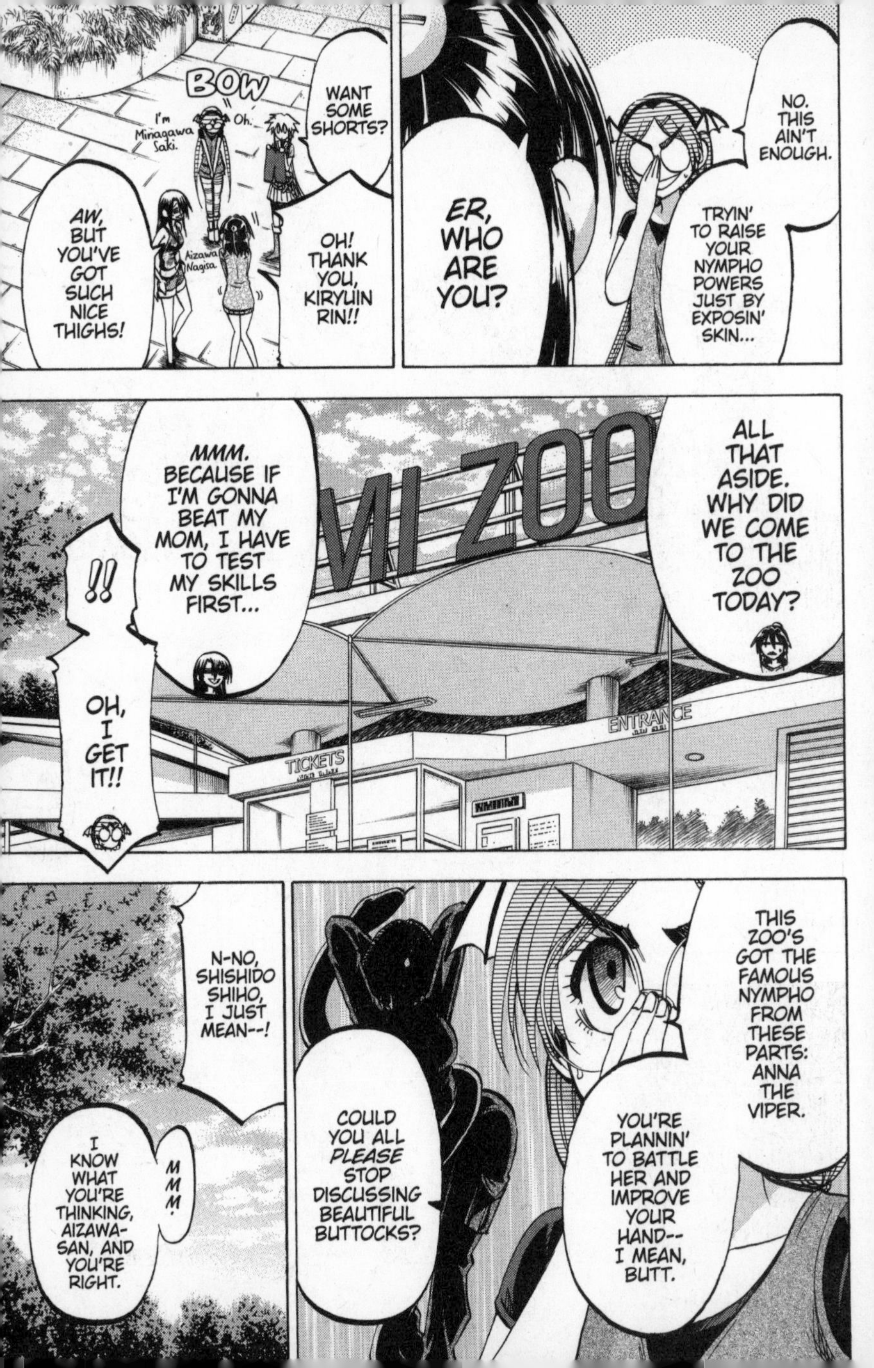
NO. THIS AIN'T ENOUGH.
TRYIN' TO RAISE YOUR NYMPHO POWERS JUST BY EXPOSIN' SKIN...
ER, WHO ARE YOU?
WANT SOME SHORTS?
OH! THANK YOU, KIRYUIN RIN!!
BOW
Oh.
I'm Minagawa Saki.
Aizawa Nagisa.
AW, BUT YOU'VE GOT SUCH NICE THIGHS!
ALL THAT ASIDE. WHY DID WE COME TO THE ZOO TODAY?
MI ZOO
ENTRANCE
TICKETS
MMM. BECAUSE IF I'M GONNA BEAT MY MOM, I HAVE TO TEST MY SKILLS FIRST...
!!
OH, I GET IT!!
THIS ZOO'S GOT THE FAMOUS NYMPHO FROM THESE PARTS: ANNA THE VIPER.
YOU'RE PLANNIN' TO BATTLE HER AND IMPROVE YOUR HAND-- I MEAN, BUTT.
COULD YOU ALL *PLEASE* STOP DISCUSSING BEAUTIFUL BUTTOCKS?
N-NO, SHISHIDO SHIHO, I JUST MEAN--!
MMM!
I KNOW WHAT YOU'RE THINKING, AIZAWA-SAN, AND YOU'RE RIGHT.

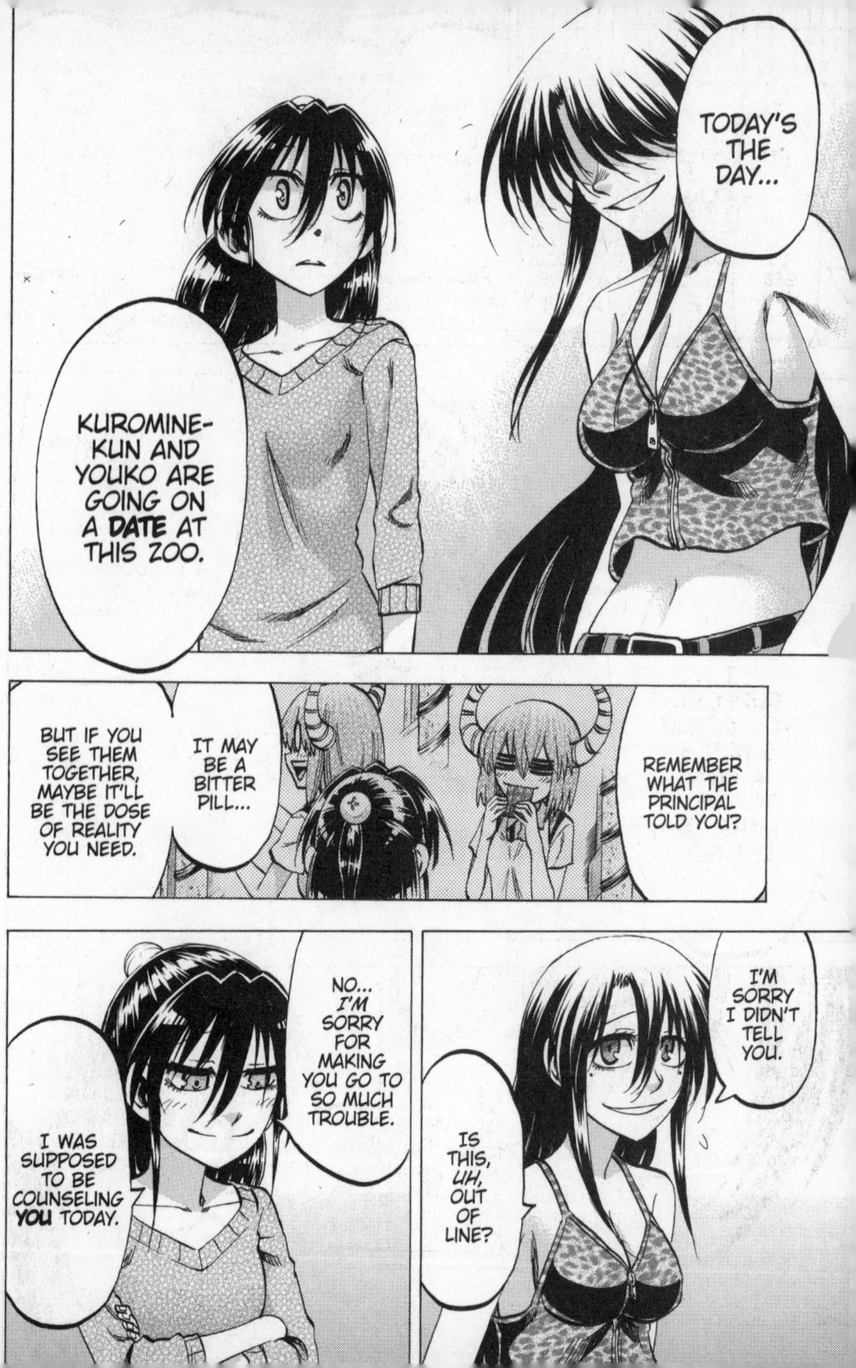
TODAY'S THE DAY...
KUROMINE-KUN AND YOUKO ARE GOING ON A **DATE** AT THIS ZOO.
REMEMBER WHAT THE PRINCIPAL TOLD YOU?
IT MAY BE A BITTER PILL...
BUT IF YOU SEE THEM TOGETHER, MAYBE IT'LL BE THE DOSE OF REALITY YOU NEED.
I'M SORRY I DIDN'T TELL YOU.
IS THIS, *UH,* OUT OF LINE?
NO... *I'M* SORRY FOR MAKING YOU GO TO SO MUCH TROUBLE.
I WAS SUPPOSED TO BE COUNSELING **YOU** TODAY.

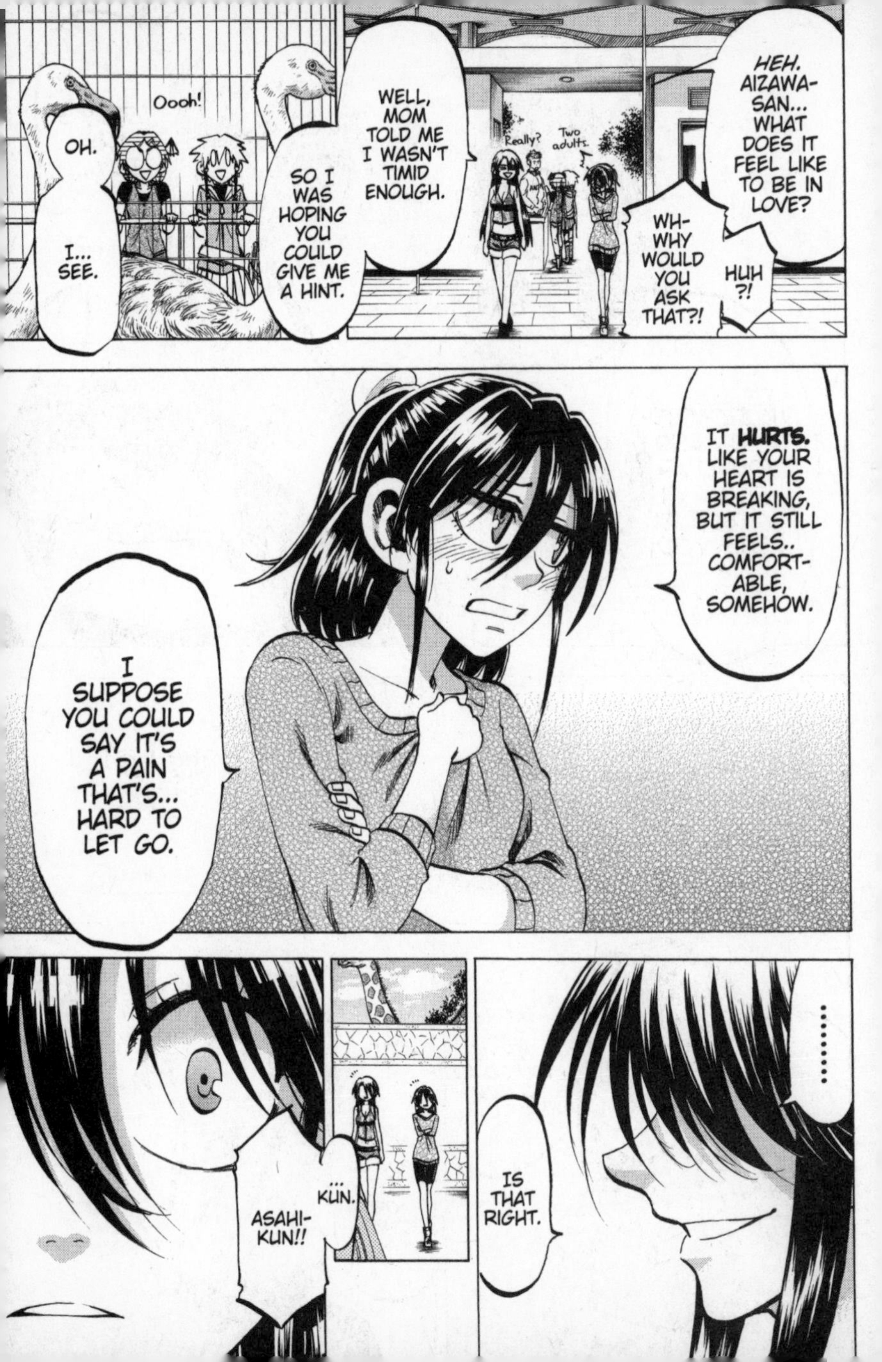
HEH. AIZAWA-SAN... WHAT DOES IT FEEL LIKE TO BE IN LOVE?
HUH?!
WH-WHY WOULD YOU ASK THAT?!
Two adults.
Really?
WELL, MOM TOLD ME I WASN'T TIMID ENOUGH.
SO I WAS HOPING YOU COULD GIVE ME A HINT.
Oooh!
OH.
I... SEE.
IT **HURTS.** LIKE YOUR HEART IS BREAKING, BUT IT STILL FEELS.. COMFORTABLE, SOMEHOW.
I SUPPOSE YOU COULD SAY IT'S A PAIN THAT'S... HARD TO LET GO.
....
IS THAT RIGHT.
...KUN.
ASAHI-KUN!!

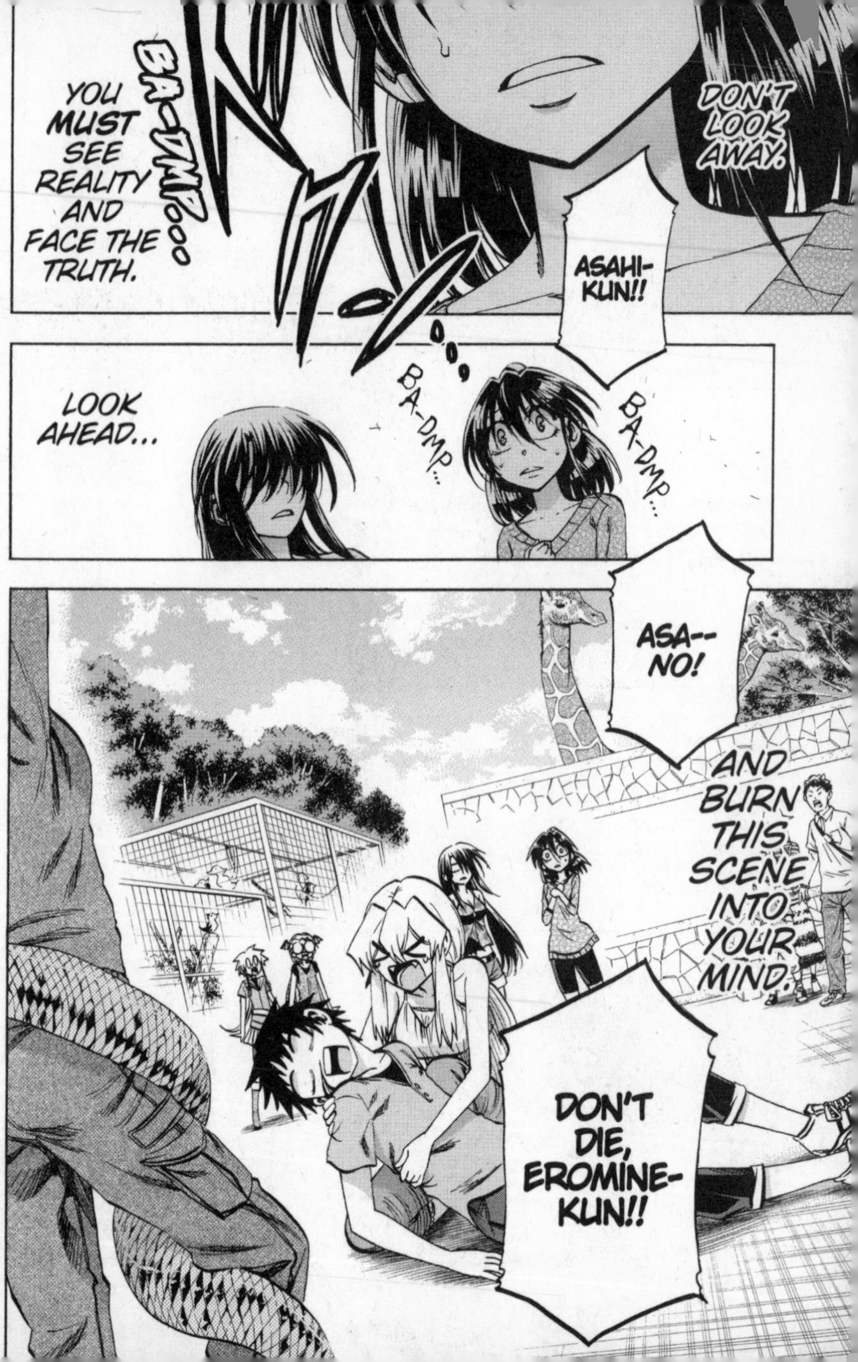
DON'T LOOK AWAY.
ASAHI-KUN!!
BA-DMPooo
YOU MUST SEE REALITY AND FACE THE TRUTH.
BA-DMP...
BA-DMP...
LOOK AHEAD...
ASA--NO!
AND BURN THIS SCENE INTO YOUR MIND.
DON'T DIE, EROMINE-KUN!!

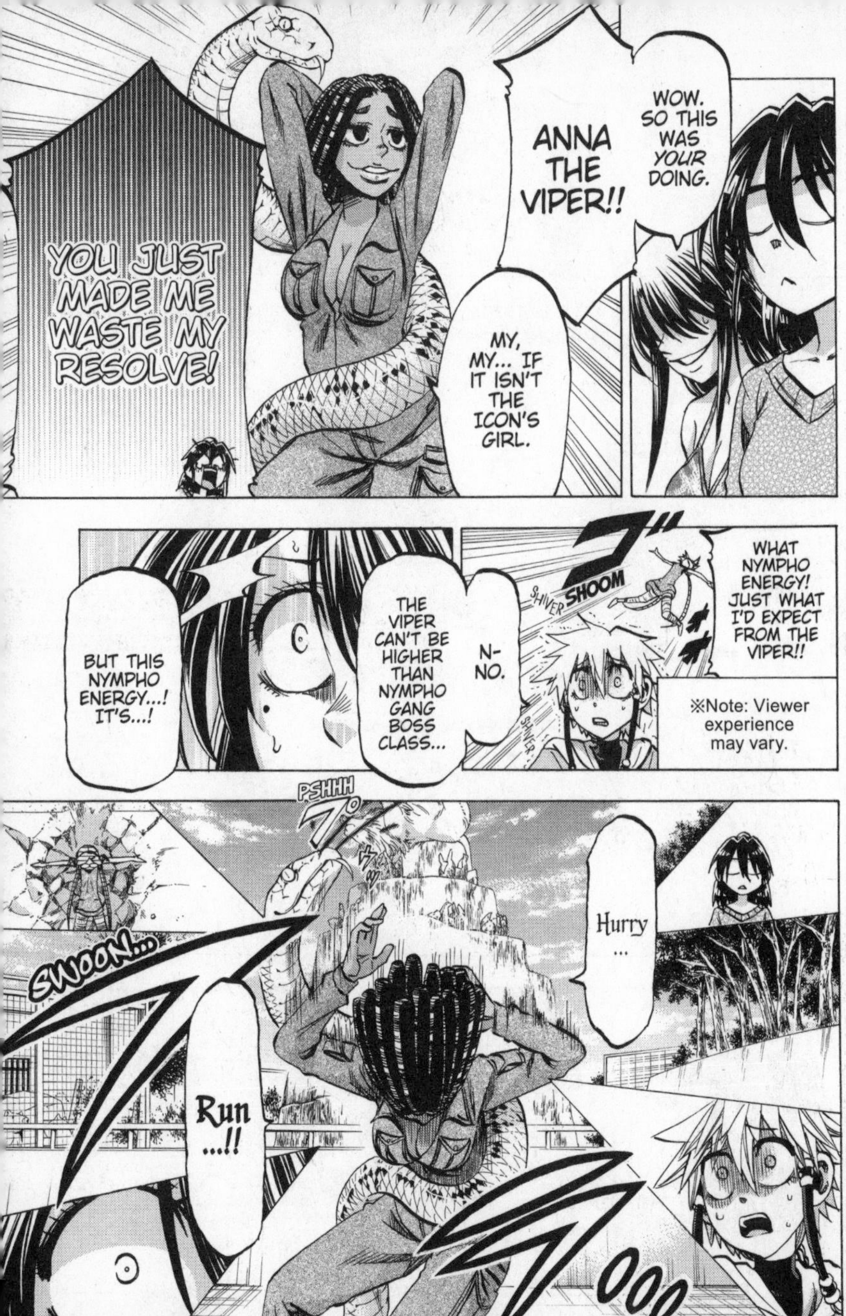
WOW. SO THIS WAS YOUR DOING.
ANNA THE VIPER!!
MY, MY... IF IT ISN'T THE ICON'S GIRL.
YOU JUST MADE ME WASTE MY RESOLVE!
WHAT NYMPHO ENERGY! JUST WHAT I'D EXPECT FROM THE VIPER!!
SHOOM
SHIVER
SHIVER
※Note: Viewer experience may vary.
N- NO.
THE VIPER CAN'T BE HIGHER THAN NYMPHO GANG BOSS CLASS...
BUT THIS NYMPHO ENERGY...! IT'S...!
PSHHH
Hurry ...
Run ...!!
SWOON...
OOO

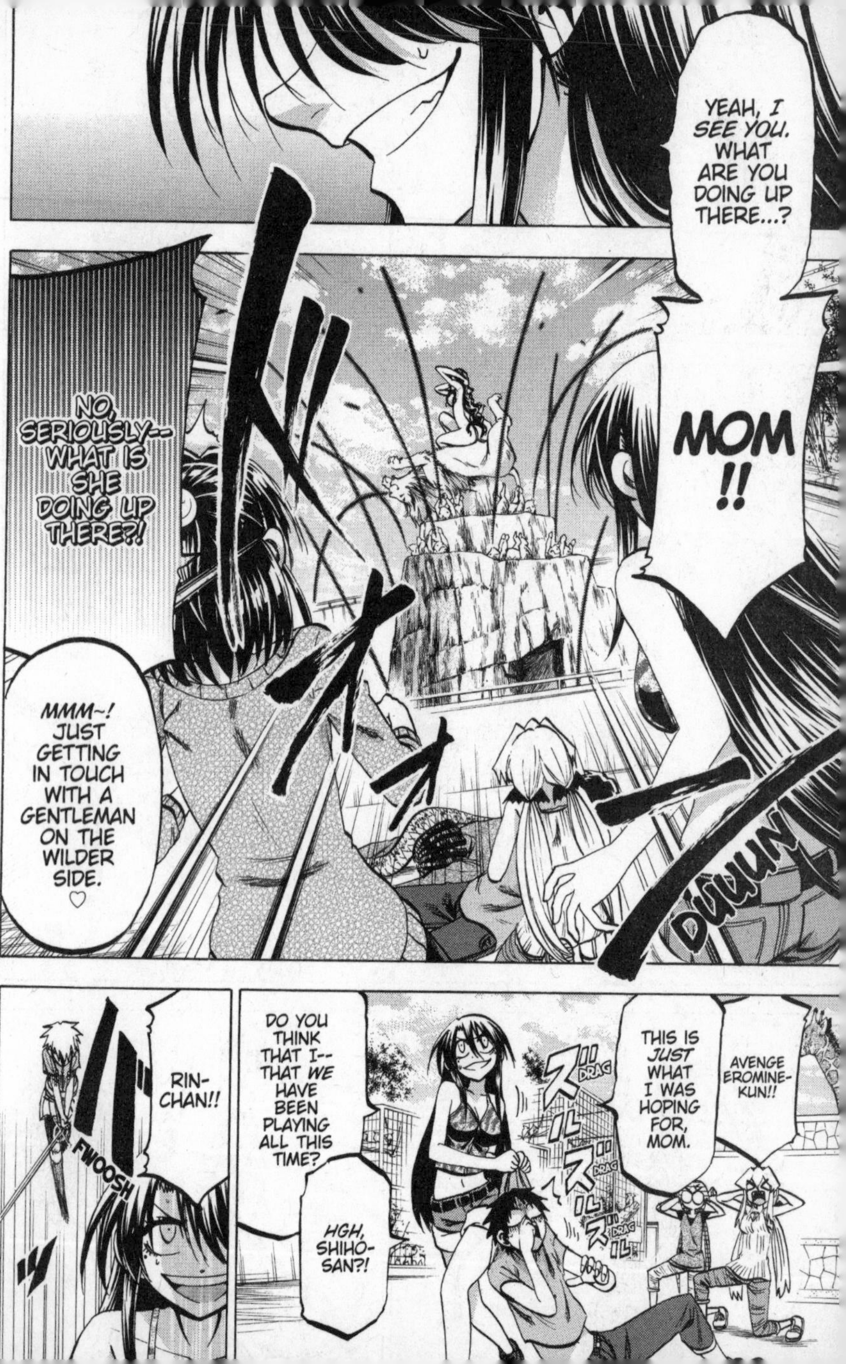
YEAH, I SEE YOU. WHAT ARE YOU DOING UP THERE...?
MOM!!
NO, SERIOUSLY-- WHAT IS SHE DOING UP THERE?!
MMM~! JUST GETTING IN TOUCH WITH A GENTLEMAN ON THE WILDER SIDE. ♡
DUUUN
AVENGE EROMINE-KUN!!
THIS IS JUST WHAT I WAS HOPING FOR, MOM.
DRAG
DRAG
DRAG
DO YOU THINK THAT I-- THAT WE HAVE BEEN PLAYING ALL THIS TIME?
HGH, SHIHO-SAN?!
RIN-CHAN!!
FWOOSH

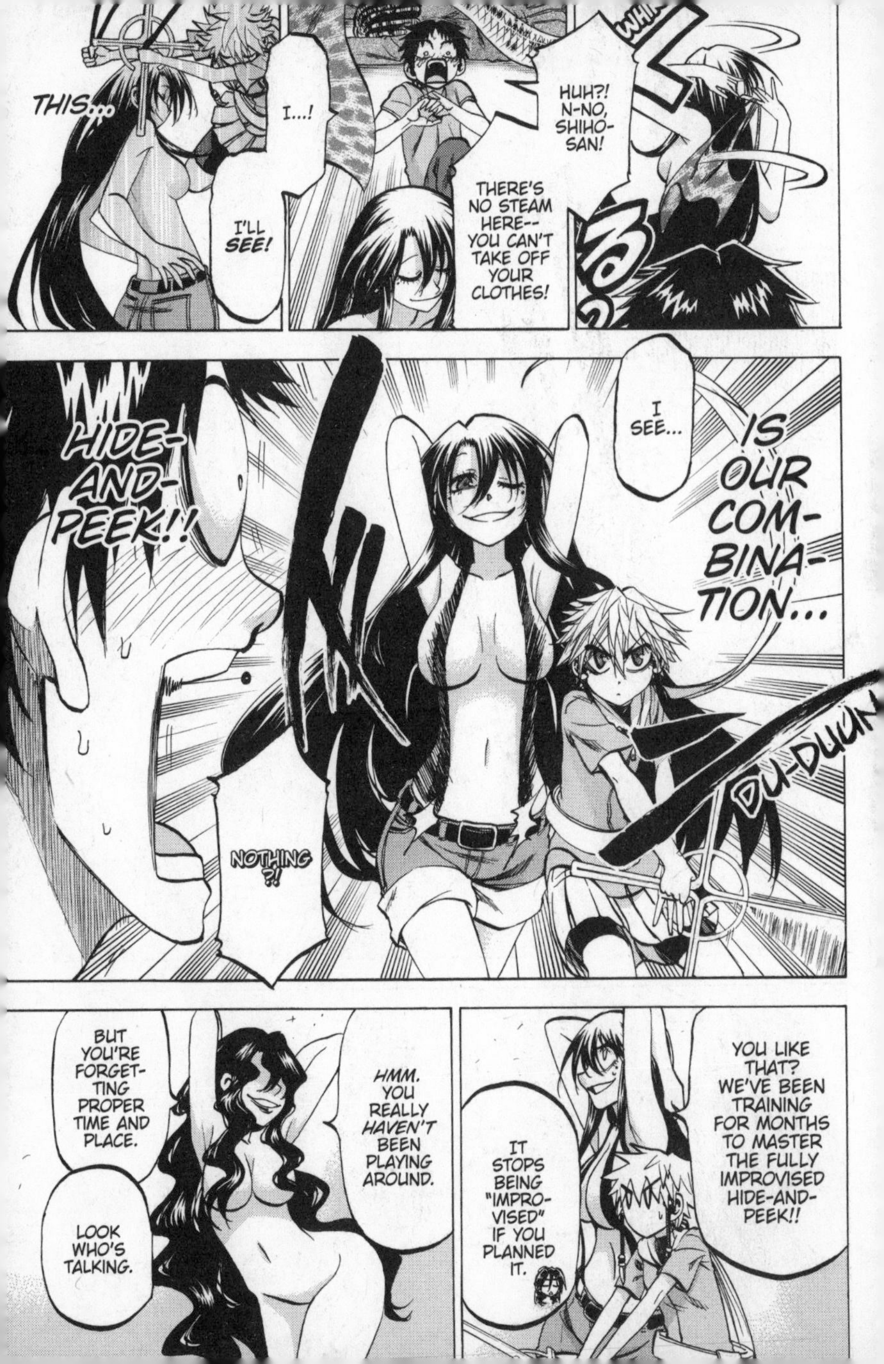
HUH?! N-NO, SHIHO-SAN!
THERE'S NO STEAM HERE-- YOU CAN'T TAKE OFF YOUR CLOTHES!
I...!
I'LL SEE!
THIS...
I SEE...
IS OUR COMBINATION...
DU-DUUN
HIDE-AND-PEEK!!
NOTHING?!
YOU LIKE THAT? WE'VE BEEN TRAINING FOR MONTHS TO MASTER THE FULLY IMPROVISED HIDE-AND-PEEK!!
IT STOPS BEING "IMPROVISED" IF YOU PLANNED IT.
HMM. YOU REALLY HAVEN'T BEEN PLAYING AROUND.
BUT YOU'RE FORGETTING PROPER TIME AND PLACE.
LOOK WHO'S TALKING.

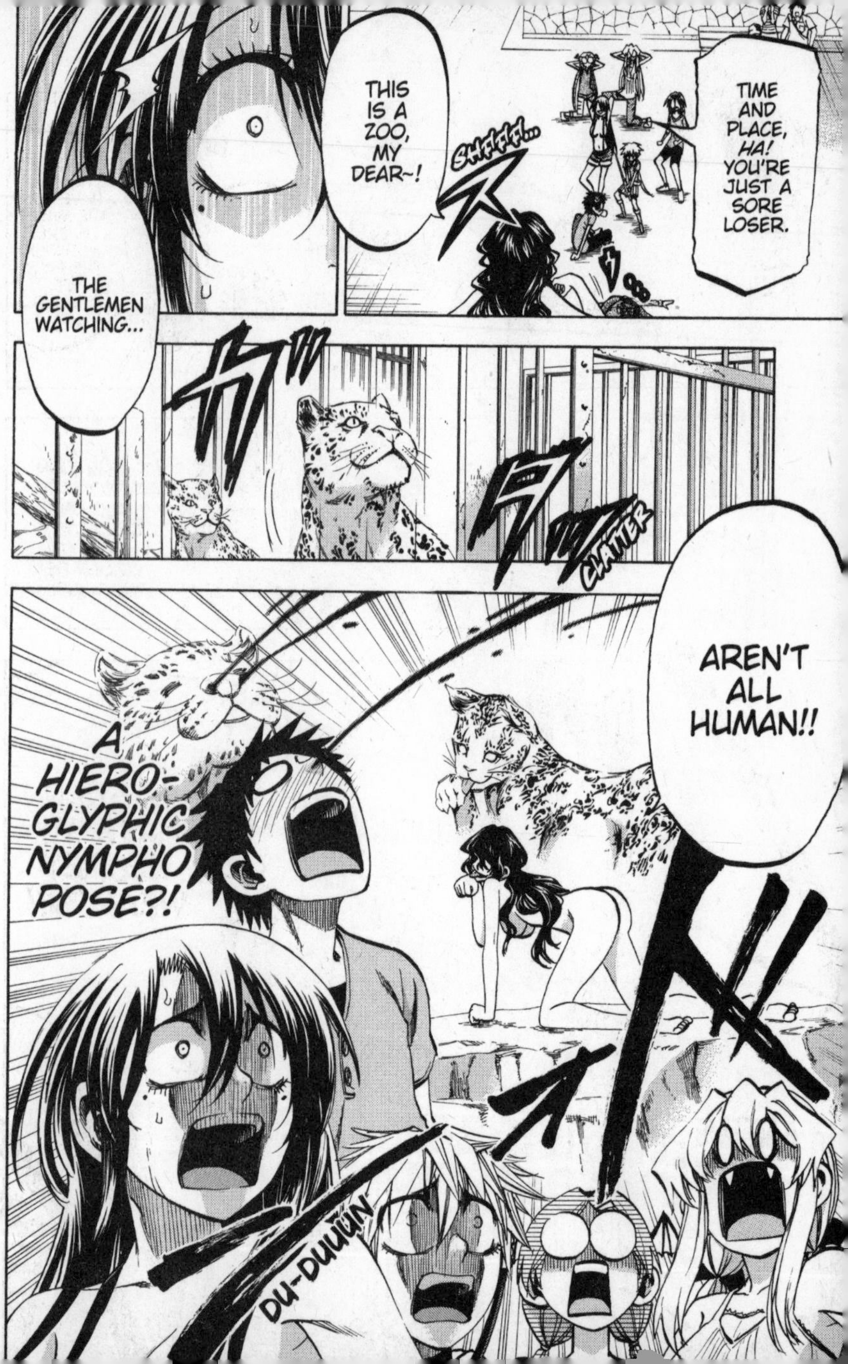
TIME AND PLACE, HA! YOU'RE JUST A SORE LOSER.
THIS IS A ZOO, MY DEAR~!
SHFFF...
THE GENTLEMEN WATCHING...
CLATTER
AREN'T ALL HUMAN!!
A HIERO-GLYPHIC NYMPHO POSE?!
DU-DUUUN

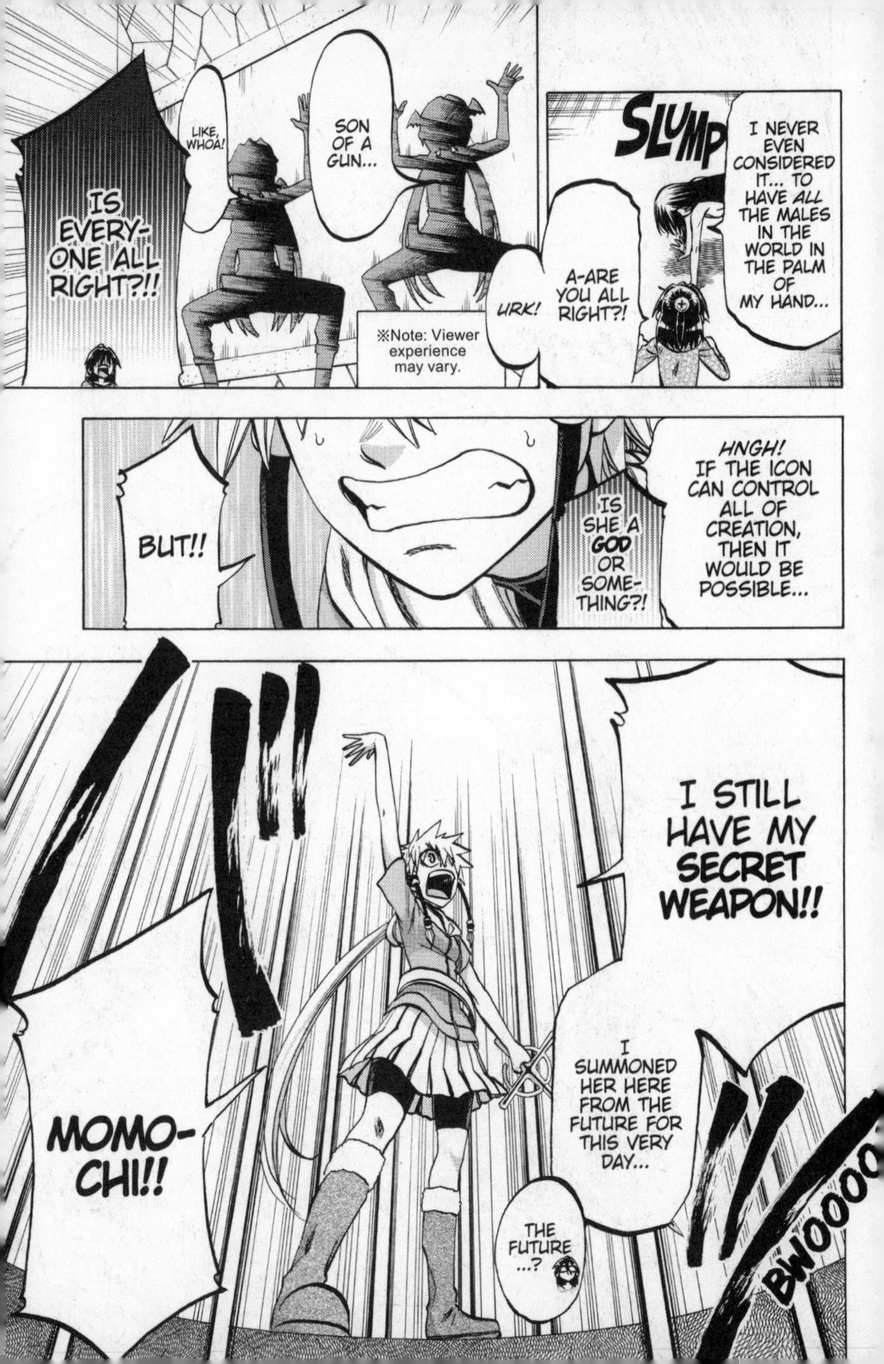
SLUMP
I NEVER EVEN CONSIDERED IT... TO HAVE *ALL* THE MALES IN THE WORLD IN THE PALM OF MY HAND...
A-ARE YOU ALL RIGHT?!
URK!
SON OF A GUN...
LIKE, WHOA!
IS EVERY-ONE ALL RIGHT?!!
※Note: Viewer experience may vary.
HNGH! IF THE ICON CAN CONTROL ALL OF CREATION, THEN IT WOULD BE POSSIBLE...
IS SHE A **GOD** OR SOME-THING?!
BUT!!
I STILL HAVE MY **SECRET WEAPON!!**
I SUMMONED HER HERE FROM THE FUTURE FOR THIS VERY DAY...
BWOOOO
THE FUTURE ...?
MOMO-CHI!!

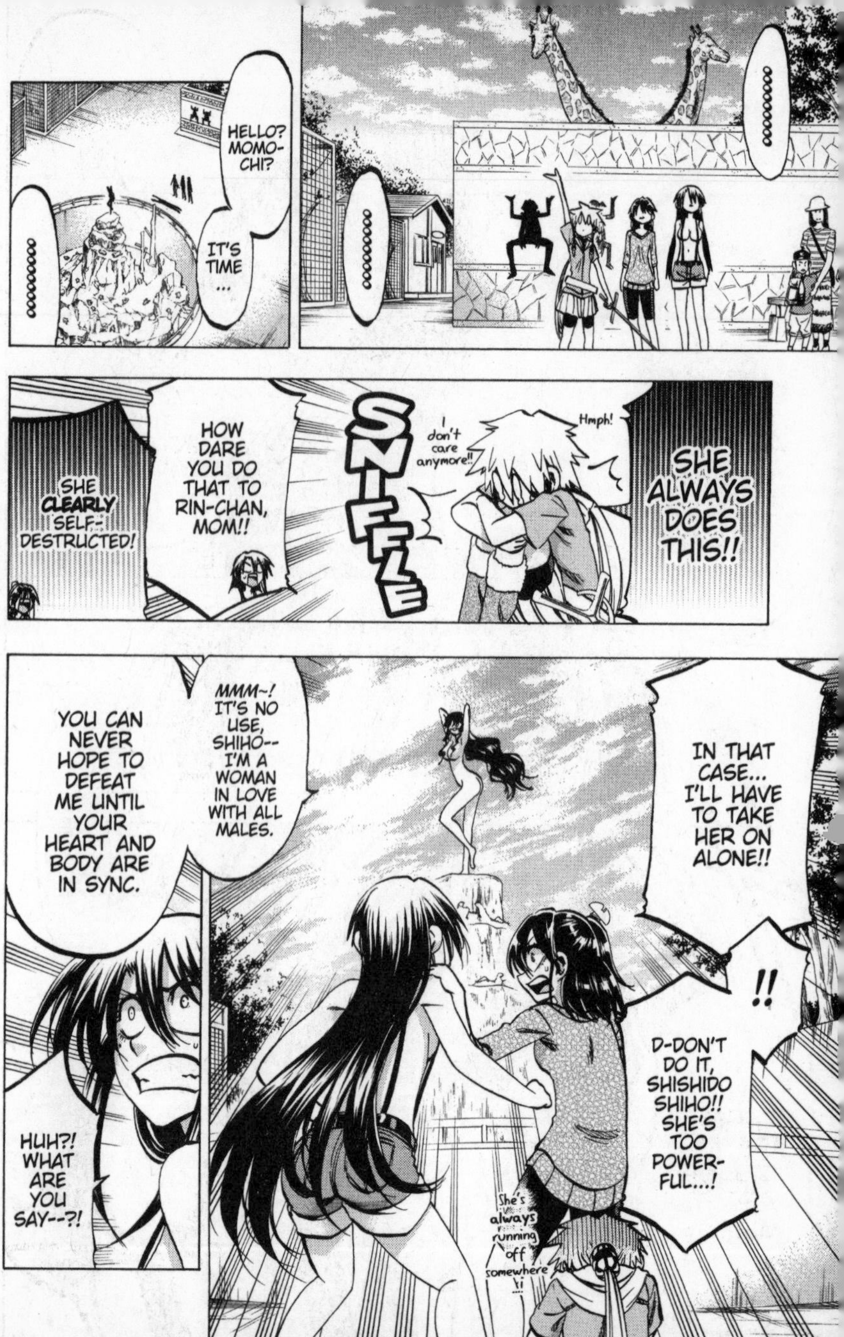
OOOOOOOO
OOOOOOOO
HELLO? MOMO-CHI?
IT'S TIME ...
OOOOOOO
SHE ALWAYS DOES THIS!!
Hmph!
I don't care anymore!!
SNIFFLE
HOW DARE YOU DO THAT TO RIN-CHAN, MOM!!
SHE CLEARLY SELF-DESTRUCTED!
IN THAT CASE... I'LL HAVE TO TAKE HER ON ALONE!!
MMM~! IT'S NO USE, SHIHO-- I'M A WOMAN IN LOVE WITH ALL MALES.
!!
D-DON'T DO IT, SHISHIDO SHIHO!! SHE'S TOO POWER-FUL...!
She's always running off somewhere
YOU CAN NEVER HOPE TO DEFEAT ME UNTIL YOUR HEART AND BODY ARE IN SYNC.
HUH?! WHAT ARE YOU SAY--?!

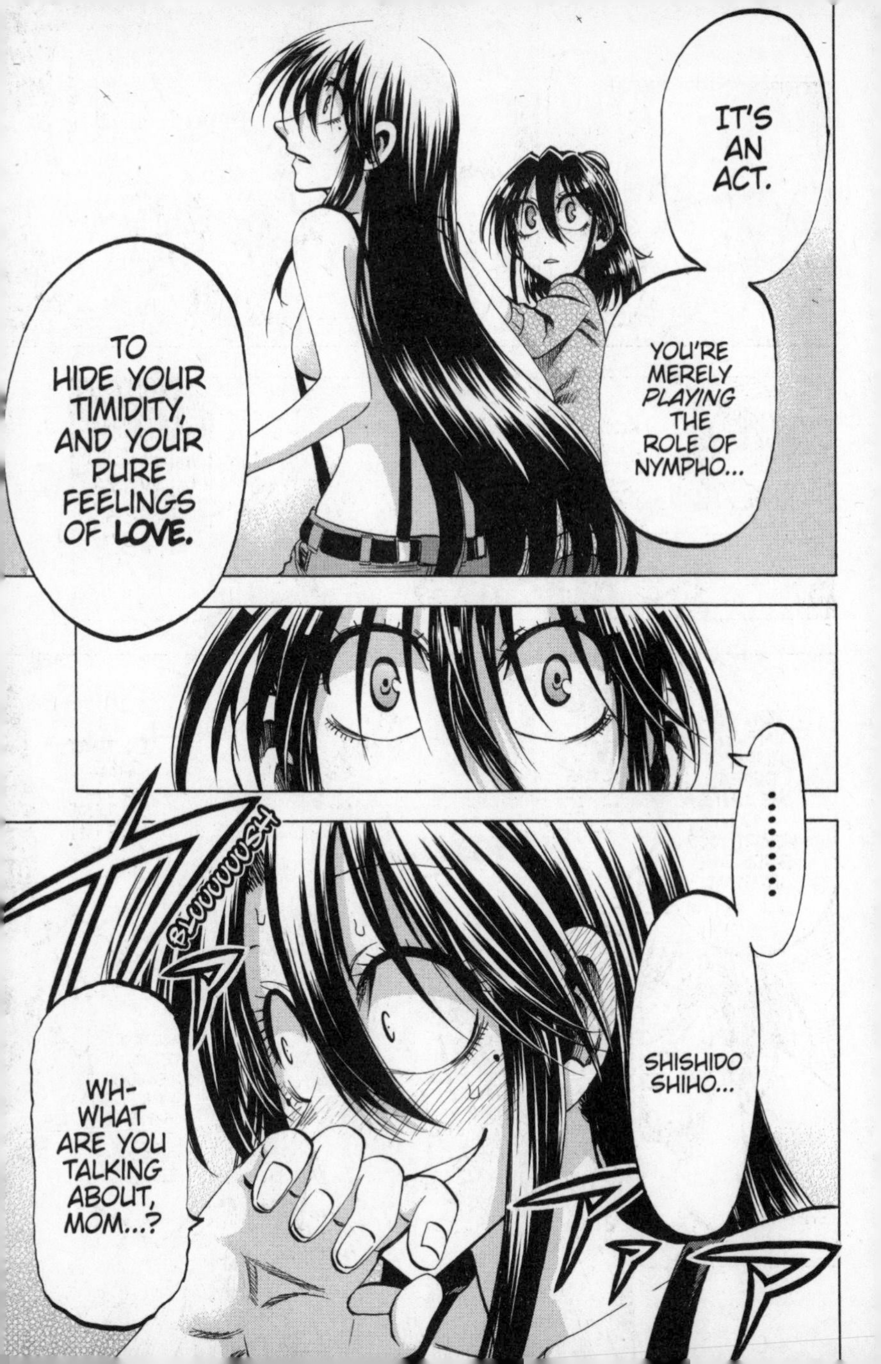
IT'S AN ACT.
YOU'RE MERELY *PLAYING* THE ROLE OF NYMPHO...
TO HIDE YOUR TIMIDITY, AND YOUR PURE FEELINGS OF **LOVE.**
......
SHISHIDO SHIHO...
BLOOOOOOSH
WH- WHAT ARE YOU TALKING ABOUT, MOM...?

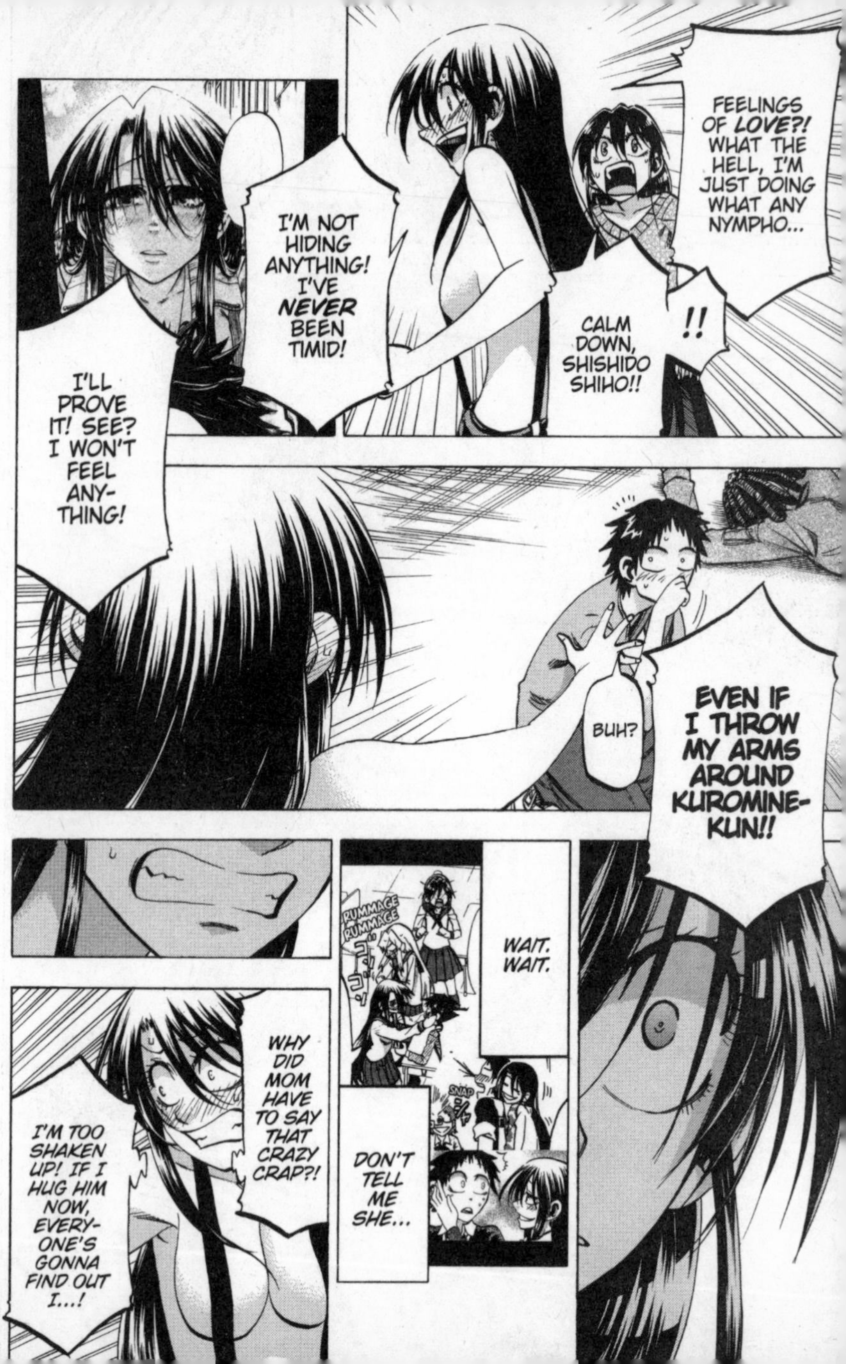

FEELINGS OF LOVE?! WHAT THE HELL, I'M JUST DOING WHAT ANY NYMPHO...
!!
CALM DOWN, SHISHIDO SHIHO!!
I'M NOT HIDING ANYTHING! I'VE NEVER BEEN TIMID!
I'LL PROVE IT! SEE? I WON'T FEEL ANYTHING!
EVEN IF I THROW MY ARMS AROUND KUROMINE-KUN!!
BUH?
WAIT. WAIT.
RUMMAGE RUMMAGE
SNAP
DON'T TELL ME SHE...
WHY DID MOM HAVE TO SAY THAT CRAZY CRAP?!
I'M TOO SHAKEN UP! IF I HUG HIM NOW, EVERYONE'S GONNA FIND OUT I...!

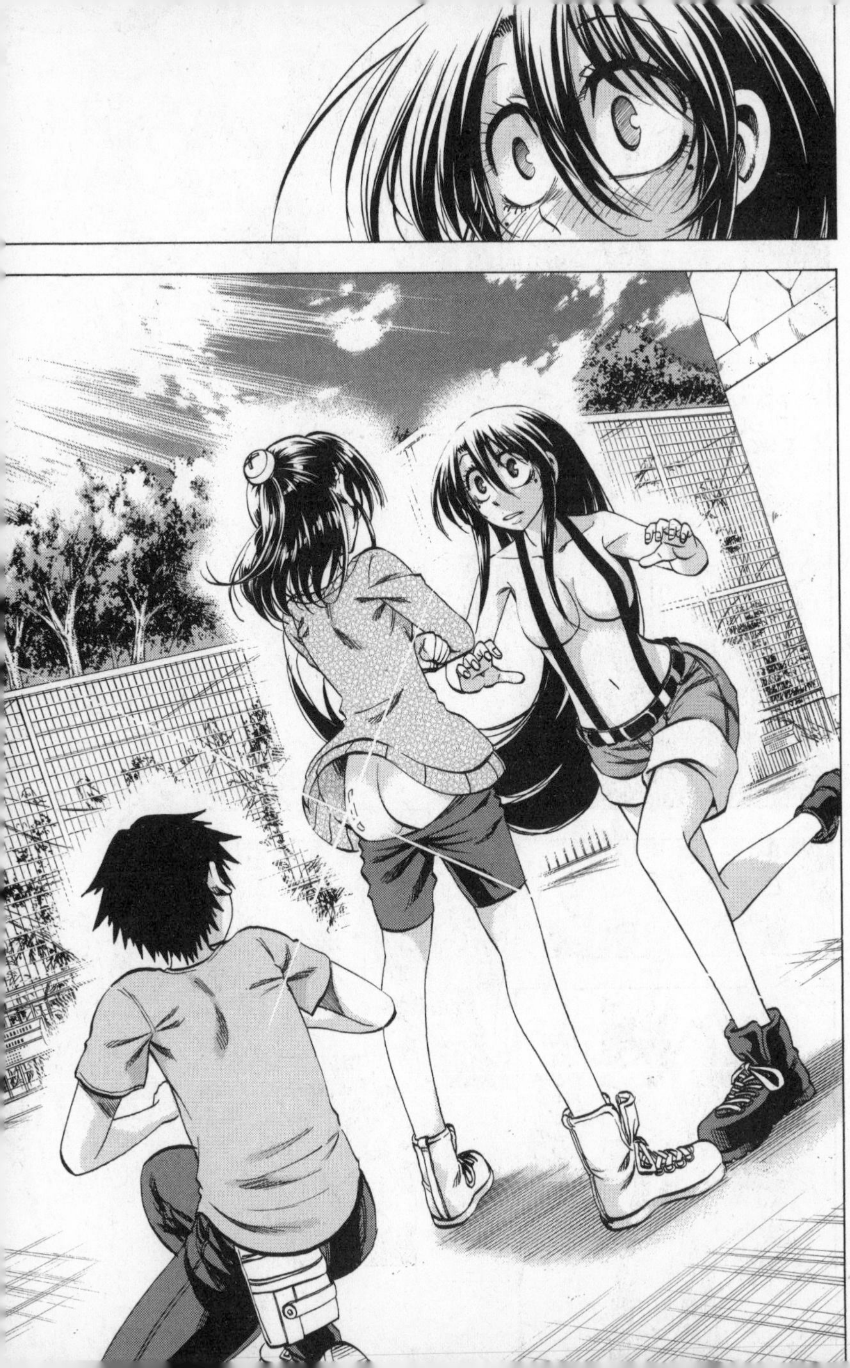

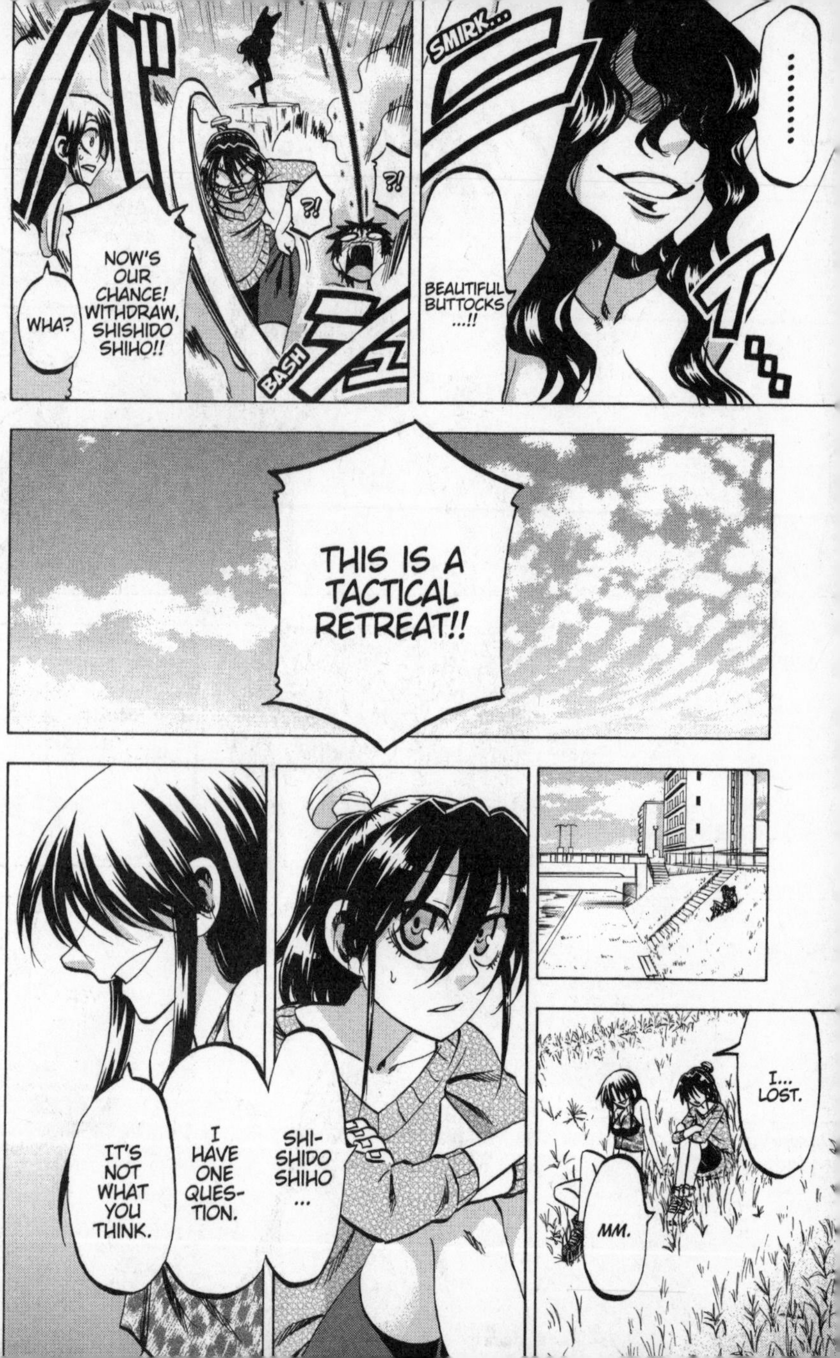
SMIRK...
......
BEAUTIFUL BUTTOCKS ...!!
?!
?!
NOW'S OUR CHANCE! WITHDRAW, SHISHIDO SHIHO!!
BASH
WHA?
THIS IS A TACTICAL RETREAT!!
I... LOST.
MM.
SHI-SHIDO SHIHO ...
I HAVE ONE QUES-TION.
IT'S NOT WHAT YOU THINK.

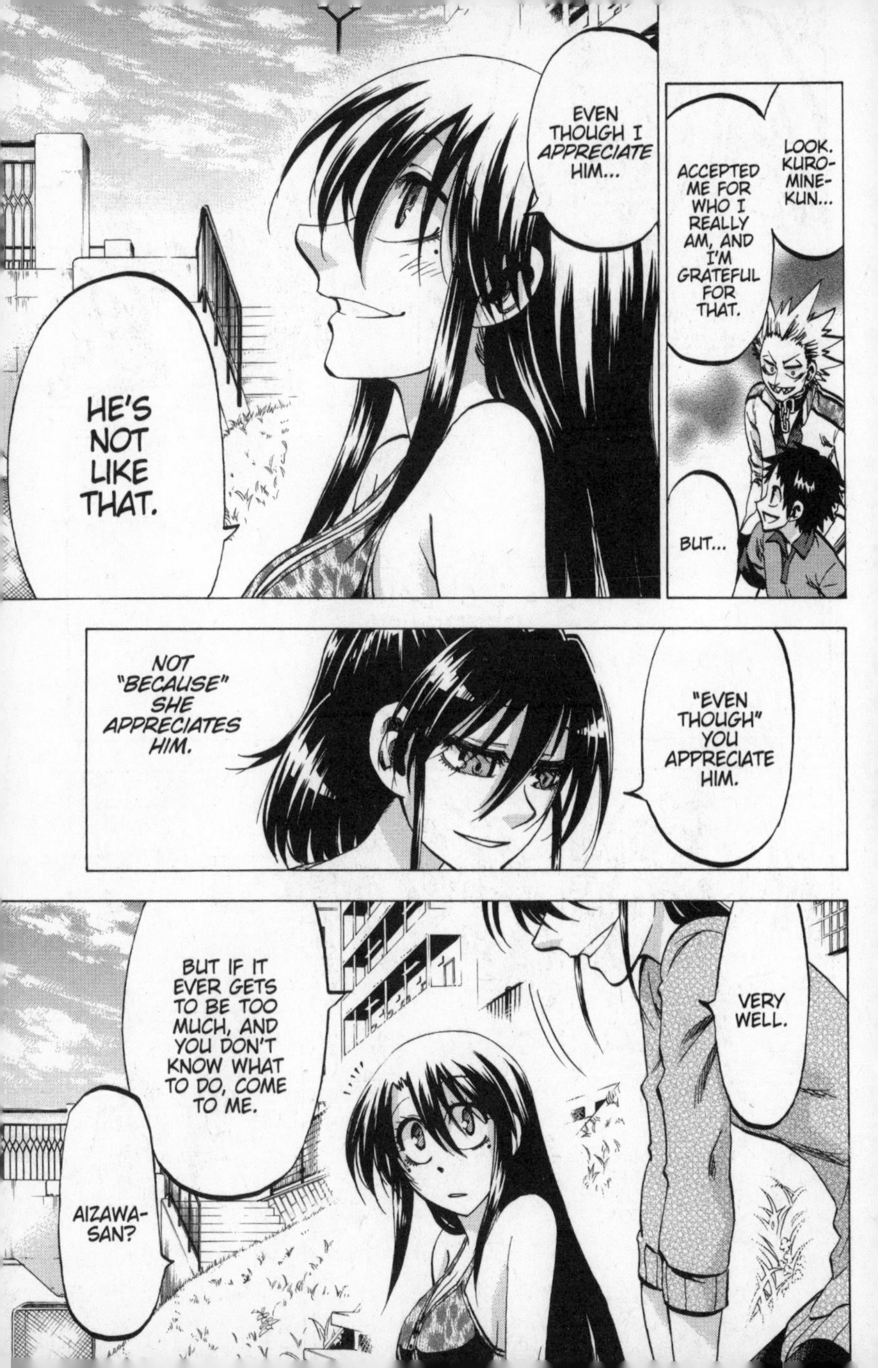
LOOK. KURO-MINE-KUN...
ACCEPTED ME FOR WHO I REALLY AM, AND I'M GRATEFUL FOR THAT.
BUT...
EVEN THOUGH I *APPRECIATE* HIM...
HE'S NOT LIKE THAT.
"EVEN THOUGH" YOU APPRECIATE HIM.
NOT "BECAUSE" SHE APPRECIATES HIM.
VERY WELL.
BUT IF IT EVER GETS TO BE TOO MUCH, AND YOU DON'T KNOW WHAT TO DO, COME TO ME.
AIZAWA-SAN?

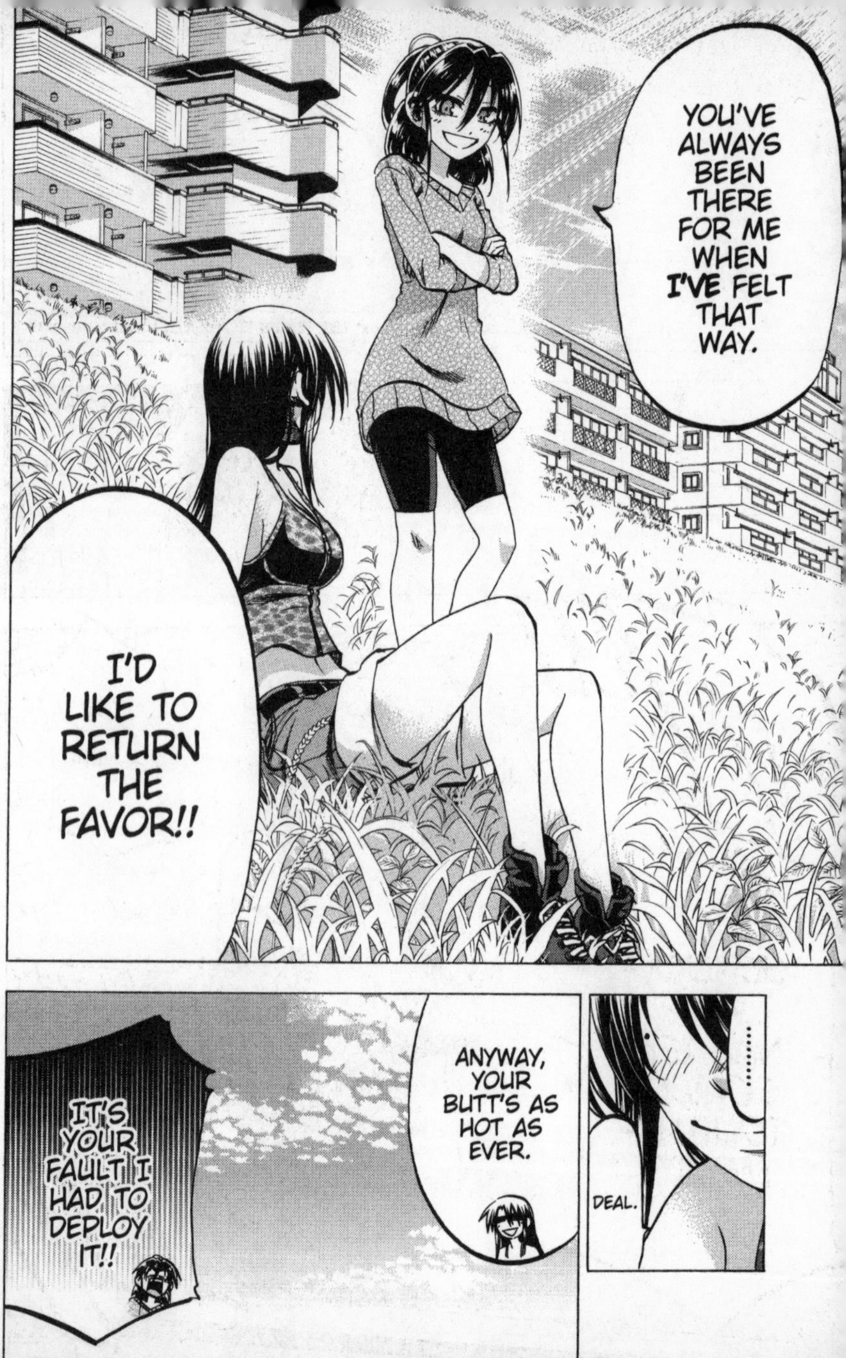
YOU'VE ALWAYS BEEN THERE FOR ME WHEN I'VE FELT THAT WAY.
I'D LIKE TO RETURN THE FAVOR!!
......
DEAL.
ANYWAY, YOUR BUTT'S AS HOT AS EVER.
IT'S YOUR FAULT I HAD TO DEPLOY IT!!

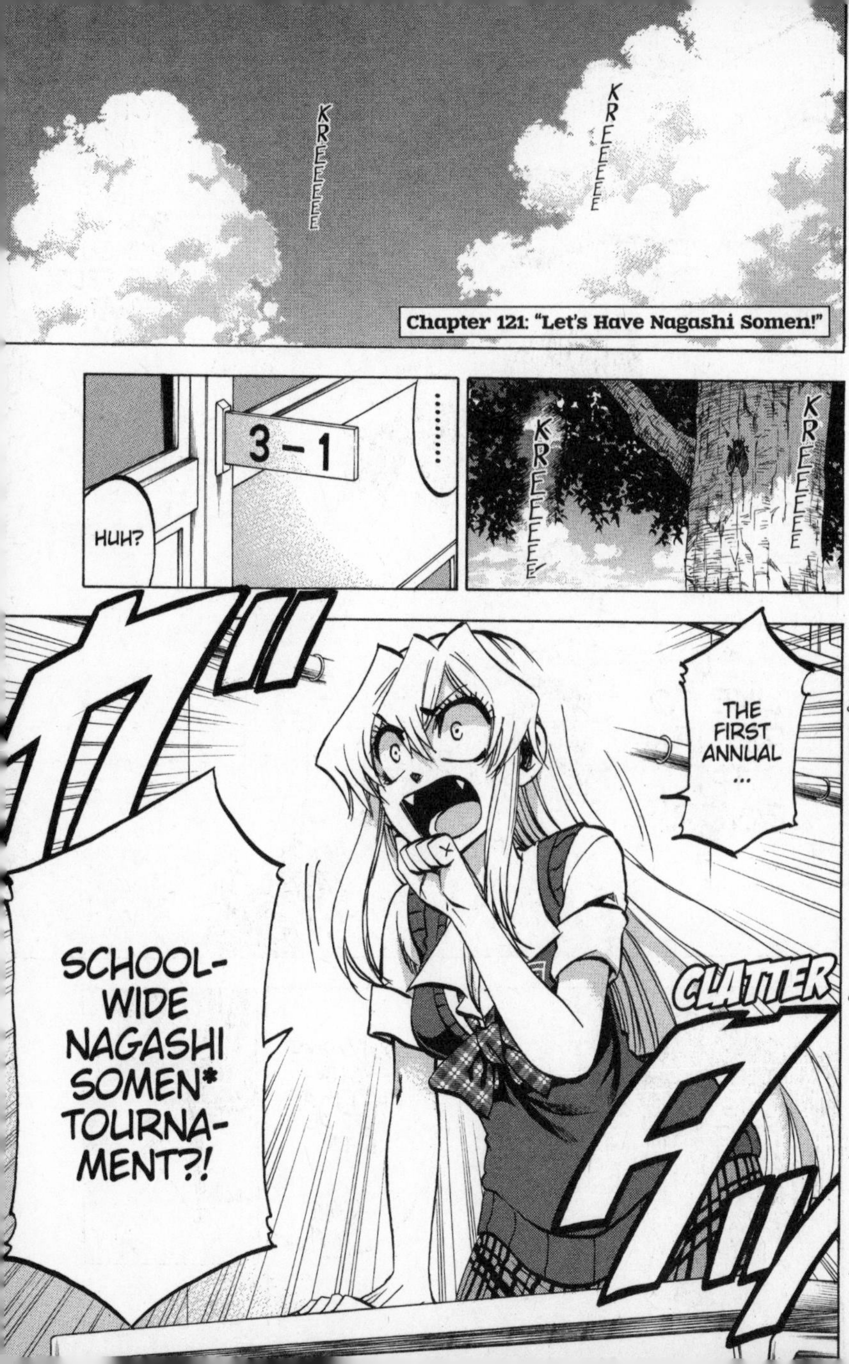
KREEEEEE
KREEEEEE
Chapter 121: "Let's Have Nagashi Somen!"
KREEEEE
KREEEEEE
......
HUH?
THE FIRST ANNUAL ...
SCHOOL-WIDE NAGASHI SOMEN* TOURNAMENT?!
CLATTER

*"Flowing noodles" served in cold water that shoot through a bamboo flume--to be picked out with chopsticks.

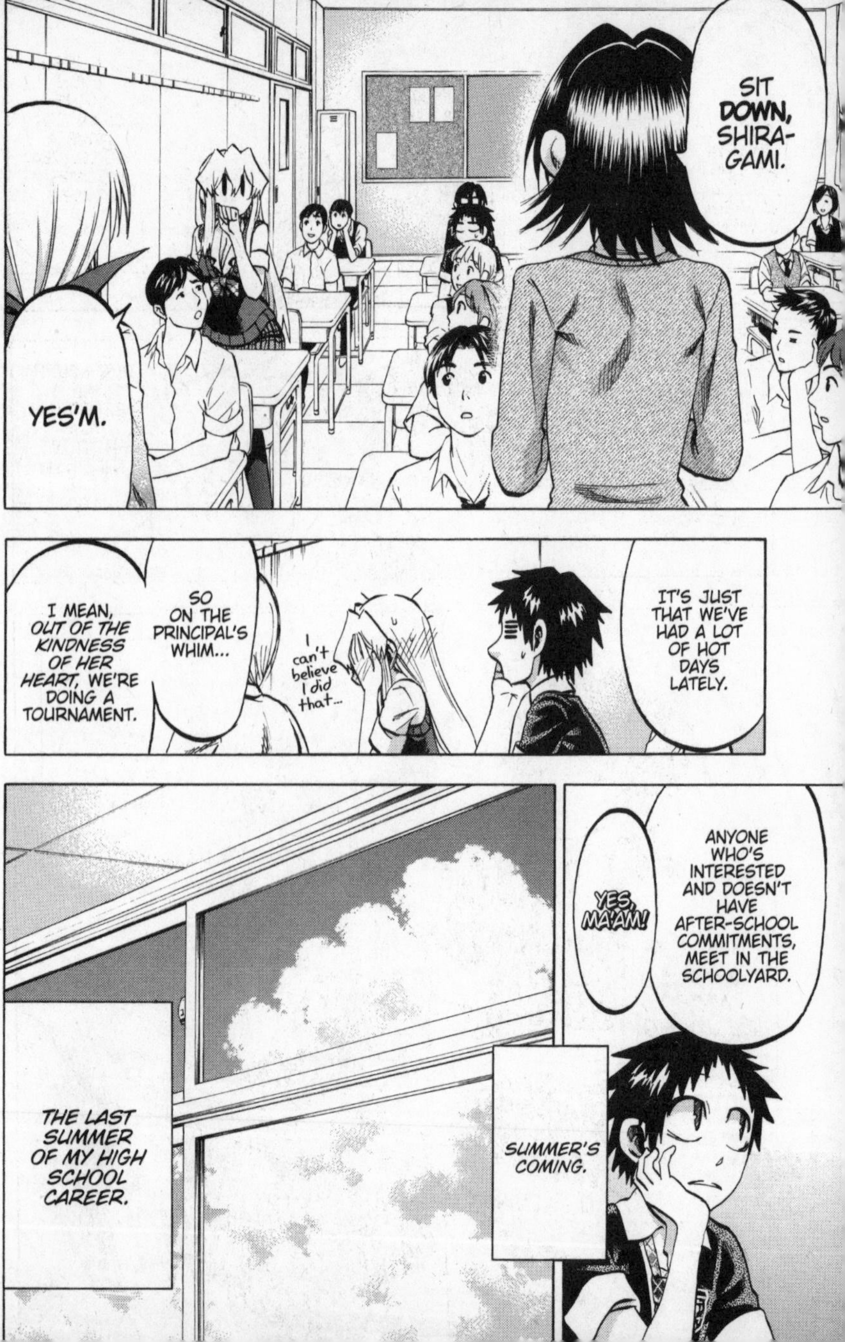
SIT DOWN, SHIRA-GAMI.
YES'M.
IT'S JUST THAT WE'VE HAD A LOT OF HOT DAYS LATELY.
I can't believe I did that...
SO ON THE PRINCIPAL'S WHIM...
I MEAN, OUT OF THE KINDNESS OF HER HEART, WE'RE DOING A TOURNAMENT.
ANYONE WHO'S INTERESTED AND DOESN'T HAVE AFTER-SCHOOL COMMITMENTS, MEET IN THE SCHOOLYARD.
YES, MA'AM!
SUMMER'S COMING.
THE LAST SUMMER OF MY HIGH SCHOOL CAREER.

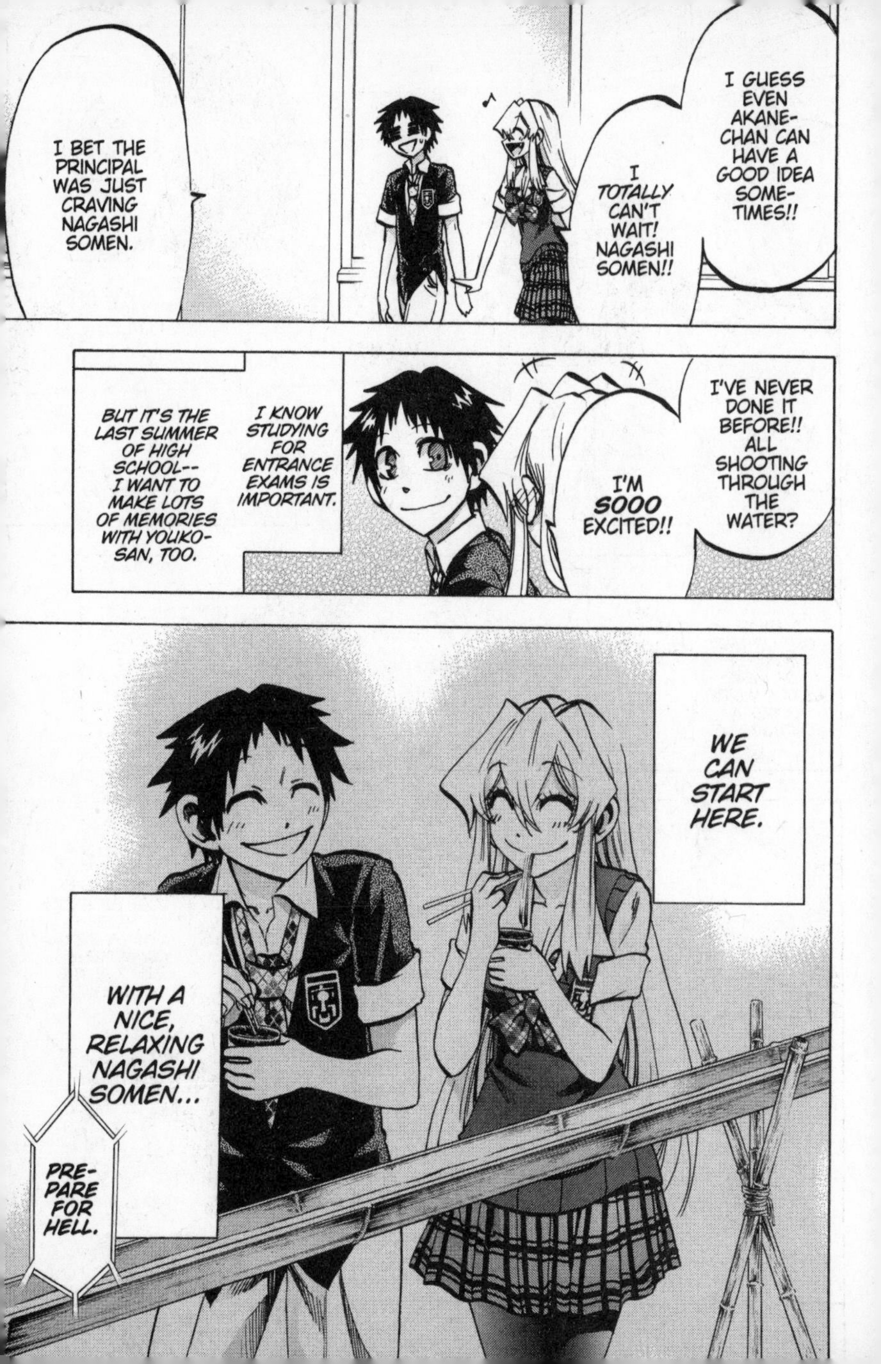
I GUESS EVEN AKANE-CHAN CAN HAVE A GOOD IDEA SOME-TIMES!!
I TOTALLY CAN'T WAIT! NAGASHI SOMEN!!
I BET THE PRINCIPAL WAS JUST CRAVING NAGASHI SOMEN.
I'VE NEVER DONE IT BEFORE!! ALL SHOOTING THROUGH THE WATER?
I'M SOOO EXCITED!!
I KNOW STUDYING FOR ENTRANCE EXAMS IS IMPORTANT.
BUT IT'S THE LAST SUMMER OF HIGH SCHOOL-- I WANT TO MAKE LOTS OF MEMORIES WITH YOUKO-SAN, TOO.
WE CAN START HERE.
WITH A NICE, RELAXING NAGASHI SOMEN...
PRE-PARE FOR HELL.

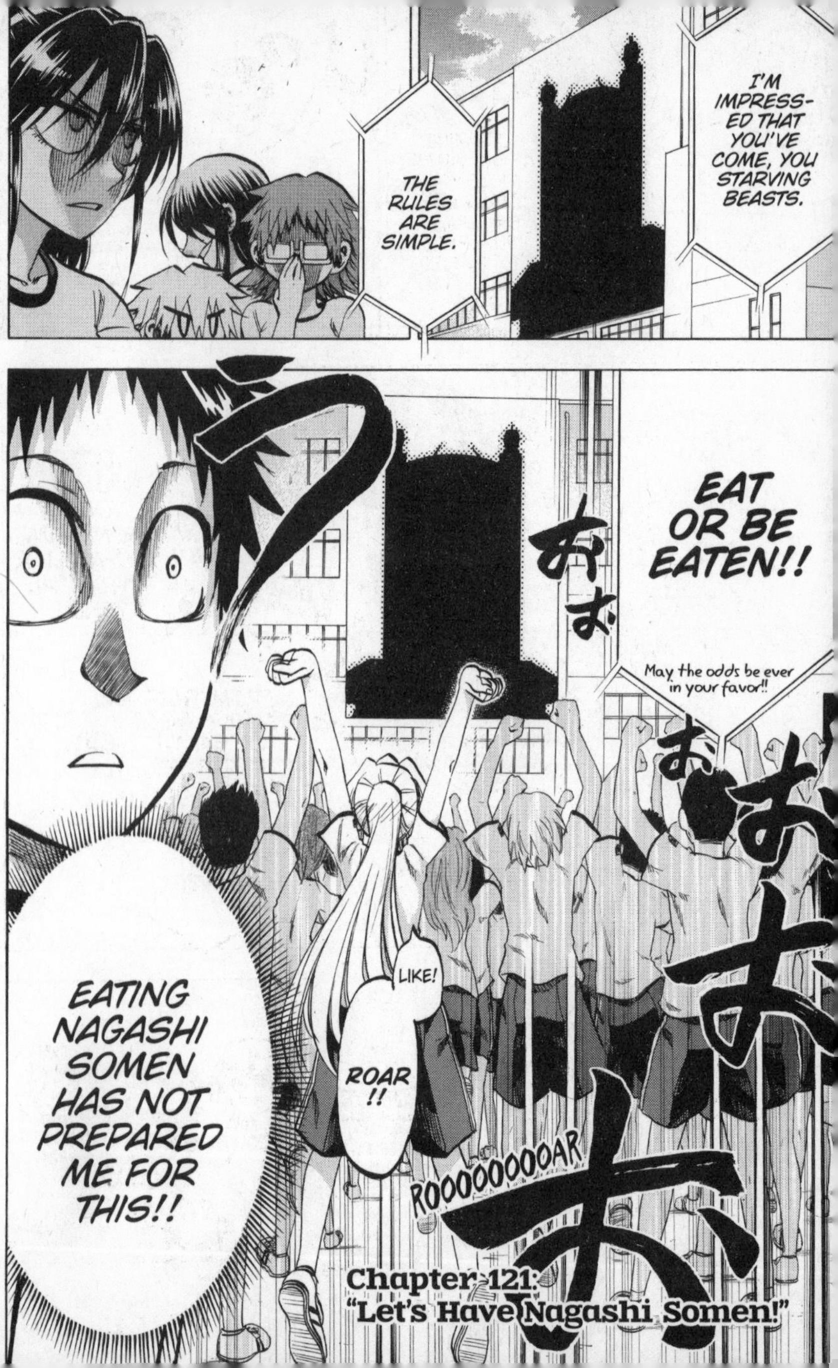
I'M IMPRESSED THAT YOU'VE COME, YOU STARVING BEASTS.
THE RULES ARE SIMPLE.
EAT OR BE EATEN!!
May the odds be ever in your favor!!
おぉぉぉぉぉ
LIKE!
ROAR!!
ROOOOOOOOAR
EATING NAGASHI SOMEN HAS NOT PREPARED ME FOR THIS!!
Chapter 121: "Let's Have Nagashi Somen!"

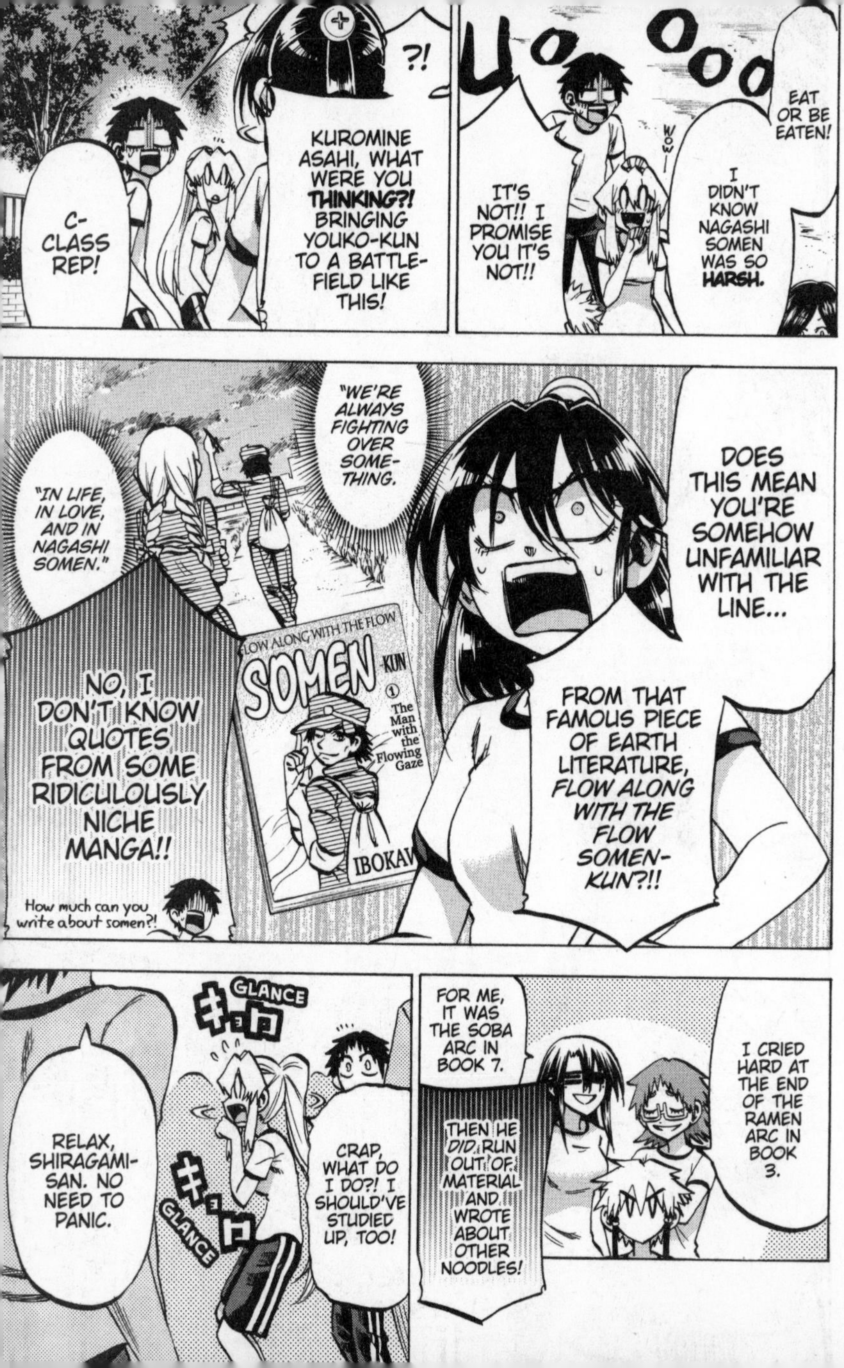
UOOOO
EAT OR BE EATEN!
I DIDN'T KNOW NAGASHI SOMEN WAS SO **HARSH.**
WOW!
IT'S NOT!! I PROMISE YOU IT'S NOT!!
?!
KUROMINE ASAHI, WHAT WERE YOU **THINKING?!** BRINGING YOUKO-KUN TO A BATTLEFIELD LIKE THIS!
C-CLASS REP!
DOES THIS MEAN YOU'RE SOMEHOW UNFAMILIAR WITH THE LINE...
FROM THAT FAMOUS PIECE OF EARTH LITERATURE, *FLOW ALONG WITH THE FLOW SOMEN-KUN?!!*
"WE'RE ALWAYS FIGHTING OVER SOMETHING.
"IN LIFE, IN LOVE, AND IN NAGASHI SOMEN."
FLOW ALONG WITH THE FLOW
SOMEN-KUN
1
The Man with the Flowing Gaze
IBOKAV
NO, I DON'T KNOW QUOTES FROM SOME RIDICULOUSLY NICHE MANGA!!
How much can you write about somen?!
I CRIED HARD AT THE END OF THE RAMEN ARC IN BOOK 3.
FOR ME, IT WAS THE SOBA ARC IN BOOK 7.
THEN HE *DID* RUN OUT OF MATERIAL AND WROTE ABOUT OTHER NOODLES!
キョロ GLANCE
キョロ GLANCE
CRAP, WHAT DO I DO?! I SHOULD'VE STUDIED UP, TOO!
RELAX, SHIRAGAMI-SAN. NO NEED TO PANIC.

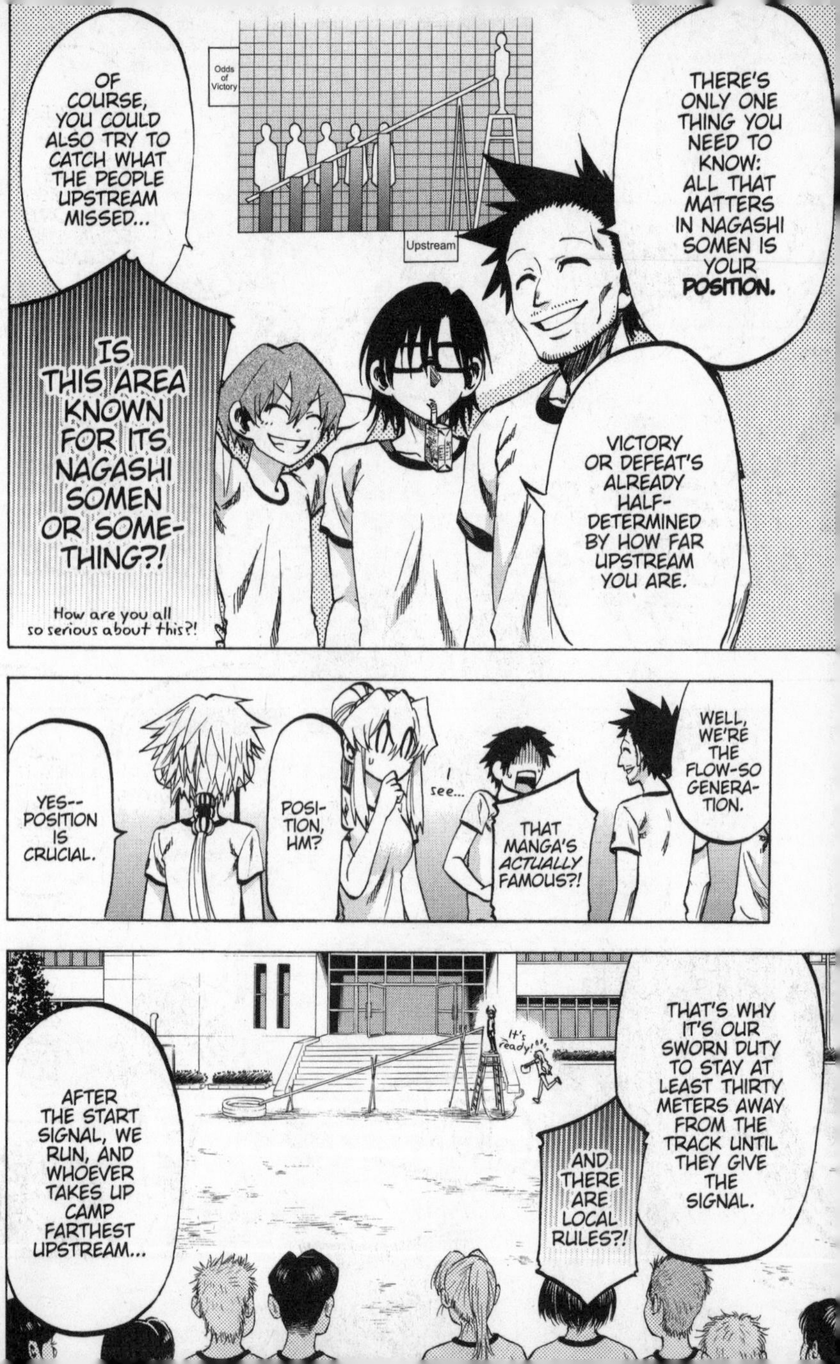
THERE'S ONLY ONE THING YOU NEED TO KNOW: ALL THAT MATTERS IN NAGASHI SOMEN IS YOUR **POSITION.**
OF COURSE, YOU COULD ALSO TRY TO CATCH WHAT THE PEOPLE UPSTREAM MISSED...
Odds of Victory
Upstream
VICTORY OR DEFEAT'S ALREADY HALF-DETERMINED BY HOW FAR UPSTREAM YOU ARE.
IS THIS AREA KNOWN FOR ITS NAGASHI SOMEN OR SOME-THING?!
How are you all so serious about this?!
WELL, WE'RE THE FLOW-SO GENERA-TION.
THAT MANGA'S *ACTUALLY* FAMOUS?!
I see...
POSI-TION, HM?
YES-- POSITION IS CRUCIAL.
THAT'S WHY IT'S OUR SWORN DUTY TO STAY AT LEAST THIRTY METERS AWAY FROM THE TRACK UNTIL THEY GIVE THE SIGNAL.
AND THERE ARE LOCAL RULES?!
It's ready!
AFTER THE START SIGNAL, WE RUN, AND WHOEVER TAKES UP CAMP FARTHEST UPSTREAM...

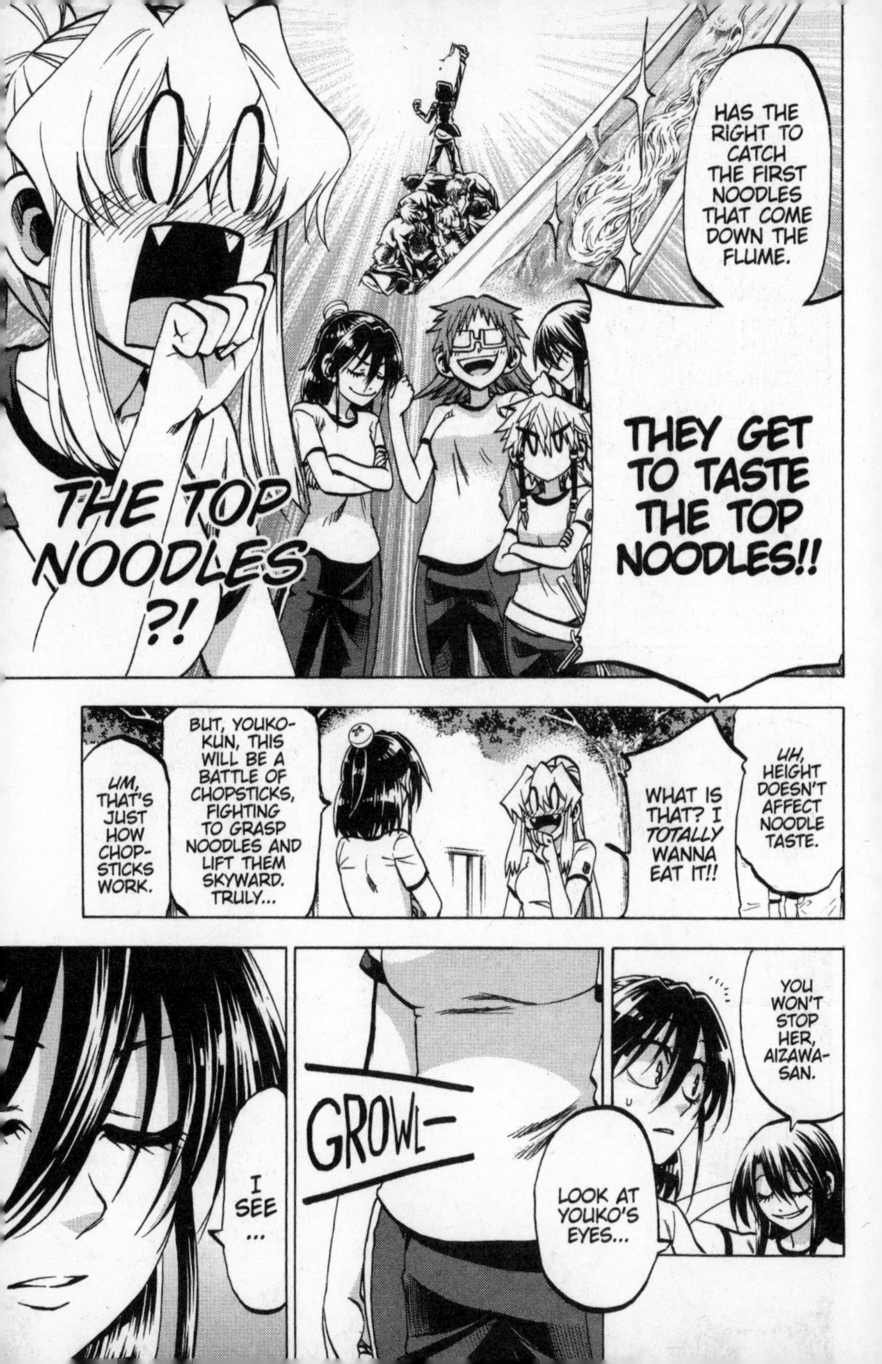
HAS THE RIGHT TO CATCH THE FIRST NOODLES THAT COME DOWN THE FLUME.
THEY GET TO TASTE THE TOP NOODLES!!
THE TOP NOODLES ?!
UH, HEIGHT DOESN'T AFFECT NOODLE TASTE.
WHAT IS THAT? I TOTALLY WANNA EAT IT!!
BUT, YOUKO-KUN, THIS WILL BE A BATTLE OF CHOPSTICKS, FIGHTING TO GRASP NOODLES AND LIFT THEM SKYWARD. TRULY...
UM, THAT'S JUST HOW CHOP-STICKS WORK.
YOU WON'T STOP HER, AIZAWA-SAN.
LOOK AT YOUKO'S EYES...
GROWL-
I SEE ...

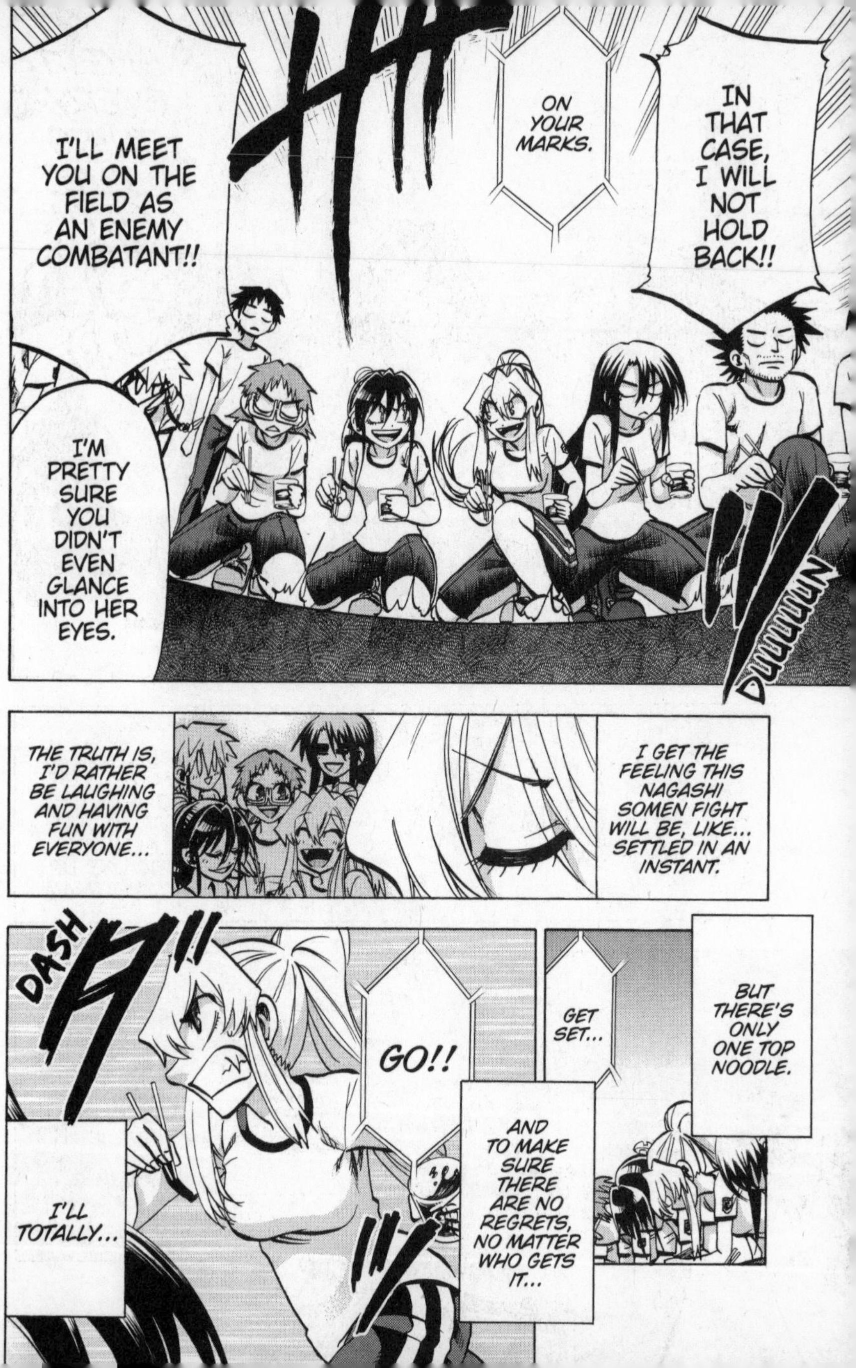
IN THAT CASE, I WILL NOT HOLD BACK!!
ON YOUR MARKS.
I'LL MEET YOU ON THE FIELD AS AN ENEMY COMBATANT!!
I'M PRETTY SURE YOU DIDN'T EVEN GLANCE INTO HER EYES.
DUUUUUUN
I GET THE FEELING THIS NAGASHI SOMEN FIGHT WILL BE, LIKE... SETTLED IN AN INSTANT.
THE TRUTH IS, I'D RATHER BE LAUGHING AND HAVING FUN WITH EVERYONE...
BUT THERE'S ONLY ONE TOP NOODLE.
GET SET...
AND TO MAKE SURE THERE ARE NO REGRETS, NO MATTER WHO GETS IT...
GO!!
DASH
I'LL TOTALLY...

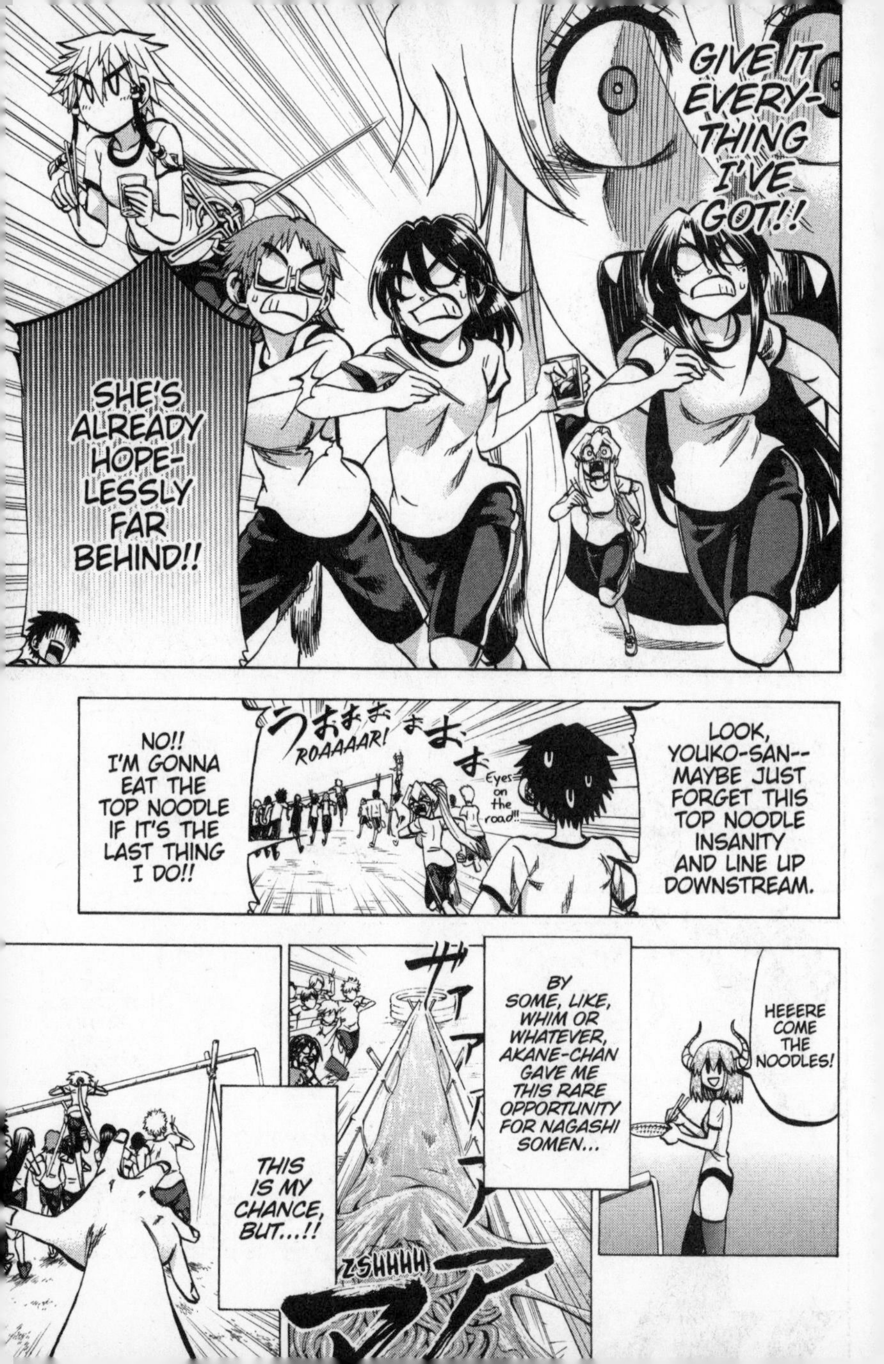
GIVE IT EVERY-THING I'VE GOT!!
SHE'S ALREADY HOPE-LESSLY FAR BEHIND!!
LOOK, YOUKO-SAN-- MAYBE JUST FORGET THIS TOP NOODLE INSANITY AND LINE UP DOWNSTREAM.
Eyes on the road!!
ROAAAAR!
NO!! I'M GONNA EAT THE TOP NOODLE IF IT'S THE LAST THING I DO!!
HEEERE COME THE NOODLES!
BY SOME, LIKE, WHIM OR WHATEVER, AKANE-CHAN GAVE ME THIS RARE OPPORTUNITY FOR NAGASHI SOMEN...
THIS IS MY CHANCE, BUT...!!
ZSHHHH

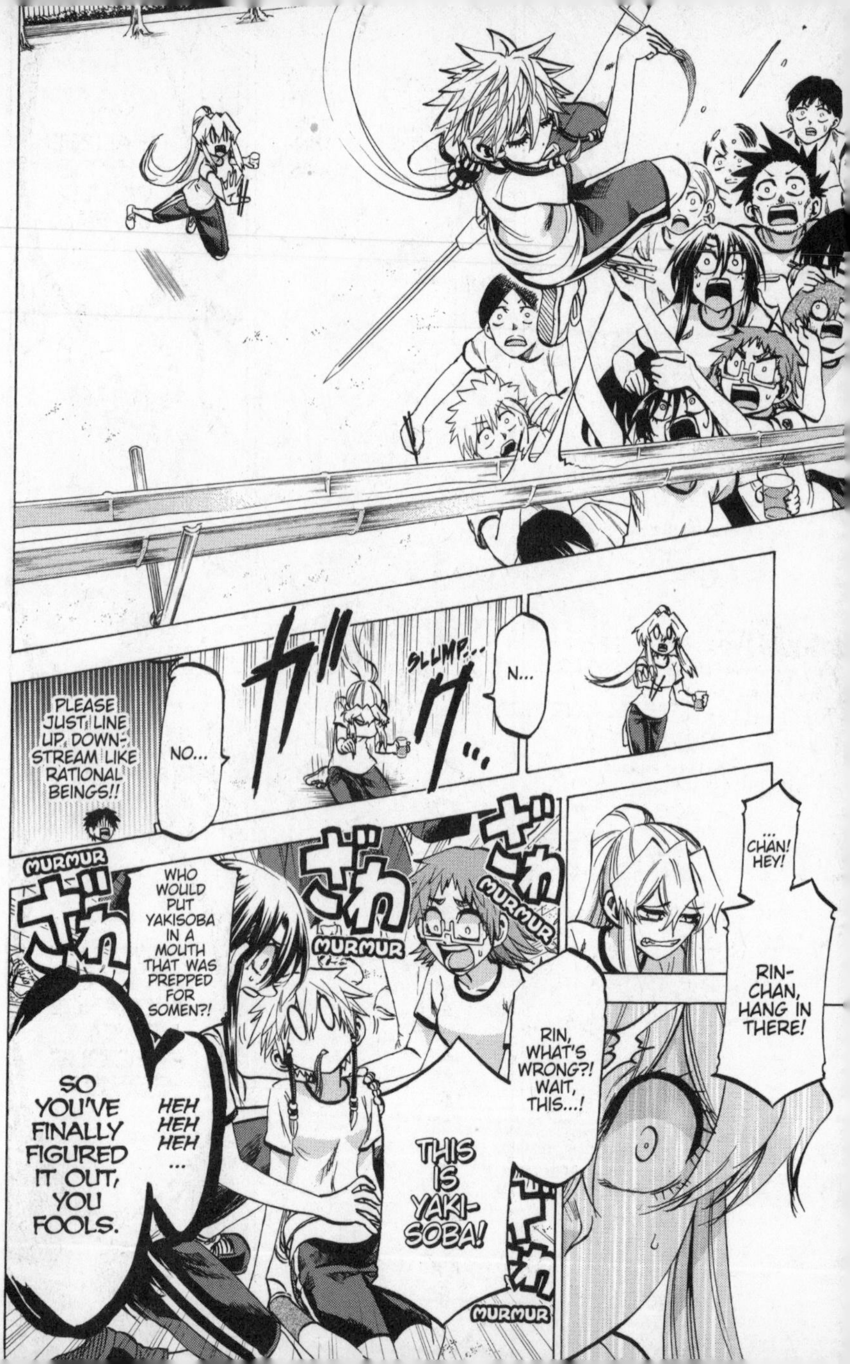
N...
SLUMP...
ガク...
NO...
PLEASE JUST LINE UP DOWN-STREAM LIKE RATIONAL BEINGS!!
...CHAN! HEY!
RIN-CHAN, HANG IN THERE!
ざわ
MURMUR
RIN, WHAT'S WRONG?! WAIT, THIS...!
THIS IS YAKI-SOBA!
ざわ
MURMUR
WHO WOULD PUT YAKISOBA IN A MOUTH THAT WAS PREPPED FOR SOMEN?!
ざわ
MURMUR
HEH HEH HEH...
SO YOU'VE FINALLY FIGURED IT OUT, YOU FOOLS.

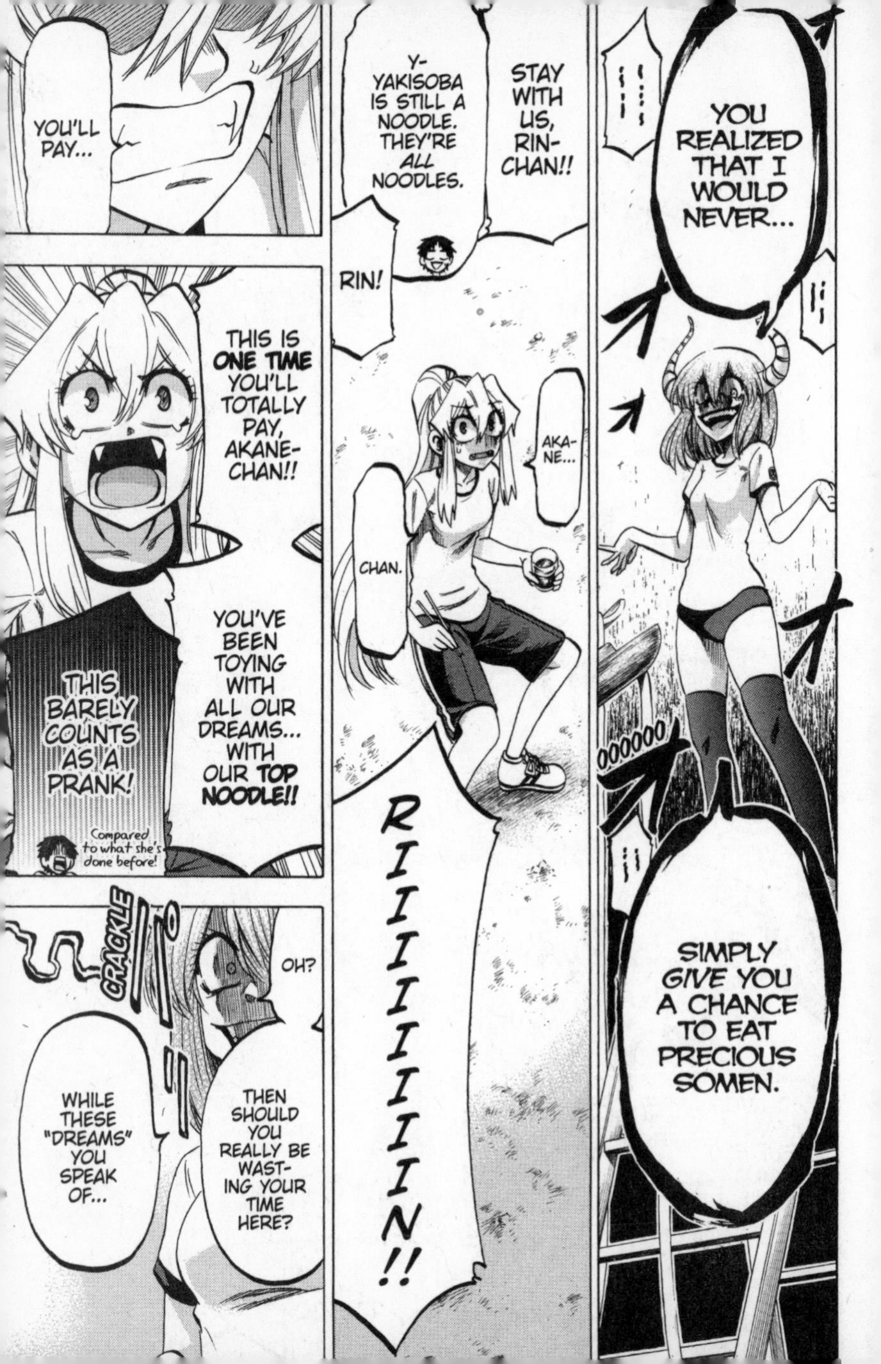
YOU REALIZED THAT I WOULD NEVER...
OOOOOO
SIMPLY GIVE YOU A CHANCE TO EAT PRECIOUS SOMEN.
STAY WITH US, RIN-CHAN!!
Y-YAKISOBA IS STILL A NOODLE. THEY'RE ALL NOODLES.
RIN!
AKA-NE...
CHAN.
RIIIIIIIIN!!
YOU'LL PAY...
THIS IS ONE TIME YOU'LL TOTALLY PAY, AKANE-CHAN!!
YOU'VE BEEN TOYING WITH ALL OUR DREAMS... WITH OUR TOP NOODLE!!
THIS BARELY COUNTS AS A PRANK!
Compared to what she's done before!
CRACKLE
OH?
THEN SHOULD YOU REALLY BE WASTING YOUR TIME HERE?
WHILE THESE "DREAMS" YOU SPEAK OF...

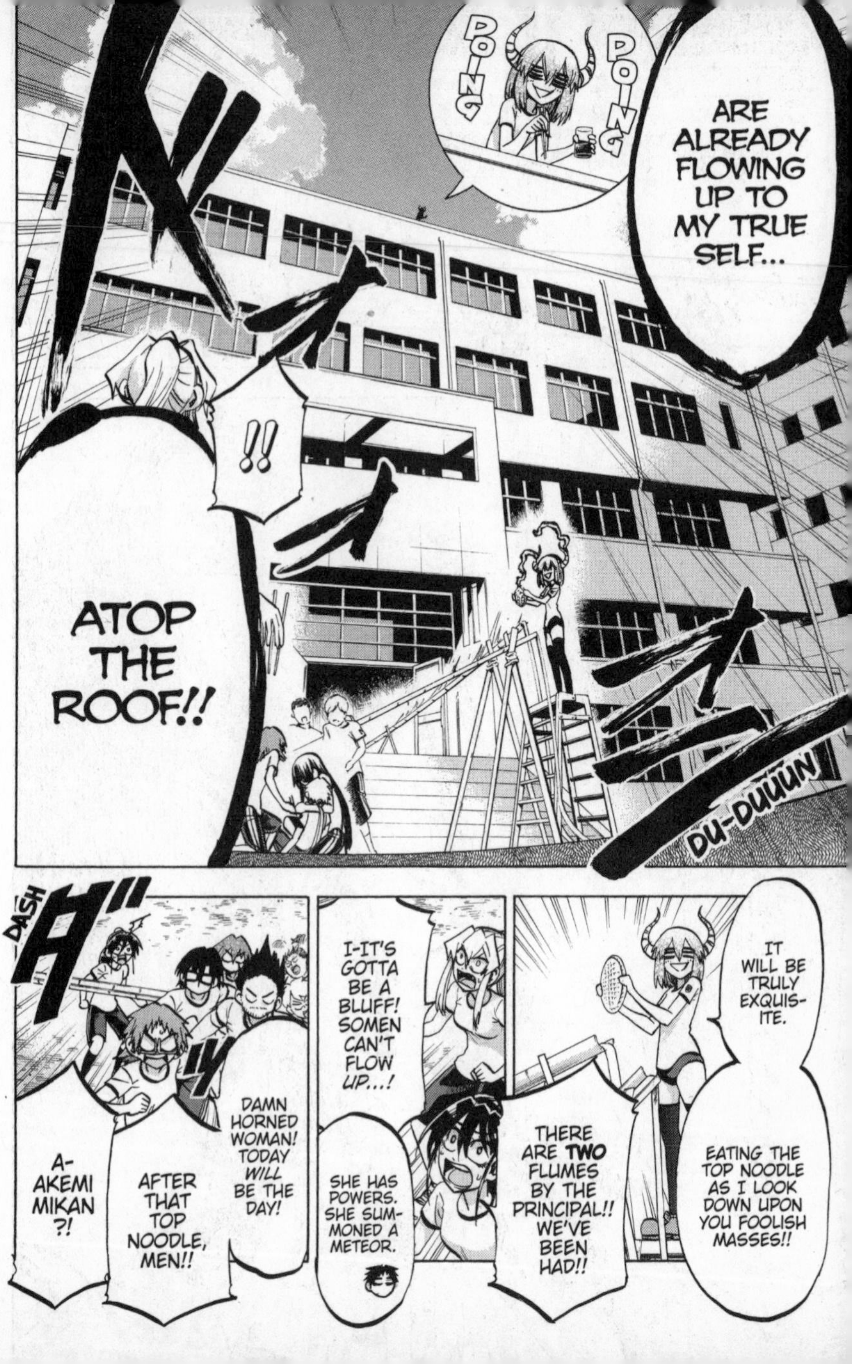
ARE ALREADY FLOWING UP TO MY TRUE SELF...
POING POING
!!
ATOP THE ROOF!!
DU-DUUUN
IT WILL BE TRULY EXQUISITE.
EATING THE TOP NOODLE AS I LOOK DOWN UPON YOU FOOLISH MASSES!!
I-IT'S GOTTA BE A BLUFF! SOMEN CAN'T FLOW *UP*...!
THERE ARE **TWO** FLUMES BY THE PRINCIPAL!! WE'VE BEEN HAD!!
SHE HAS POWERS. SHE SUMMONED A METEOR.
DASH
DAMN HORNED WOMAN! TODAY *WILL* BE THE DAY!
AFTER THAT TOP NOODLE, MEN!!
A-AKEMI MIKAN?!

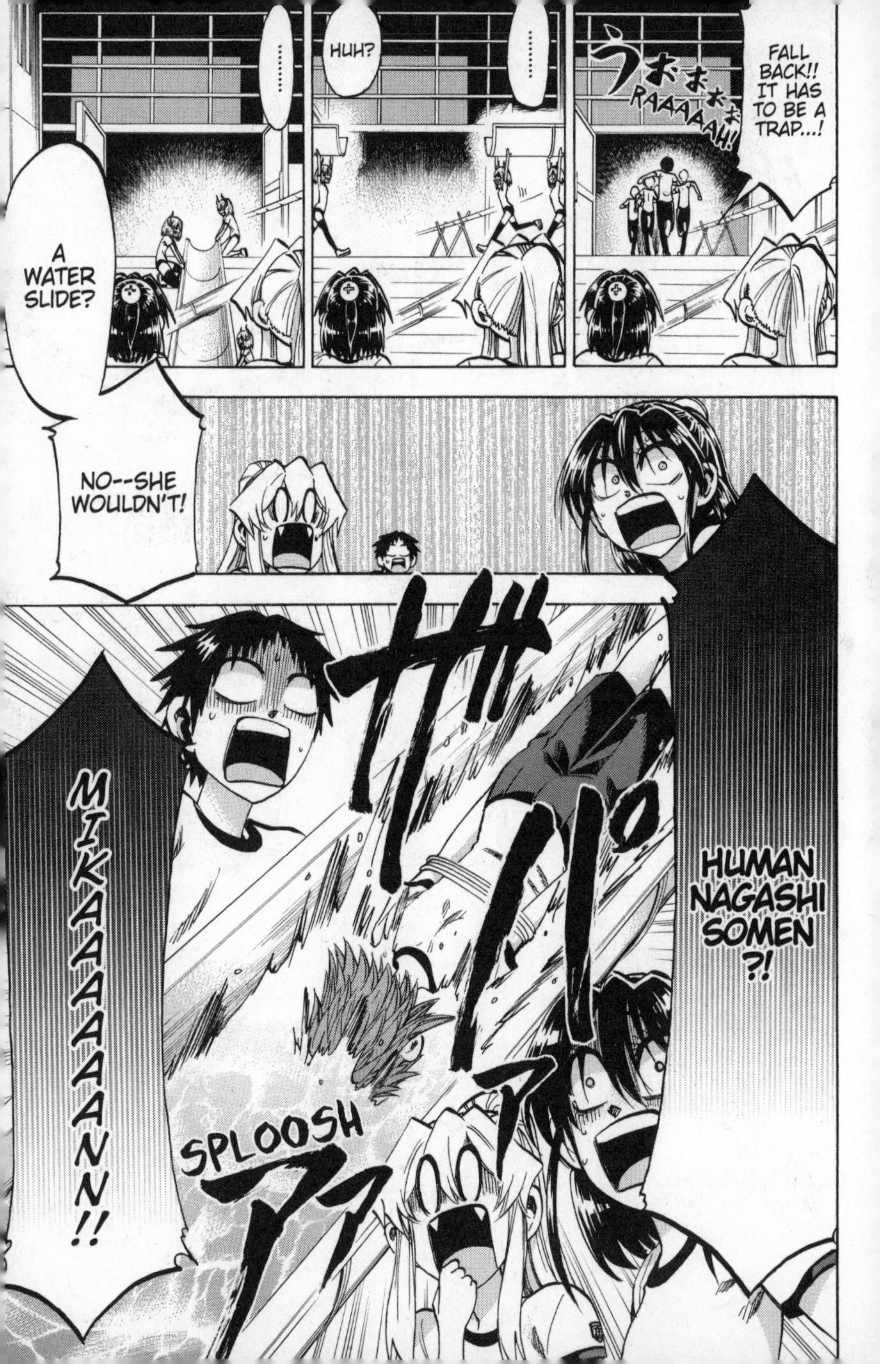
FALL BACK!! IT HAS TO BE A TRAP...!
RAAAAAAH!
......
HUH?
......
A WATER SLIDE?
NO--SHE WOULDN'T!
HUMAN NAGASHI SOMEN?!
MIKAAAAAAAAANN!!
SPLOOSH

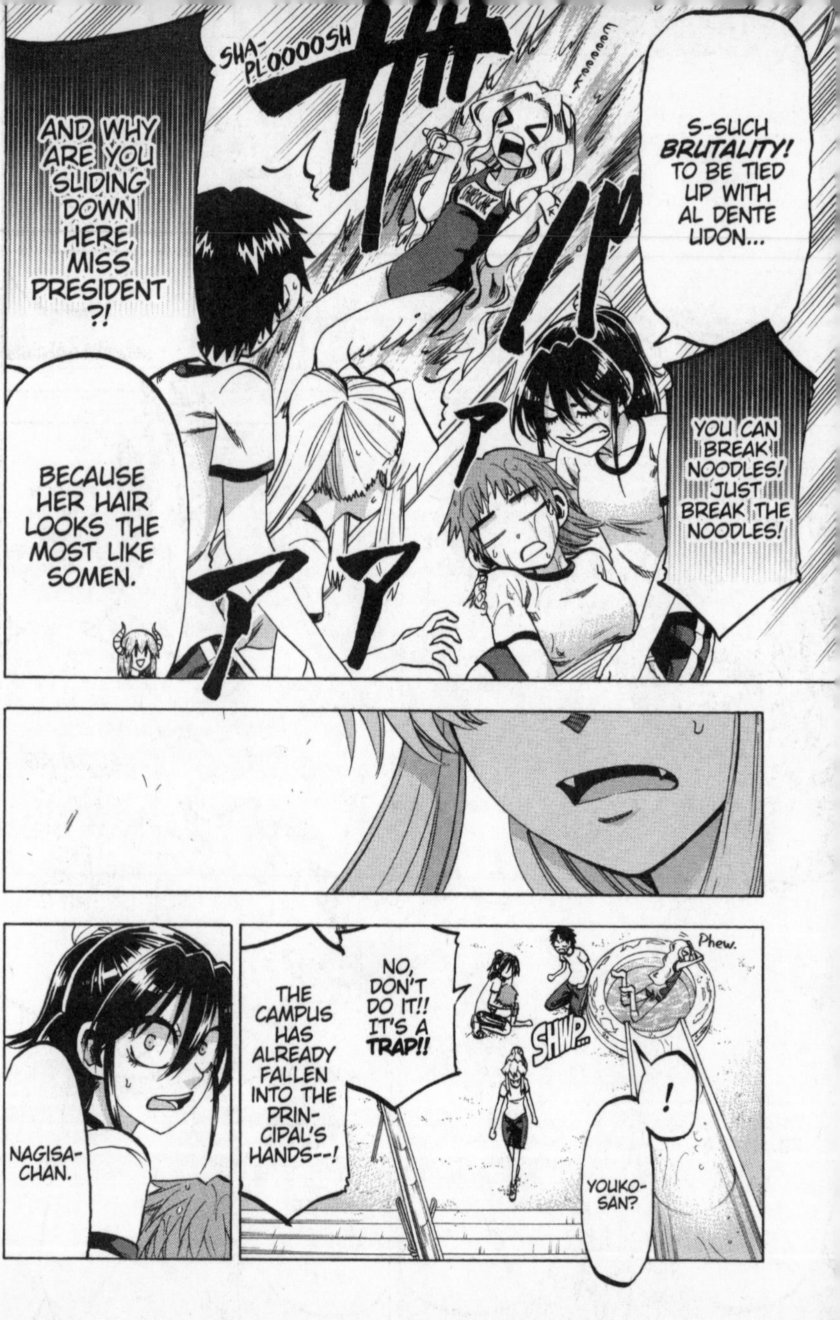
S-SUCH BRUTALITY! TO BE TIED UP WITH AL DENTE UDON...
SHA-PLOOOOOSH
AND WHY ARE YOU SLIDING DOWN HERE, MISS PRESIDENT?!
YOU CAN BREAK NOODLES! JUST BREAK THE NOODLES!
BECAUSE HER HAIR LOOKS THE MOST LIKE SOMEN.
Phew.
SHWP...
!
YOUKO-SAN?
NO, DON'T DO IT!! IT'S A TRAP!!
THE CAMPUS HAS ALREADY FALLEN INTO THE PRINCIPAL'S HANDS--!
NAGISA-CHAN.

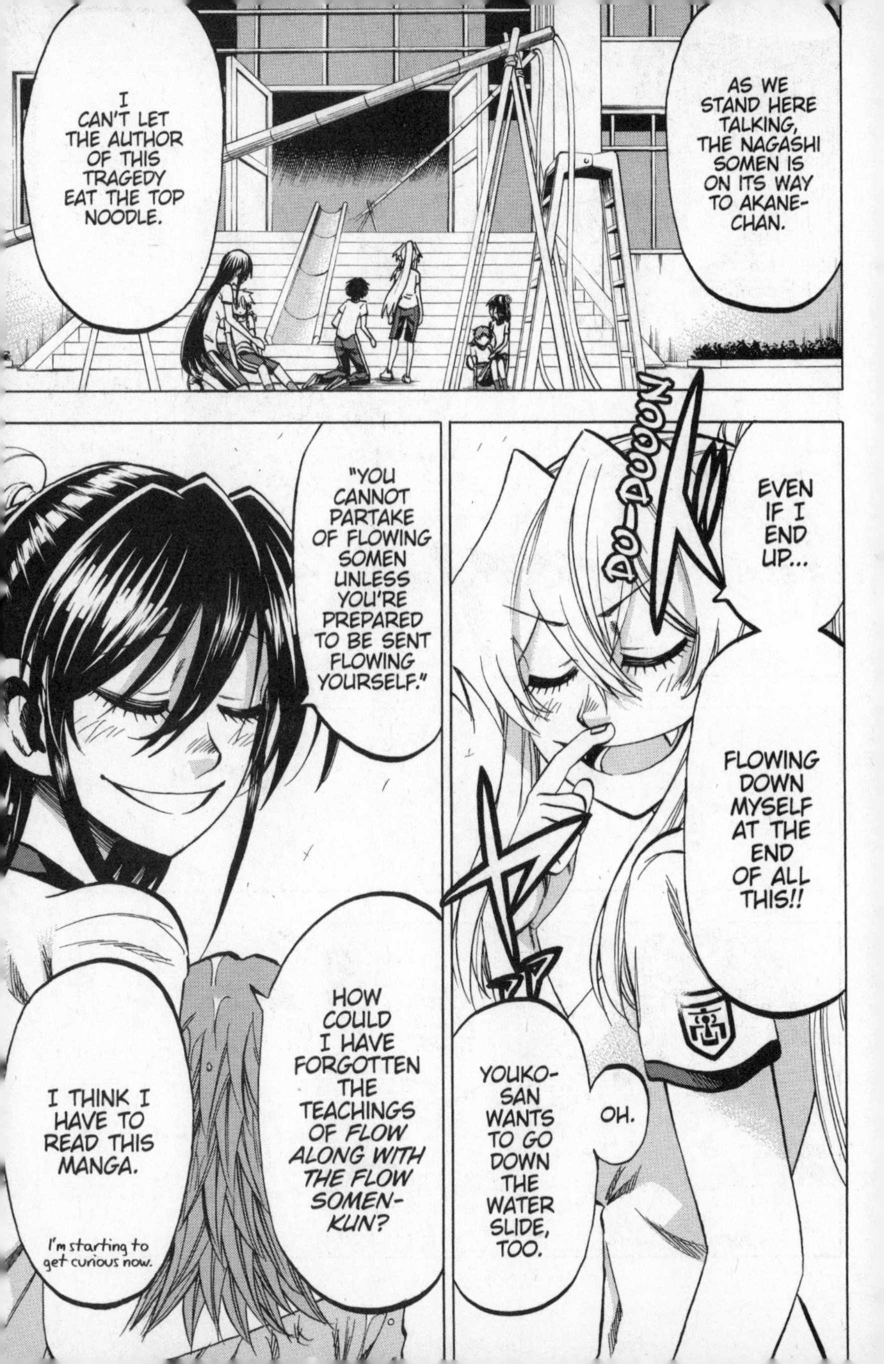
AS WE STAND HERE TALKING, THE NAGASHI SOMEN IS ON ITS WAY TO AKANE-CHAN.
I CAN'T LET THE AUTHOR OF THIS TRAGEDY EAT THE TOP NOODLE.
DO-DOOOON
EVEN IF I END UP...
FLOWING DOWN MYSELF AT THE END OF ALL THIS!!
OH.
YOUKO-SAN WANTS TO GO DOWN THE WATER SLIDE, TOO.
"YOU CANNOT PARTAKE OF FLOWING SOMEN UNLESS YOU'RE PREPARED TO BE SENT FLOWING YOURSELF."
HOW COULD I HAVE FORGOTTEN THE TEACHINGS OF *FLOW ALONG WITH THE FLOW SOMEN-KUN*?
I THINK I HAVE TO READ THIS MANGA.
I'm starting to get curious now.

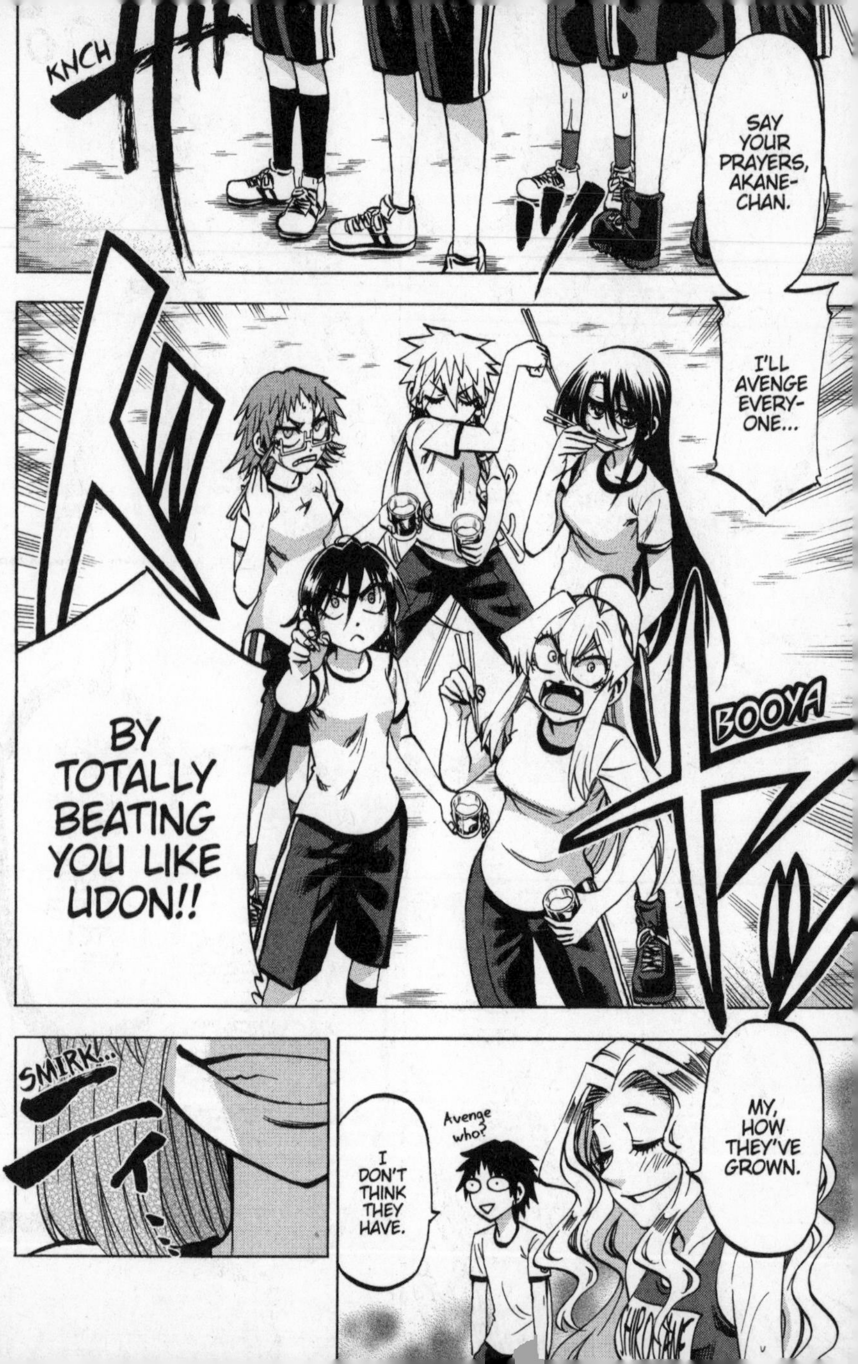

SAY YOUR PRAYERS, AKANE-CHAN.
KNCH
I'LL AVENGE EVERY-ONE...
BOOYA
BY TOTALLY BEATING YOU LIKE UDON!!
MY, HOW THEY'VE GROWN.
Avenge who?
I DON'T THINK THEY HAVE.
SMIRK...

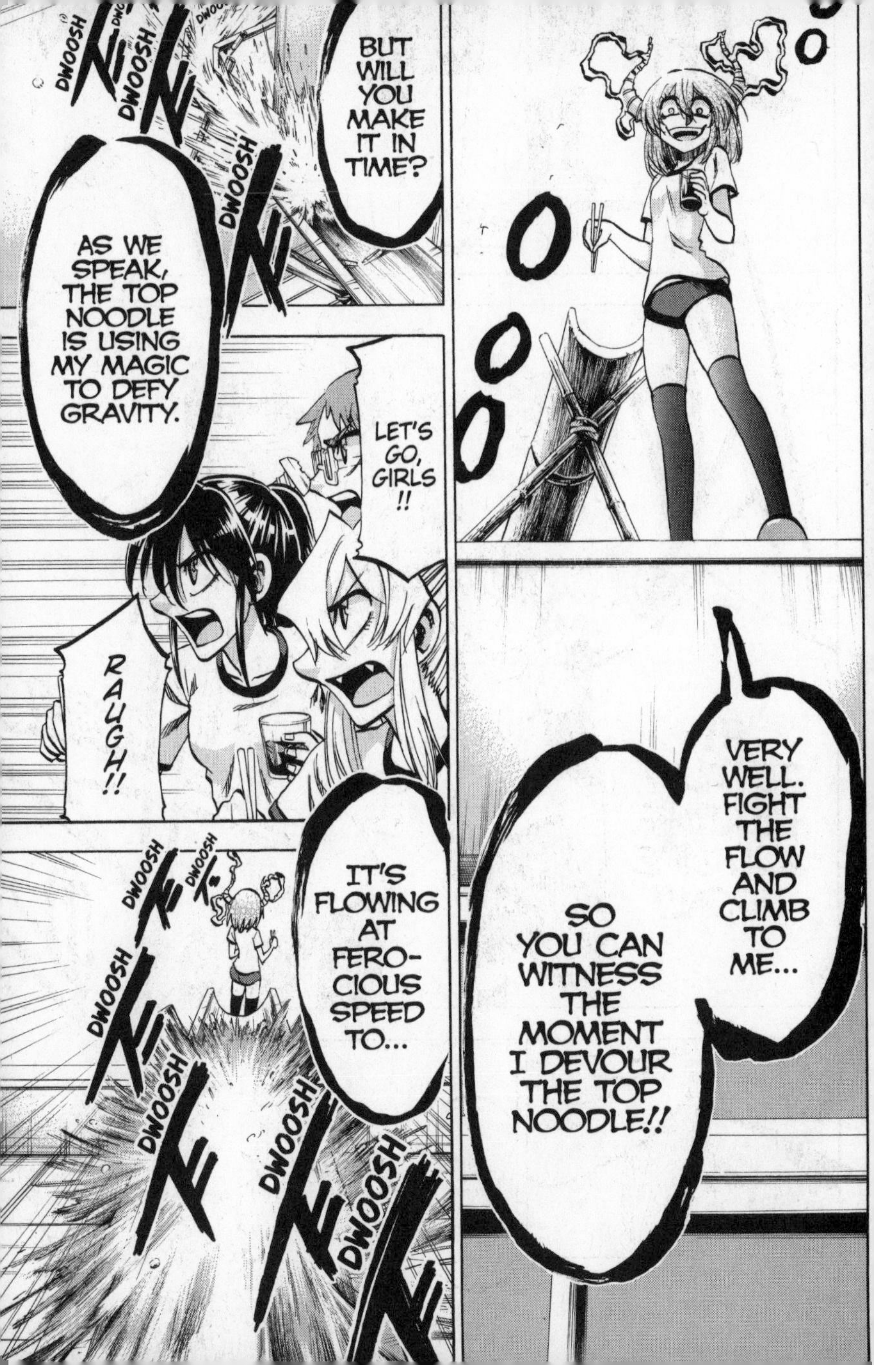
O O O O
BUT WILL YOU MAKE IT IN TIME?
AS WE SPEAK, THE TOP NOODLE IS USING MY MAGIC TO DEFY GRAVITY.
DWOOSH DWOOSH DWOOSH DWOOSH
LET'S GO, GIRLS!!
RAUGH!!
VERY WELL. FIGHT THE FLOW AND CLIMB TO ME...
SO YOU CAN WITNESS THE MOMENT I DEVOUR THE TOP NOODLE!!
IT'S FLOWING AT FERO-CIOUS SPEED TO...
DWOOSH DWOOSH DWOOSH DWOOSH DWOOSH DWOOSH

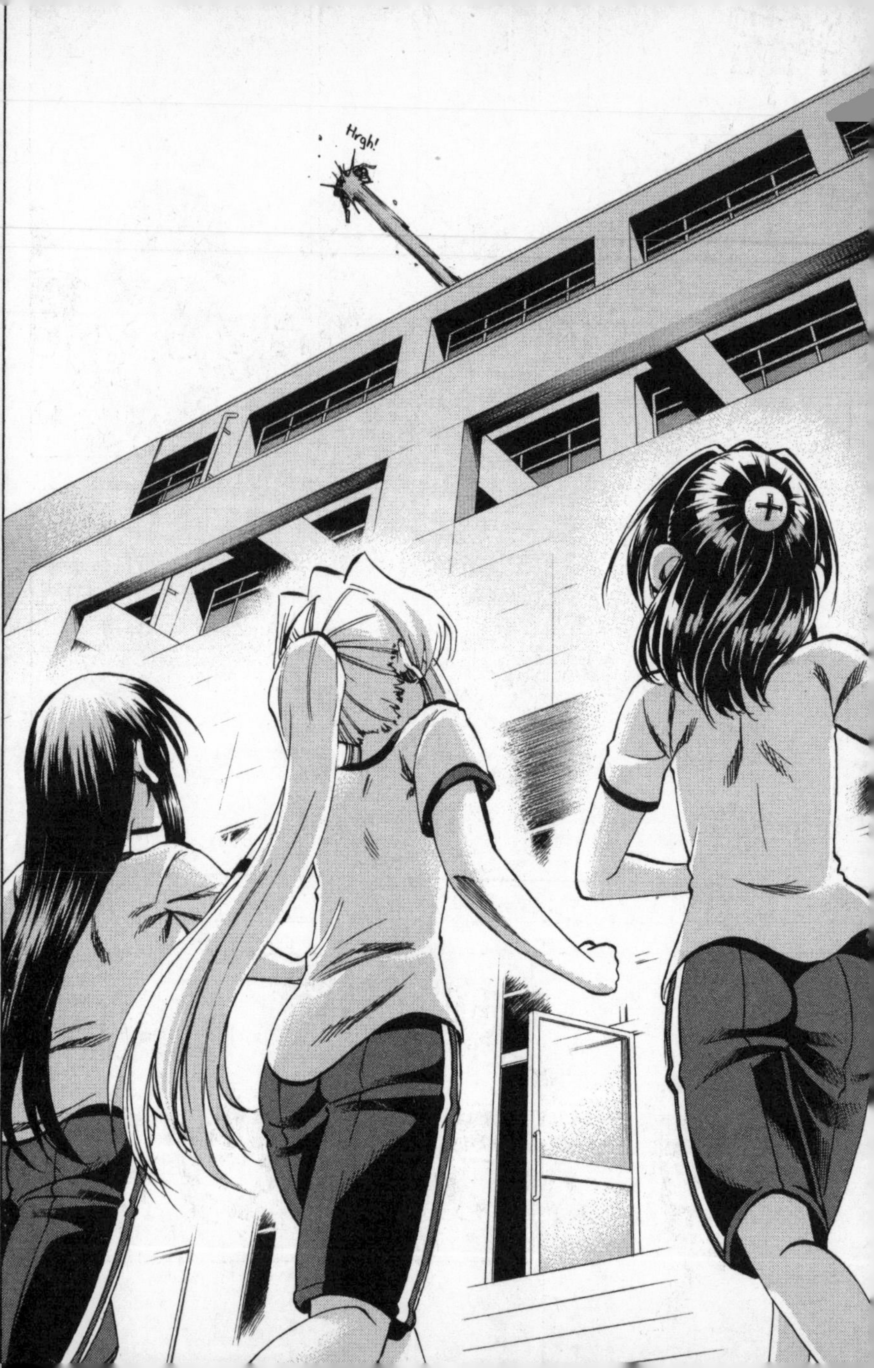
Hrgh!

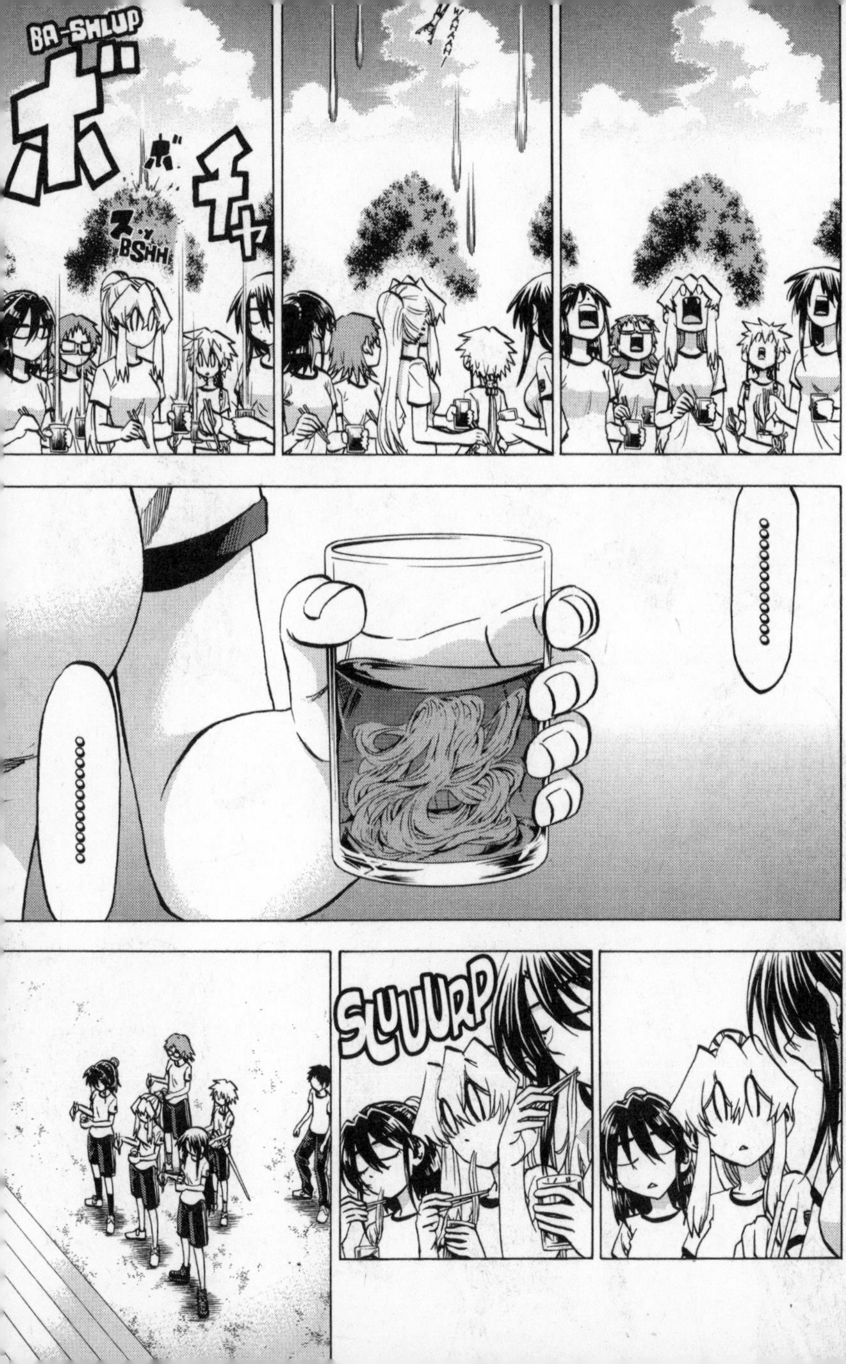
WAHAAH!
BA-SHLUP
ボボチャ
ズッ BSHH
....
....
SLUUURP

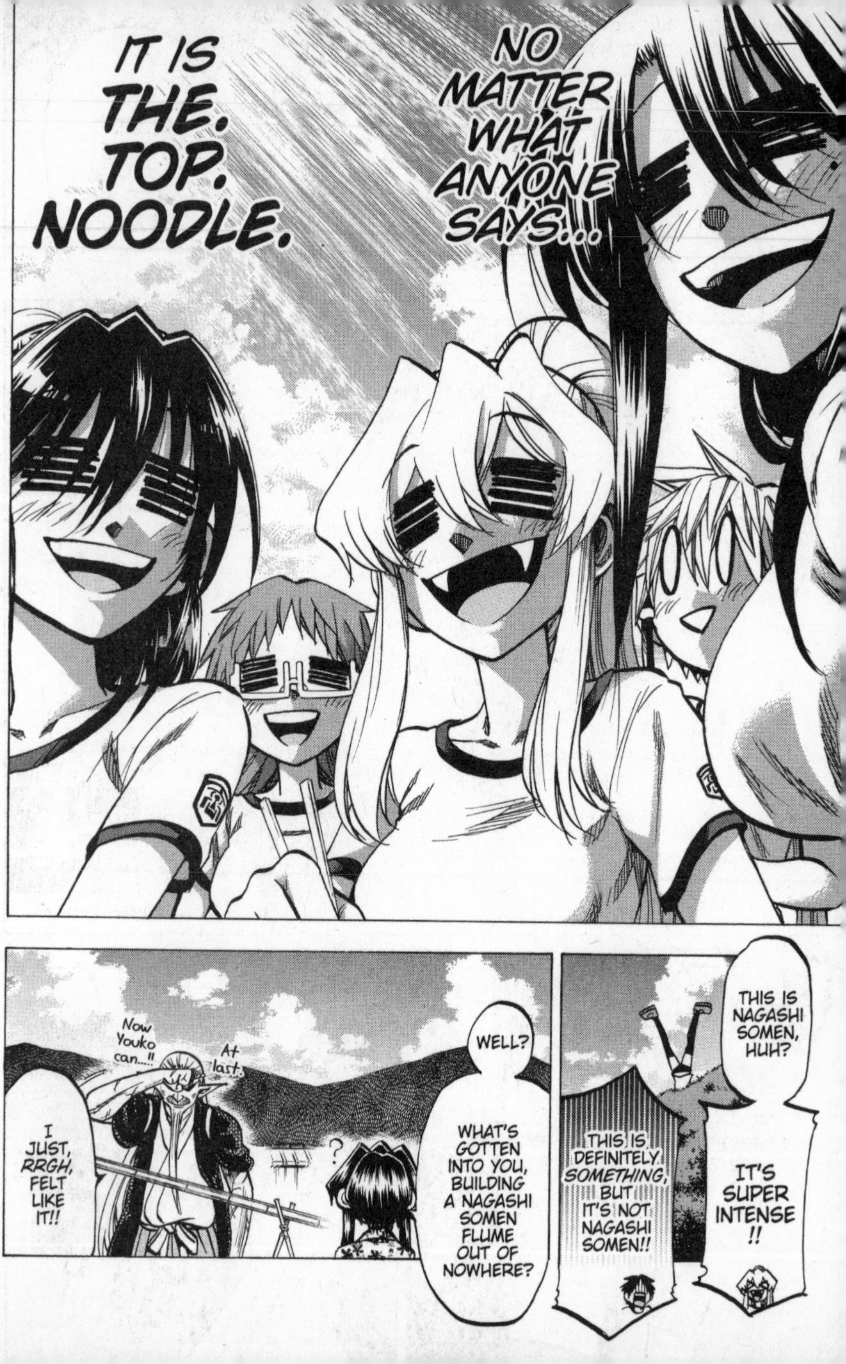
NO MATTER WHAT ANYONE SAYS...
IT IS THE. TOP. NOODLE.
THIS IS NAGASHI SOMEN, HUH?
IT'S SUPER INTENSE!!
THIS IS DEFINITELY SOMETHING, BUT IT'S NOT NAGASHI SOMEN!!
WELL?
WHAT'S GOTTEN INTO YOU, BUILDING A NAGASHI SOMEN FLUME OUT OF NOWHERE?
At last.
Now Youko can....!!
I JUST, RRGH, FELT LIKE IT!!

Chapter 122: "Let's Catch Rhinoceros Beetles!"

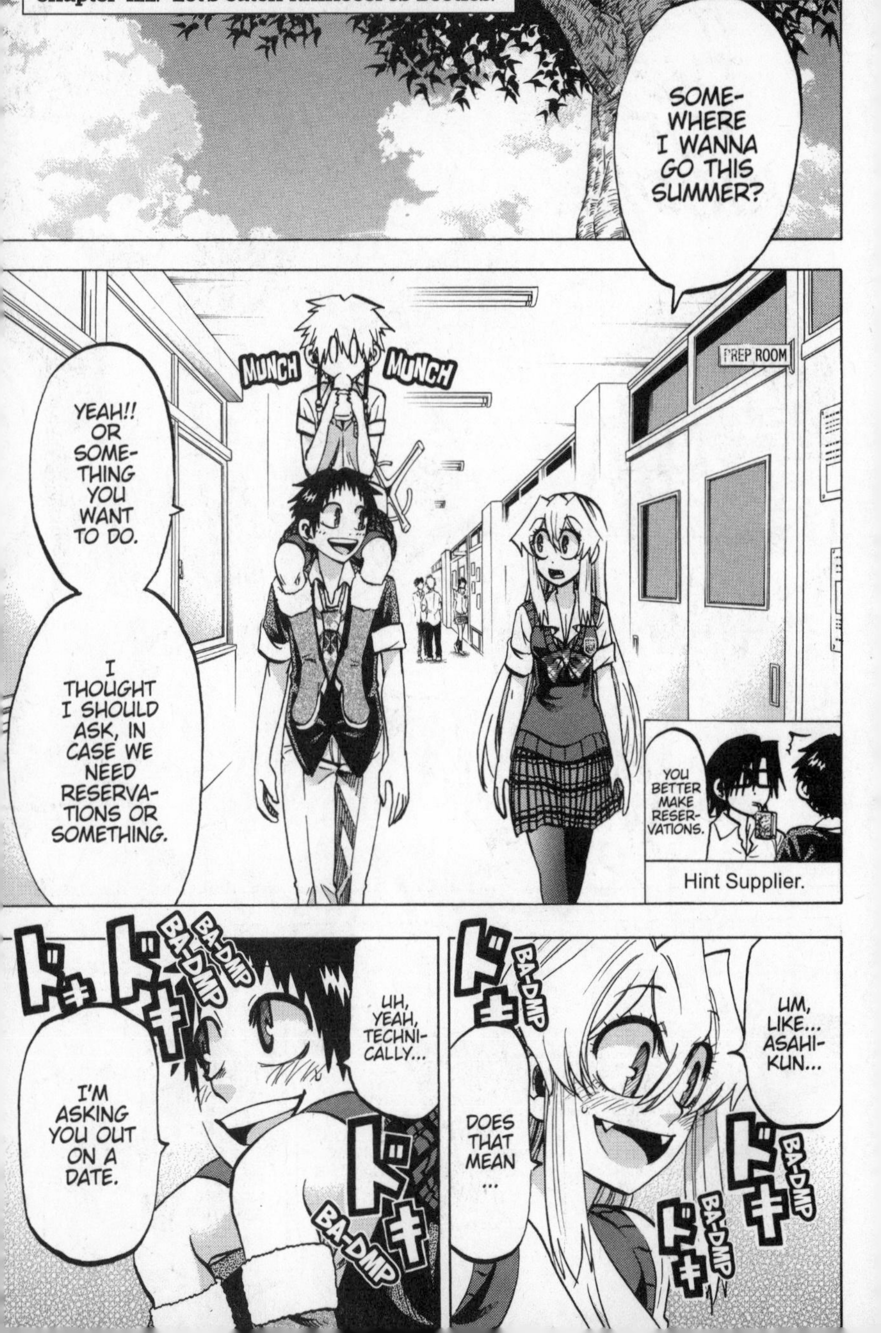
SOME-WHERE I WANNA GO THIS SUMMER?
MUNCH MUNCH
YEAH!! OR SOME-THING YOU WANT TO DO.
I THOUGHT I SHOULD ASK, IN CASE WE NEED RESERVA-TIONS OR SOMETHING.
PREP ROOM
YOU BETTER MAKE RESER-VATIONS.
Hint Supplier.
ドキ BA-DMP
UM, LIKE... ASAHI-KUN...
DOES THAT MEAN ...
ドキ BA-DMP ドキ BA-DMP
ドキ ドキ BA-DMP BA-DMP
UH, YEAH, TECHNI-CALLY...
I'M ASKING YOU OUT ON A DATE.
ドキ BA-DMP

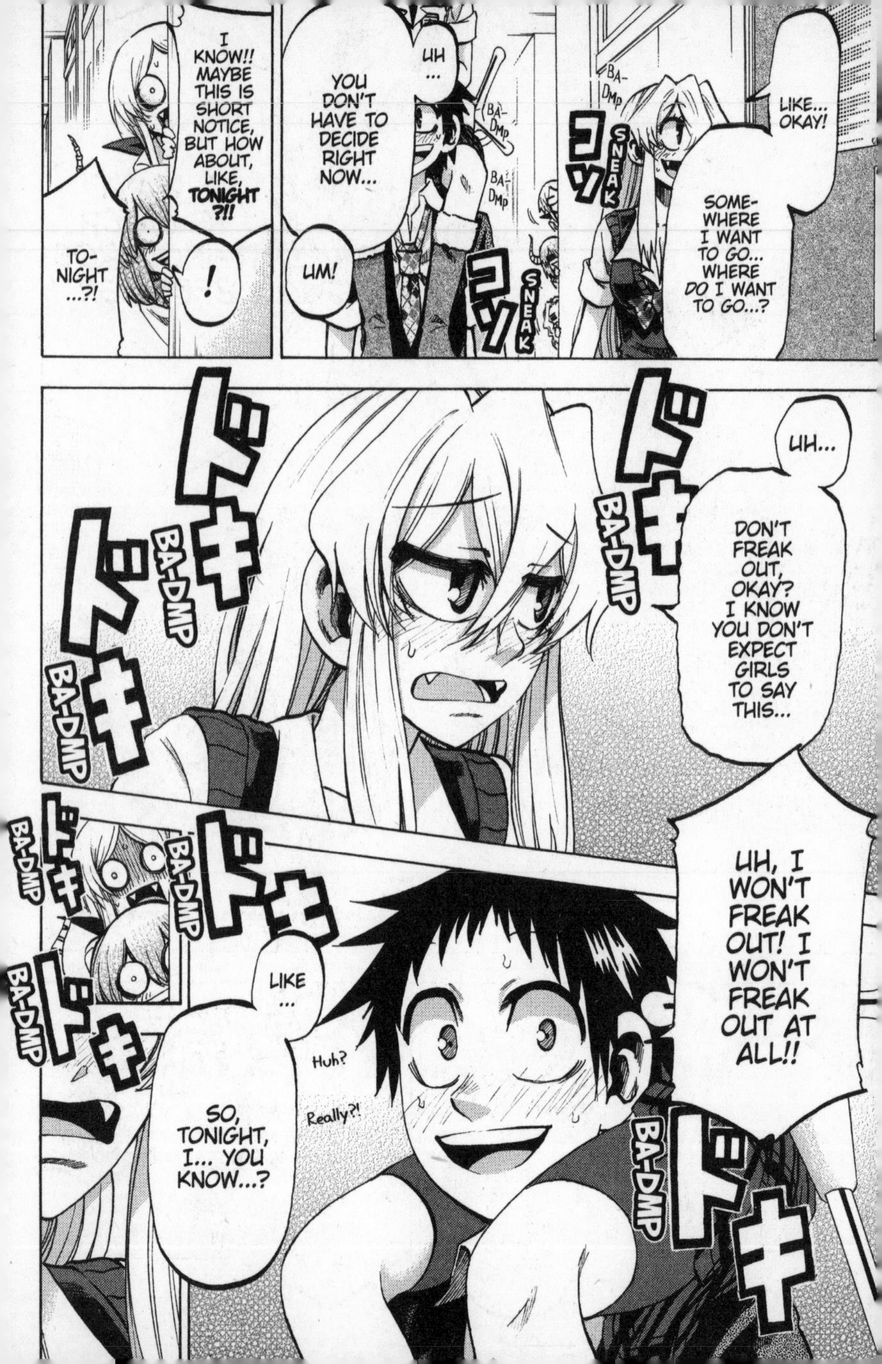
LIKE... OKAY!
SOME-WHERE I WANT TO GO... WHERE DO I WANT TO GO...?
BA-DMP
SNEAK
UH ...
YOU DON'T HAVE TO DECIDE RIGHT NOW...
UM!
BA-DMP
BA-DMP
SNEAK
I KNOW!! MAYBE THIS IS SHORT NOTICE, BUT HOW ABOUT, LIKE, **TONIGHT?!!**
!
TO-NIGHT ...?!
UH...
DON'T FREAK OUT, OKAY? I KNOW YOU DON'T EXPECT GIRLS TO SAY THIS...
BA-DMP
BA-DMP
BA-DMP
UH, I WON'T FREAK OUT! I WON'T FREAK OUT AT ALL!!
BA-DMP
BA-DMP
BA-DMP
BA-DMP
LIKE ...
Huh?
Really?!
SO, TONIGHT, I... YOU KNOW...?

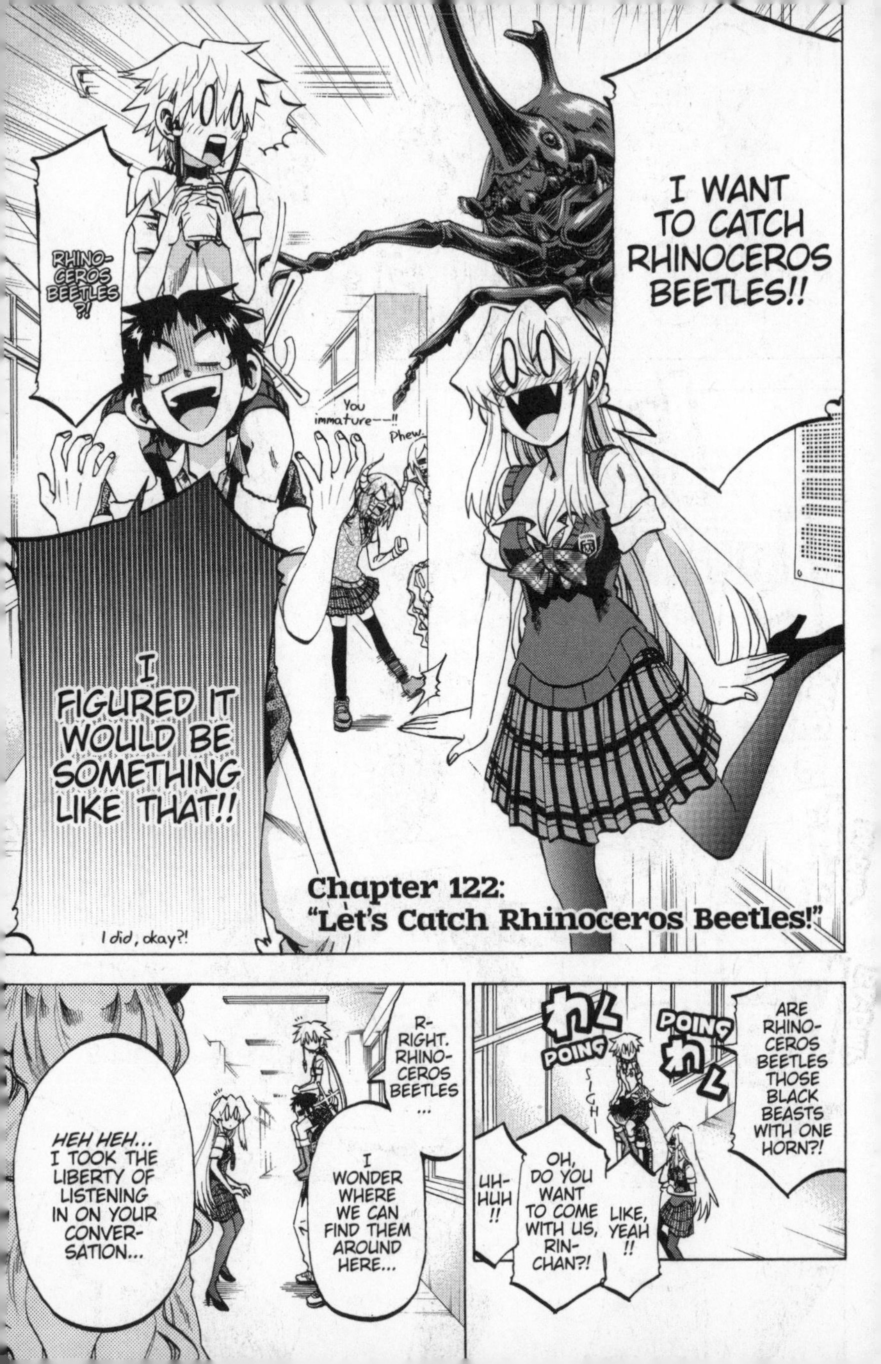
I WANT TO CATCH RHINOCEROS BEETLES!!
RHINOCEROS BEETLES?!
You immature--!!
Phew.
I FIGURED IT WOULD BE SOMETHING LIKE THAT!!
Chapter 122: "Let's Catch Rhinoceros Beetles!"
I did, okay?!
ARE RHINOCEROS BEETLES THOSE BLACK BEASTS WITH ONE HORN?!
POING
わく
POING
わく
SIGH
OH, DO YOU WANT TO COME WITH US, RIN-CHAN?!
LIKE, YEAH!!
UH-HUH!!
R-RIGHT. RHINOCEROS BEETLES...
I WONDER WHERE WE CAN FIND THEM AROUND HERE...
HEH HEH... I TOOK THE LIBERTY OF LISTENING IN ON YOUR CONVERSATION...

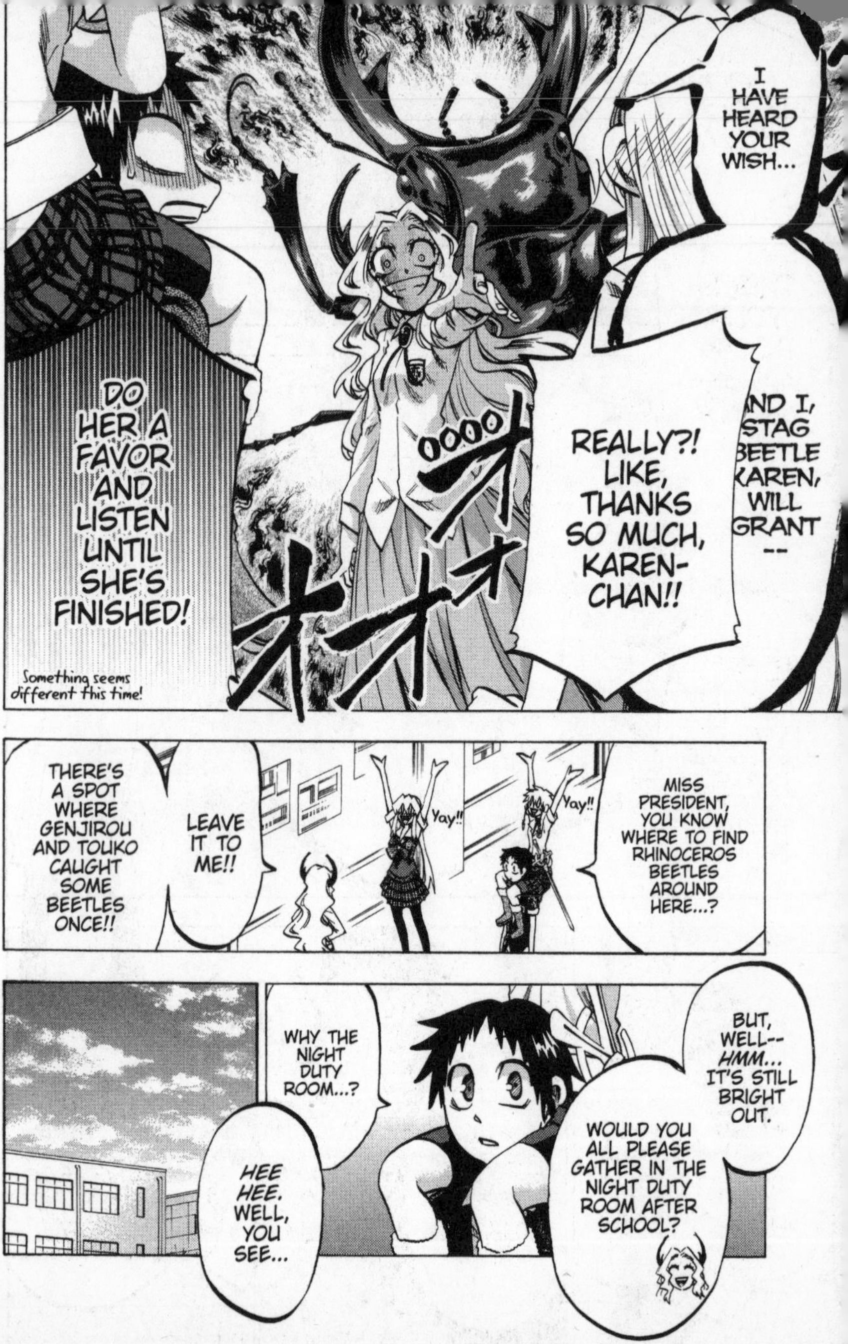
I HAVE HEARD YOUR WISH...
ND I, STAG BEETLE KAREN, WILL GRANT --
REALLY?! LIKE, THANKS SO MUCH, KAREN-CHAN!!
OOOO
オオオオ
DO HER A FAVOR AND LISTEN UNTIL SHE'S FINISHED!
Something seems different this time!
MISS PRESIDENT, YOU KNOW WHERE TO FIND RHINOCEROS BEETLES AROUND HERE...?
Yay!!
Yay!!
LEAVE IT TO ME!!
THERE'S A SPOT WHERE GENJIROU AND TOUKO CAUGHT SOME BEETLES ONCE!!
BUT, WELL-- HMM... IT'S STILL BRIGHT OUT.
WOULD YOU ALL PLEASE GATHER IN THE NIGHT DUTY ROOM AFTER SCHOOL?
WHY THE NIGHT DUTY ROOM...?
HEE HEE. WELL, YOU SEE...

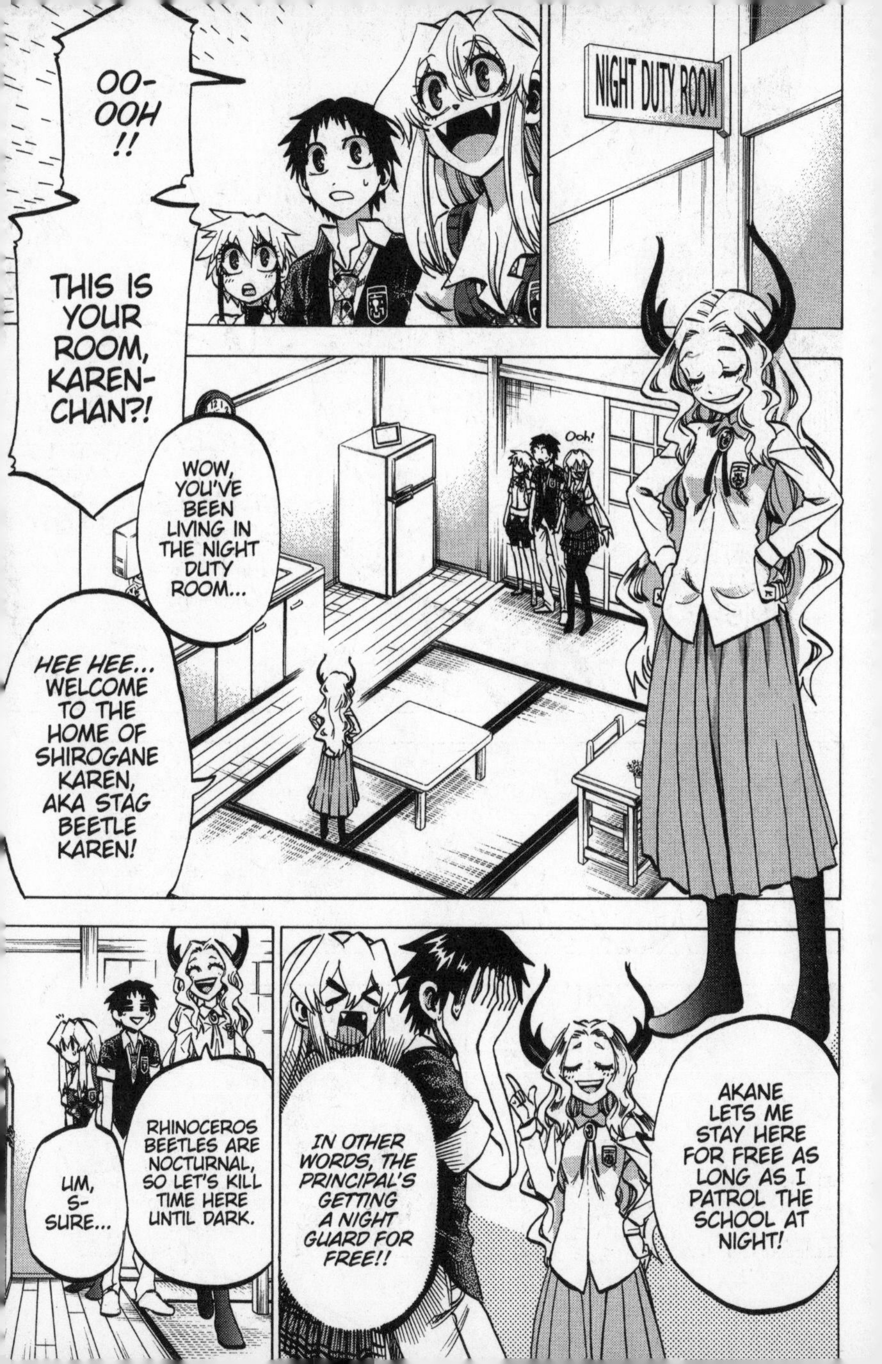
NIGHT DUTY ROOM
OO-OOH!!
Ooh!
THIS IS YOUR ROOM, KAREN-CHAN?!
WOW, YOU'VE BEEN LIVING IN THE NIGHT DUTY ROOM...
HEE HEE... WELCOME TO THE HOME OF SHIROGANE KAREN, AKA STAG BEETLE KAREN!
AKANE LETS ME STAY HERE FOR FREE AS LONG AS I PATROL THE SCHOOL AT NIGHT!
IN OTHER WORDS, THE PRINCIPAL'S GETTING A NIGHT GUARD FOR FREE!!
RHINOCEROS BEETLES ARE NOCTURNAL, SO LET'S KILL TIME HERE UNTIL DARK.
UM, S-SURE...

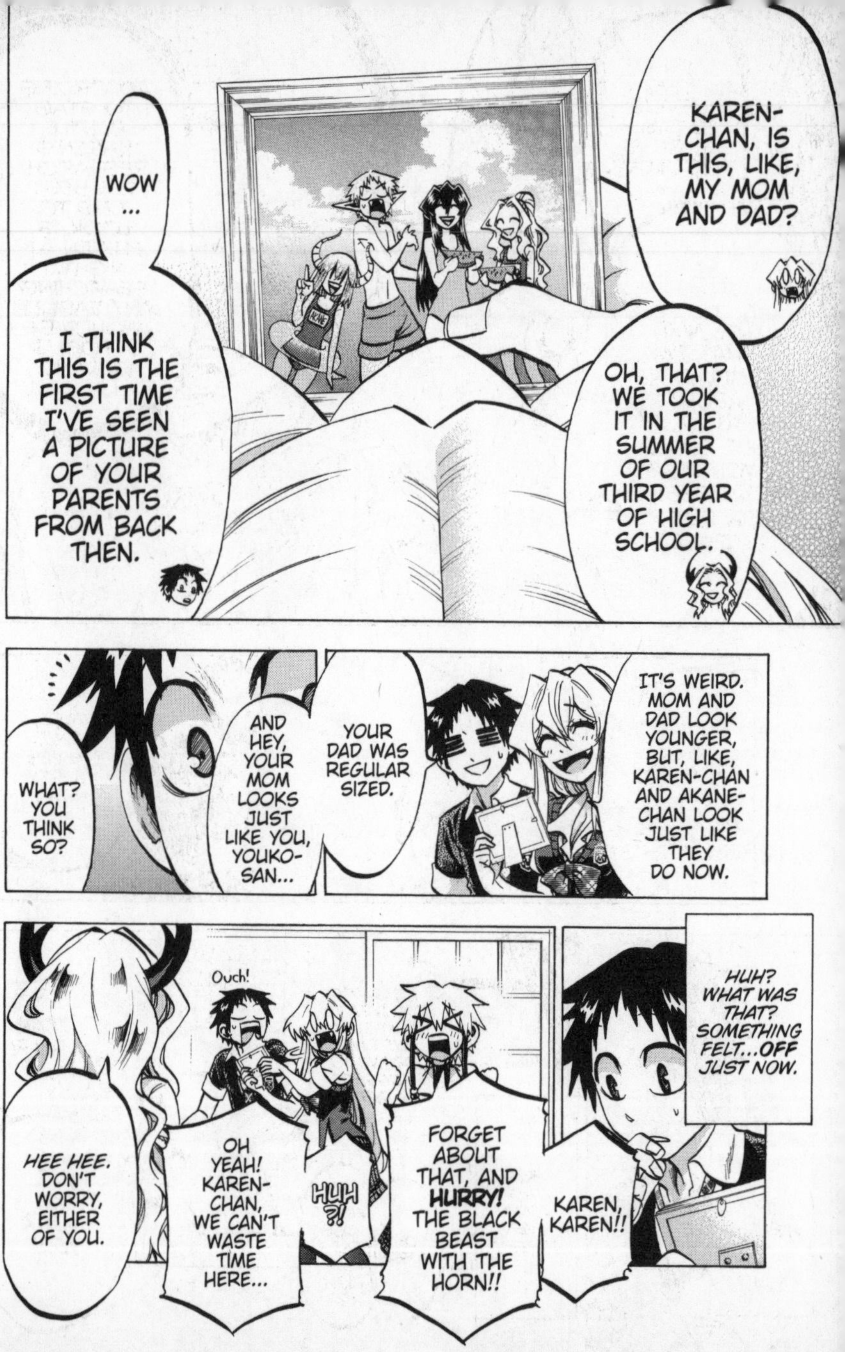
KAREN-CHAN, IS THIS, LIKE, MY MOM AND DAD?
WOW ...
OH, THAT? WE TOOK IT IN THE SUMMER OF OUR THIRD YEAR OF HIGH SCHOOL.
I THINK THIS IS THE FIRST TIME I'VE SEEN A PICTURE OF YOUR PARENTS FROM BACK THEN.
IT'S WEIRD. MOM AND DAD LOOK YOUNGER, BUT, LIKE, KAREN-CHAN AND AKANE-CHAN LOOK JUST LIKE THEY DO NOW.
YOUR DAD WAS REGULAR SIZED.
AND HEY, YOUR MOM LOOKS JUST LIKE YOU, YOUKO-SAN...
WHAT? YOU THINK SO?
*HUH? WHAT WAS THAT? SOMETHING FELT...**OFF** JUST NOW.*
Ouch!
KAREN, KAREN!!
FORGET ABOUT THAT, AND **HURRY!** THE BLACK BEAST WITH THE HORN!!
HUH?!
OH YEAH! KAREN-CHAN, WE CAN'T WASTE TIME HERE...
HEE HEE. DON'T WORRY, EITHER OF YOU.

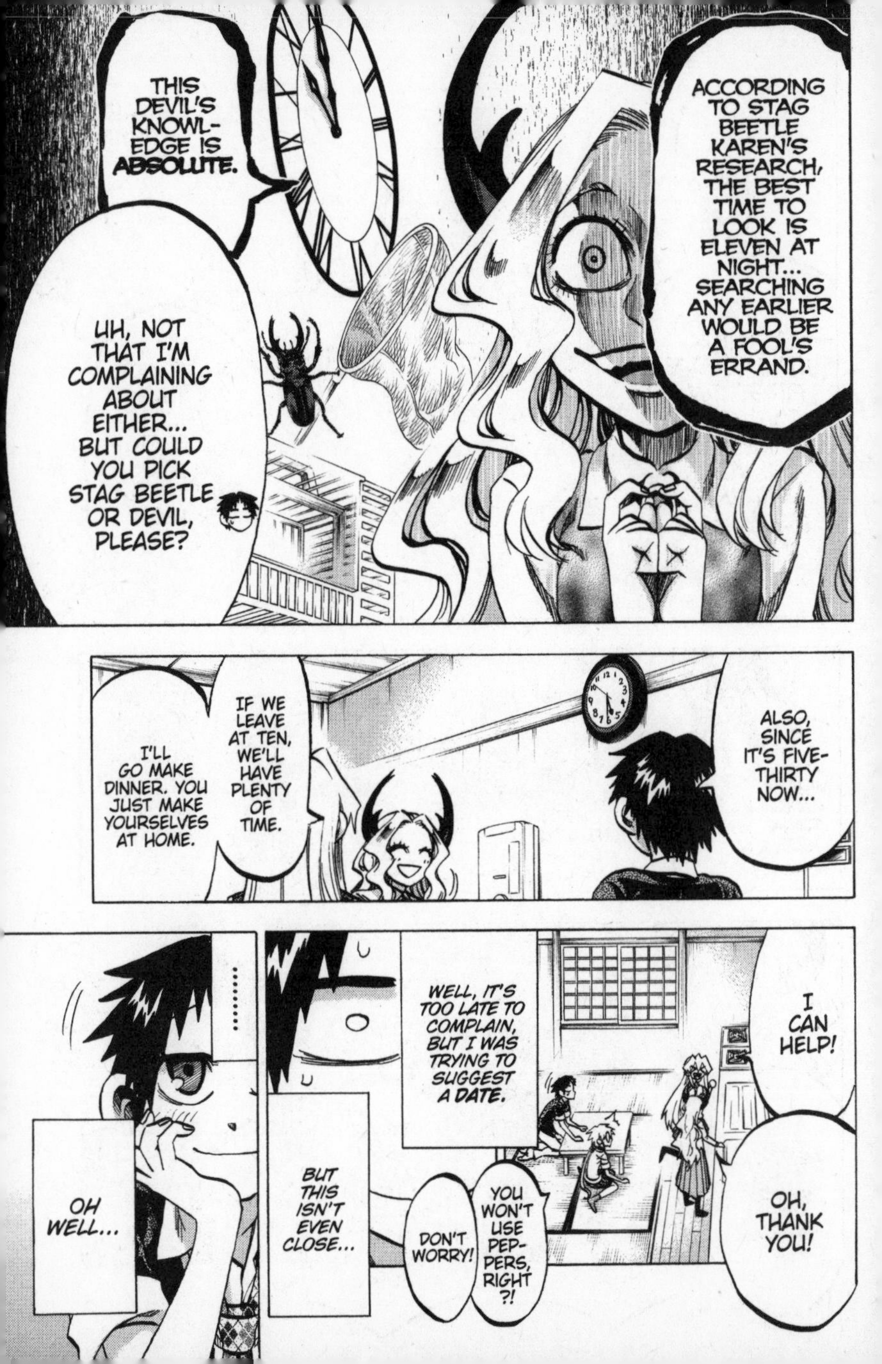
ACCORDING TO STAG BEETLE KAREN'S RESEARCH, THE BEST TIME TO LOOK IS ELEVEN AT NIGHT... SEARCHING ANY EARLIER WOULD BE A FOOL'S ERRAND.
THIS DEVIL'S KNOWL-EDGE IS **ABSOLUTE.**
UH, NOT THAT I'M COMPLAINING ABOUT EITHER... BUT COULD YOU PICK STAG BEETLE OR DEVIL, PLEASE?
ALSO, SINCE IT'S FIVE-THIRTY NOW...
IF WE LEAVE AT TEN, WE'LL HAVE PLENTY OF TIME.
I'LL GO MAKE DINNER. YOU JUST MAKE YOURSELVES AT HOME.
I CAN HELP!
OH, THANK YOU!
WELL, IT'S TOO LATE TO COMPLAIN, BUT I WAS TRYING TO SUGGEST A **DATE.**
YOU WON'T USE PEP-PERS, RIGHT?!
DON'T WORRY!
BUT THIS ISN'T EVEN CLOSE...
......
OH WELL...

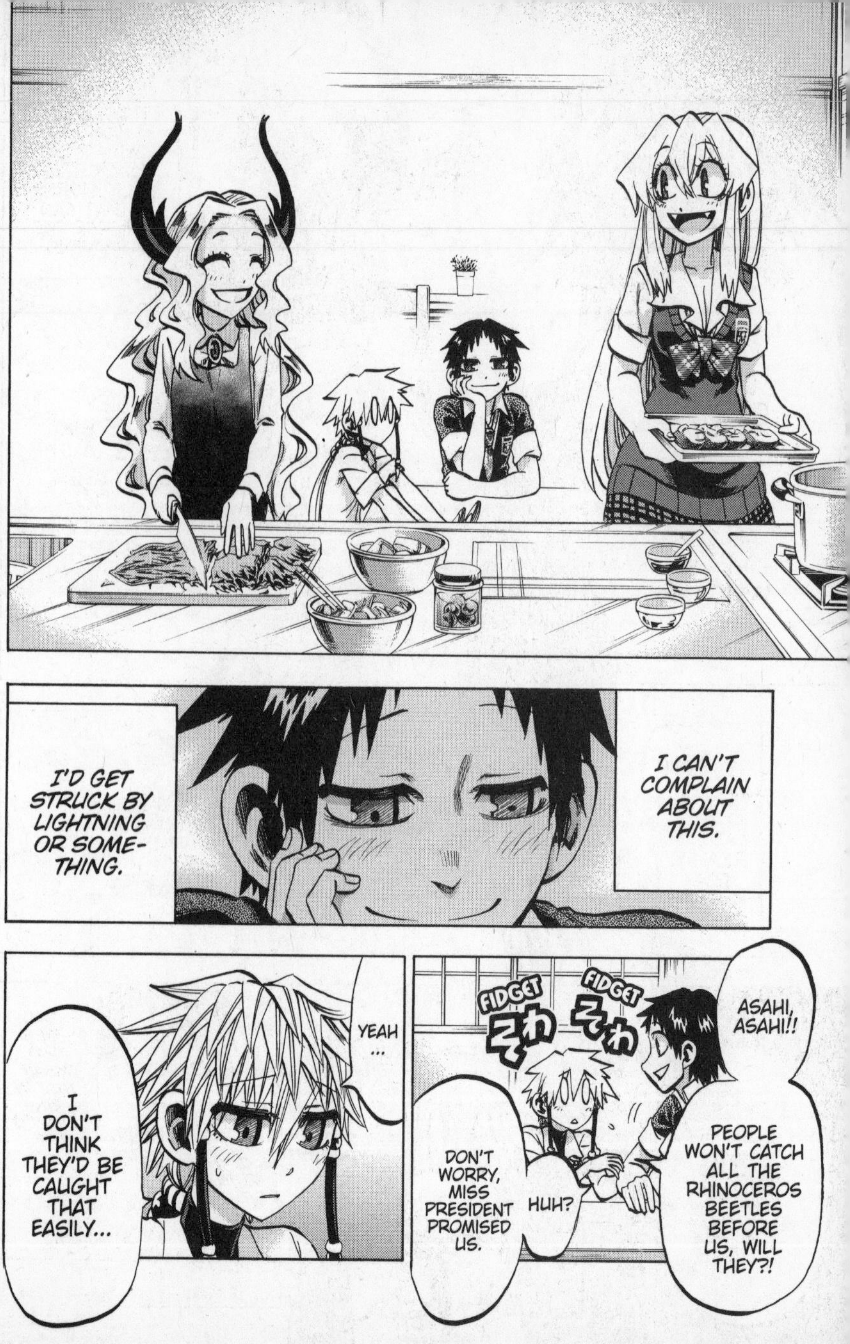
I CAN'T COMPLAIN ABOUT THIS.
I'D GET STRUCK BY LIGHTNING OR SOME-THING.
ASAHI, ASAHI!!
FIDGET FIDGET
そわ そわ
PEOPLE WON'T CATCH ALL THE RHINOCEROS BEETLES BEFORE US, WILL THEY?!
HUH?
DON'T WORRY, MISS PRESIDENT PROMISED US.
YEAH ...
I DON'T THINK THEY'D BE CAUGHT THAT EASILY...

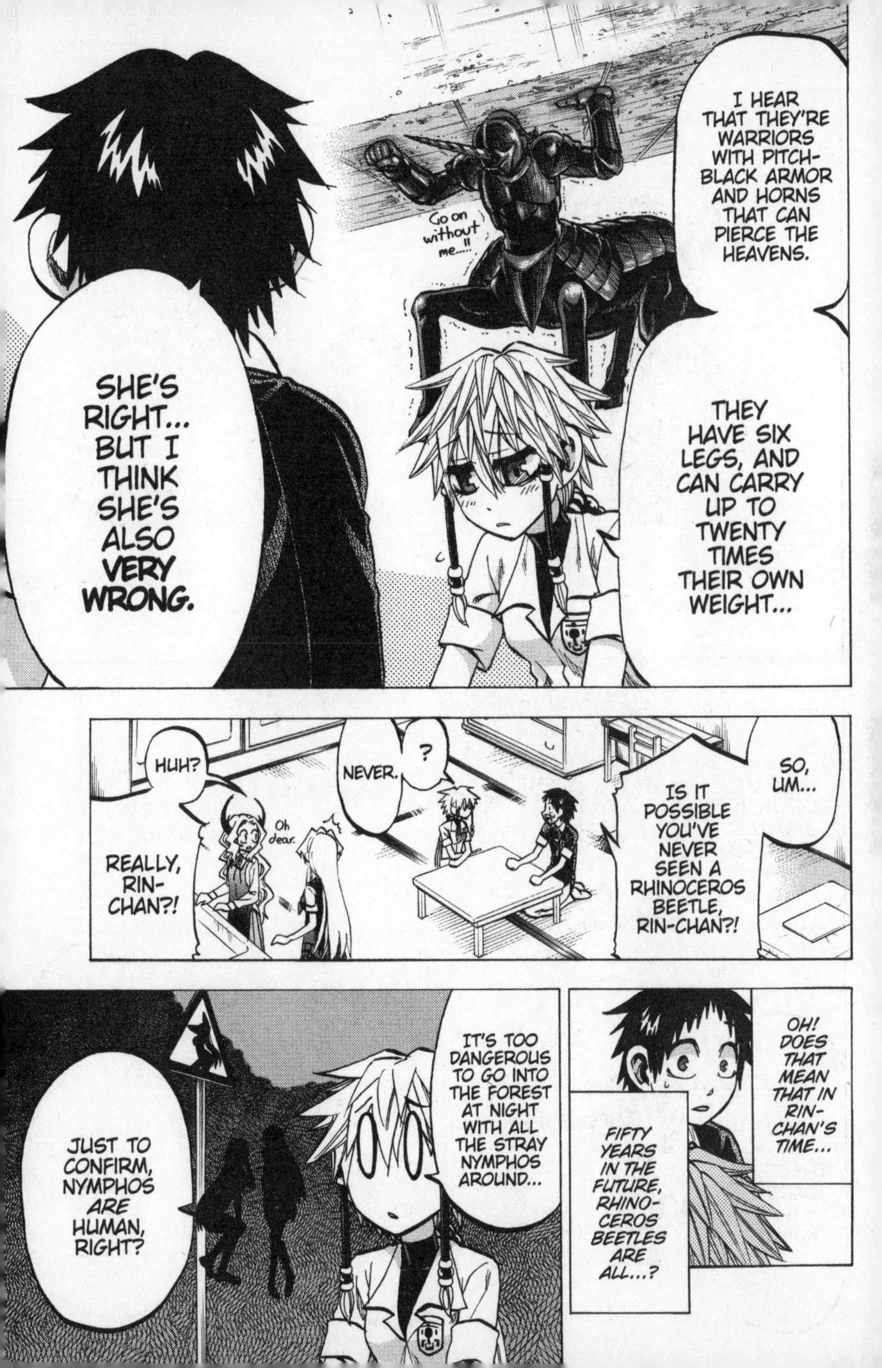
I HEAR THAT THEY'RE WARRIORS WITH PITCH-BLACK ARMOR AND HORNS THAT CAN PIERCE THE HEAVENS.
Go on without me...!!
THEY HAVE SIX LEGS, AND CAN CARRY UP TO TWENTY TIMES THEIR OWN WEIGHT...
SHE'S RIGHT... BUT I THINK SHE'S ALSO **VERY WRONG.**
SO, UM...
IS IT POSSIBLE YOU'VE NEVER SEEN A RHINOCEROS BEETLE, RIN-CHAN?!
?
NEVER.
Oh dear.
HUH?
REALLY, RIN-CHAN?!
OH! DOES THAT MEAN THAT IN RIN-CHAN'S TIME...
FIFTY YEARS IN THE FUTURE, RHINOCEROS BEETLES ARE ALL...?
IT'S TOO DANGEROUS TO GO INTO THE FOREST AT NIGHT WITH ALL THE STRAY NYMPHOS AROUND...
JUST TO CONFIRM, NYMPHOS *ARE* HUMAN, RIGHT?

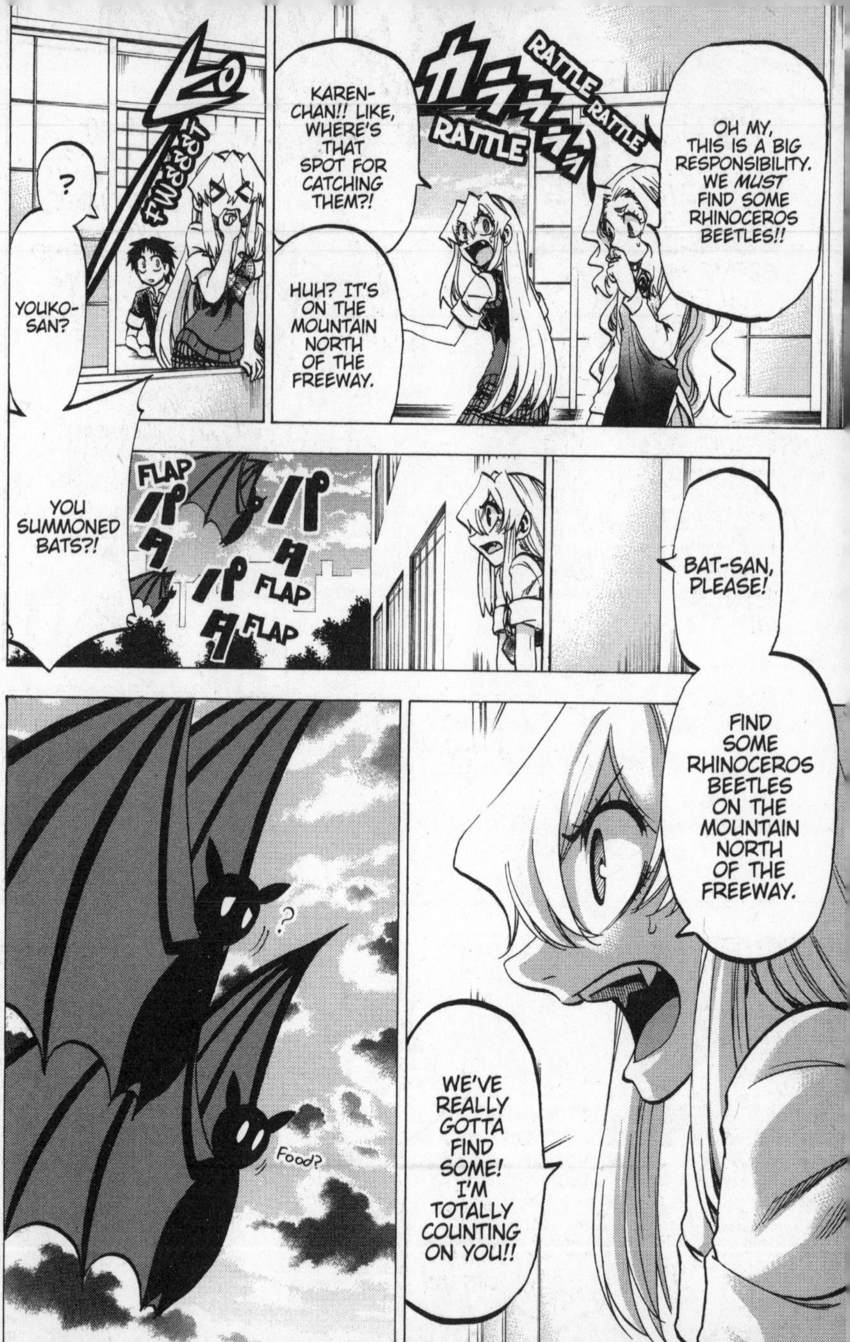

OH MY, THIS IS A BIG RESPONSIBILITY. WE *MUST* FIND SOME RHINOCEROS BEETLES!!
RATTLE RATTLE RATTLE
KAREN-CHAN!! LIKE, WHERE'S THAT SPOT FOR CATCHING THEM?!
HUH? IT'S ON THE MOUNTAIN NORTH OF THE FREEWAY.
FWEEEET
?
YOUKO-SAN?
BAT-SAN, PLEASE!
FLAP FLAP FLAP
YOU SUMMONED BATS?!
FIND SOME RHINOCEROS BEETLES ON THE MOUNTAIN NORTH OF THE FREEWAY.
WE'VE REALLY GOTTA FIND SOME! I'M TOTALLY COUNTING ON YOU!!
?
Food?

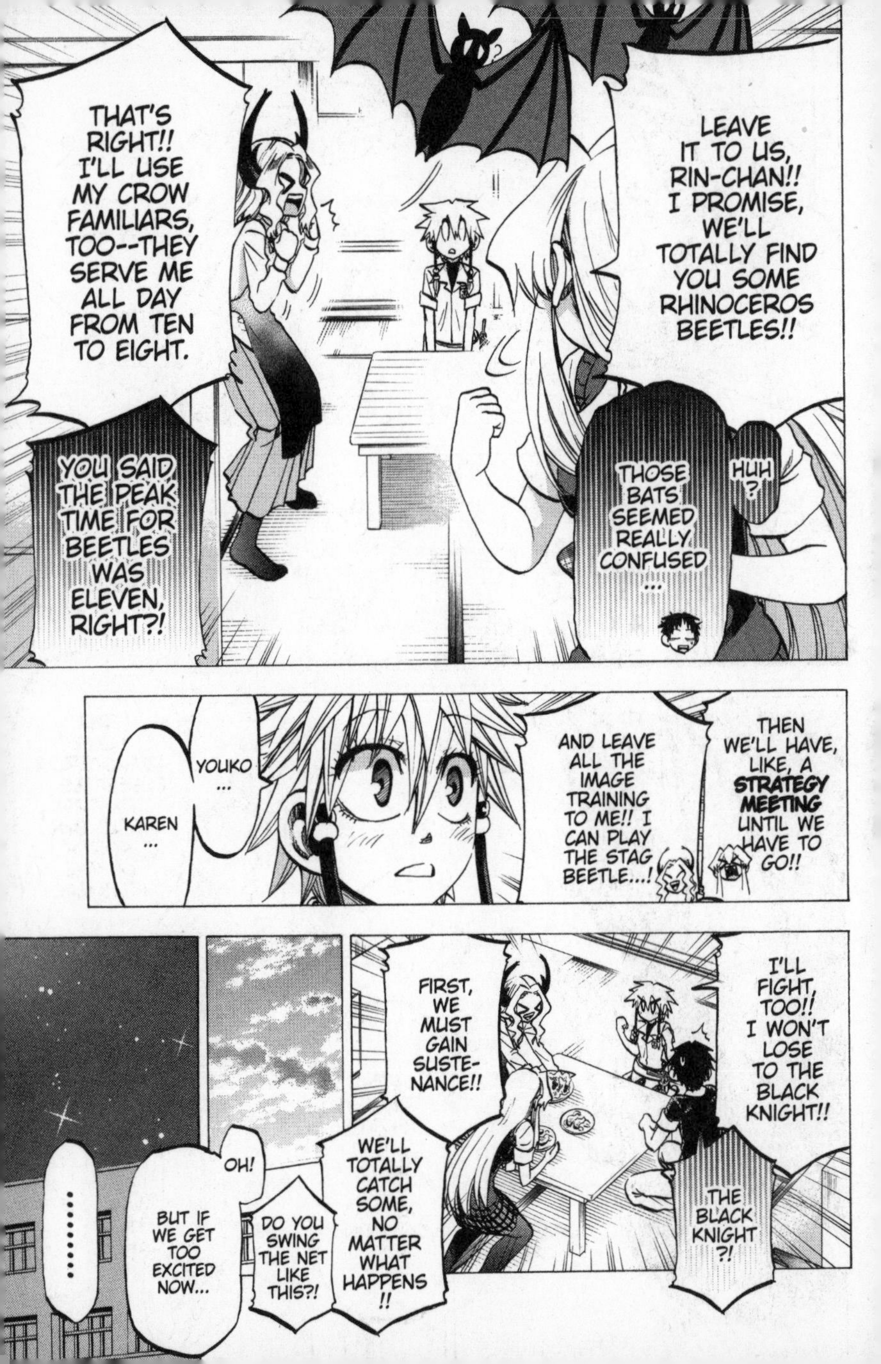

LEAVE IT TO US, RIN-CHAN!! I PROMISE, WE'LL TOTALLY FIND YOU SOME RHINOCEROS BEETLES!!
THAT'S RIGHT!! I'LL USE MY CROW FAMILIARS, TOO--THEY SERVE ME ALL DAY FROM TEN TO EIGHT.
HUH?
THOSE BATS SEEMED REALLY CONFUSED...
YOU SAID THE PEAK TIME FOR BEETLES WAS ELEVEN, RIGHT?!
THEN WE'LL HAVE, LIKE, A **STRATEGY MEETING** UNTIL WE HAVE TO GO!!
AND LEAVE ALL THE IMAGE TRAINING TO ME!! I CAN PLAY THE STAG BEETLE...!
YOUKO...
KAREN...
I'LL FIGHT, TOO!! I WON'T LOSE TO THE BLACK KNIGHT!!
FIRST, WE MUST GAIN SUSTE-NANCE!!
THE BLACK KNIGHT?!
WE'LL TOTALLY CATCH SOME, NO MATTER WHAT HAPPENS!!
DO YOU SWING THE NET LIKE THIS?!
OH!
BUT IF WE GET TOO EXCITED NOW...
......

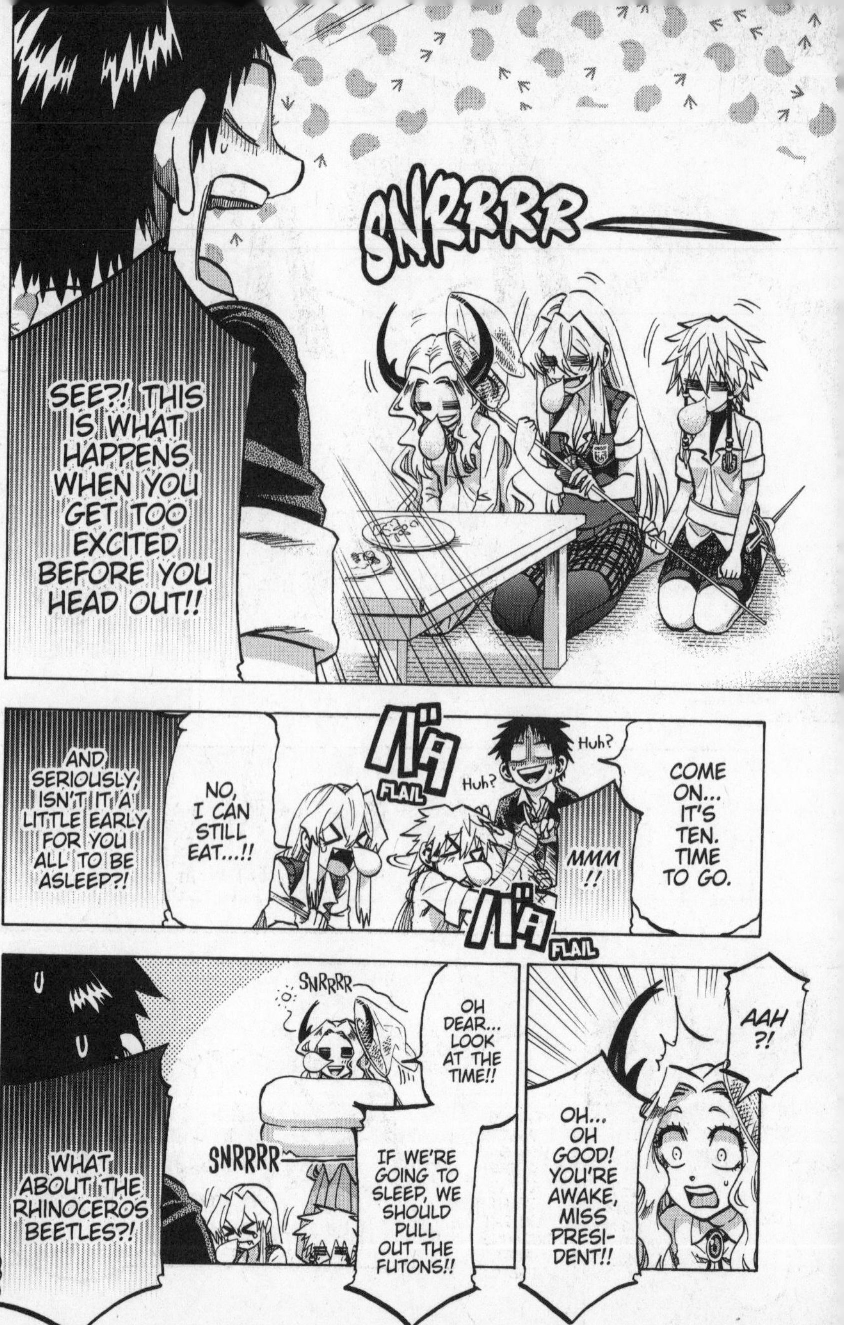
SNRRRR
SEE?! THIS IS WHAT HAPPENS WHEN YOU GET TOO EXCITED BEFORE YOU HEAD OUT!!
COME ON... IT'S TEN. TIME TO GO.
Huh?
Huh?
MMM!!
バタ
FLAIL
NO, I CAN STILL EAT...!!
バタ
FLAIL
AND SERIOUSLY, ISN'T IT A LITTLE EARLY FOR YOU ALL TO BE ASLEEP?!
AAH?!
OH... OH GOOD! YOU'RE AWAKE, MISS PRESIDENT!!
SNRRRR
OH DEAR... LOOK AT THE TIME!!
IF WE'RE GOING TO SLEEP, WE SHOULD PULL OUT THE FUTONS!!
SNRRRR
WHAT ABOUT THE RHINOCEROS BEETLES?!

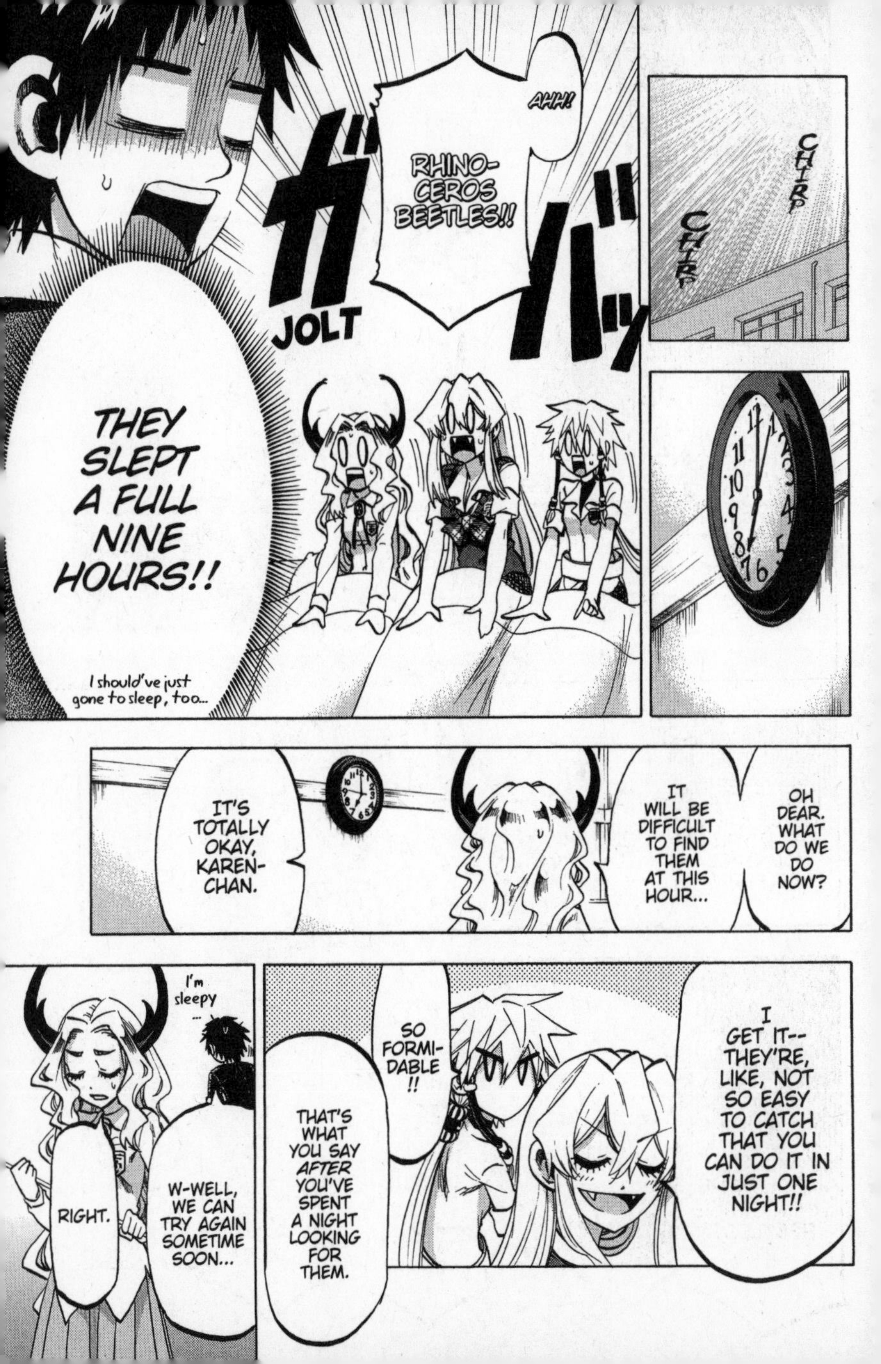

CHIRP
CHIRP
AHH!
RHINO-CEROS BEETLES!!
JOLT
THEY SLEPT A FULL NINE HOURS!!
I should've just gone to sleep, too...
OH DEAR. WHAT DO WE DO NOW?
IT WILL BE DIFFICULT TO FIND THEM AT THIS HOUR...
IT'S TOTALLY OKAY, KAREN-CHAN.
I GET IT--THEY'RE, LIKE, NOT SO EASY TO CATCH THAT YOU CAN DO IT IN JUST ONE NIGHT!!
SO FORMIDABLE!!
THAT'S WHAT YOU SAY *AFTER* YOU'VE SPENT A NIGHT LOOKING FOR THEM.
I'm sleepy...
W-WELL, WE CAN TRY AGAIN SOMETIME SOON...
RIGHT.

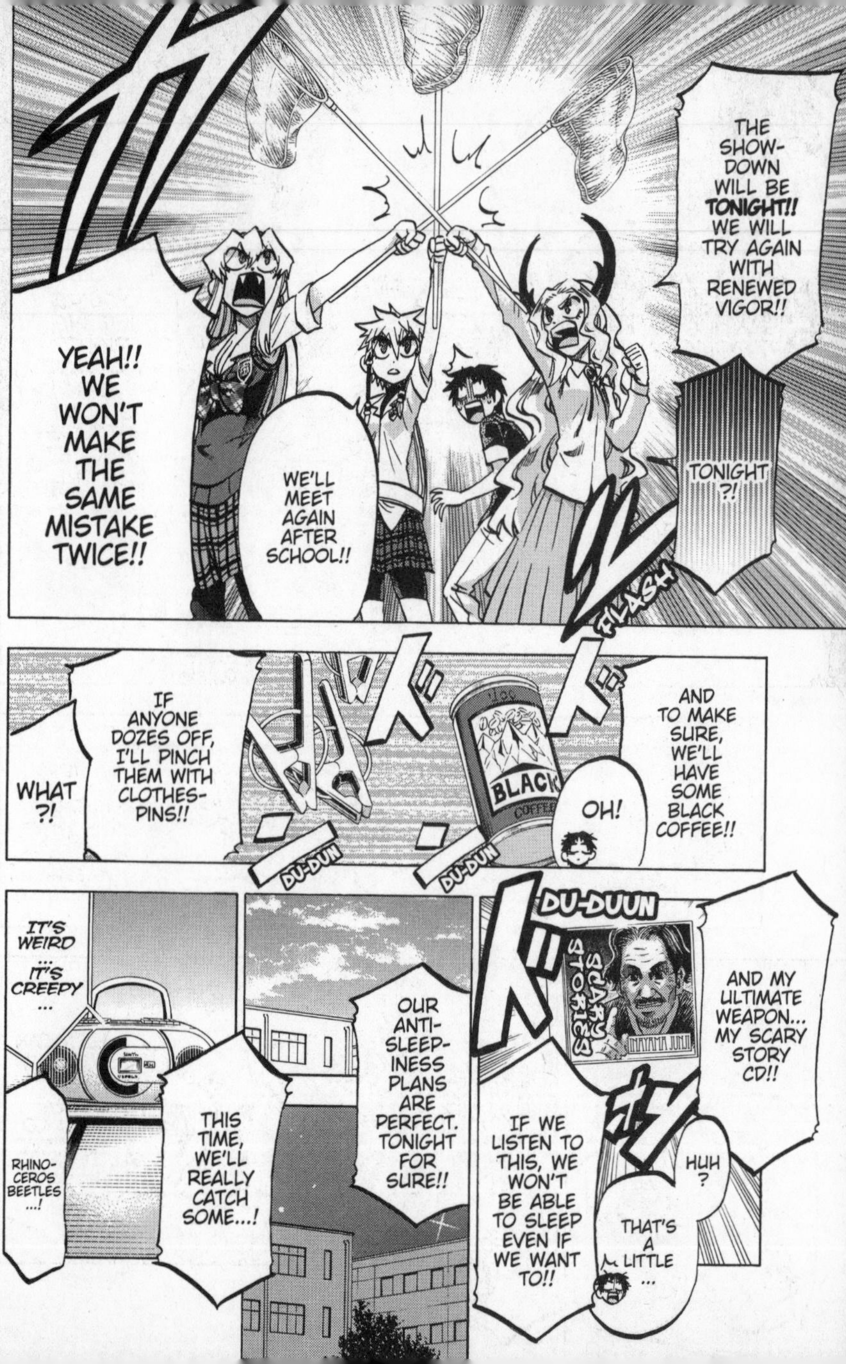
THE SHOWDOWN WILL BE **TONIGHT!!** WE WILL TRY AGAIN WITH RENEWED VIGOR!!
TONIGHT?!
WE'LL MEET AGAIN AFTER SCHOOL!!
YEAH!! WE WON'T MAKE THE SAME MISTAKE TWICE!!
FLASH
AND TO MAKE SURE, WE'LL HAVE SOME BLACK COFFEE!!
OH!
BLACK COFFEE
DU-DUN
DU-DUN
IF ANYONE DOZES OFF, I'LL PINCH THEM WITH CLOTHES-PINS!!
WHAT?!
DU-DUUN
AND MY ULTIMATE WEAPON... MY SCARY STORY CD!!
SCARY STORIES 3
INAYAMA JUNJI
IF WE LISTEN TO THIS, WE WON'T BE ABLE TO SLEEP EVEN IF WE WANT TO!!
HUH?
THAT'S A LITTLE ...
OUR ANTI-SLEEP-INESS PLANS ARE PERFECT. TONIGHT FOR SURE!!
THIS TIME, WE'LL REALLY CATCH SOME...!
IT'S WEIRD ... IT'S CREEPY ...
RHINO-CEROS BEETLES ...!

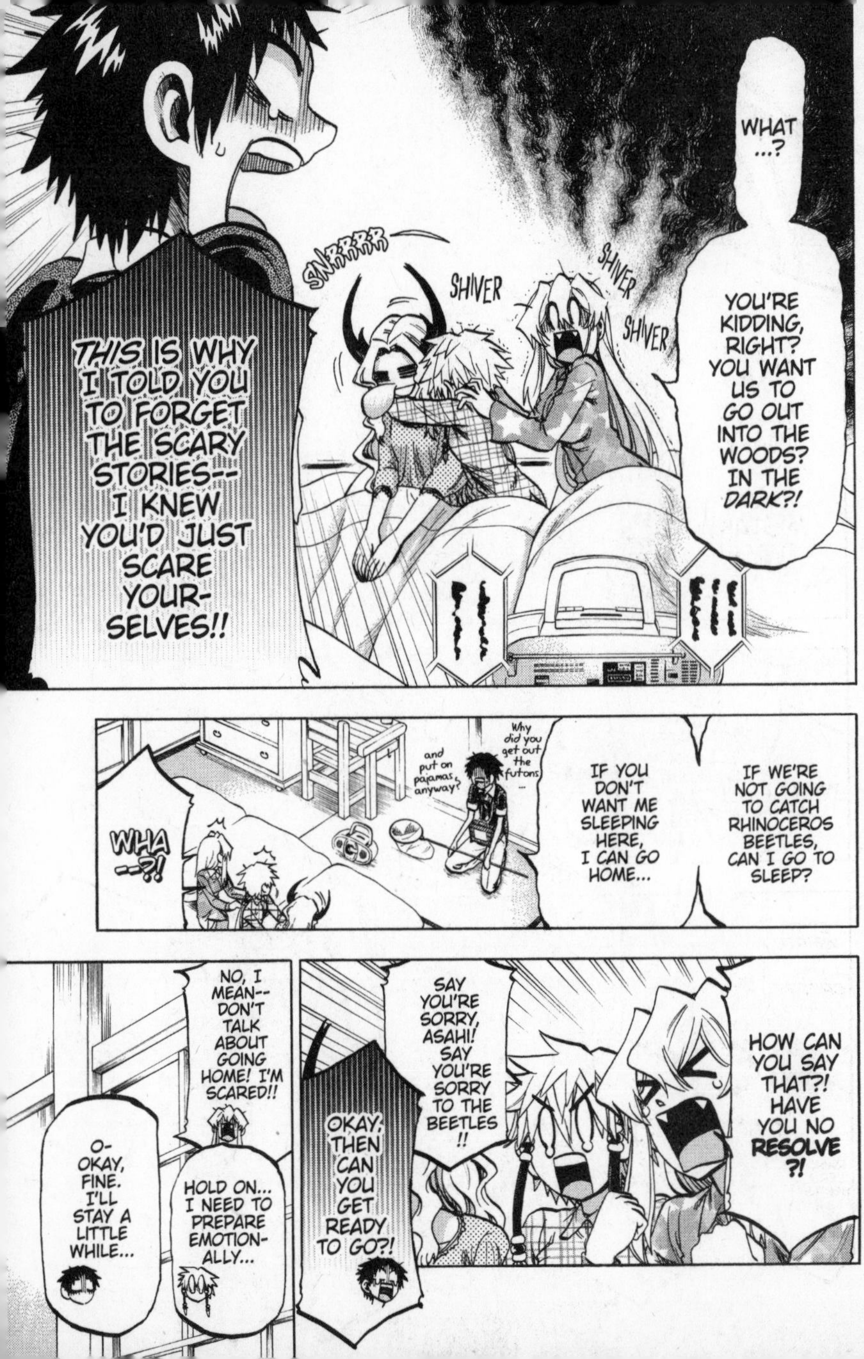

WHAT ...?
YOU'RE KIDDING, RIGHT? YOU WANT US TO GO OUT INTO THE WOODS? IN THE DARK?!
SHIVER
SHIVER
SHIVER
SNRRRRR
THIS IS WHY I TOLD YOU TO FORGET THE SCARY STORIES-- I KNEW YOU'D JUST SCARE YOUR-SELVES!!
IF WE'RE NOT GOING TO CATCH RHINOCEROS BEETLES, CAN I GO TO SLEEP?
IF YOU DON'T WANT ME SLEEPING HERE, I CAN GO HOME...
Why did you get out the futons...
and put on pajamas anyway?
WHA--?!
HOW CAN YOU SAY THAT?! HAVE YOU NO RESOLVE?!
SAY YOU'RE SORRY, ASAHI! SAY YOU'RE SORRY TO THE BEETLES!!
OKAY. THEN CAN YOU GET READY TO GO?!
NO, I MEAN-- DON'T TALK ABOUT GOING HOME! I'M SCARED!!
HOLD ON... I NEED TO PREPARE EMOTION-ALLY...
O-OKAY, FINE. I'LL STAY A LITTLE WHILE...

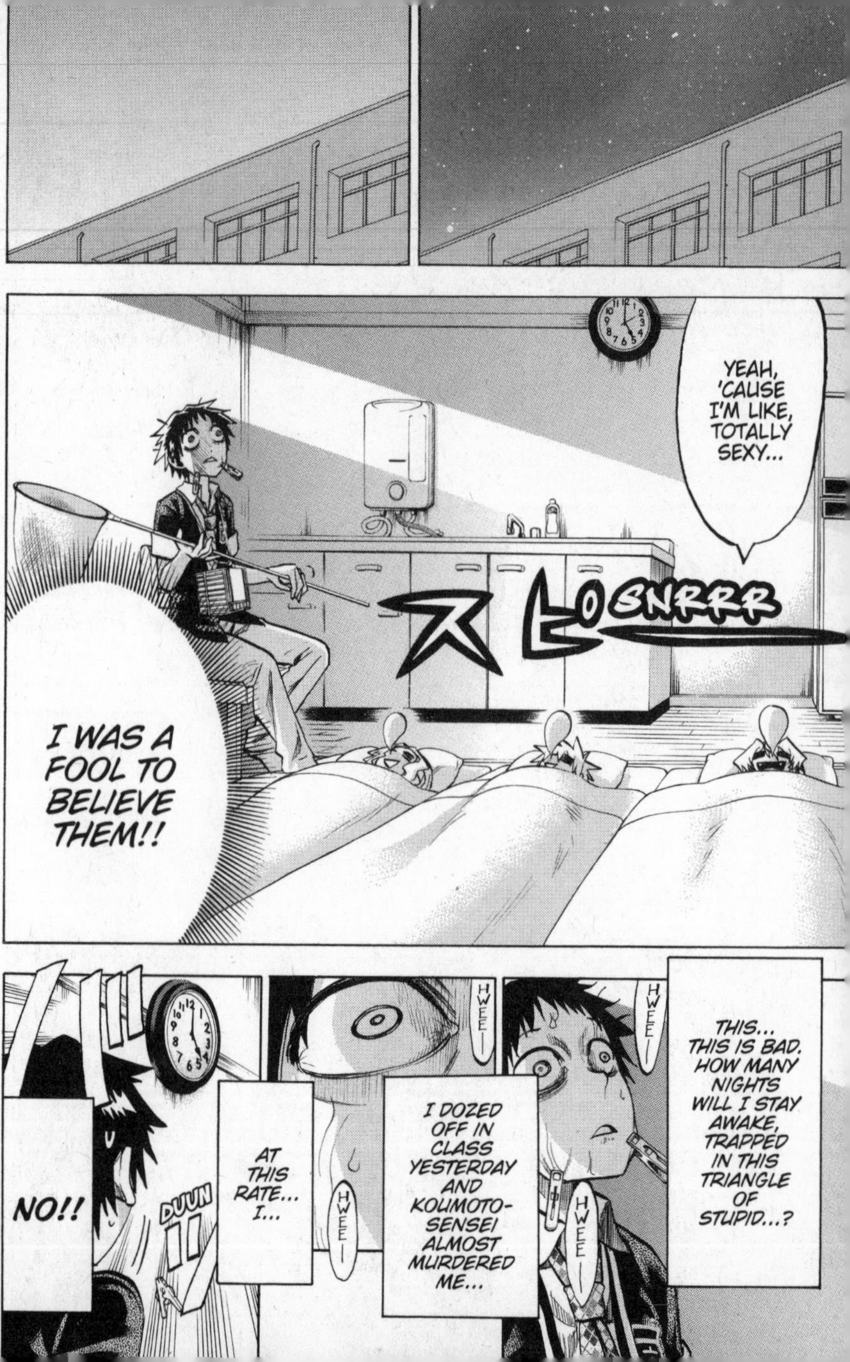
YEAH, 'CAUSE I'M LIKE, TOTALLY SEXY...
SNRRR
I WAS A FOOL TO BELIEVE THEM!!
THIS... THIS IS BAD. HOW MANY NIGHTS WILL I STAY AWAKE, TRAPPED IN THIS TRIANGLE OF STUPID...?
HWEE—
HWEE—
I DOZED OFF IN CLASS YESTERDAY AND KOUMOTO-SENSEI ALMOST MURDERED ME...
HWEE—
HWEE—
AT THIS RATE... I...
NO!!
DUUN

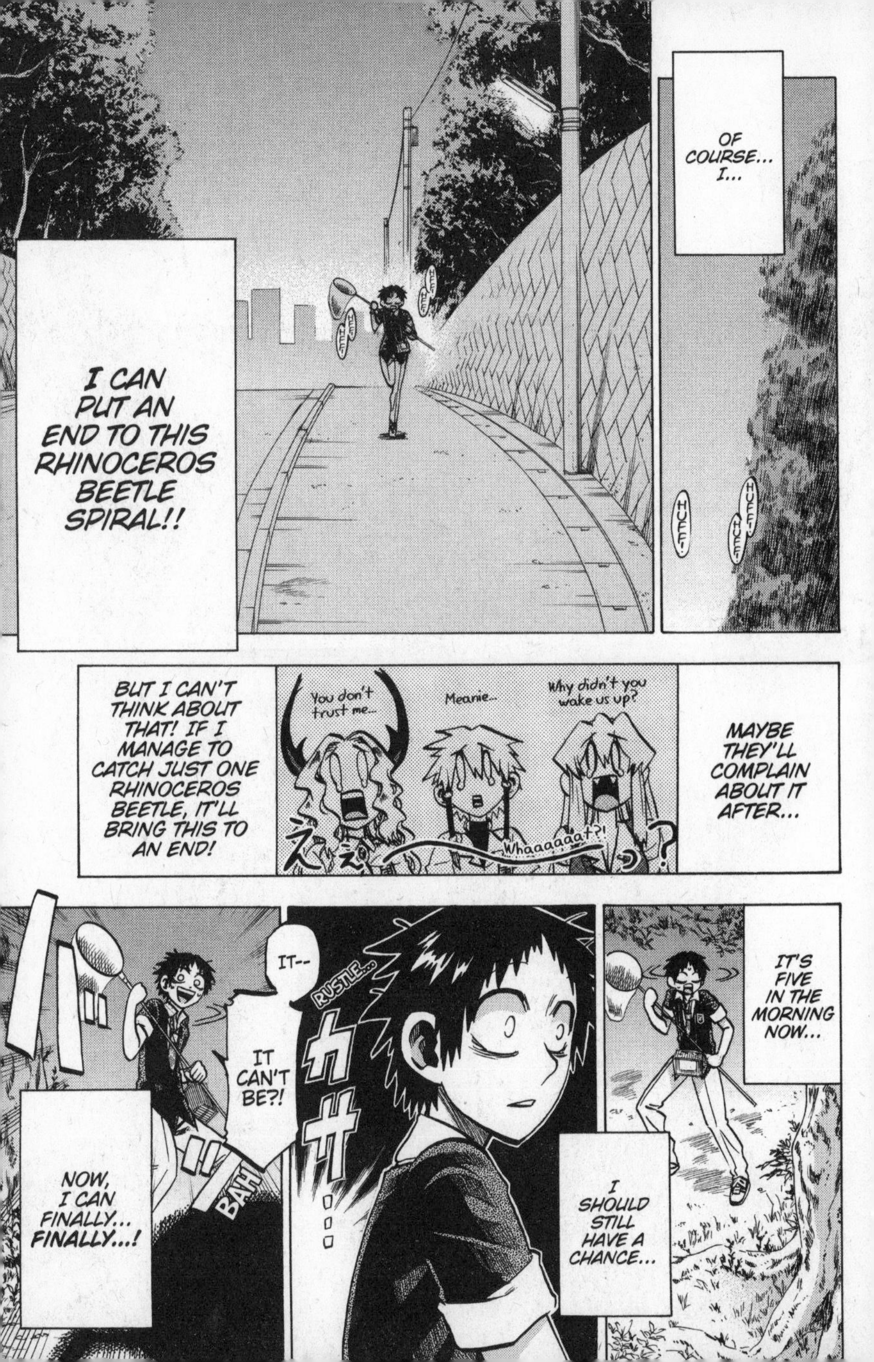
OF COURSE... I...
HUFF!
HUFF!
HUFF!
I CAN PUT AN END TO THIS RHINOCEROS BEETLE SPIRAL!!
MAYBE THEY'LL COMPLAIN ABOUT IT AFTER...
Why didn't you wake us up?
Meanie...
You don't trust me...
Whaaaaaat?!
BUT I CAN'T THINK ABOUT THAT! IF I MANAGE TO CATCH JUST ONE RHINOCEROS BEETLE, IT'LL BRING THIS TO AN END!
IT'S FIVE IN THE MORNING NOW...
I SHOULD STILL HAVE A CHANCE...
RUSTLE...
IT--
IT CAN'T BE?!
BAH
NOW, I CAN FINALLY... FINALLY...!

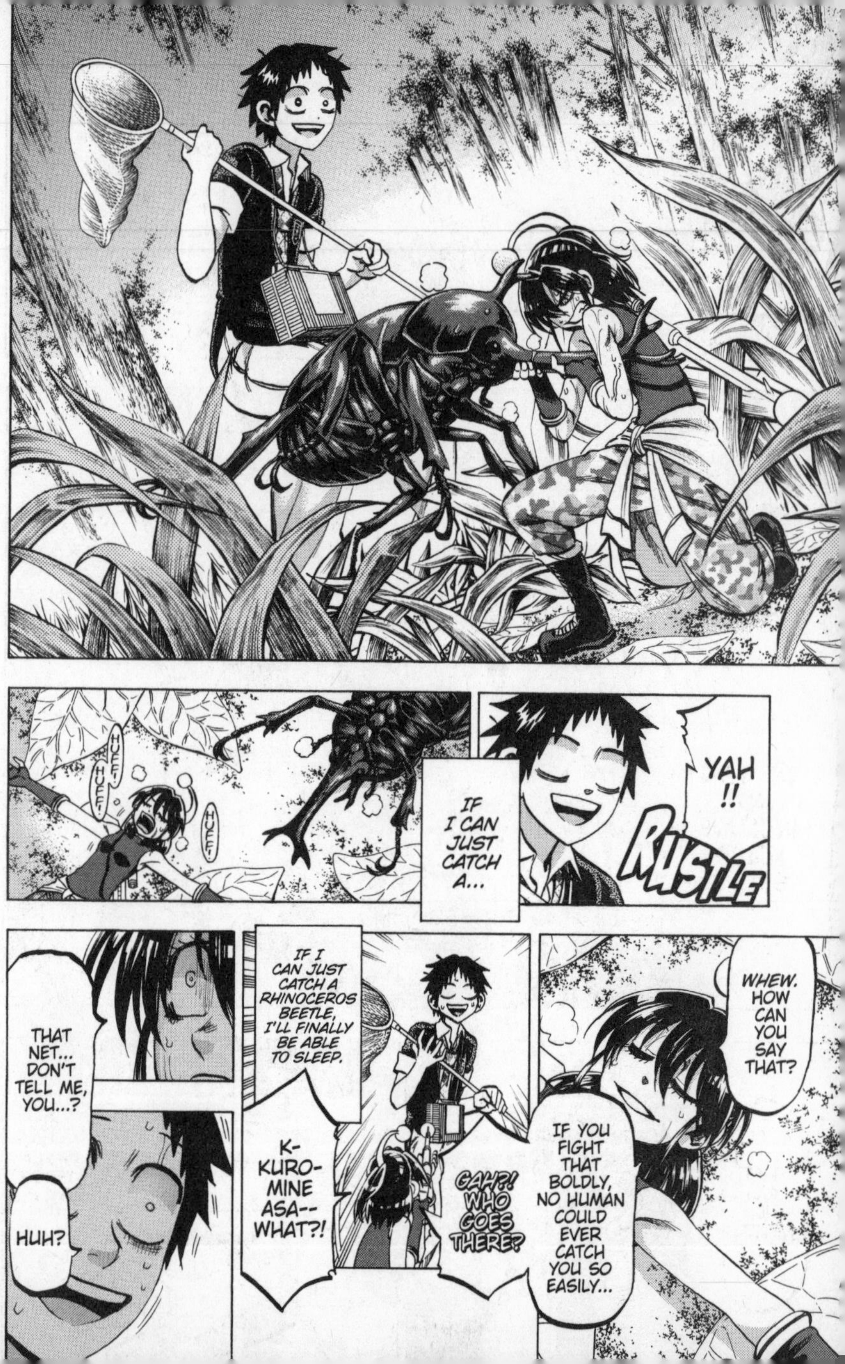
YAH!!
RUSTLE
IF I CAN JUST CATCH A...
HUFF! HUFF! HUFF!
WHEW. HOW CAN YOU SAY THAT?
IF YOU FIGHT THAT BOLDLY, NO HUMAN COULD EVER CATCH YOU SO EASILY...
GAH?! WHO GOES THERE?
IF I CAN JUST CATCH A RHINOCEROS BEETLE, I'LL FINALLY BE ABLE TO SLEEP.
K-KUROMINE ASA--WHAT?!
THAT NET... DON'T TELL ME, YOU...?
HUH?

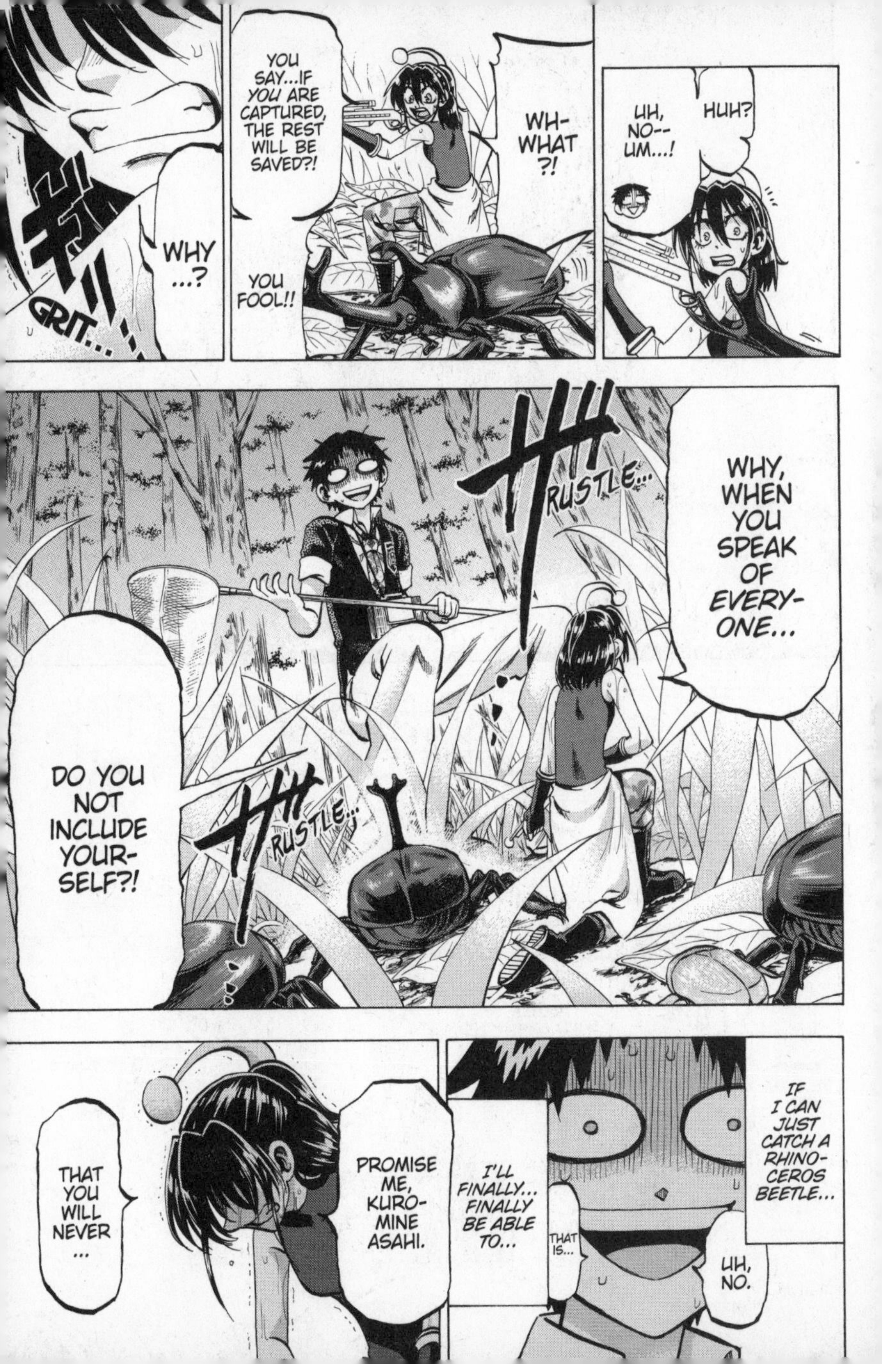
HUH?
UH, NO-- UM...!
WH- WHAT ?!
YOU SAY...IF YOU ARE CAPTURED, THE REST WILL BE SAVED?!
YOU FOOL!!
WHY ...?
GRIT...
WHY, WHEN YOU SPEAK OF EVERY-ONE...
RUSTLE...
RUSTLE...
DO YOU NOT INCLUDE YOUR-SELF?!
IF I CAN JUST CATCH A RHINO-CEROS BEETLE...
UH, NO.
THAT IS...
I'LL FINALLY... FINALLY BE ABLE TO...
PROMISE ME, KURO-MINE ASAHI.
THAT YOU WILL NEVER ...

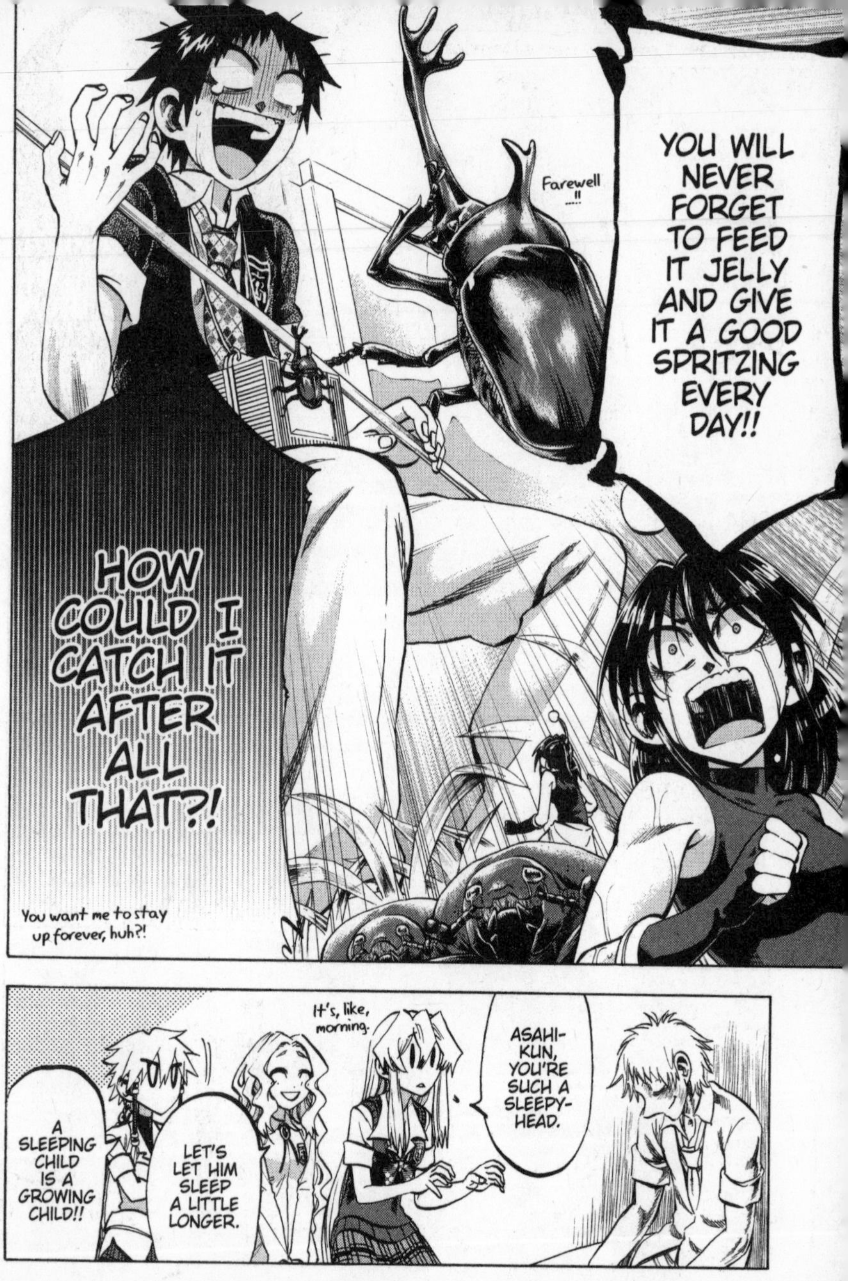
YOU WILL NEVER FORGET TO FEED IT JELLY AND GIVE IT A GOOD SPRITZING EVERY DAY!!
Farewell!!
HOW COULD I CATCH IT AFTER ALL THAT?!
You want me to stay up forever, huh?!
ASAHI-KUN, YOU'RE SUCH A SLEEPY-HEAD.
It's, like, morning.
LET'S LET HIM SLEEP A LITTLE LONGER.
A SLEEPING CHILD IS A GROWING CHILD!!

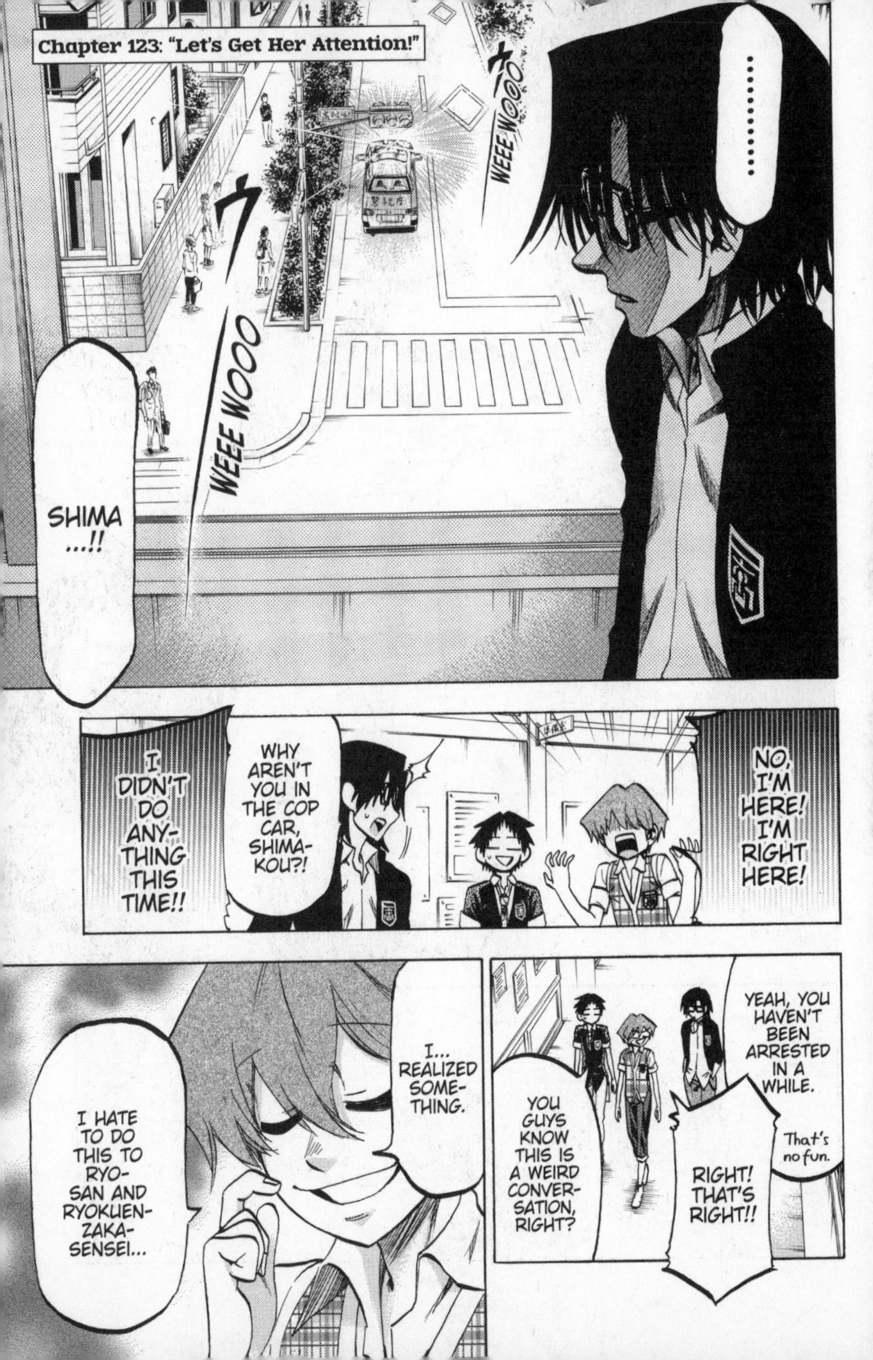
Chapter 123: "Let's Get Her Attention!"
......
WEEE WOOO
WEEE WOOO
SHIMA ...!!
NO, I'M HERE! I'M RIGHT HERE!
WHY AREN'T YOU IN THE COP CAR, SHIMA-KOU?!
I DIDN'T DO ANY-THING THIS TIME!!
YEAH, YOU HAVEN'T BEEN ARRESTED IN A WHILE.
That's no fun.
RIGHT! THAT'S RIGHT!!
YOU GUYS KNOW THIS IS A WEIRD CONVER-SATION, RIGHT?
I... REALIZED SOME-THING.
I HATE TO DO THIS TO RYO-SAN AND RYOKUEN-ZAKA-SENSEI...

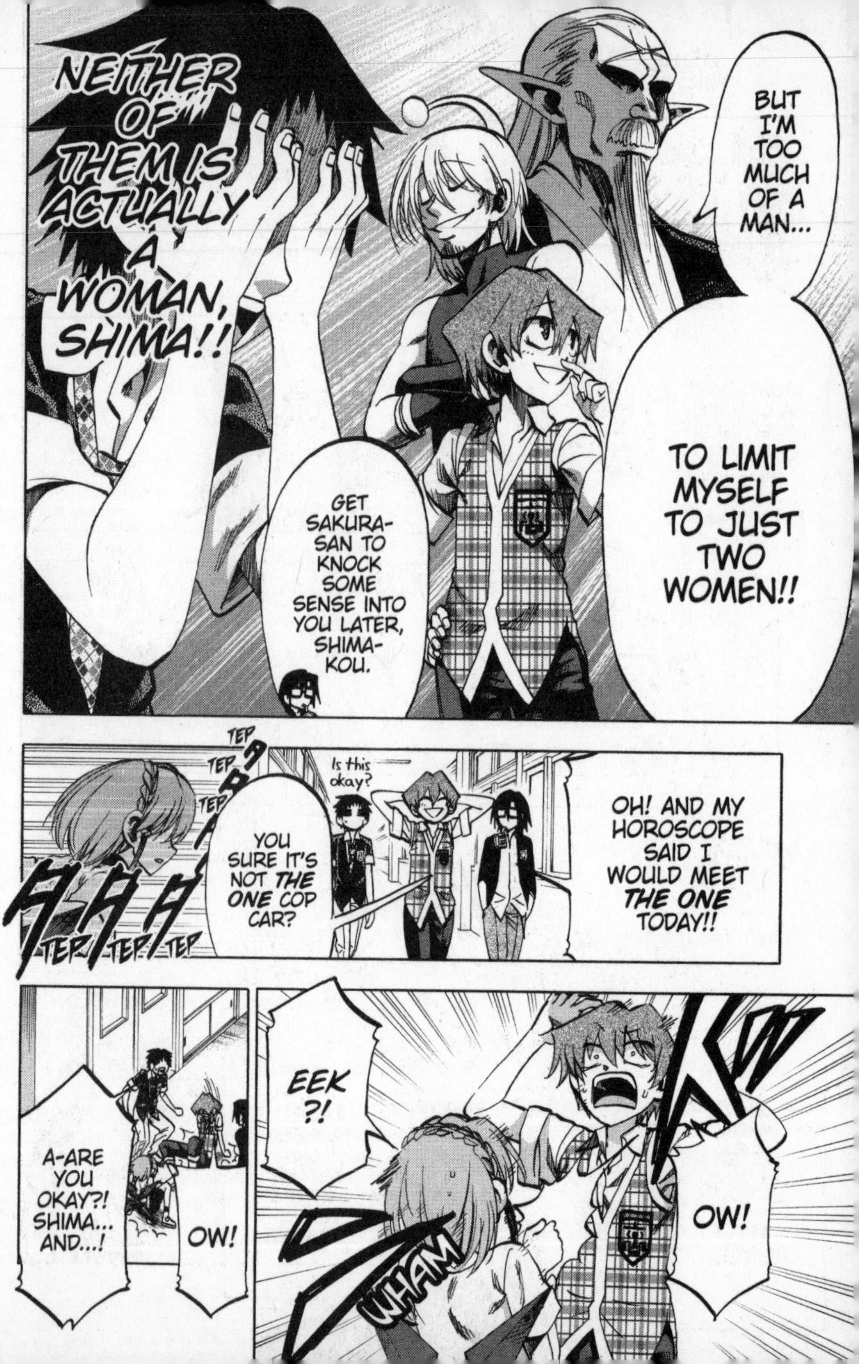
BUT I'M TOO MUCH OF A MAN...
TO LIMIT MYSELF TO JUST TWO WOMEN!!
NEITHER OF THEM IS ACTUALLY A WOMAN, SHIMA!!
GET SAKURA-SAN TO KNOCK SOME SENSE INTO YOU LATER, SHIMA-KOU.
OH! AND MY HOROSCOPE SAID I WOULD MEET *THE ONE* TODAY!!
Is this okay?
YOU SURE IT'S NOT *THE ONE* COP CAR?
TEP TEP TEP
TEP TEP TEP
OW!
EEK ?!
WHAM
A-ARE YOU OKAY?! SHIMA... AND...!
OW!

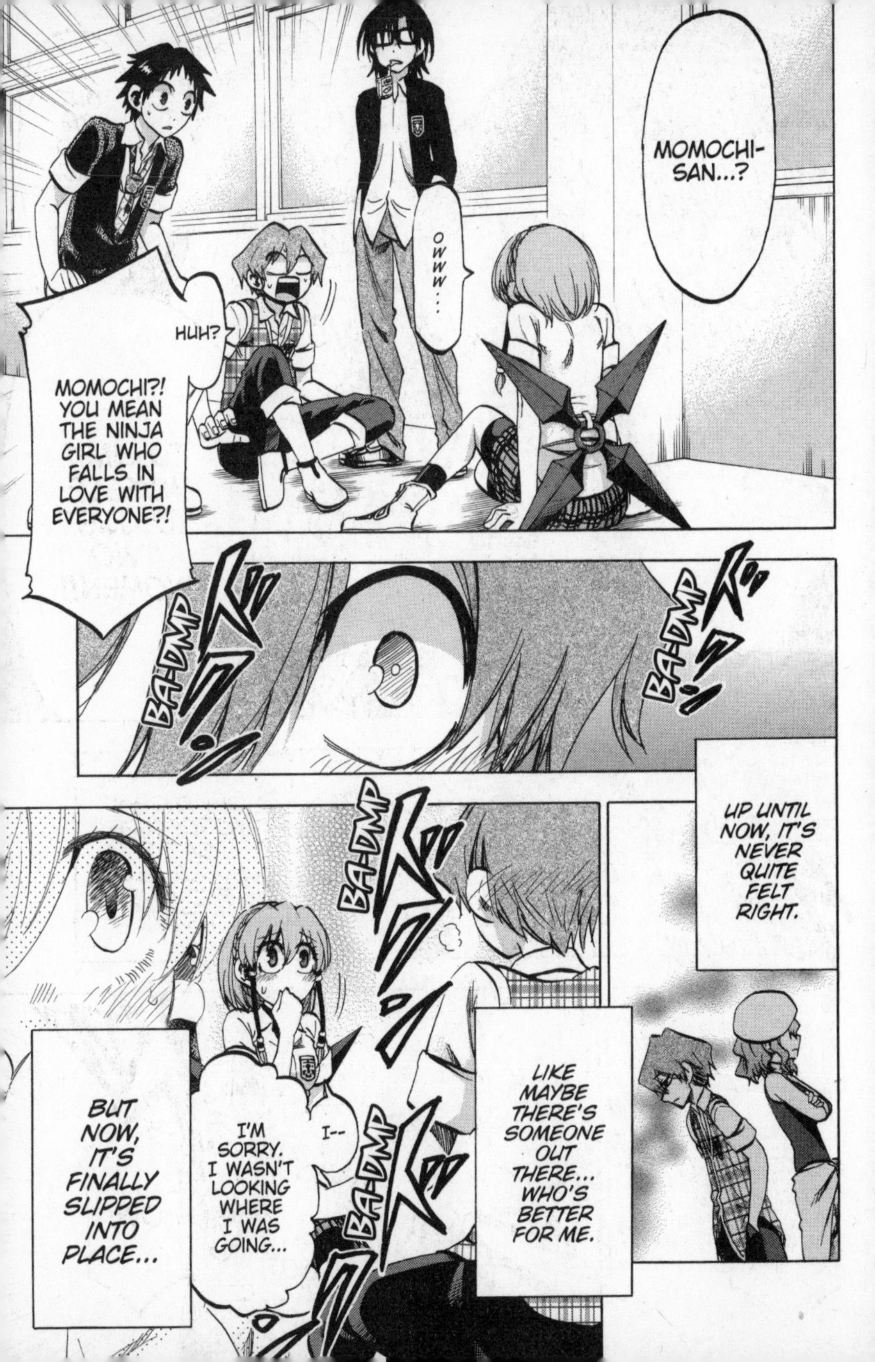
MOMOCHI-SAN...?
OWWW...
HUH?
MOMOCHI?! YOU MEAN THE NINJA GIRL WHO FALLS IN LOVE WITH EVERYONE?!
BA-DMP
BA-DMP
UP UNTIL NOW, IT'S NEVER QUITE FELT RIGHT.
BA-DMP
LIKE MAYBE THERE'S SOMEONE OUT THERE... WHO'S BETTER FOR ME.
BA-DMP
I--
I'M SORRY. I WASN'T LOOKING WHERE I WAS GOING...
BUT NOW, IT'S FINALLY SLIPPED INTO PLACE...

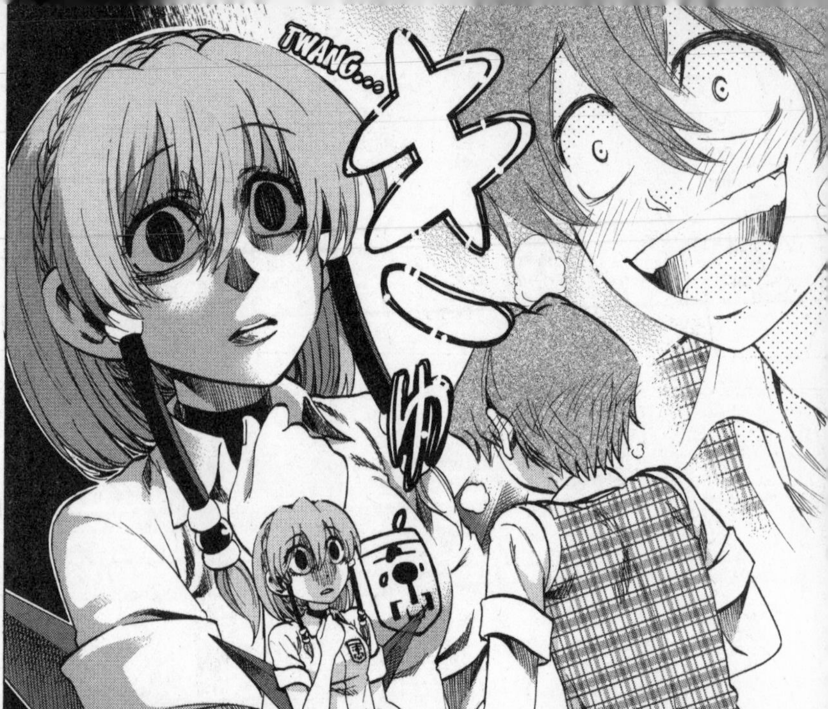
TWANG...
Chapter 123:
"Let's Get Her Attention!"

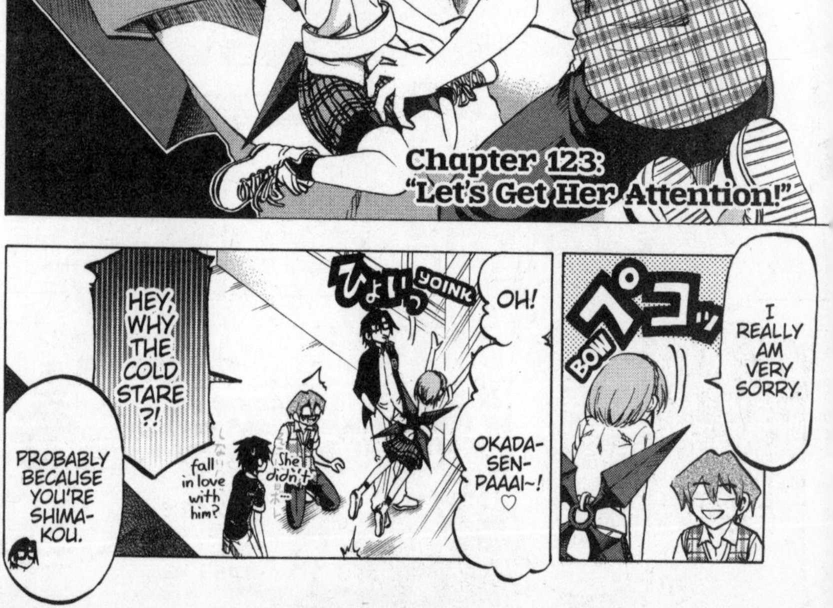
ペコッ
BOW
I REALLY AM VERY SORRY.
ひょいっ
YOINK
OH!
OKADA-SEN-PAAAI~! ♡
She didn't...
fall in love with him?
HEY, WHY THE COLD STARE?!
PROBABLY BECAUSE YOU'RE SHIMA-KOU.

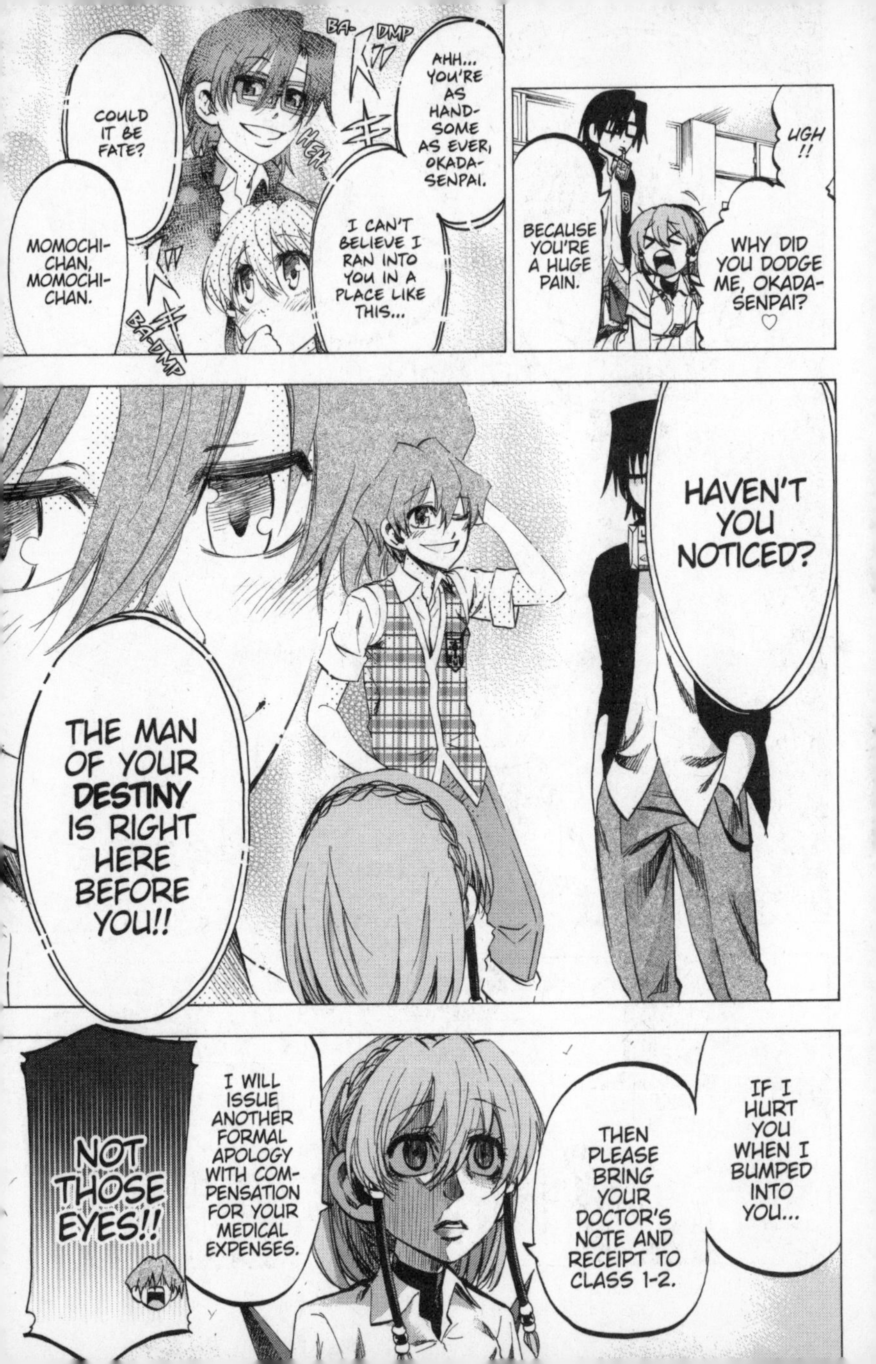
UGH!!
WHY DID YOU DODGE ME, OKADA-SENPAI? ♡
BECAUSE YOU'RE A HUGE PAIN.
BA-DMP
AHH... YOU'RE AS HANDSOME AS EVER, OKADA-SENPAI.
I CAN'T BELIEVE I RAN INTO YOU IN A PLACE LIKE THIS...
HEH...
COULD IT BE FATE?
MOMOCHI-CHAN, MOMOCHI-CHAN.
BA-DMP
HAVEN'T YOU NOTICED?
THE MAN OF YOUR DESTINY IS RIGHT HERE BEFORE YOU!!
IF I HURT YOU WHEN I BUMPED INTO YOU...
THEN PLEASE BRING YOUR DOCTOR'S NOTE AND RECEIPT TO CLASS 1-2.
I WILL ISSUE ANOTHER FORMAL APOLOGY WITH COMPENSATION FOR YOUR MEDICAL EXPENSES.
NOT THOSE EYES!!

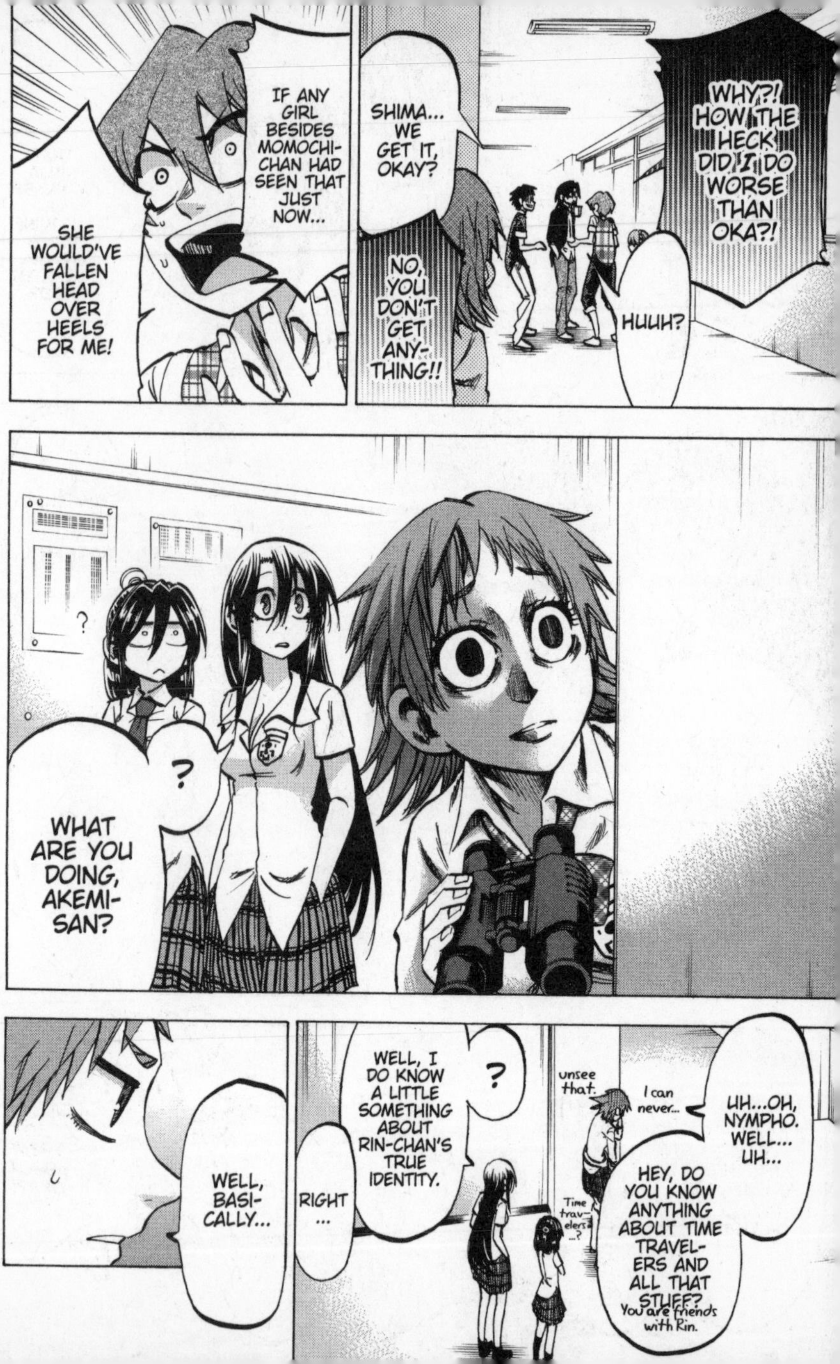
WHY?! HOW THE HECK DID I DO WORSE THAN OKA?!
SHIMA... WE GET IT, OKAY?
HUUH?
NO, YOU DON'T GET ANY-THING!!
IF ANY GIRL BESIDES MOMOCHI-CHAN HAD SEEN THAT JUST NOW...
SHE WOULD'VE FALLEN HEAD OVER HEELS FOR ME!
?
?
WHAT ARE YOU DOING, AKEMI-SAN?
UH...OH, NYMPHO. WELL... UH...
I can never...
unsee that.
HEY, DO YOU KNOW ANYTHING ABOUT TIME TRAVEL-ERS AND ALL THAT STUFF?
You are friends with Rin.
Time trav-elers...?
?
WELL, I DO KNOW A LITTLE SOMETHING ABOUT RIN-CHAN'S TRUE IDENTITY.
RIGHT...
WELL, BASI-CALLY...

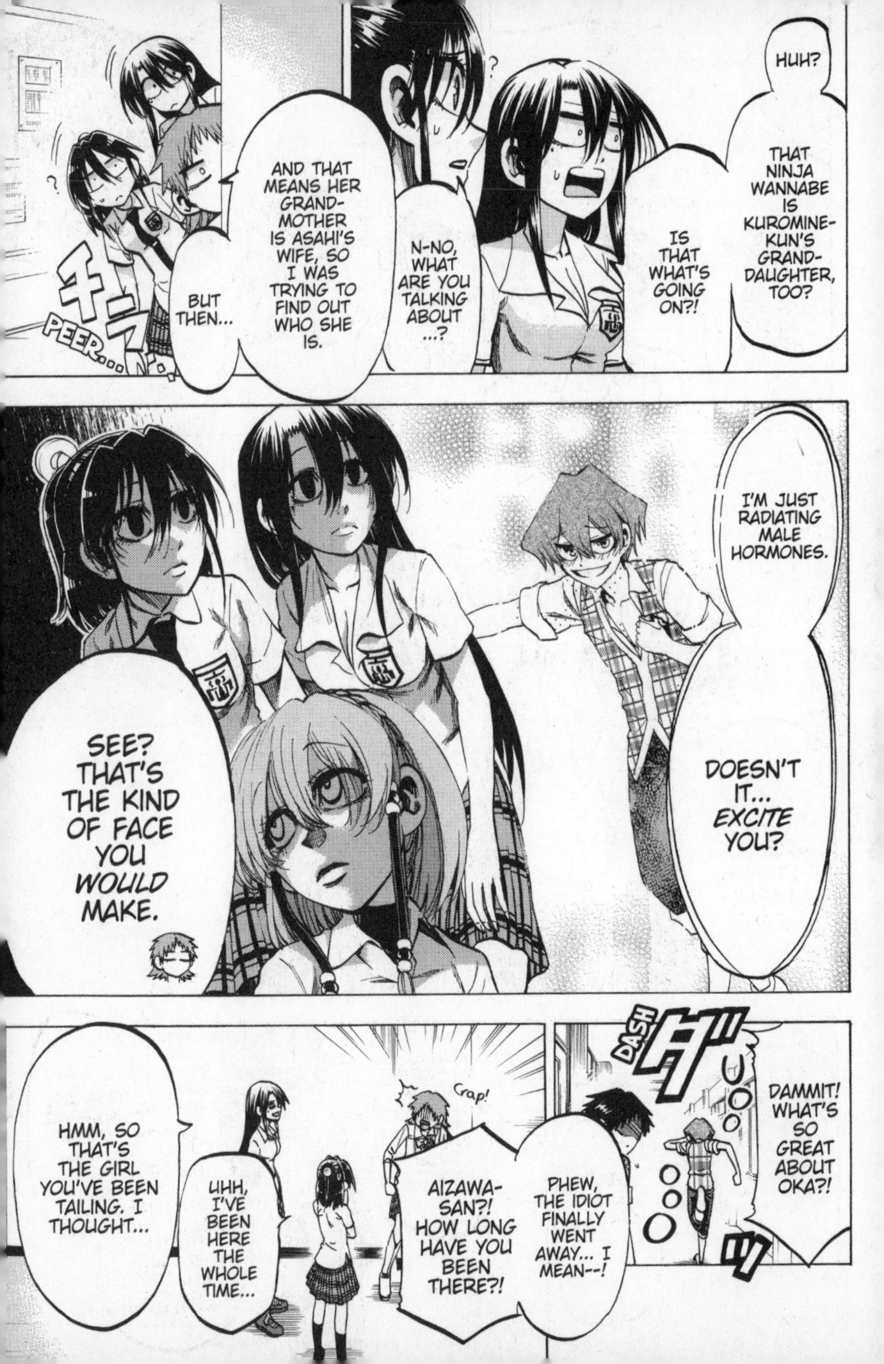
HUH?
THAT NINJA WANNABE IS KUROMINE-KUN'S GRAND-DAUGHTER, TOO?
IS THAT WHAT'S GOING ON?!
N-NO, WHAT ARE YOU TALKING ABOUT ...?
AND THAT MEANS HER GRAND-MOTHER IS ASAHI'S WIFE, SO I WAS TRYING TO FIND OUT WHO SHE IS.
BUT THEN...
PEER...
I'M JUST RADIATING MALE HORMONES.
DOESN'T IT... *EXCITE* YOU?
SEE? THAT'S THE KIND OF FACE YOU *WOULD* MAKE.
DASH
DAMMIT! WHAT'S SO GREAT ABOUT OKA?!
PHEW, THE IDIOT FINALLY WENT AWAY... I MEAN--!
Crap!
AIZAWA-SAN?! HOW LONG HAVE YOU BEEN THERE?!
UHH, I'VE BEEN HERE THE WHOLE TIME...
HMM, SO THAT'S THE GIRL YOU'VE BEEN TAILING. I THOUGHT...

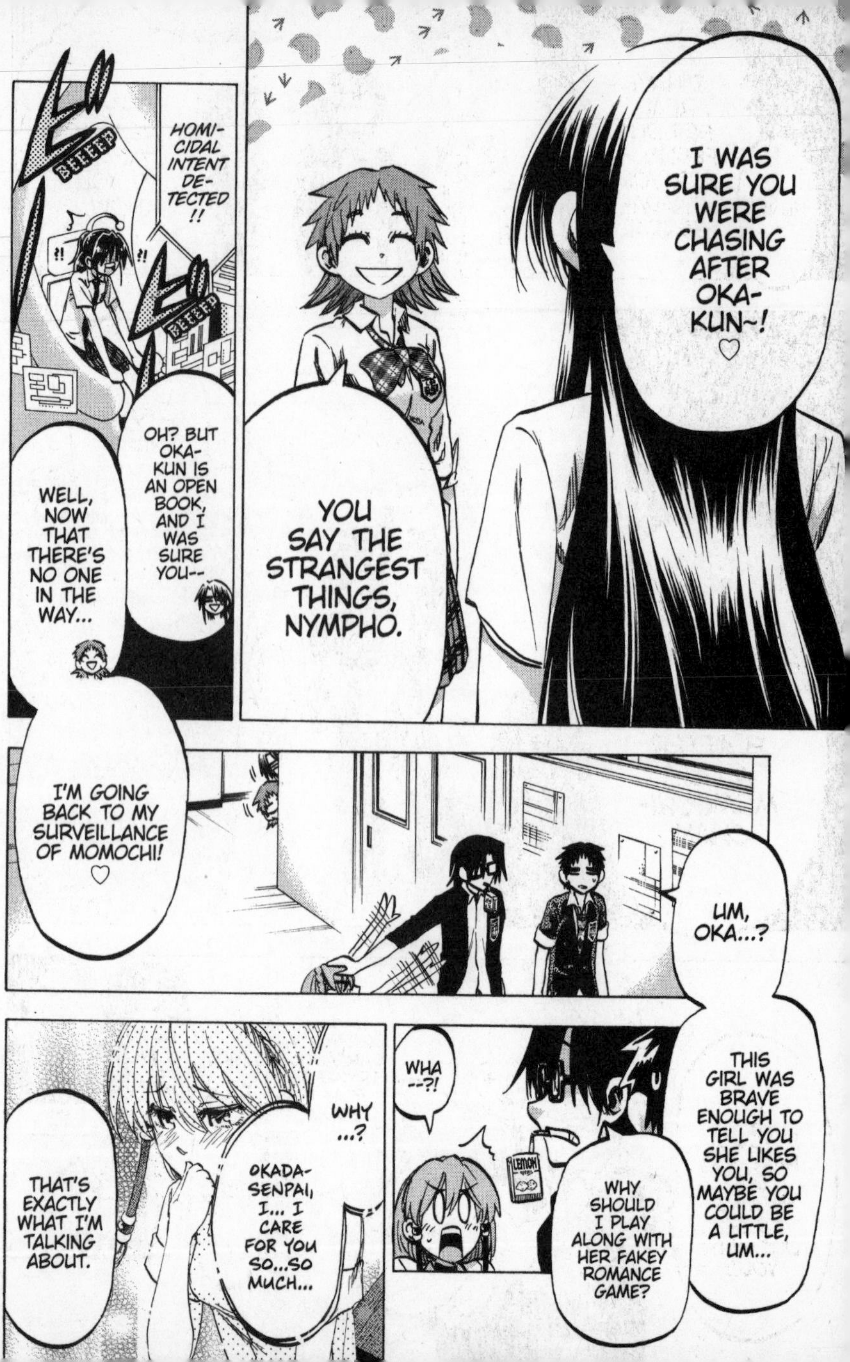
I WAS SURE YOU WERE CHASING AFTER OKA-KUN~! ♡
YOU SAY THE STRANGEST THINGS, NYMPHO.
HOMICIDAL INTENT DETECTED!!
?!
?!
OH? BUT OKA-KUN IS AN OPEN BOOK, AND I WAS SURE YOU--
WELL, NOW THAT THERE'S NO ONE IN THE WAY...
I'M GOING BACK TO MY SURVEILLANCE OF MOMOCHI! ♡
UM, OKA...?
THIS GIRL WAS BRAVE ENOUGH TO TELL YOU SHE LIKES YOU, SO MAYBE YOU COULD BE A LITTLE, UM...
WHY SHOULD I PLAY ALONG WITH HER FAKEY ROMANCE GAME?
WHA--?!
LEMON
WHY...?
OKADA-SENPAI, I... I CARE FOR YOU SO...SO MUCH...
THAT'S EXACTLY WHAT I'M TALKING ABOUT.

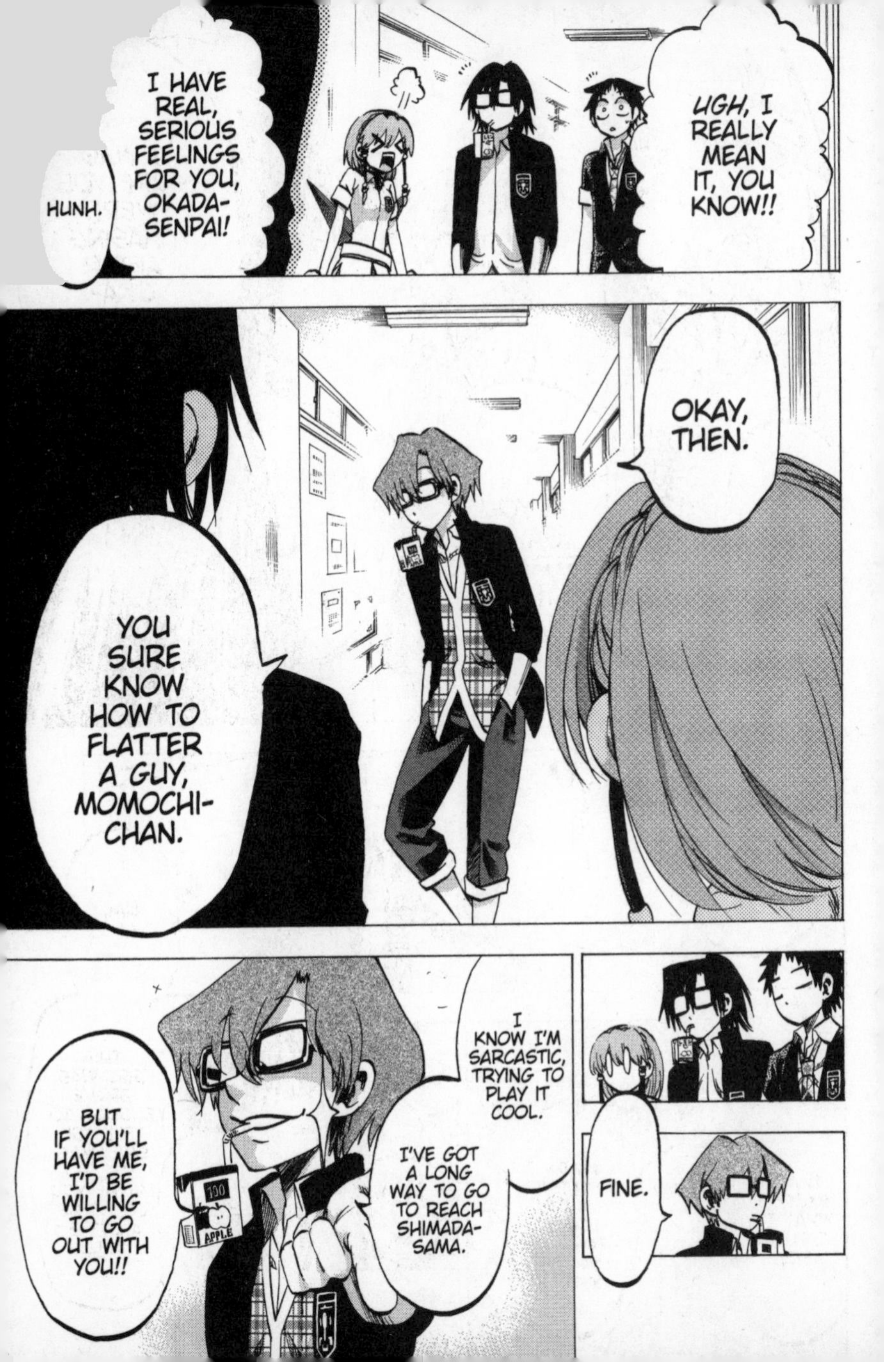
UGH, I REALLY MEAN IT, YOU KNOW!!
I HAVE REAL, SERIOUS FEELINGS FOR YOU, OKADA-SENPAI!
HUNH.
OKAY, THEN.
YOU SURE KNOW HOW TO FLATTER A GUY, MOMOCHI-CHAN.
FINE.
I KNOW I'M SARCASTIC, TRYING TO PLAY IT COOL.
I'VE GOT A LONG WAY TO GO TO REACH SHIMADA-SAMA.
BUT IF YOU'LL HAVE ME, I'D BE WILLING TO GO OUT WITH YOU!!
100
APPLE

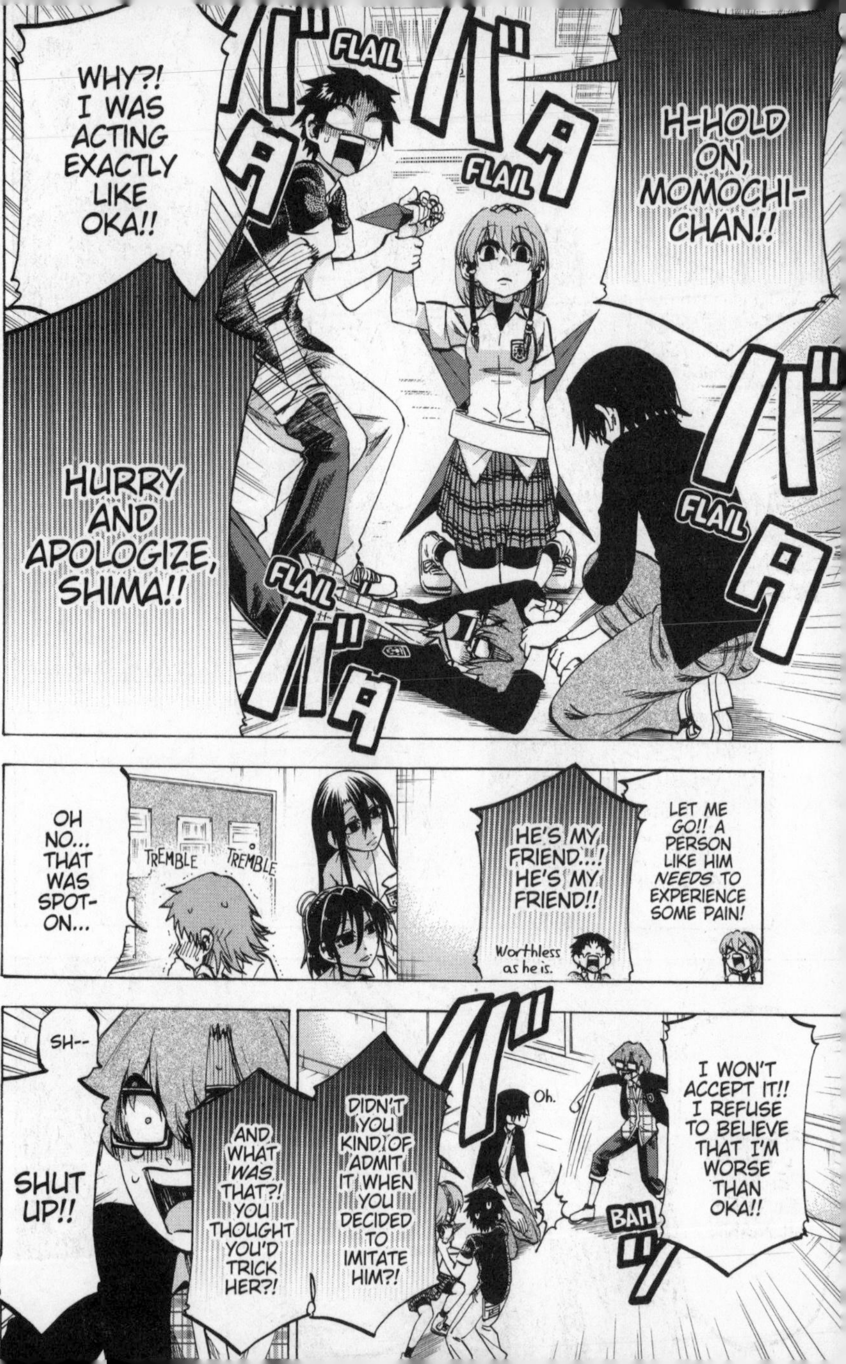
H-HOLD ON, MOMOCHI-CHAN!!
バタ FLAIL
バタ FLAIL
WHY?! I WAS ACTING EXACTLY LIKE OKA!!
バタ FLAIL
バタ FLAIL
HURRY AND APOLOGIZE, SHIMA!!
LET ME GO!! A PERSON LIKE HIM *NEEDS* TO EXPERIENCE SOME PAIN!
HE'S MY FRIEND...! HE'S MY FRIEND!!
Worthless as he is.
TREMBLE TREMBLE
OH NO... THAT WAS SPOT-ON...
I WON'T ACCEPT IT!! I REFUSE TO BELIEVE THAT I'M WORSE THAN OKA!!
Oh.
バッ BAH
DIDN'T YOU KIND OF ADMIT IT WHEN YOU DECIDED TO IMITATE HIM?!
AND WHAT *WAS* THAT?! YOU THOUGHT YOU'D TRICK HER?!
SH--
SHUT UP!!

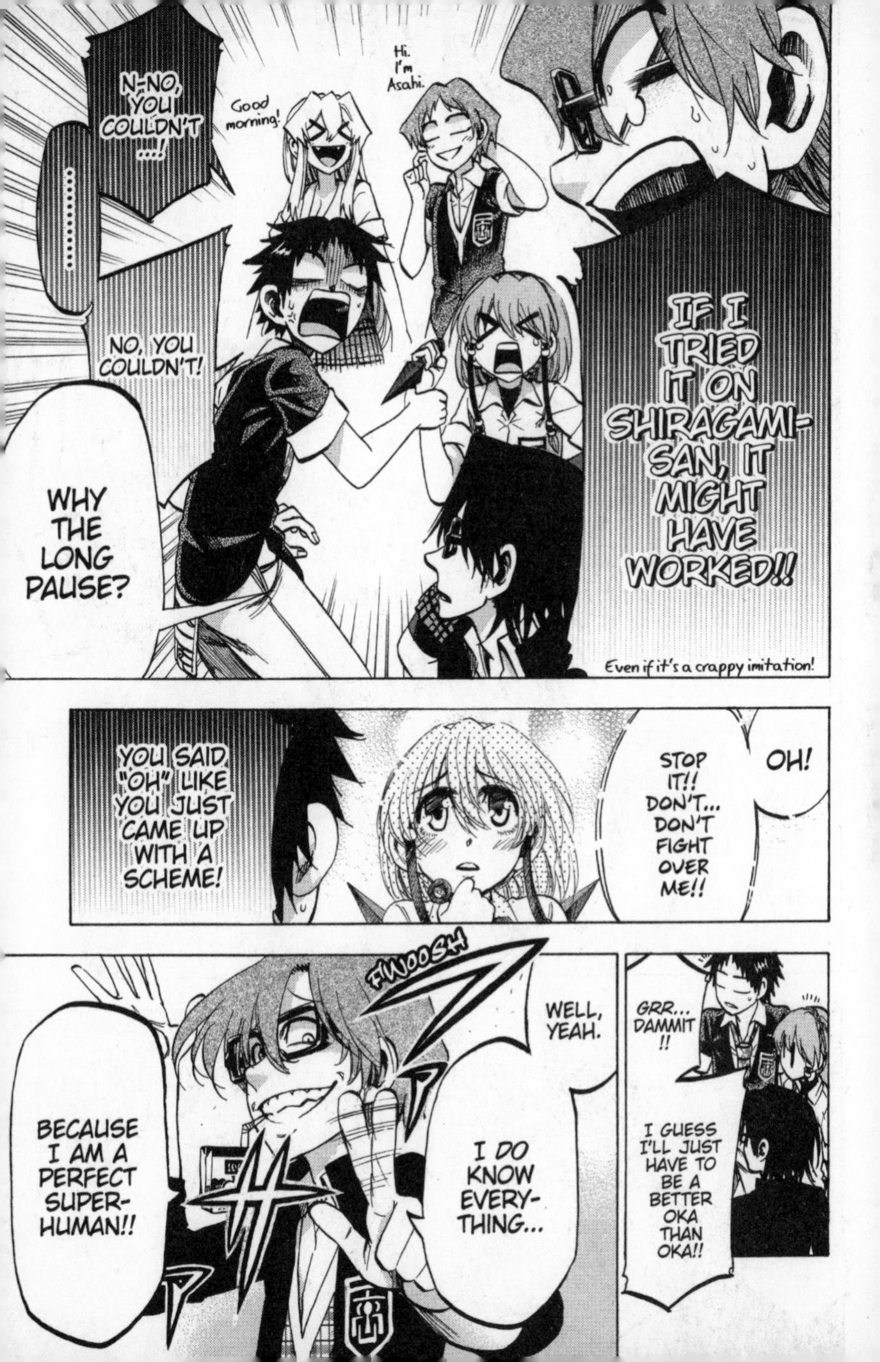
IF I TRIED IT ON SHIRAGAMI-SAN, IT MIGHT HAVE WORKED!!
Hi. I'm Asahi.
Good morning!
N-NO, YOU COULDN'T ...!
......
NO, YOU COULDN'T!
WHY THE LONG PAUSE?
Even if it's a crappy imitation!
OH!
STOP IT!! DON'T... DON'T FIGHT OVER ME!!
YOU SAID "OH" LIKE YOU JUST CAME UP WITH A SCHEME!
GRR... DAMMIT!!
I GUESS I'LL JUST HAVE TO BE A BETTER OKA THAN OKA!!
WELL, YEAH.
FWOOSH
I DO KNOW EVERY-THING...
BECAUSE I AM A PERFECT SUPER-HUMAN!!

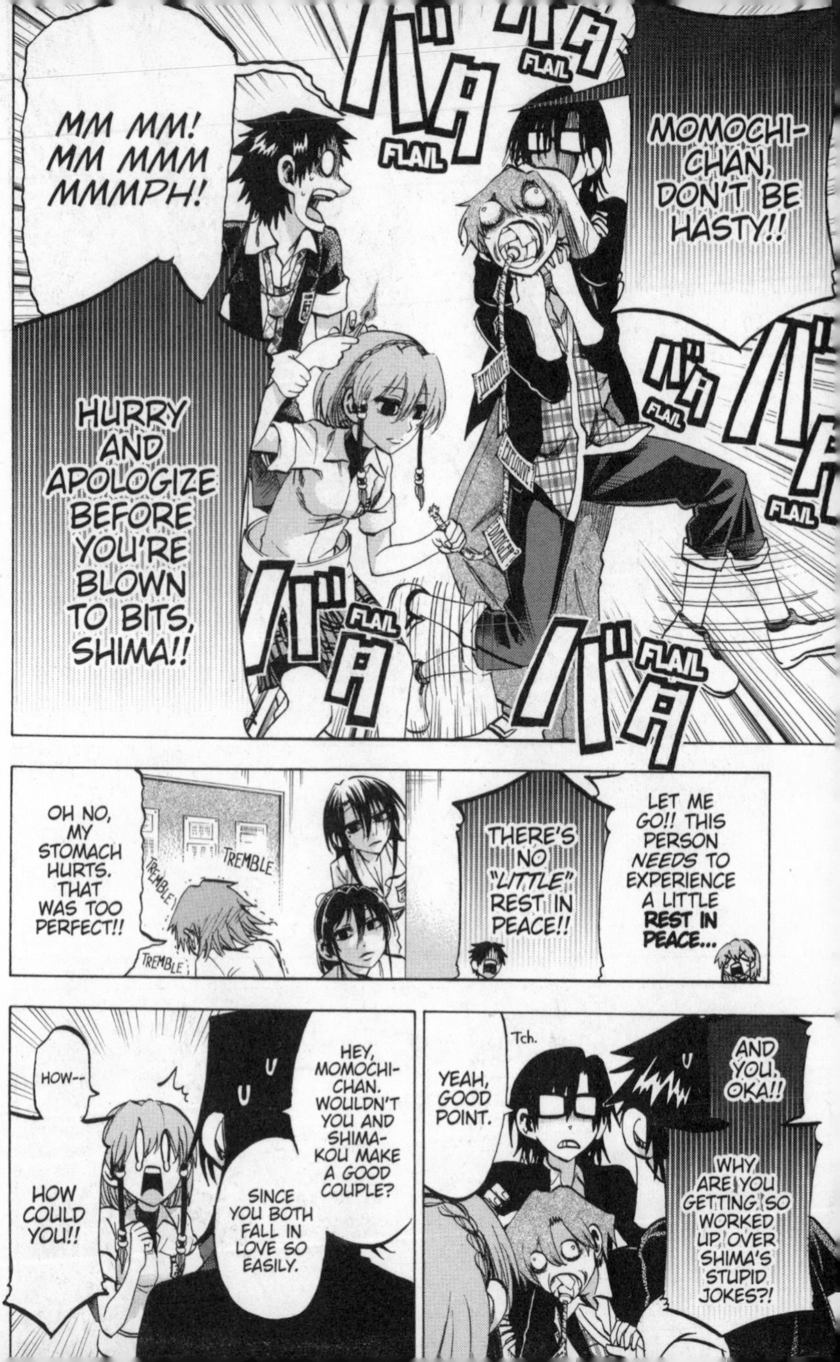
FLAIL
FLAIL
MOMOCHI-CHAN, DON'T BE HASTY!!
MM MM! MM MMM MMMPH!
FLAIL
FLAIL
HURRY AND APOLOGIZE BEFORE YOU'RE BLOWN TO BITS, SHIMA!!
FLAIL
FLAIL
LET ME GO!! THIS PERSON NEEDS TO EXPERIENCE A LITTLE REST IN PEACE...
THERE'S NO "LITTLE" REST IN PEACE!!
TREMBLE
TREMBLE
TREMBLE
OH NO, MY STOMACH HURTS. THAT WAS TOO PERFECT!!
AND YOU, OKA!!
WHY ARE YOU GETTING SO WORKED UP OVER SHIMA'S STUPID JOKES?!
Tch.
YEAH, GOOD POINT.
HEY, MOMOCHI-CHAN. WOULDN'T YOU AND SHIMA-KOU MAKE A GOOD COUPLE?
SINCE YOU BOTH FALL IN LOVE SO EASILY.
HOW--
HOW COULD YOU!!

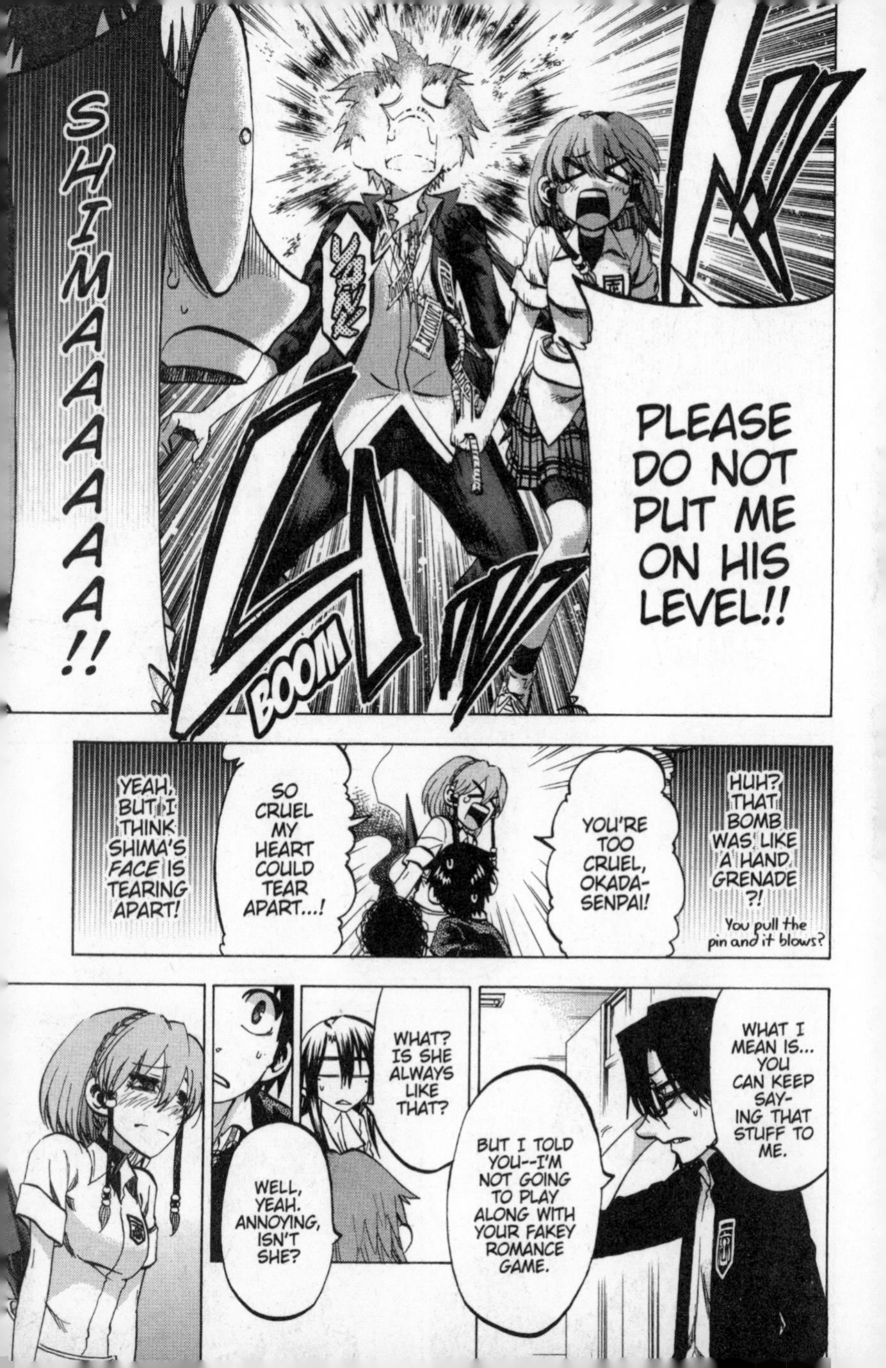
PLEASE DO NOT PUT ME ON HIS LEVEL!!
BOOM
SHIMAAAAAAA!!
HUH? THAT BOMB WAS LIKE A HAND GRENADE?!
You pull the pin and it blows?
YOU'RE TOO CRUEL, OKADA-SENPAI!
SO CRUEL MY HEART COULD TEAR APART...!
YEAH, BUT I THINK SHIMA'S FACE IS TEARING APART!
WHAT I MEAN IS... YOU CAN KEEP SAYING THAT STUFF TO ME.
BUT I TOLD YOU--I'M NOT GOING TO PLAY ALONG WITH YOUR FAKEY ROMANCE GAME.
WHAT? IS SHE ALWAYS LIKE THAT?
WELL, YEAH. ANNOYING, ISN'T SHE?

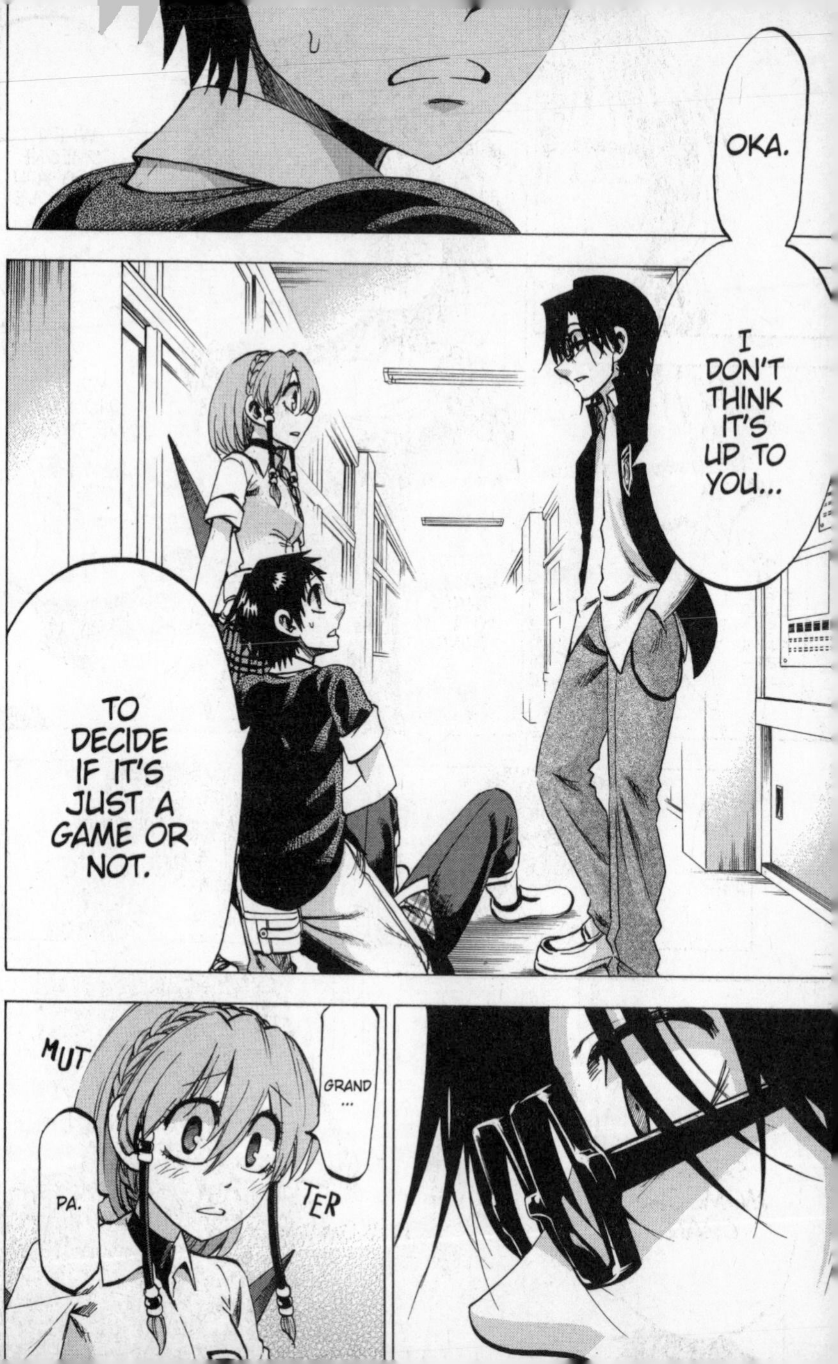
OKA.
I DON'T THINK IT'S UP TO YOU...
TO DECIDE IF IT'S JUST A GAME OR NOT.
GRAND ...
MUT
TER
PA.

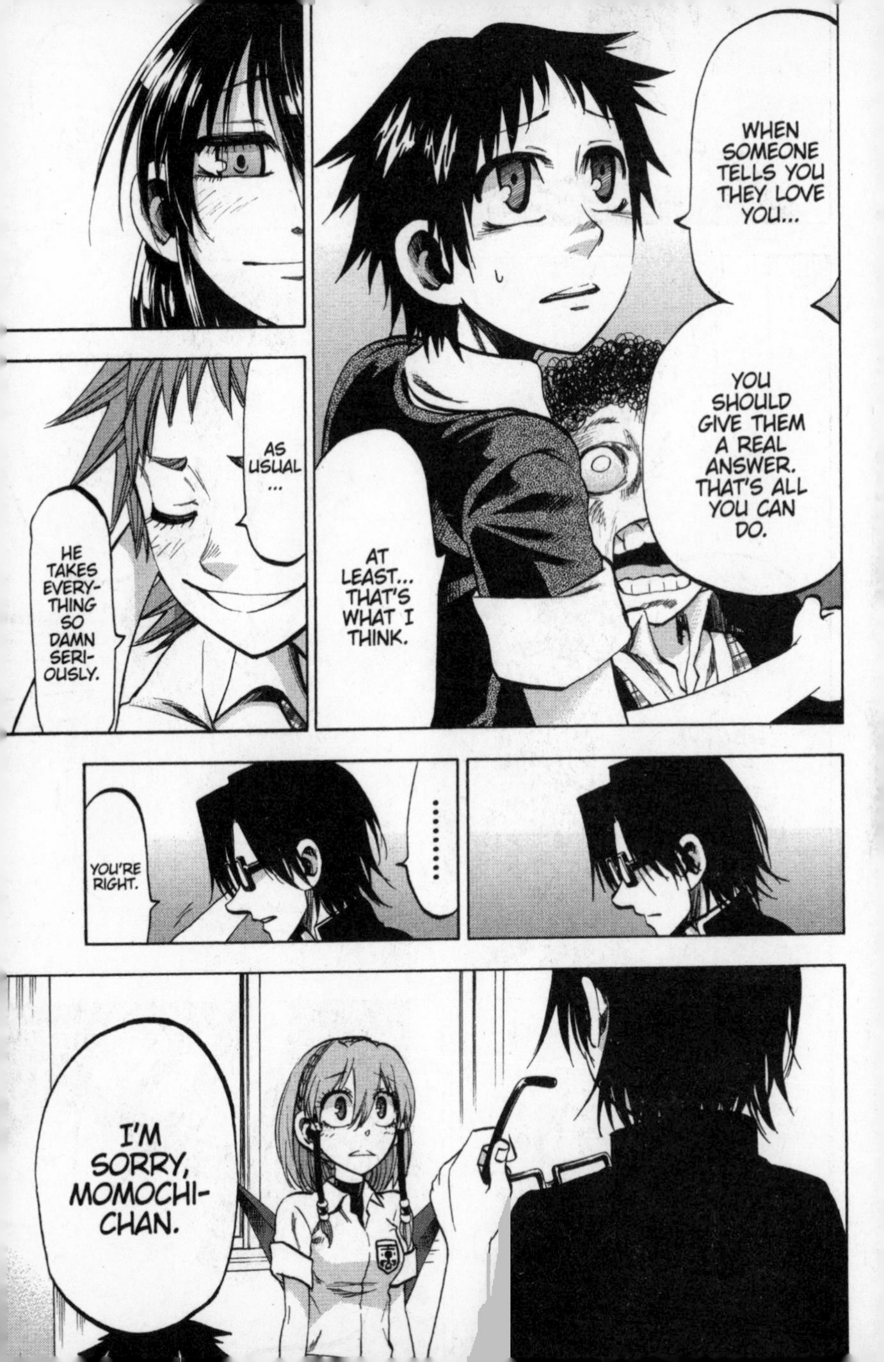
WHEN SOMEONE TELLS YOU THEY LOVE YOU...
YOU SHOULD GIVE THEM A REAL ANSWER. THAT'S ALL YOU CAN DO.
AT LEAST... THAT'S WHAT I THINK.
AS USUAL...
HE TAKES EVERYTHING SO DAMN SERIOUSLY.
......
YOU'RE RIGHT.
I'M SORRY, MOMOCHI-CHAN.

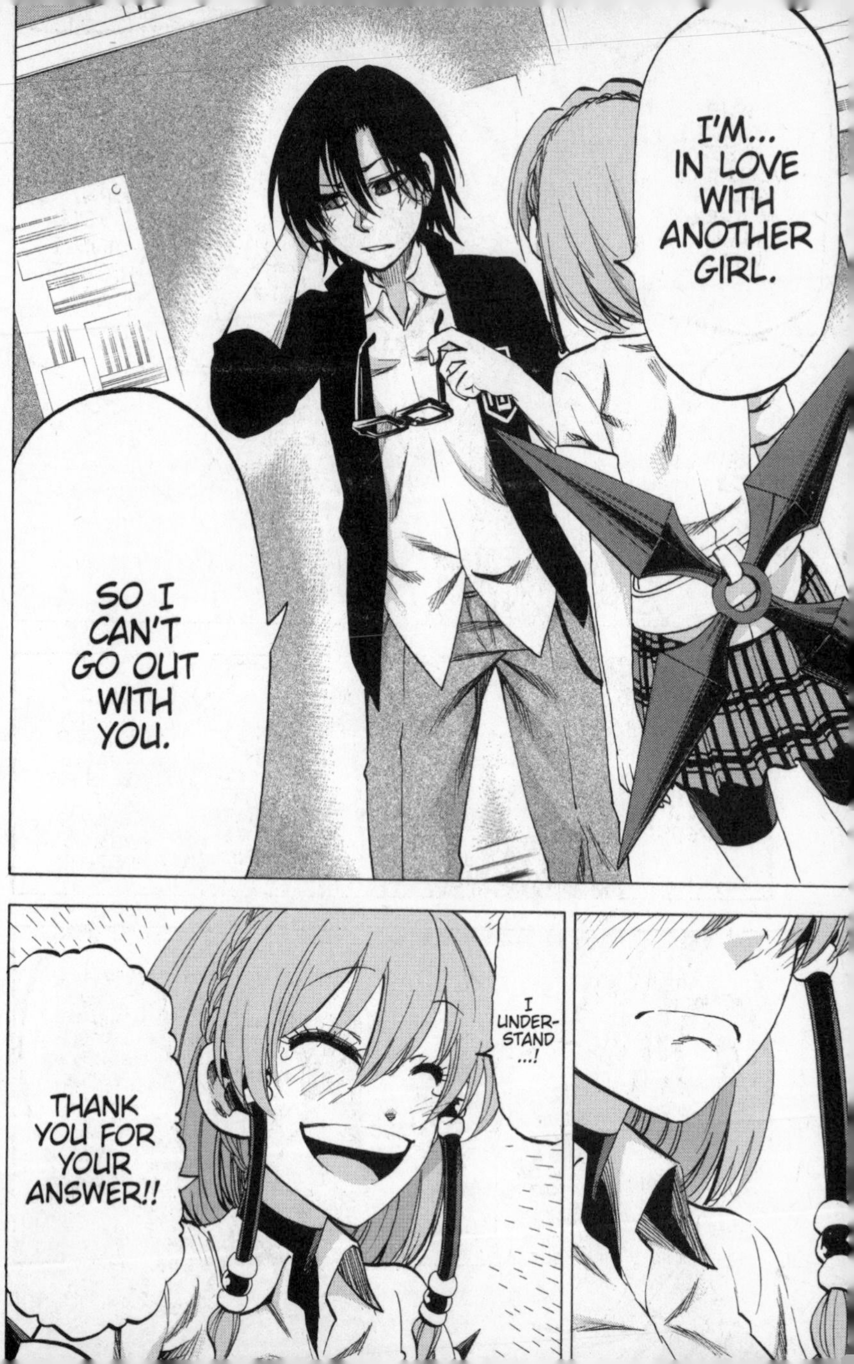

I'M... IN LOVE WITH ANOTHER GIRL.
SO I CAN'T GO OUT WITH YOU.
I UNDER-STAND ...!
THANK YOU FOR YOUR ANSWER!!

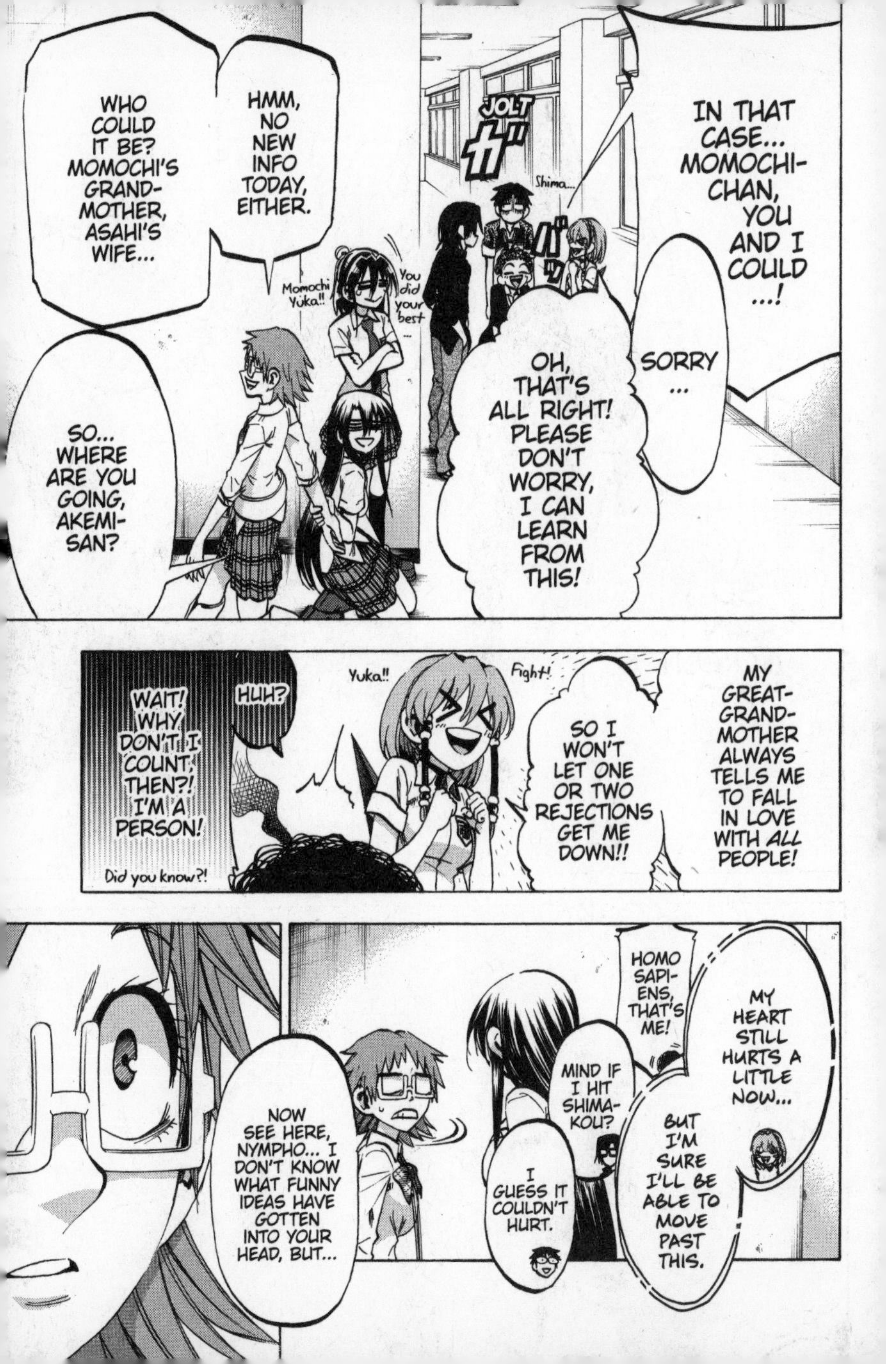
IN THAT CASE... MOMOCHI-CHAN, YOU AND I COULD ...!
SORRY ...
OH, THAT'S ALL RIGHT! PLEASE DON'T WORRY, I CAN LEARN FROM THIS!
JOLT
Shima...
You did your best ...
Momochi Yuka!!
HMM, NO NEW INFO TODAY, EITHER.
WHO COULD IT BE? MOMOCHI'S GRAND-MOTHER, ASAHI'S WIFE...
SO... WHERE ARE YOU GOING, AKEMI-SAN?
MY GREAT-GRANDMOTHER ALWAYS TELLS ME TO FALL IN LOVE WITH ALL PEOPLE!
SO I WON'T LET ONE OR TWO REJECTIONS GET ME DOWN!!
Fight!
Yuka!!
HUH?
WAIT! WHY DON'T I COUNT, THEN?! I'M A PERSON!
Did you know?!
MY HEART STILL HURTS A LITTLE NOW...
BUT I'M SURE I'LL BE ABLE TO MOVE PAST THIS.
HOMO SAPIENS, THAT'S ME!
MIND IF I HIT SHIMA-KOU?
I GUESS IT COULDN'T HURT.
NOW SEE HERE, NYMPHO... I DON'T KNOW WHAT FUNNY IDEAS HAVE GOTTEN INTO YOUR HEAD, BUT...

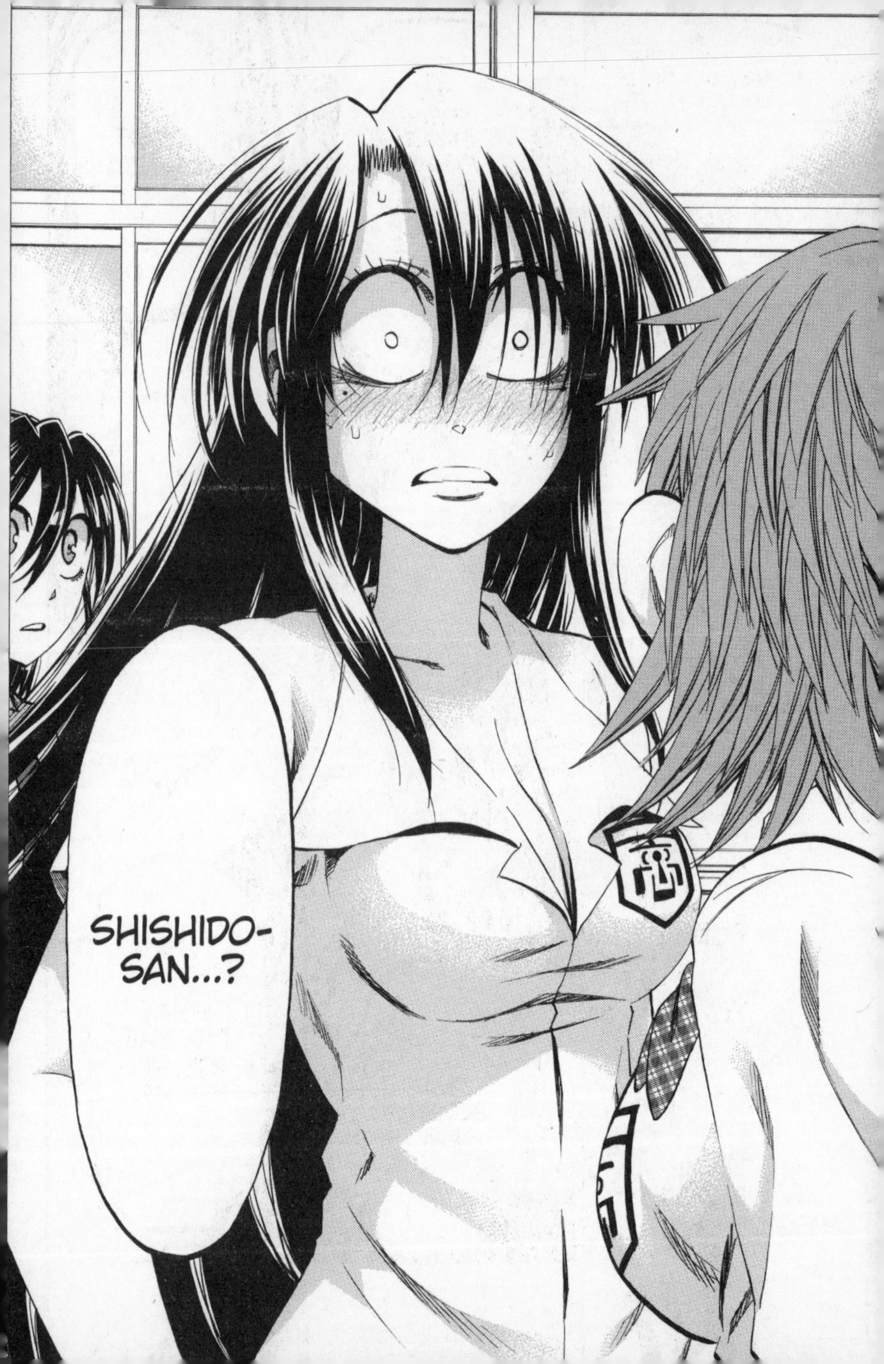
SHISHIDO-SAN...?

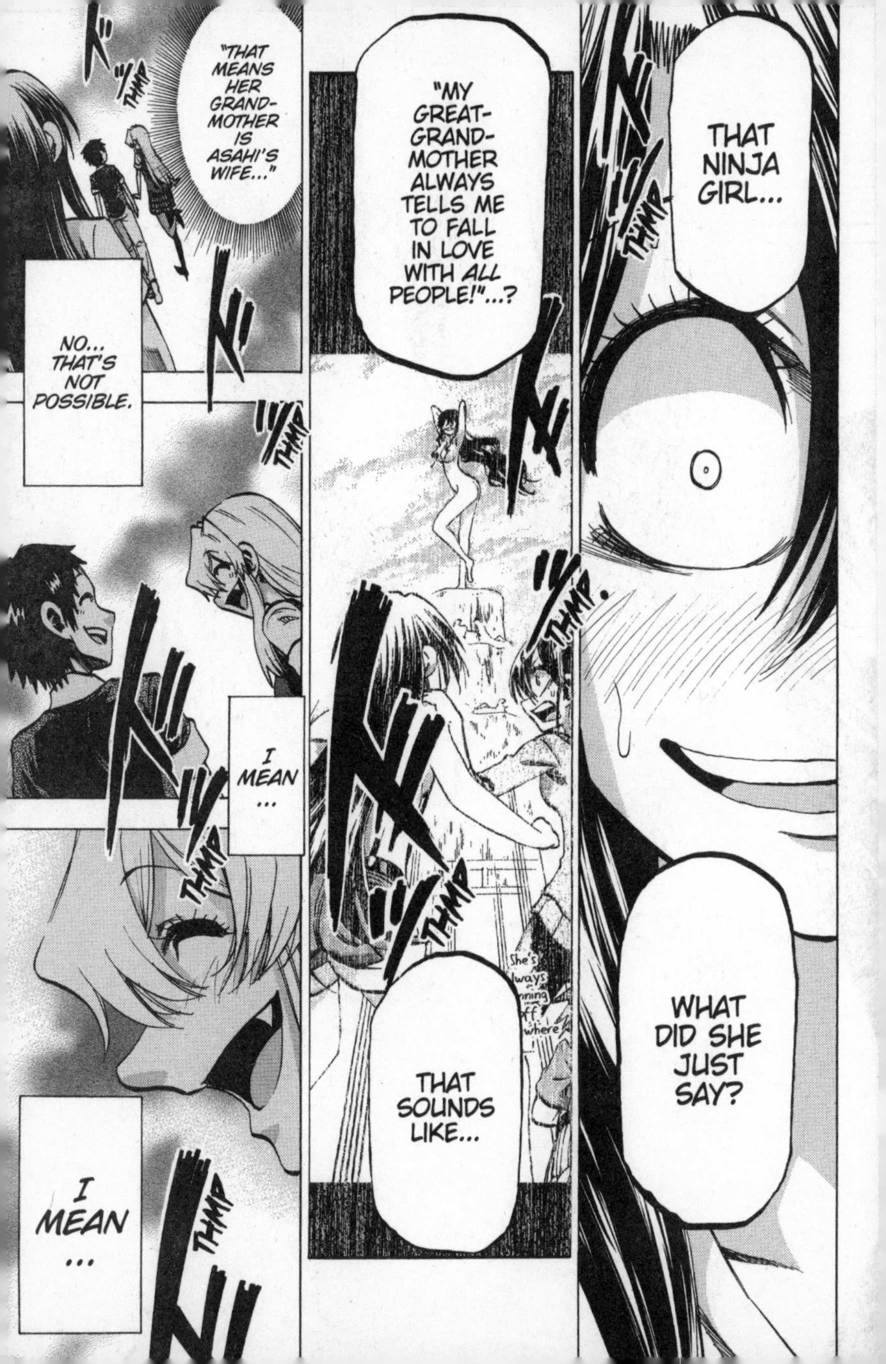
THAT NINJA GIRL...
THMP
THMP
WHAT DID SHE JUST SAY?
"MY GREAT-GRAND-MOTHER ALWAYS TELLS ME TO FALL IN LOVE WITH ALL PEOPLE!"...?
THMP
THMP
THAT SOUNDS LIKE...
"THAT MEANS HER GRAND-MOTHER IS ASAHI'S WIFE..."
THMP
NO... THAT'S NOT POSSIBLE.
THMP
I MEAN ...
THMP
I MEAN ...
THMP

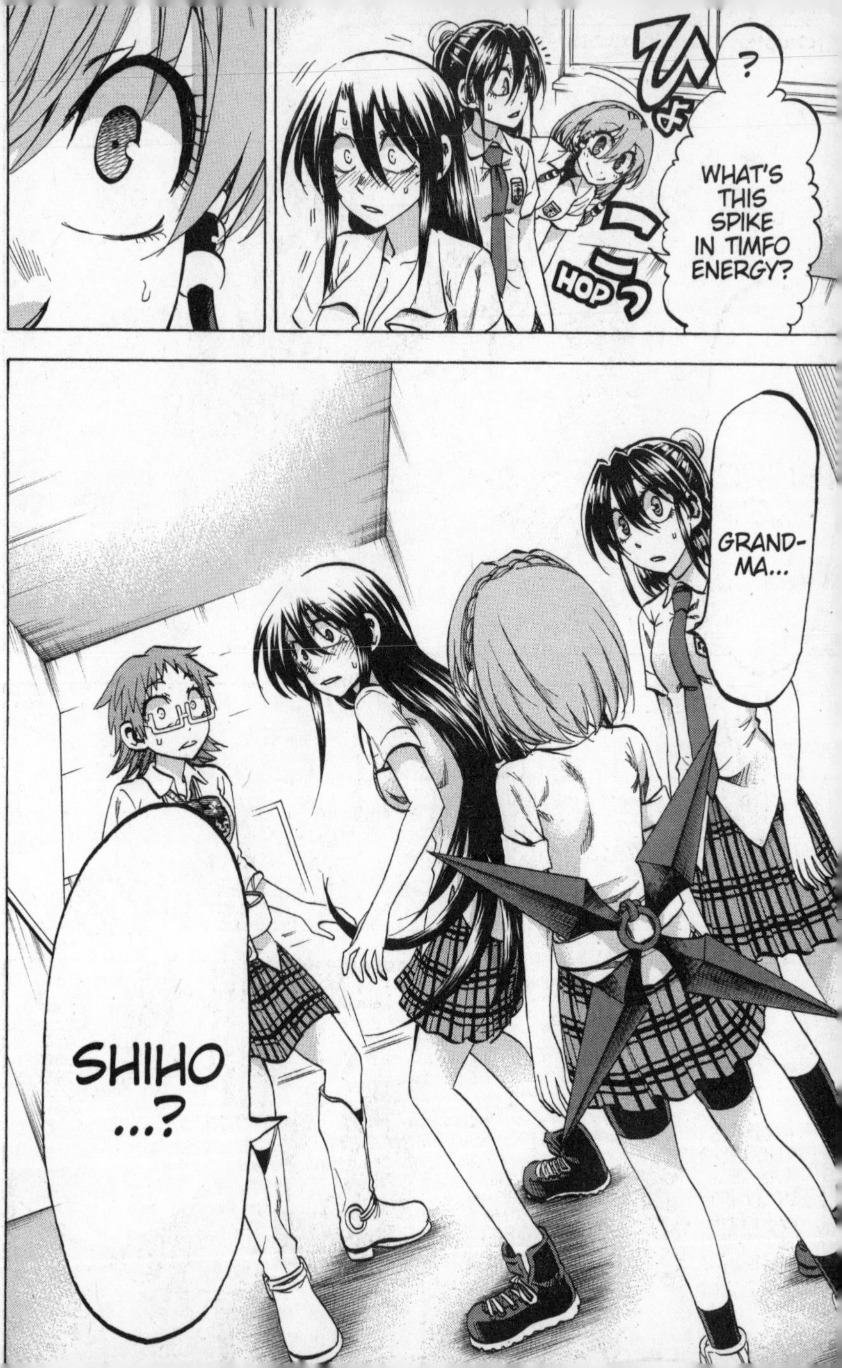
ひょ
?
WHAT'S THIS SPIKE IN TIMFO ENERGY?
HOP
GRAND-MA...
SHIHO ...?

Chapter 124: "Let's Change the Future!"

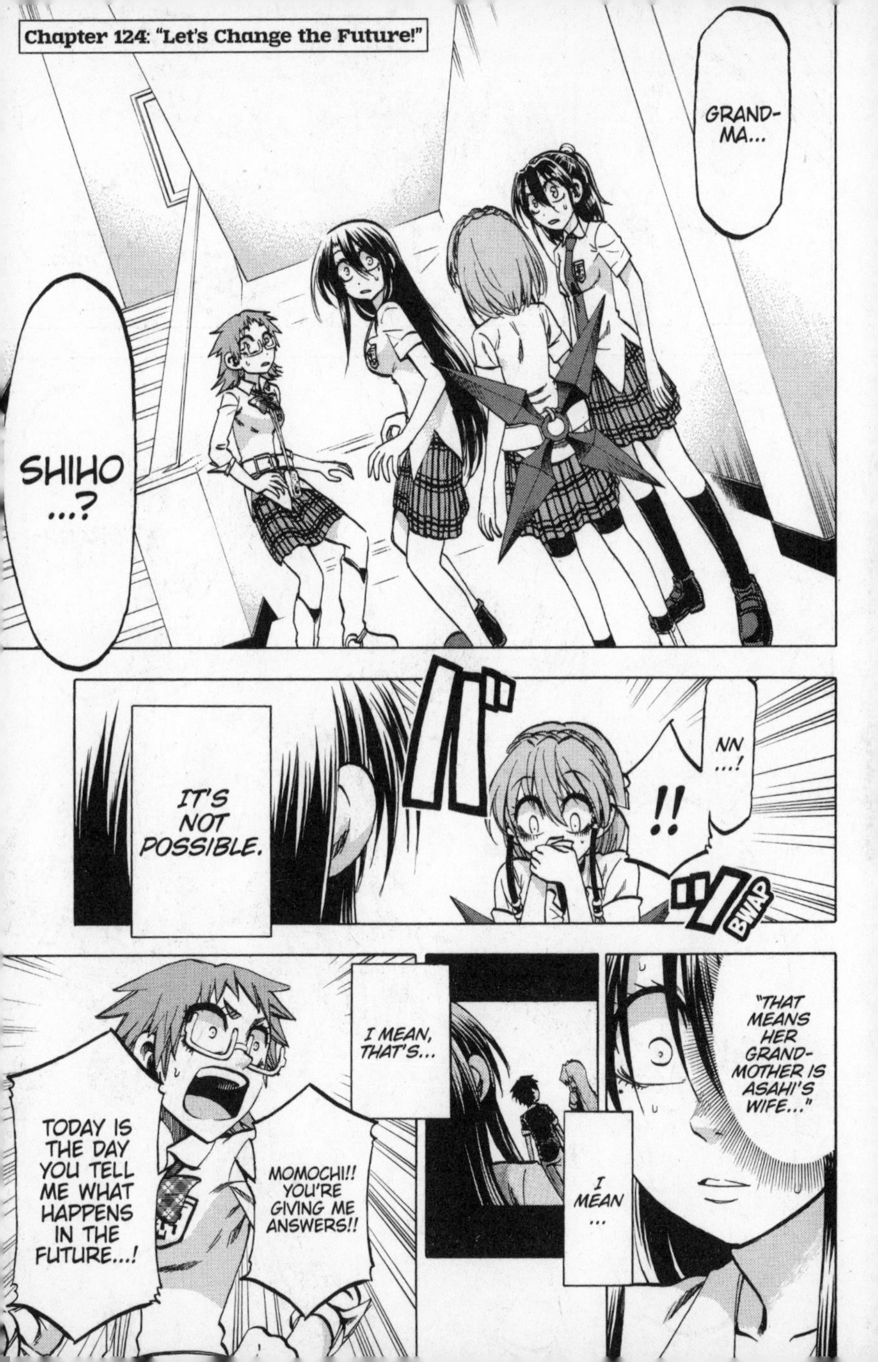
GRAND-MA...
SHIHO ...?
NN ...!
!!
BWAP
IT'S NOT POSSIBLE.
"THAT MEANS HER GRAND-MOTHER IS ASAHI'S WIFE..."
I MEAN ...
I MEAN, THAT'S...
MOMOCHI!! YOU'RE GIVING ME ANSWERS!!
TODAY IS THE DAY YOU TELL ME WHAT HAPPENS IN THE FUTURE...!

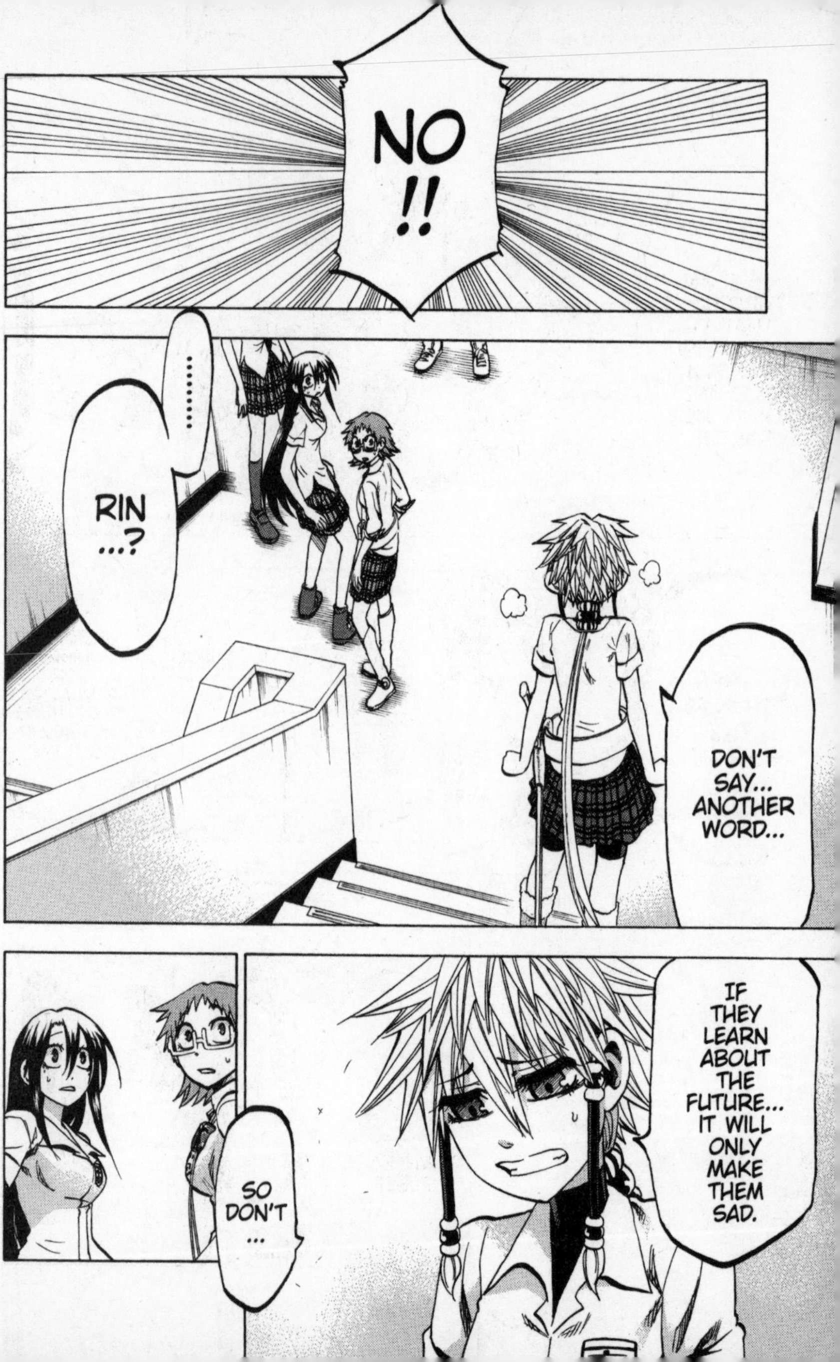
NO!!
......
RIN ...?
DON'T SAY... ANOTHER WORD...
IF THEY LEARN ABOUT THE FUTURE... IT WILL ONLY MAKE THEM SAD.
SO DON'T ...

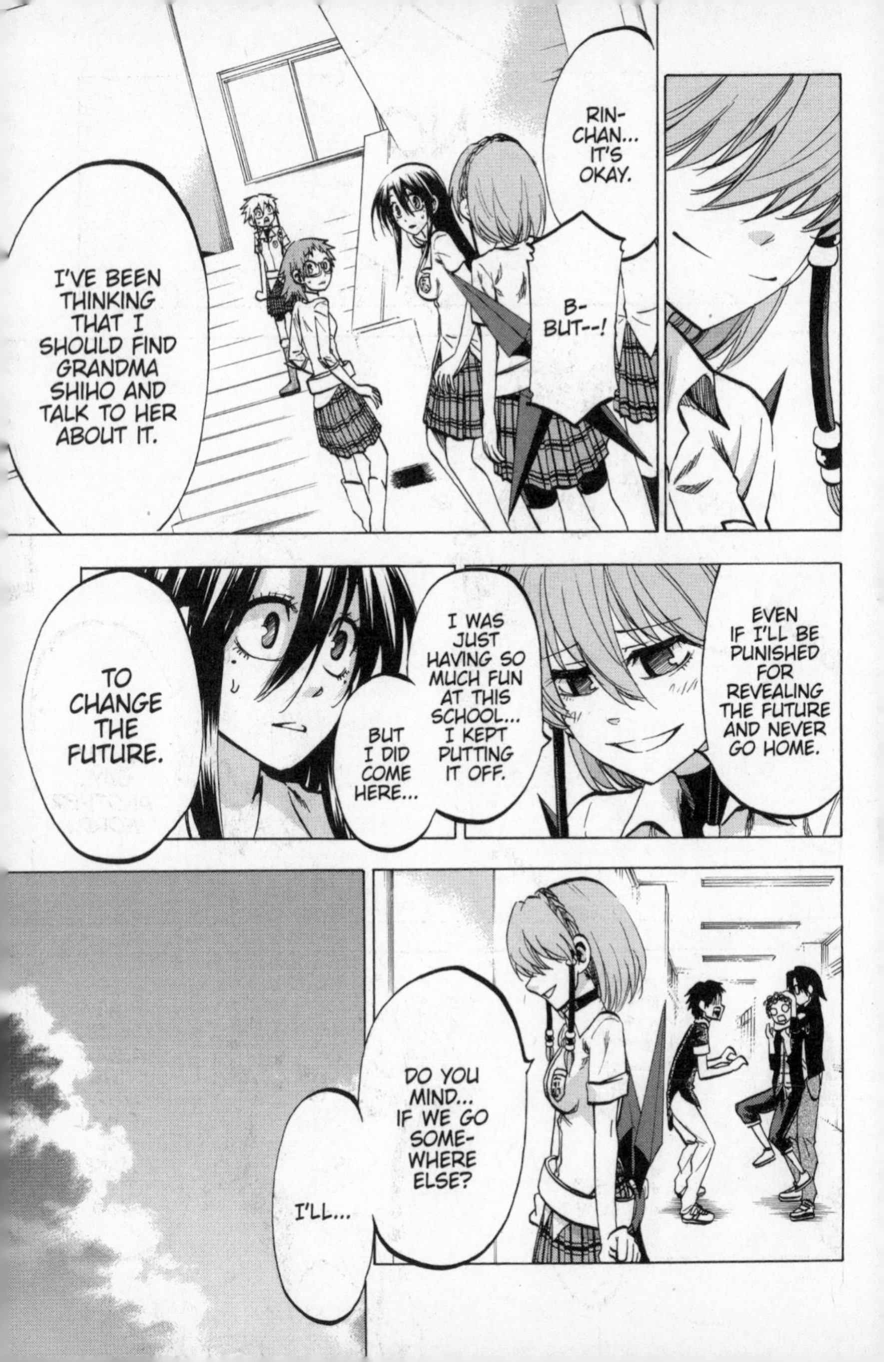
RIN-CHAN... IT'S OKAY.
B-BUT--!
I'VE BEEN THINKING THAT I SHOULD FIND GRANDMA SHIHO AND TALK TO HER ABOUT IT.
EVEN IF I'LL BE PUNISHED FOR REVEALING THE FUTURE AND NEVER GO HOME.
I WAS JUST HAVING SO MUCH FUN AT THIS SCHOOL... I KEPT PUTTING IT OFF.
BUT I DID COME HERE...
TO CHANGE THE FUTURE.
DO YOU MIND... IF WE GO SOME-WHERE ELSE?
I'LL...

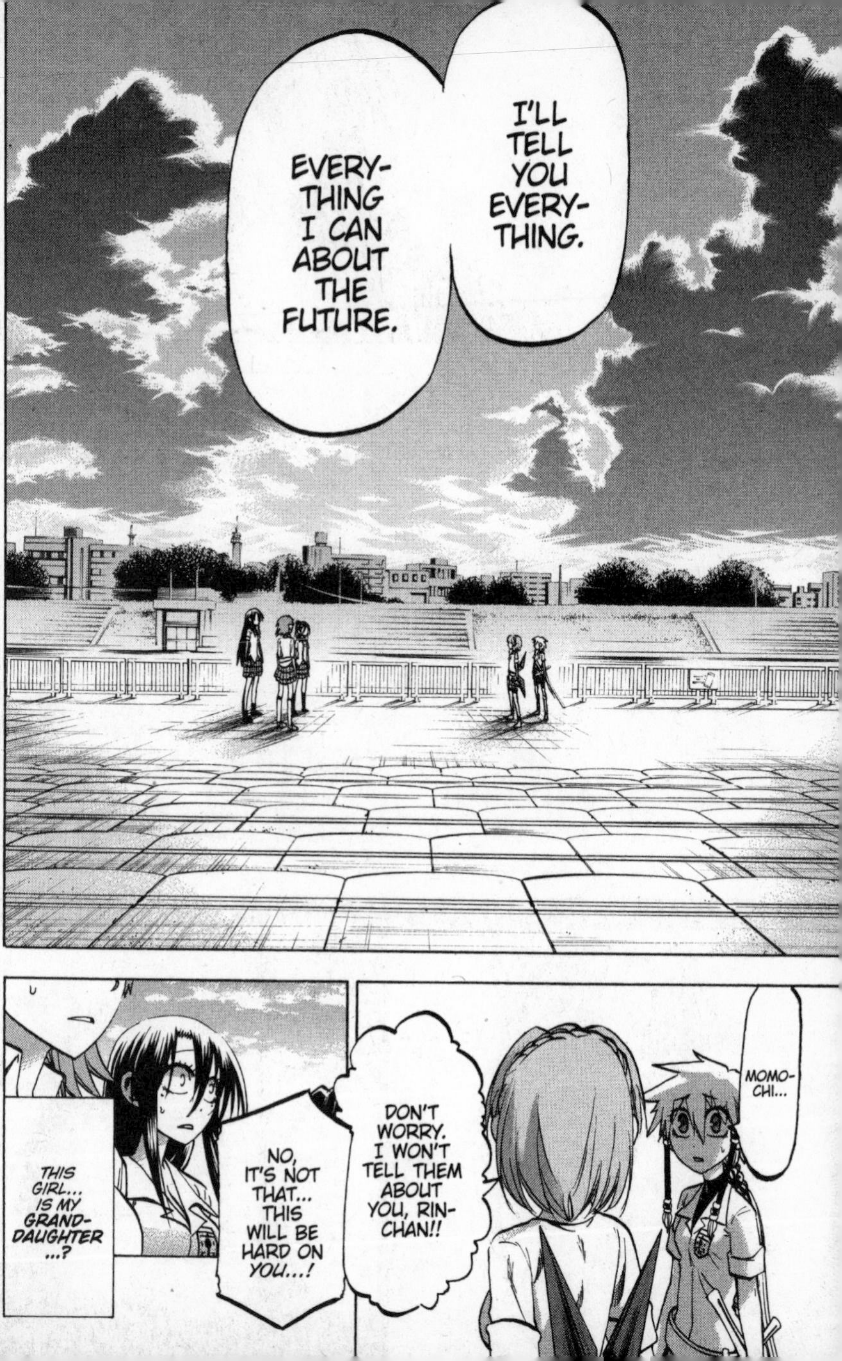
I'LL TELL YOU EVERY-THING.
EVERY-THING I CAN ABOUT THE FUTURE.
MOMO-CHI...
DON'T WORRY. I WON'T TELL THEM ABOUT YOU, RIN-CHAN!!
NO, IT'S NOT THAT... THIS WILL BE HARD ON YOU...!
THIS GIRL... IS MY GRAND-DAUGHTER ...?

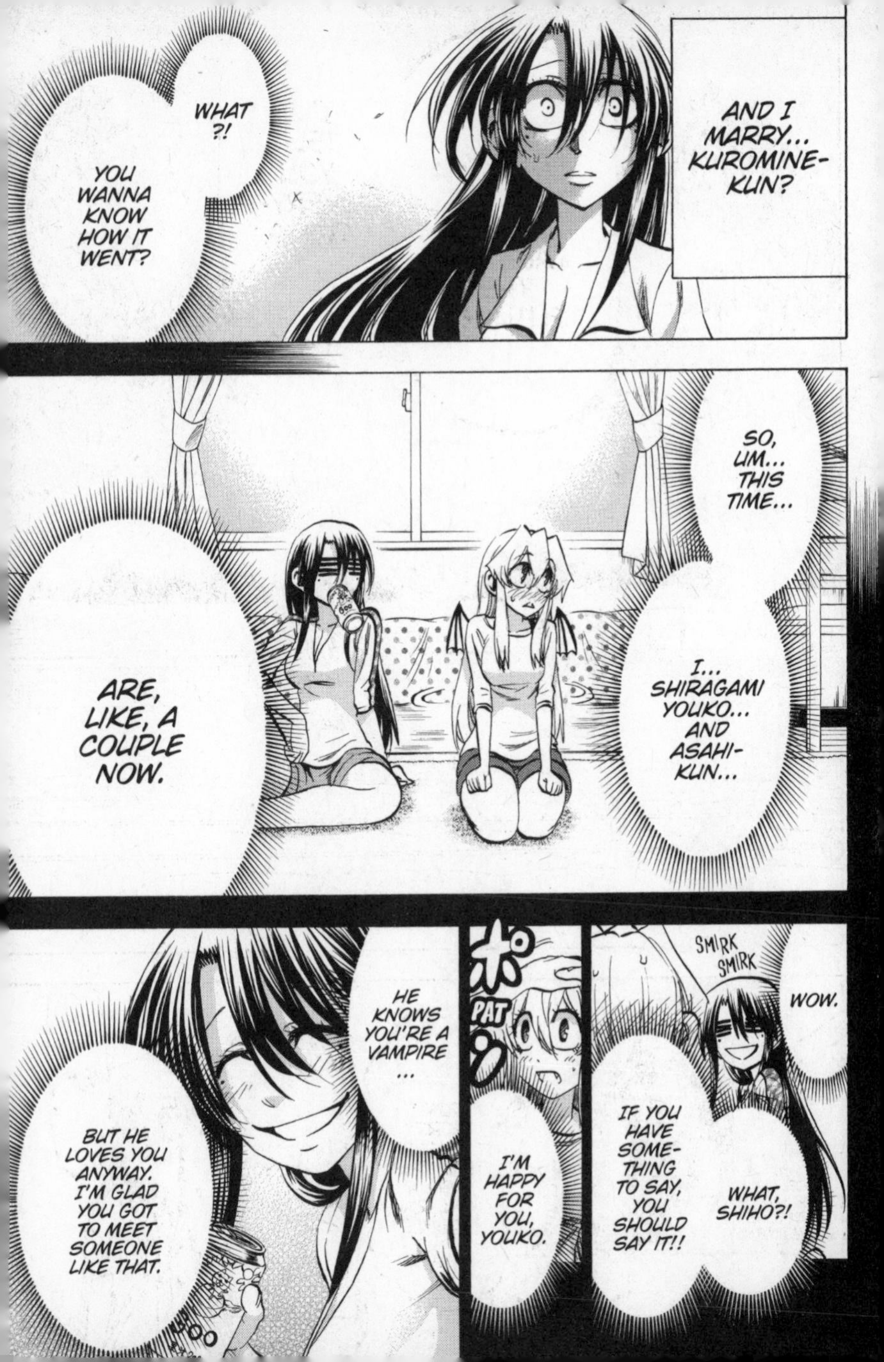

AND I MARRY... KUROMINE-KUN?
WHAT?!
YOU WANNA KNOW HOW IT WENT?
SO, UM... THIS TIME...
I... SHIRAGAMI YOUKO... AND ASAHI-KUN...
ARE, LIKE, A COUPLE NOW.
SMIRK SMIRK
WOW.
WHAT, SHIHO?!
IF YOU HAVE SOMETHING TO SAY, YOU SHOULD SAY IT!!
ポ
PAT
I'M HAPPY FOR YOU, YOUKO.
HE KNOWS YOU'RE A VAMPIRE...
BUT HE LOVES YOU ANYWAY. I'M GLAD YOU GOT TO MEET SOMEONE LIKE THAT.

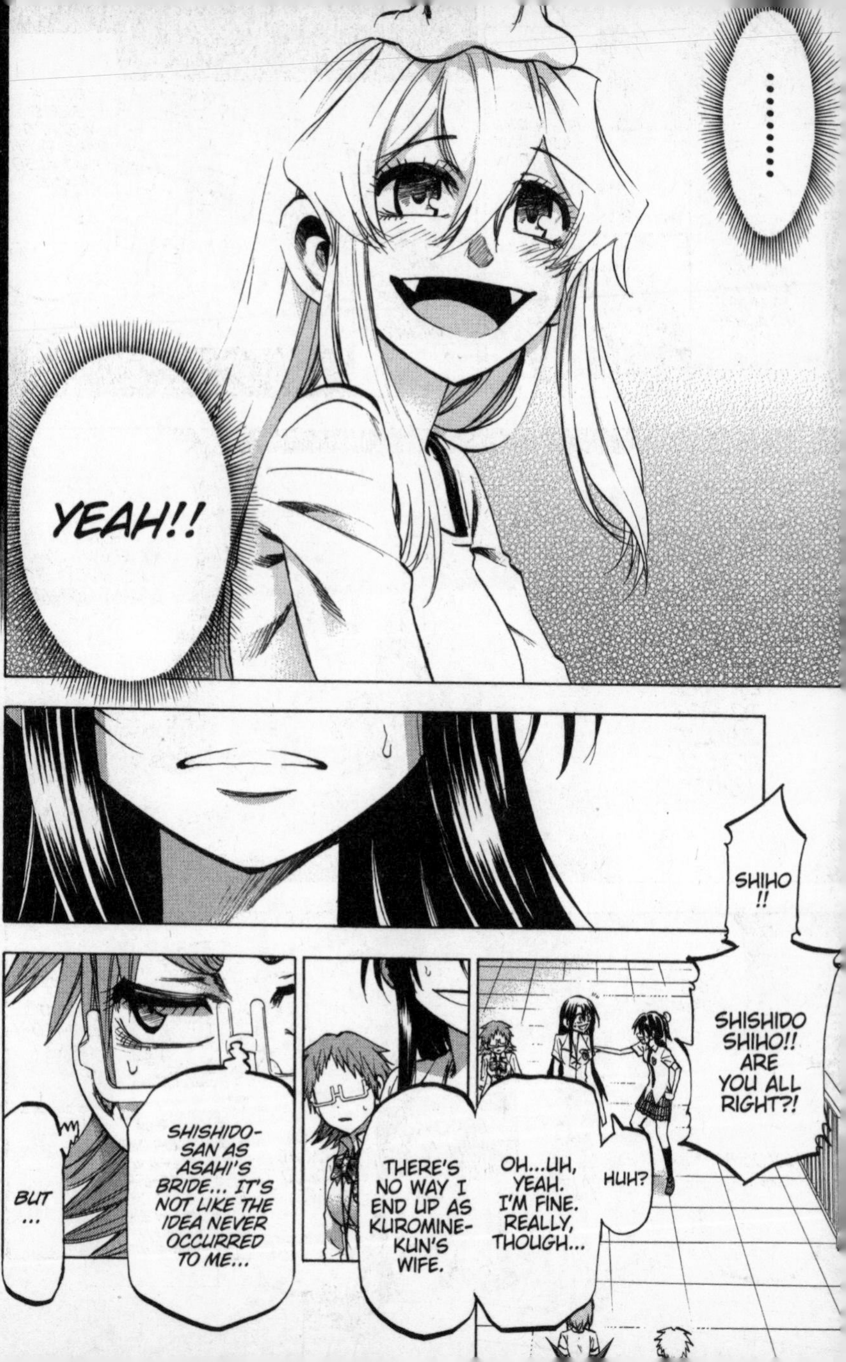
......
YEAH!!
SHIHO !!
SHISHIDO SHIHO!! ARE YOU ALL RIGHT?!
HUH?
OH...UH, YEAH. I'M FINE. REALLY, THOUGH...
THERE'S NO WAY I END UP AS KUROMINE-KUN'S WIFE.
SHISHIDO-SAN AS ASAHI'S BRIDE... IT'S NOT LIKE THE IDEA NEVER OCCURRED TO ME...
BUT ...

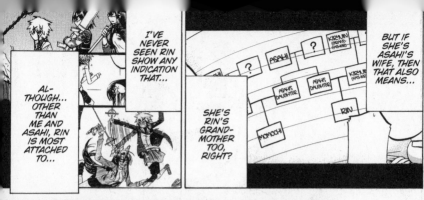

I'VE NEVER SEEN RIN SHOW ANY INDICATION THAT...

AL-THOUGH... OTHER THAN ME AND ASAHI, RIN IS MOST ATTACHED TO...

SHE'S RIN'S GRAND-MOTHER TOO, RIGHT?

BUT IF SHE'S ASAHI'S WIFE, THEN THAT ALSO MEANS...

KIRMUN (GRAND-FATHER)		
?	ASAHI	?
ASAHI'S DAUGHTER	ASAHI'S DAUGHTER	KIRMUN (FATHER)
MOMOCHI		RIN

"WELL, WHEN YOU FIND OUT WHO MOMOCHI'S GRANDMOTHER IS...

"BE NICE TO HER ABOUT IT, WILL YOU?"

FIRST... ACTUALLY, I...

MOMOCHI YUKA...

UM... WHERE SHOULD I START...?

WOULD I GET MAD AT SHISHIDO-SAN?

SHE HAS TWO GRAND-MOTHERS, SO WE DON'T KNOW SHE'S ASAHI'S WIFE YET...

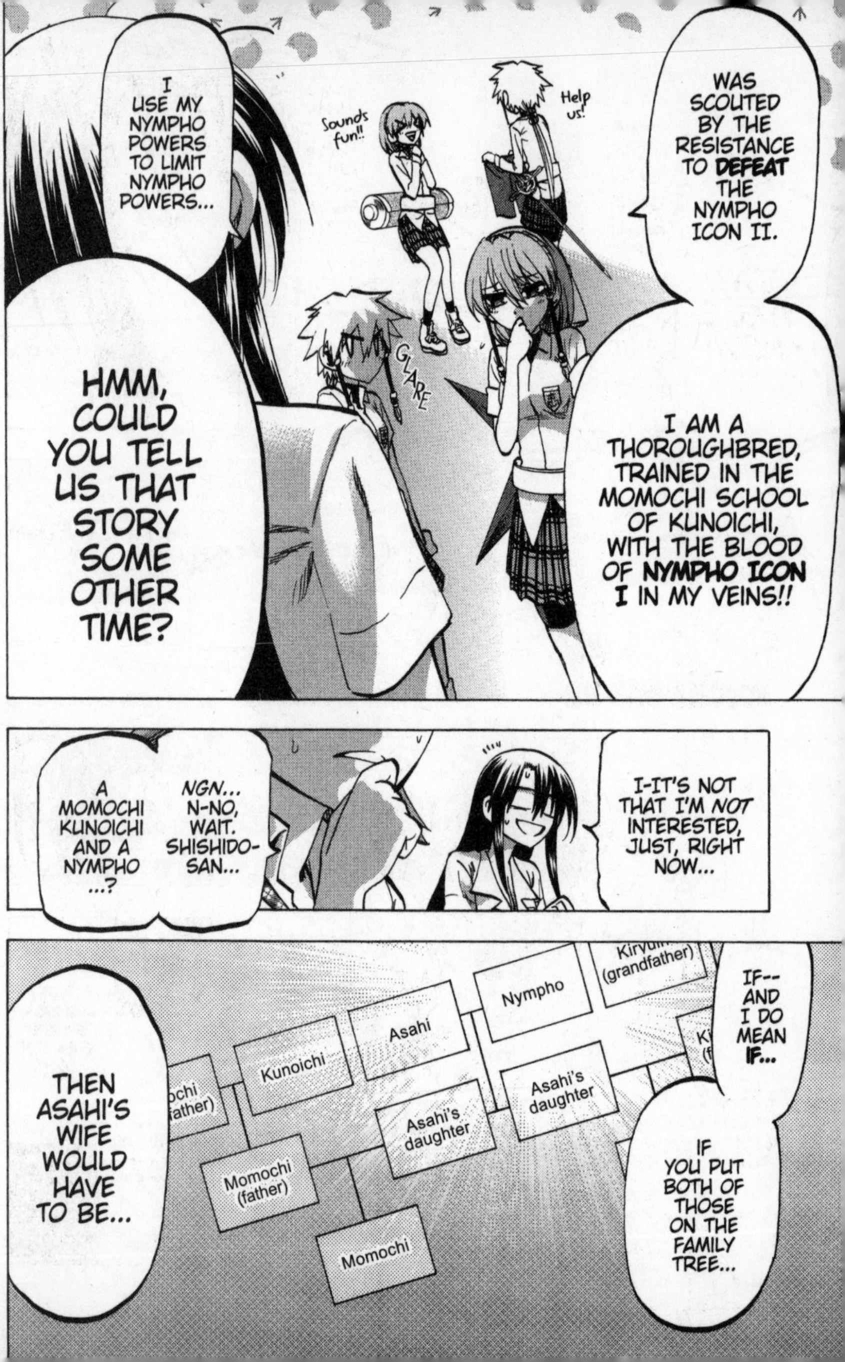
WAS SCOUTED BY THE RESISTANCE TO DEFEAT THE NYMPHO ICON II.
I AM A THOROUGHBRED, TRAINED IN THE MOMOCHI SCHOOL OF KUNOICHI, WITH THE BLOOD OF NYMPHO ICON I IN MY VEINS!!
Help us!
Sounds fun!!
GLARE
I USE MY NYMPHO POWERS TO LIMIT NYMPHO POWERS...
HMM, COULD YOU TELL US THAT STORY SOME OTHER TIME?
I-IT'S NOT THAT I'M NOT INTERESTED, JUST, RIGHT NOW...
NGN... N-NO, WAIT. SHISHIDO-SAN...
A MOMOCHI KUNOICHI AND A NYMPHO ...?
IF-- AND I DO MEAN IF...
IF YOU PUT BOTH OF THOSE ON THE FAMILY TREE...
(grandfather)
Nympho
Asahi
Kunoichi
Asahi's daughter
Asahi's daughter
Momochi (father)
Momochi
THEN ASAHI'S WIFE WOULD HAVE TO BE...

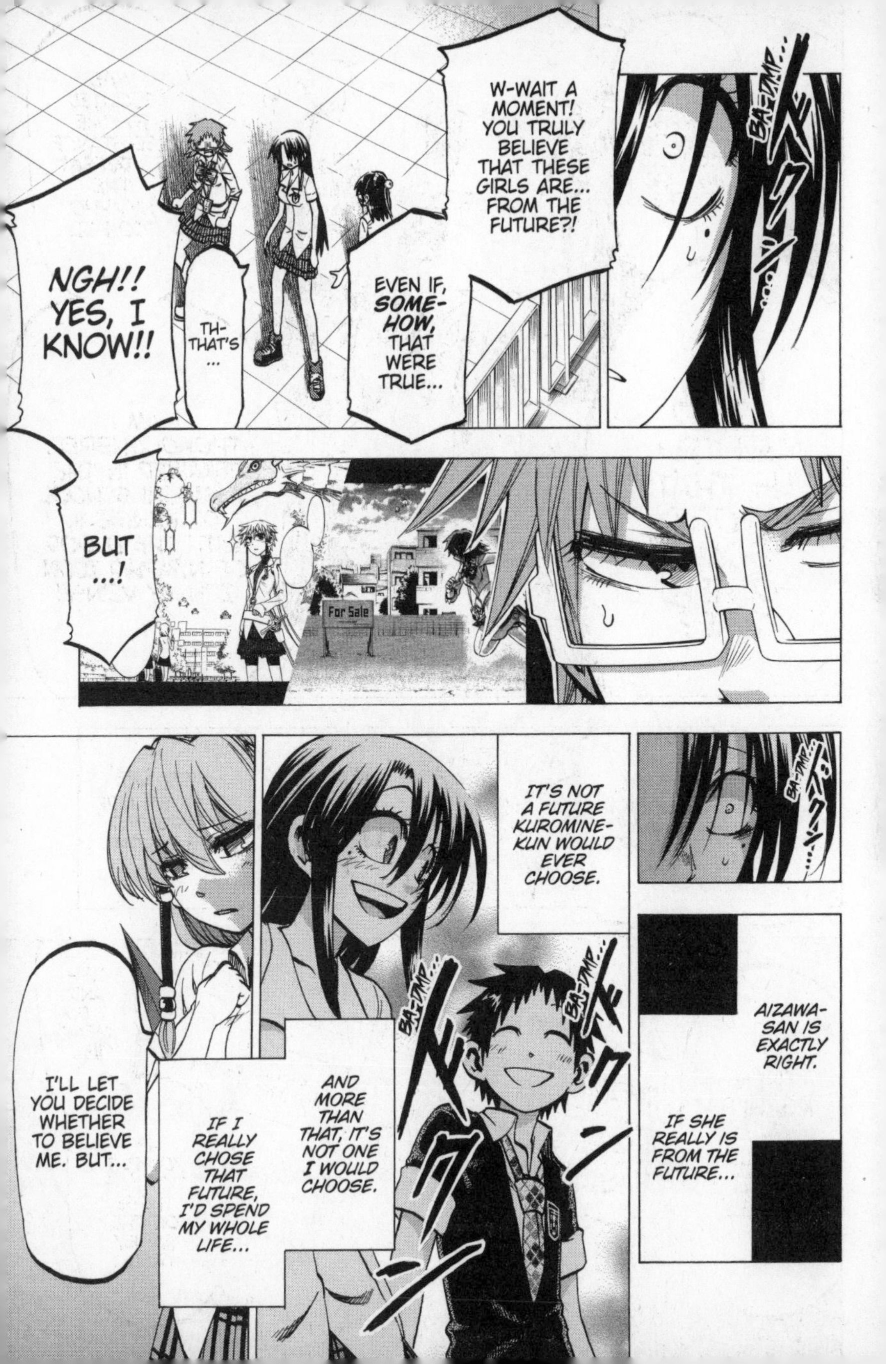
BA-DMP...
W-WAIT A MOMENT! YOU TRULY BELIEVE THAT THESE GIRLS ARE... FROM THE FUTURE?!
EVEN IF, SOMEHOW, THAT WERE TRUE...
TH-THAT'S ...
NGH!! YES, I KNOW!!
For Sale
BUT ...!
BA-DMP...
AIZAWA-SAN IS EXACTLY RIGHT.
IF SHE REALLY IS FROM THE FUTURE...
IT'S NOT A FUTURE KUROMINE-KUN WOULD EVER CHOOSE.
BA-DMP...
BA-DMP...
AND MORE THAN THAT, IT'S NOT ONE I WOULD CHOOSE.
IF I REALLY CHOSE THAT FUTURE, I'D SPEND MY WHOLE LIFE...
I'LL LET YOU DECIDE WHETHER TO BELIEVE ME. BUT...

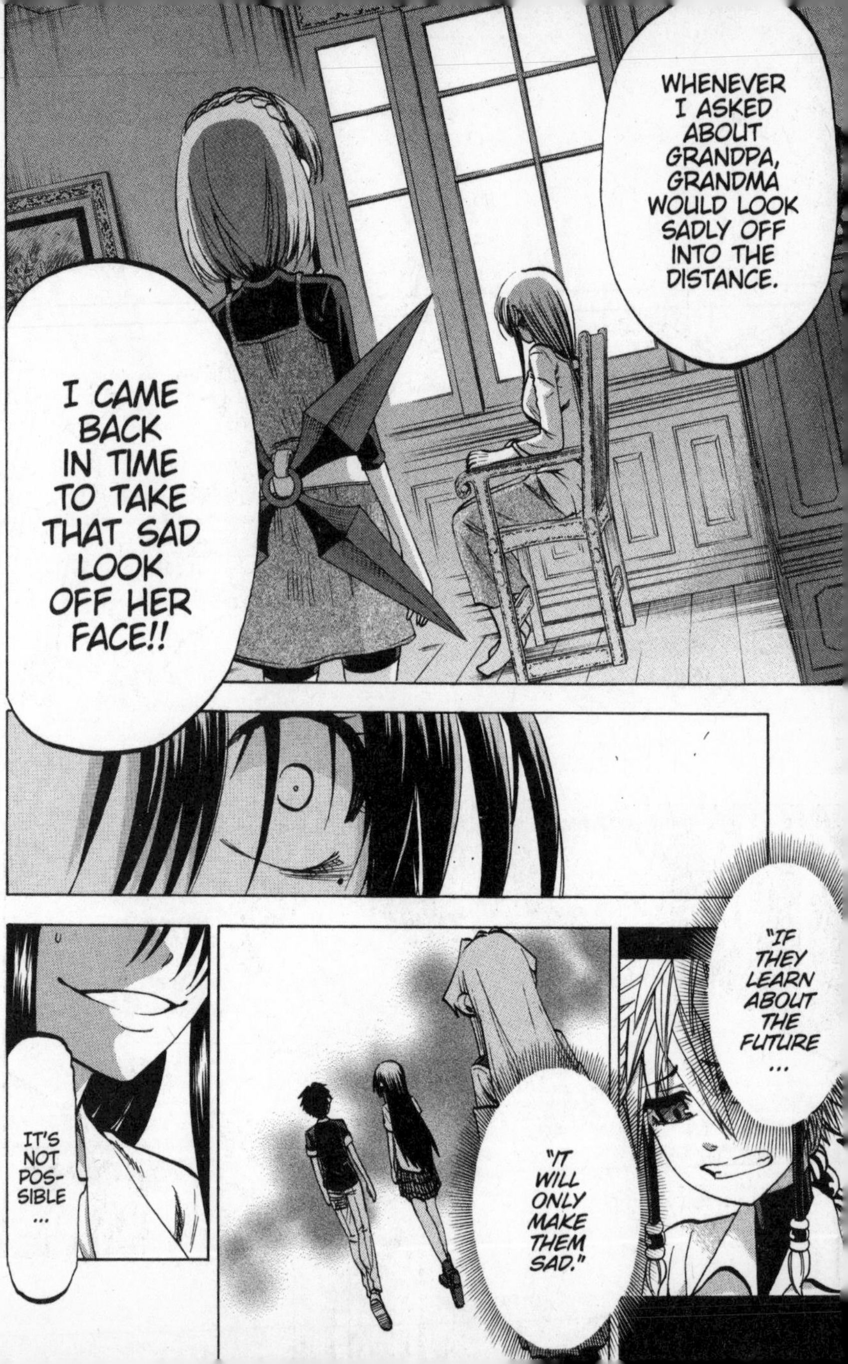
WHENEVER I ASKED ABOUT GRANDPA, GRANDMA WOULD LOOK SADLY OFF INTO THE DISTANCE.
I CAME BACK IN TIME TO TAKE THAT SAD LOOK OFF HER FACE!!
"IF THEY LEARN ABOUT THE FUTURE ...
"IT WILL ONLY MAKE THEM SAD."
IT'S NOT POS-SIBLE ...

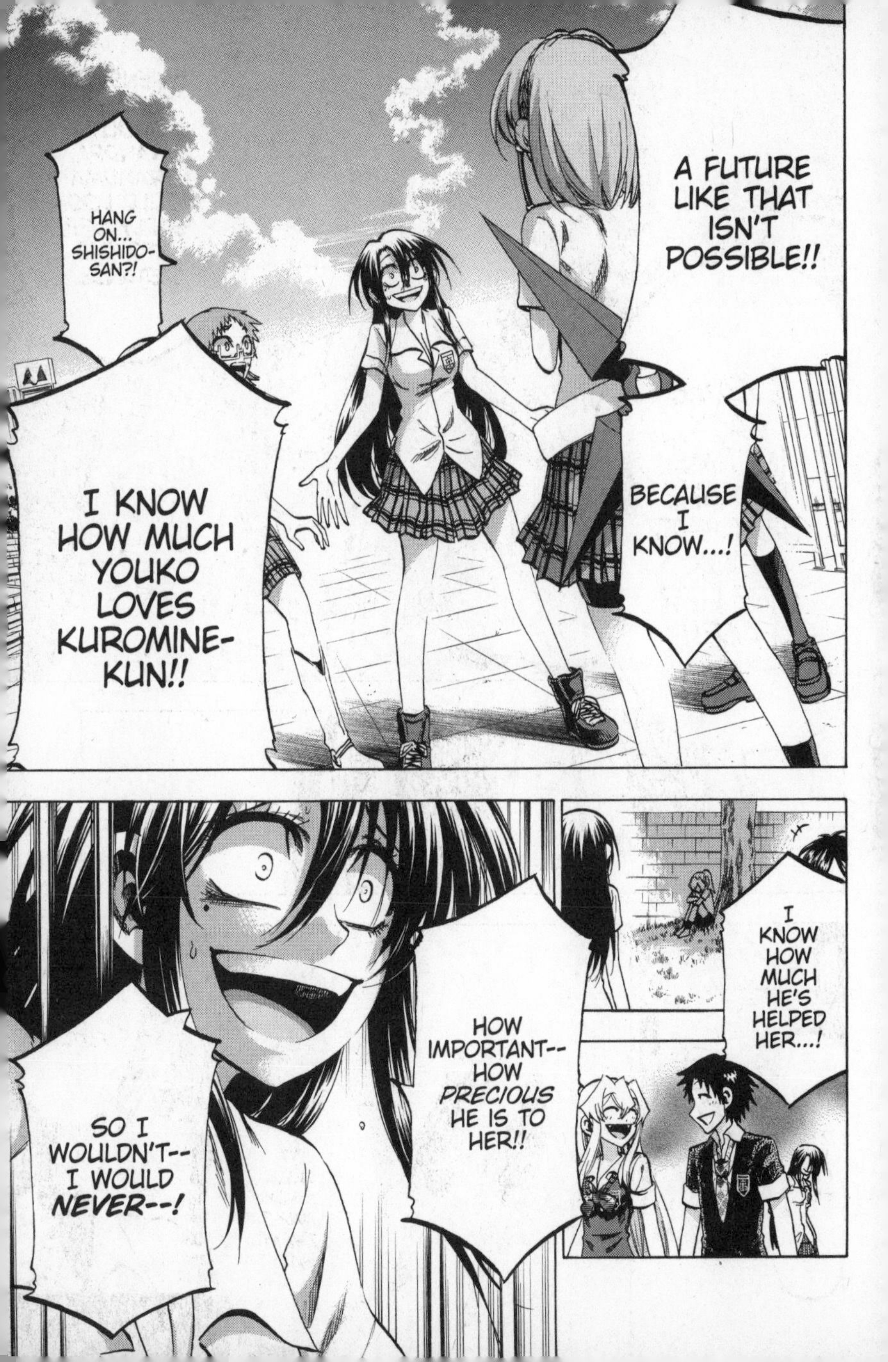
A FUTURE LIKE THAT ISN'T POSSIBLE!!
HANG ON... SHISHIDO-SAN?!
BECAUSE I KNOW...!
I KNOW HOW MUCH YOUKO LOVES KUROMINE-KUN!!
I KNOW HOW MUCH HE'S HELPED HER...!
HOW IMPORTANT--HOW *PRECIOUS* HE IS TO HER!!
SO I WOULDN'T--I WOULD *NEVER*--!

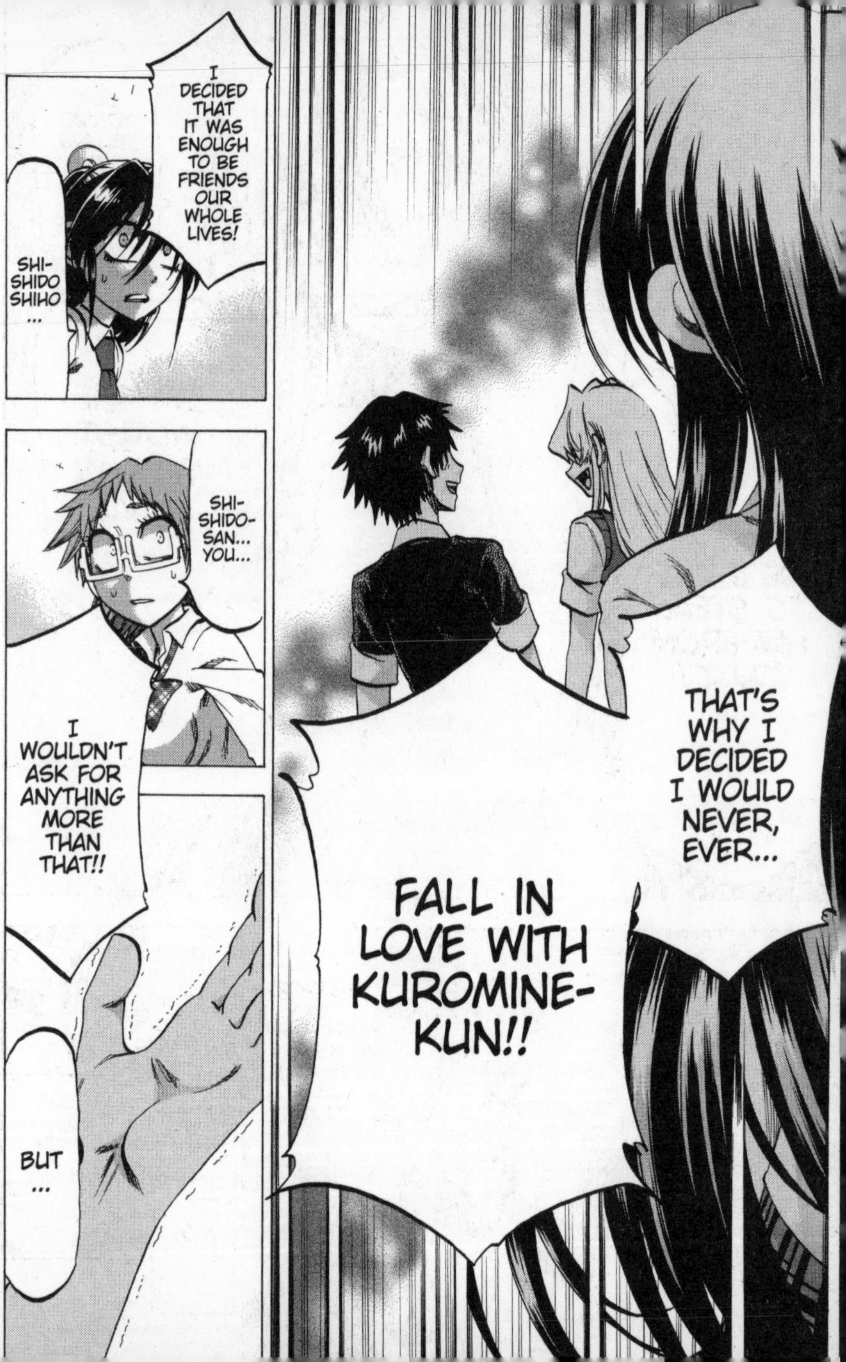
THAT'S WHY I DECIDED I WOULD NEVER, EVER...
FALL IN LOVE WITH KUROMINE-KUN!!
I DECIDED THAT IT WAS ENOUGH TO BE FRIENDS OUR WHOLE LIVES!
SHI-SHIDO SHIHO...
SHI-SHIDO-SAN... YOU...
I WOULDN'T ASK FOR ANYTHING MORE THAN THAT!!
BUT...

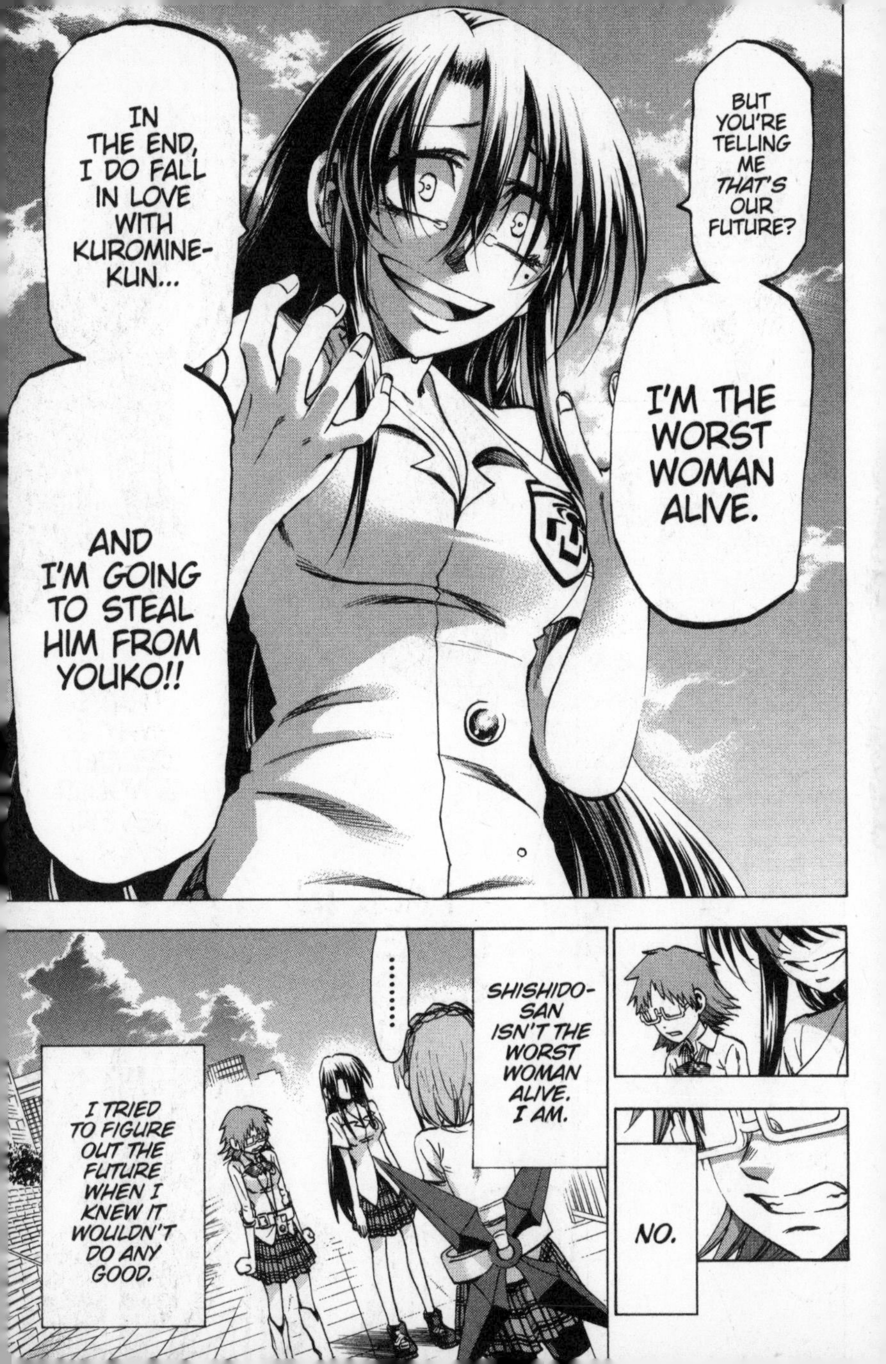
BUT YOU'RE TELLING ME *THAT'S* OUR FUTURE?
I'M THE WORST WOMAN ALIVE.
IN THE END, I DO FALL IN LOVE WITH KUROMINE-KUN...
AND I'M GOING TO STEAL HIM FROM YOUKO!!
NO.
SHISHIDO-SAN ISN'T THE WORST WOMAN ALIVE. I AM.
......
I TRIED TO FIGURE OUT THE FUTURE WHEN I KNEW IT WOULDN'T DO ANY GOOD.

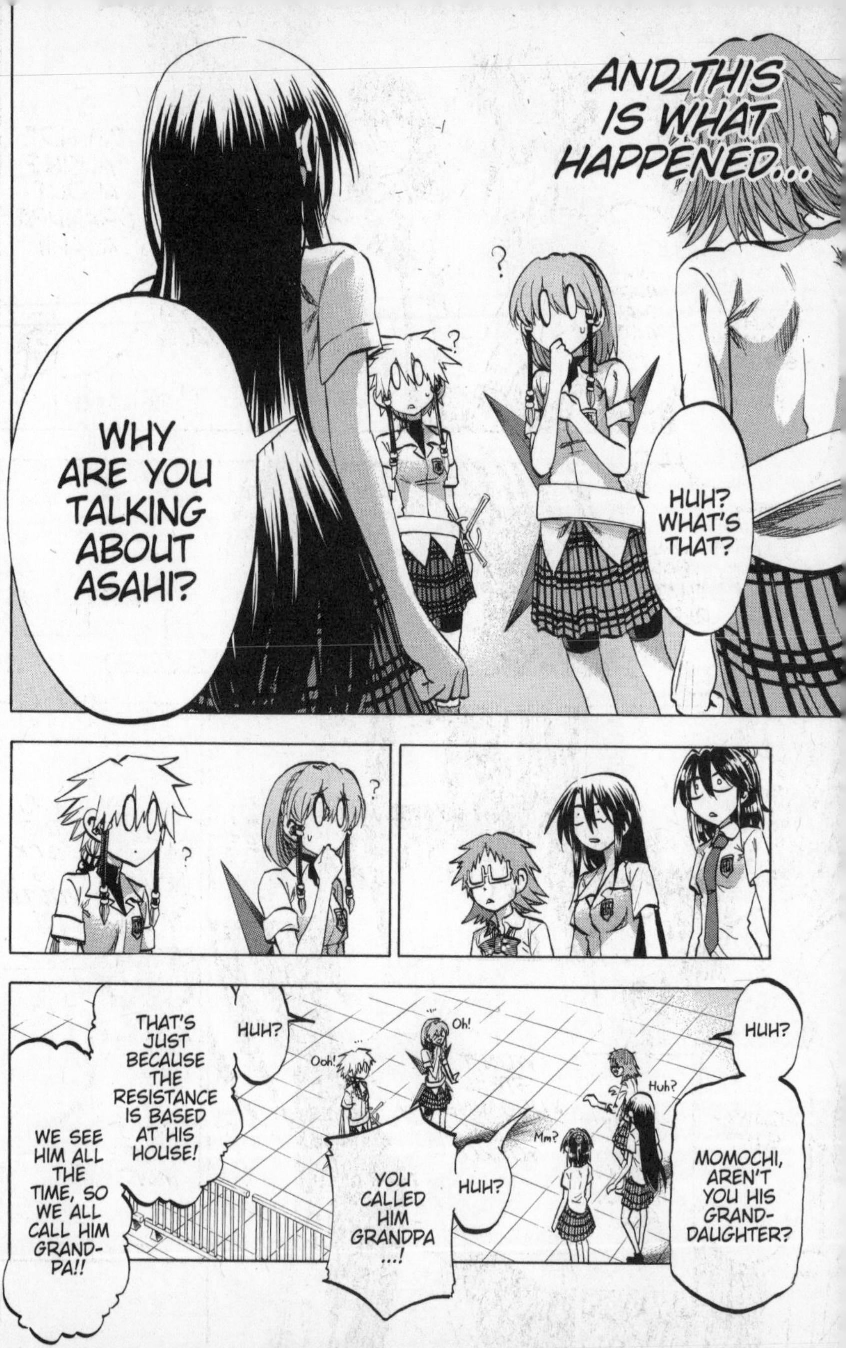
AND THIS IS WHAT HAPPENED...
HUH? WHAT'S THAT?
WHY ARE YOU TALKING ABOUT ASAHI?
?
?
?
?
HUH?
MOMOCHI, AREN'T YOU HIS GRAND-DAUGHTER?
Huh?
Mm?
HUH?
YOU CALLED HIM GRANDPA ...!
Oh!
Ooh!
HUH?
THAT'S JUST BECAUSE THE RESISTANCE IS BASED AT HIS HOUSE!
WE SEE HIM ALL THE TIME, SO WE ALL CALL HIM GRAND-PA!!

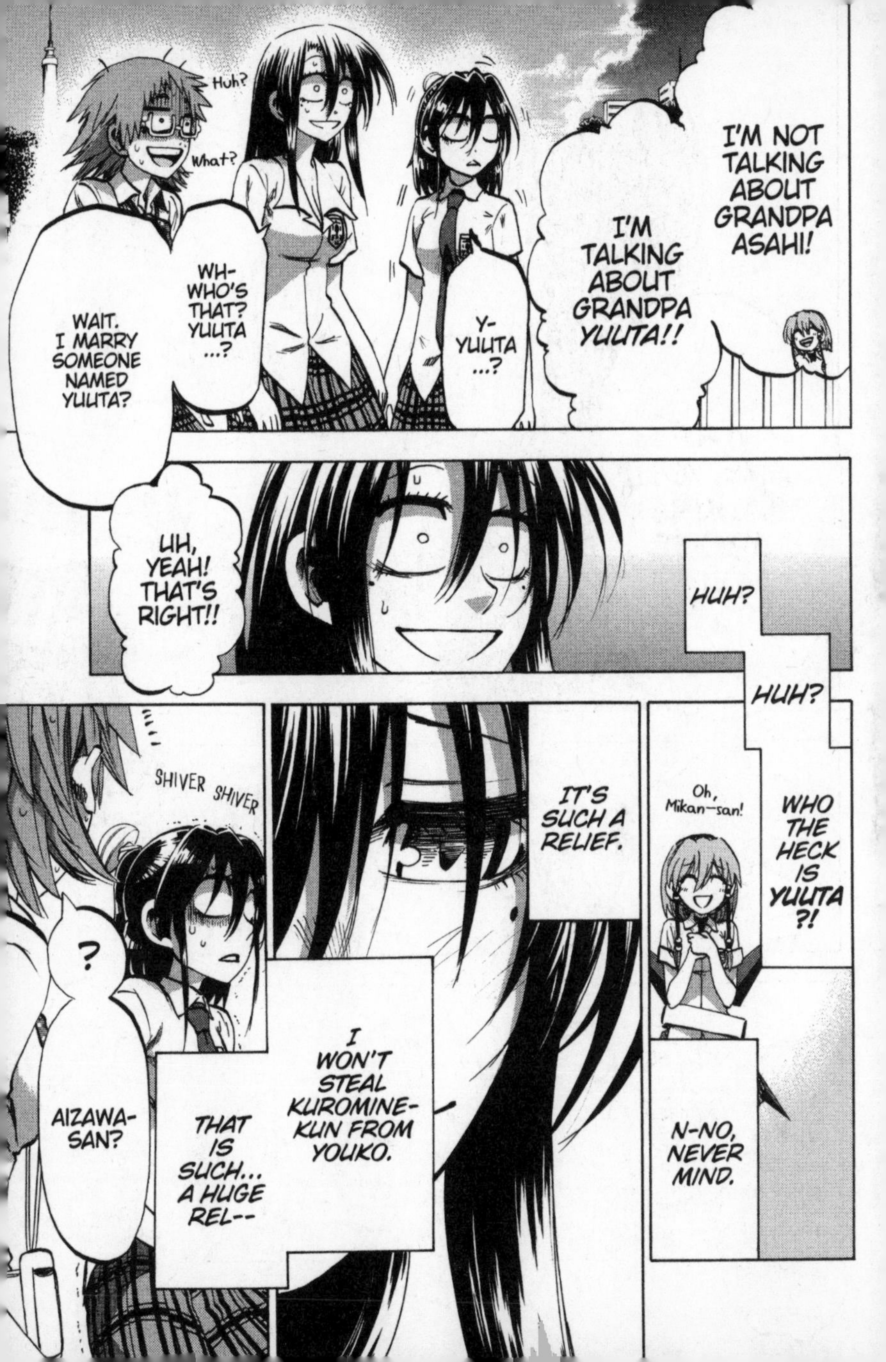
I'M NOT TALKING ABOUT GRANDPA ASAHI!
I'M TALKING ABOUT GRANDPA YUUTA!!
Y-YUUTA...?
WH-WHO'S THAT? YUUTA...?
Huh?
What?
WAIT. I MARRY SOMEONE NAMED YUUTA?
UH, YEAH! THAT'S RIGHT!!
HUH?
HUH?
WHO THE HECK IS YUUTA?!
Oh, Mikan-san!
N-NO, NEVER MIND.
IT'S SUCH A RELIEF.
I WON'T STEAL KUROMINE-KUN FROM YOUKO.
THAT IS SUCH... A HUGE REL--
SHIVER SHIVER
?
AIZAWA-SAN?

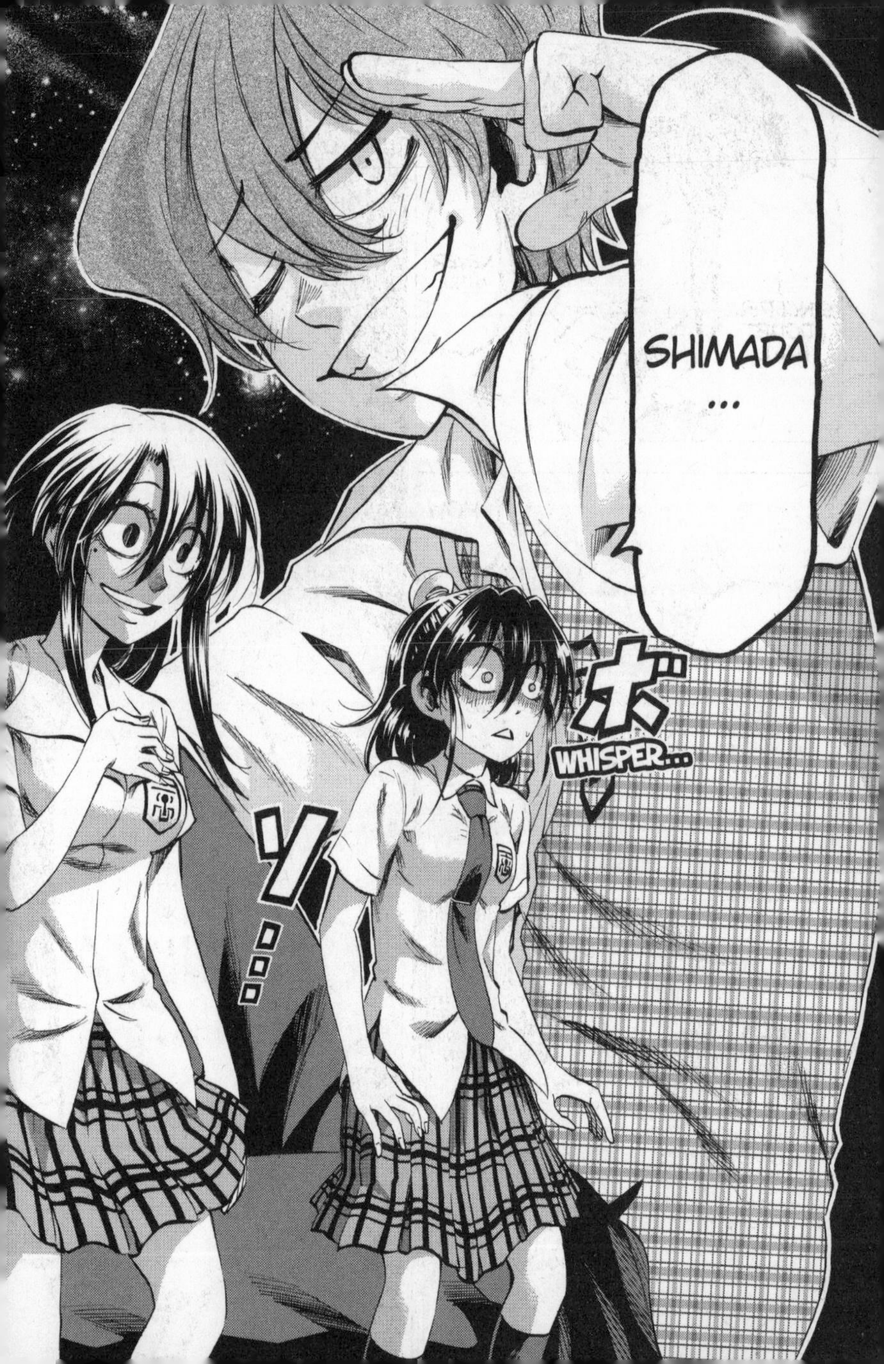
SHIMADA ...
ボ
WHISPER...
ソ...

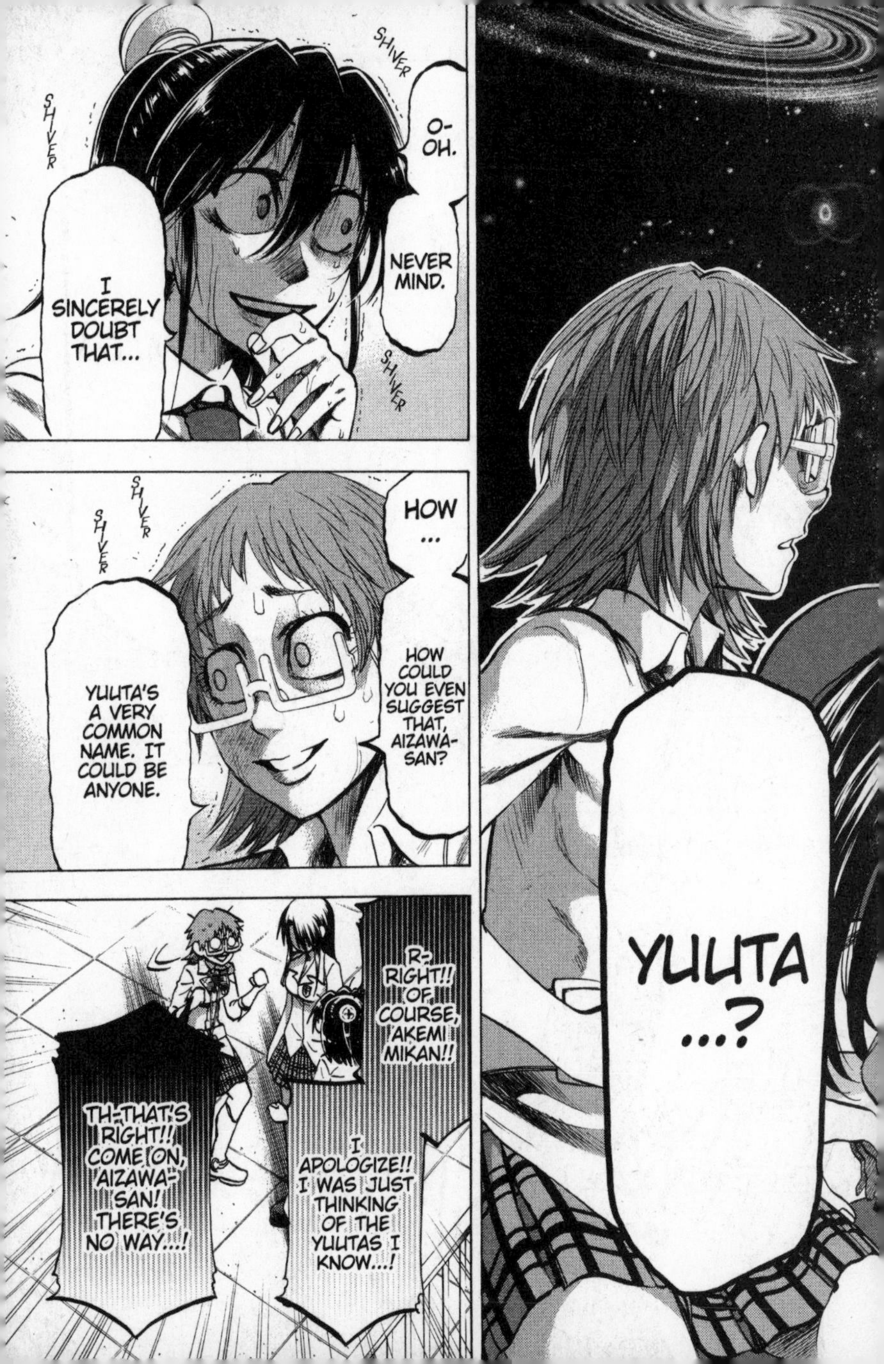
YUUTA ...?
SHIVER
O-OH.
NEVER MIND.
SHIVER
SHIVER
I SINCERELY DOUBT THAT...
HOW ...
HOW COULD YOU EVEN SUGGEST THAT, AIZAWA-SAN?
SHIVER
SHIVER
YUUTA'S A VERY COMMON NAME. IT COULD BE ANYONE.
R-RIGHT!! OF COURSE, AKEMI MIKAN!!
I APOLOGIZE!! I WAS JUST THINKING OF THE YUUTAS I KNOW...!
TH-THAT'S RIGHT!! COME ON, AIZAWA-SAN! THERE'S NO WAY...!

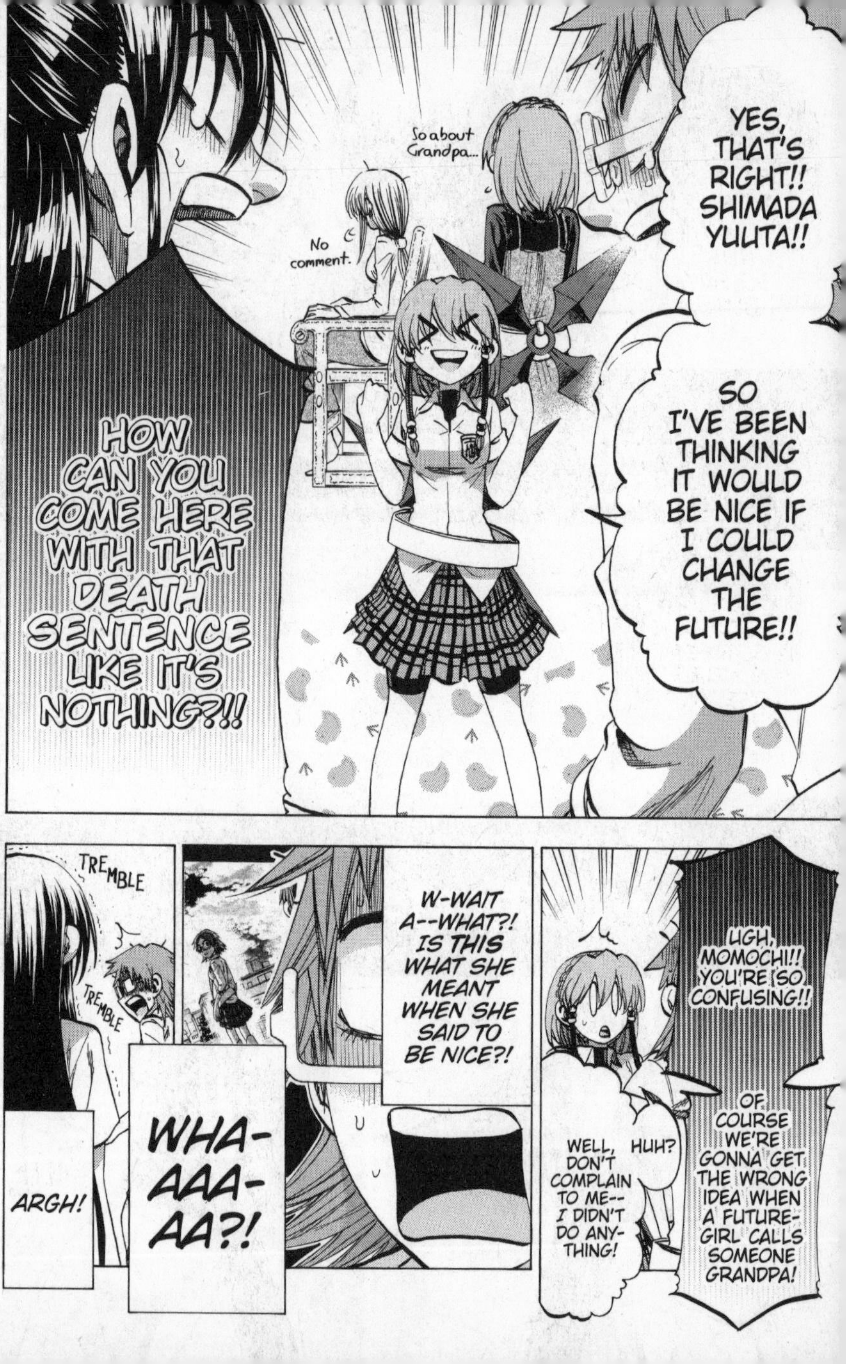
YES, THAT'S RIGHT!! SHIMADA YUUTA!!
SO I'VE BEEN THINKING IT WOULD BE NICE IF I COULD CHANGE THE FUTURE!!
So about Grandpa...
No comment.
HOW CAN YOU COME HERE WITH THAT DEATH SENTENCE LIKE IT'S NOTHING?!!
UGH, MOMOCHI!! YOU'RE SO CONFUSING!!
OF COURSE WE'RE GONNA GET THE WRONG IDEA WHEN A FUTURE-GIRL CALLS SOMEONE GRANDPA!
HUH?
WELL, DON'T COMPLAIN TO ME-- I DIDN'T DO ANYTHING!
W-WAIT A--WHAT?! IS THIS WHAT SHE MEANT WHEN SHE SAID TO BE NICE?!
WHA-AAAA-AA?!
TREMBLE
TREMBLE
ARGH!

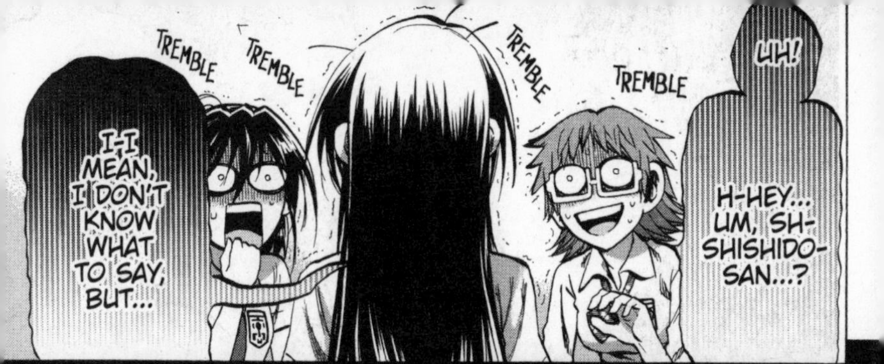
UH!
H-HEY... UM, SH-SHISHIDO-SAN...?
TREMBLE
TREMBLE
TREMBLE
TREMBLE
I-I MEAN, I DON'T KNOW WHAT TO SAY, BUT...

My Monster Secret

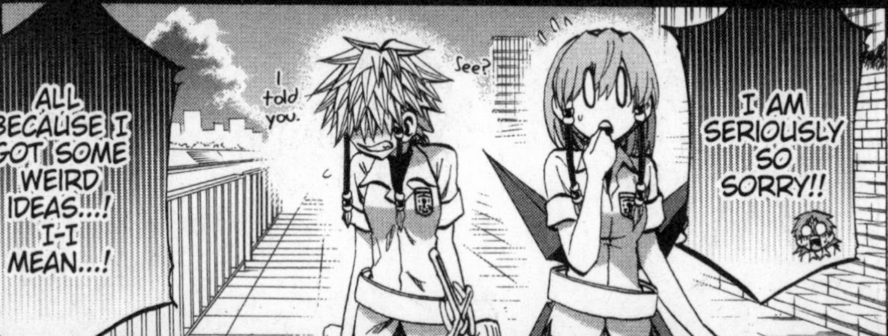
I AM SERIOUSLY SO SORRY!!
See?
I told you.
ALL BECAUSE I GOT SOME WEIRD IDEAS...! I-I MEAN...!

Chapter 124

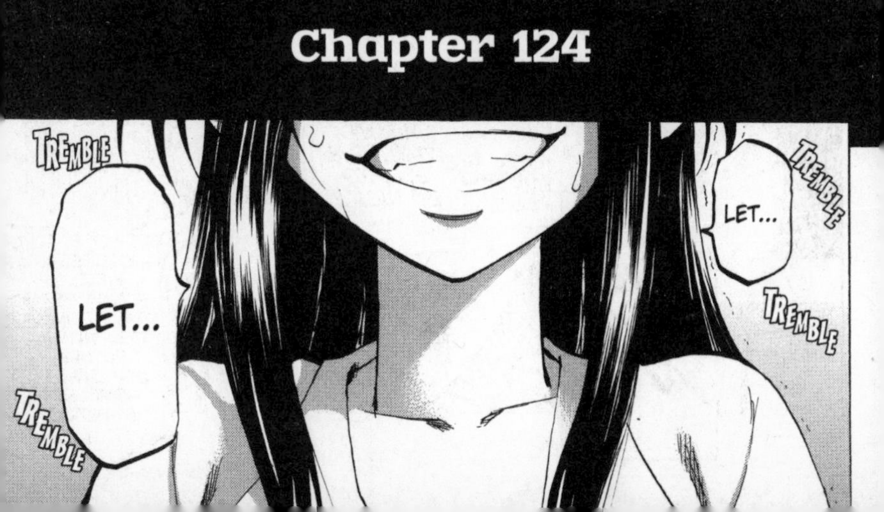
TREMBLE
LET...
TREMBLE
TREMBLE
LET...
TREMBLE

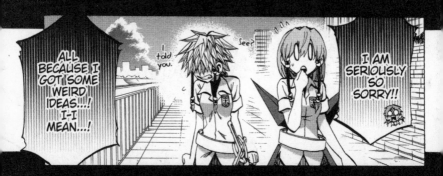

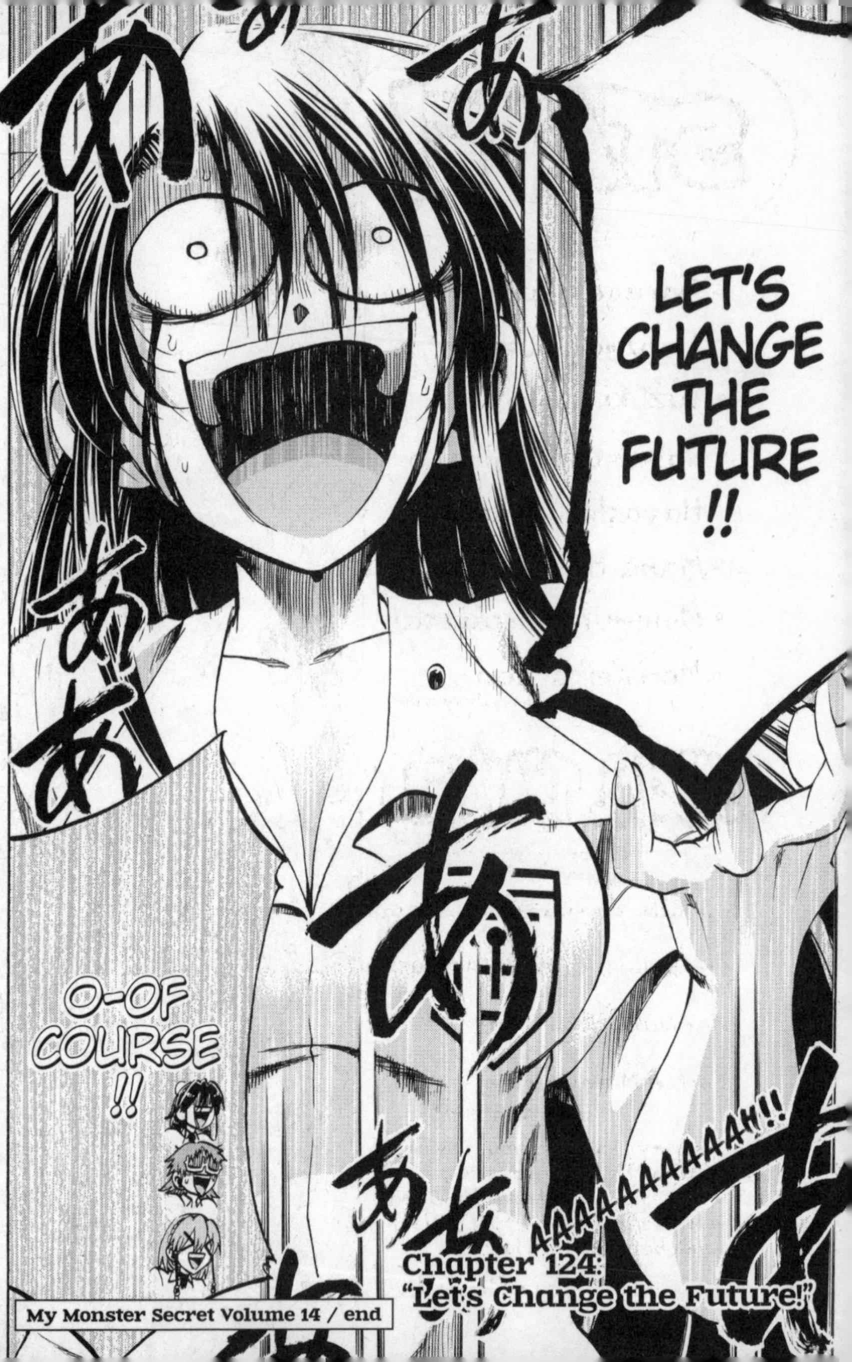
LET'S CHANGE THE FUTURE!!
AAAAAAAAAAAAH!!
O-OF COURSE!!
Chapter 124: "Let's Change the Future!"
My Monster Secret Volume 14 / end

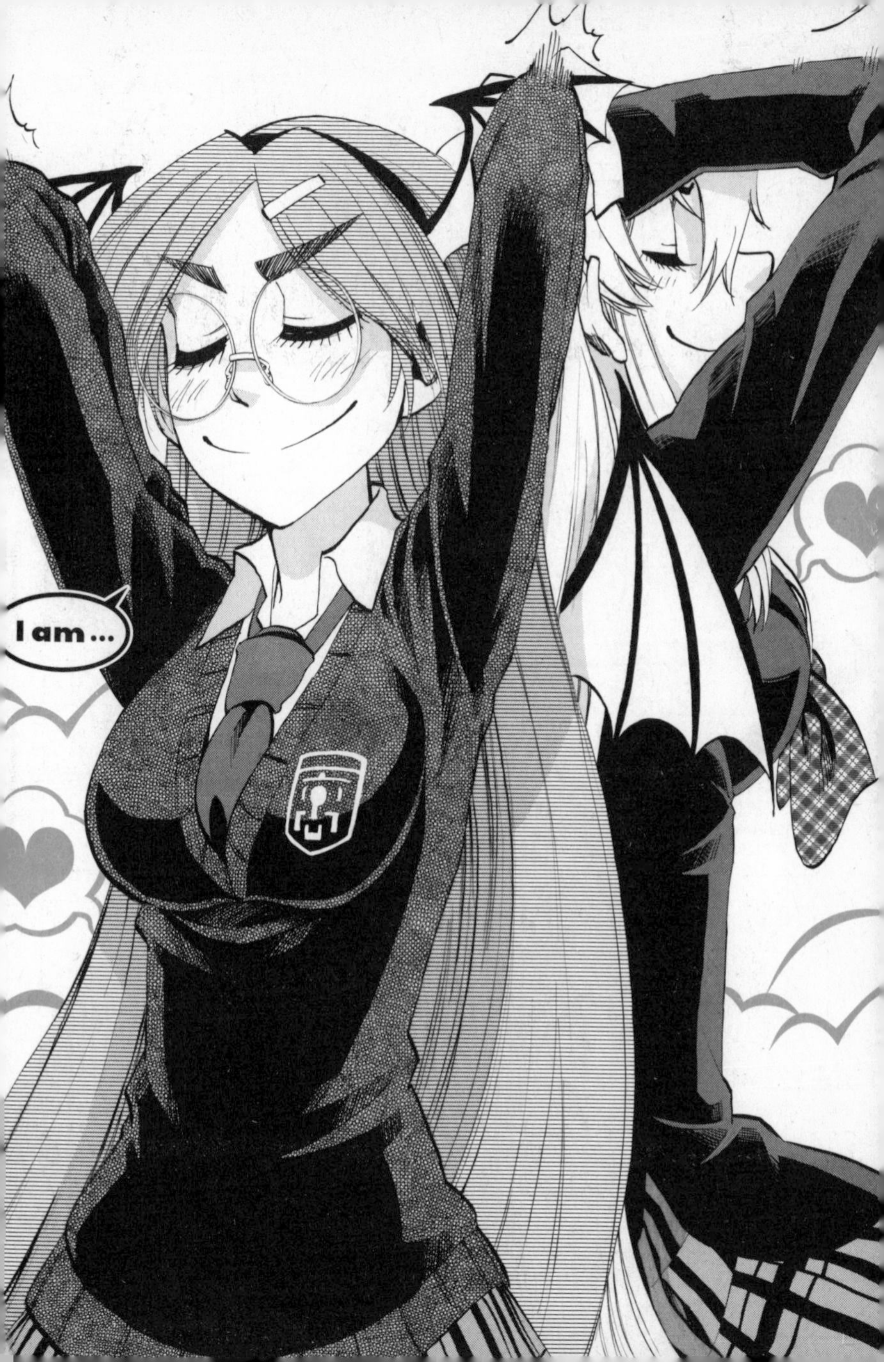
I am...

I am 14

After Teacher ①

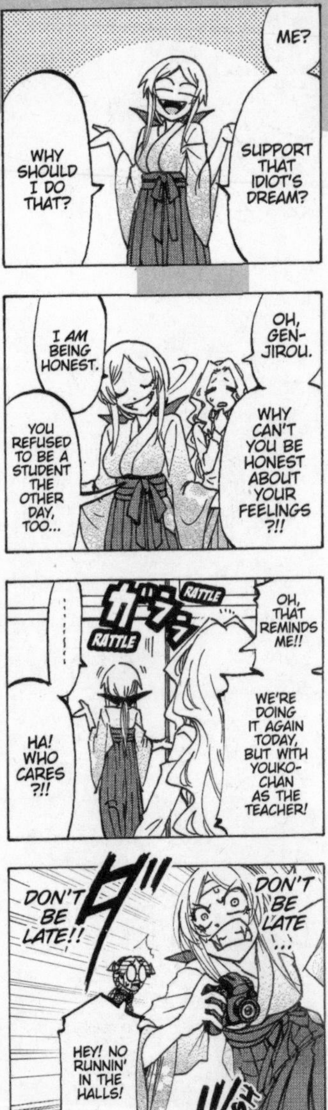
ME?
SUPPORT THAT IDIOT'S DREAM?
WHY SHOULD I DO THAT?
OH, GEN-JIROU.
WHY CAN'T YOU BE HONEST ABOUT YOUR FEELINGS?!!
I AM BEING HONEST.
YOU REFUSED TO BE A STUDENT THE OTHER DAY, TOO...
OH, THAT REMINDS ME!!
RATTLE
RATTLE
WE'RE DOING IT AGAIN TODAY, BUT WITH YOUKO-CHAN AS THE TEACHER!
......
HA! WHO CARES?!!
DON'T BE LATE...
DON'T BE LATE!!
HEY! NO RUNNIN' IN THE HALLS!
DASH

After Teacher ②

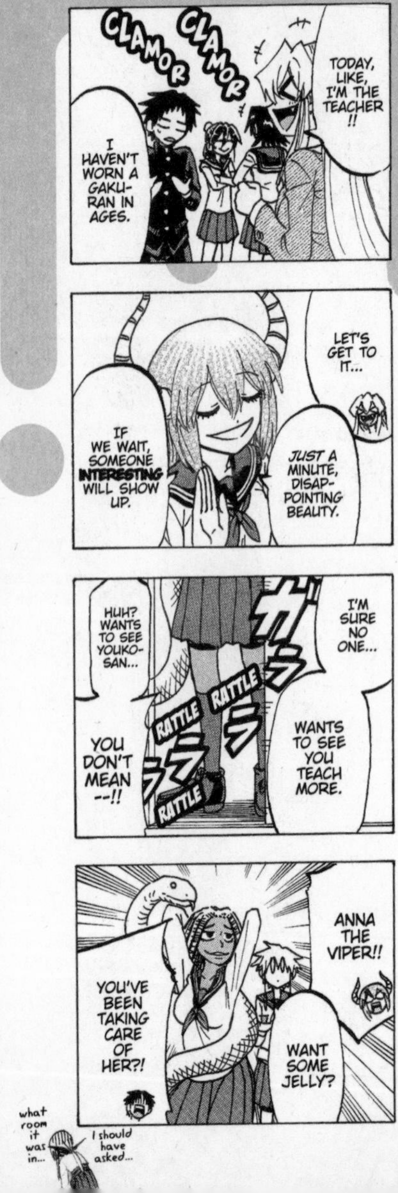
CLAMOR
CLAMOR
TODAY, LIKE, I'M THE TEACHER!!
I HAVEN'T WORN A GAKU-RAN IN AGES.
LET'S GET TO IT...
JUST A MINUTE, DISAP-POINTING BEAUTY.
IF WE WAIT, SOMEONE INTERESTING WILL SHOW UP.
I'M SURE NO ONE...
WANTS TO SEE YOU TEACH MORE.
HUH? WANTS TO SEE YOUKO-SAN...
YOU DON'T MEAN--!!
RATTLE
RATTLE
RATTLE
RATTLE
ANNA THE VIPER!!
WANT SOME JELLY?
YOU'VE BEEN TAKING CARE OF HER?!
I should have asked...
what room it was in...

I am... 14

After Nagashi Somen

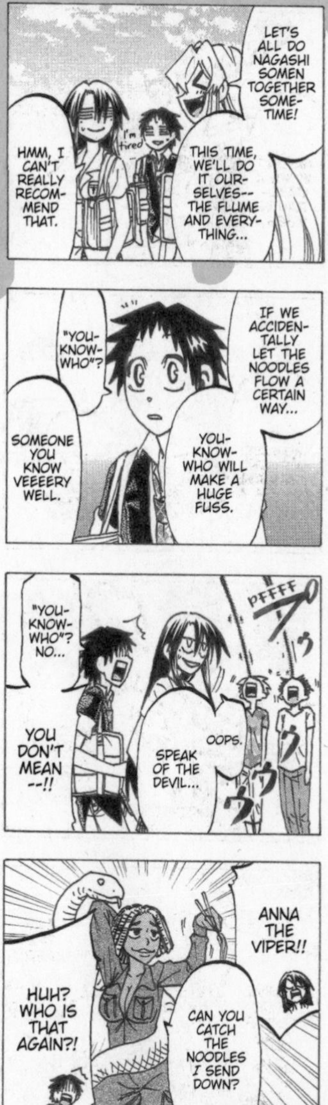
LET'S ALL DO NAGASHI SOMEN TOGETHER SOMETIME!
I'm tired
THIS TIME, WE'LL DO IT OURSELVES-- THE FLUME AND EVERYTHING...
HMM, I CAN'T REALLY RECOMMEND THAT.
IF WE ACCIDENTALLY LET THE NOODLES FLOW A CERTAIN WAY...
"YOU-KNOW-WHO"?
YOU-KNOW-WHO WILL MAKE A HUGE FUSS.
SOMEONE YOU KNOW VEEEERY WELL.
PFFFF
"YOU-KNOW-WHO"? NO...
OOPS.
SPEAK OF THE DEVIL...
YOU DON'T MEAN--!!
ANNA THE VIPER!!
CAN YOU CATCH THE NOODLES *I* SEND DOWN?
HUH? WHO IS THAT AGAIN?!

After Rhinoceros Beetles

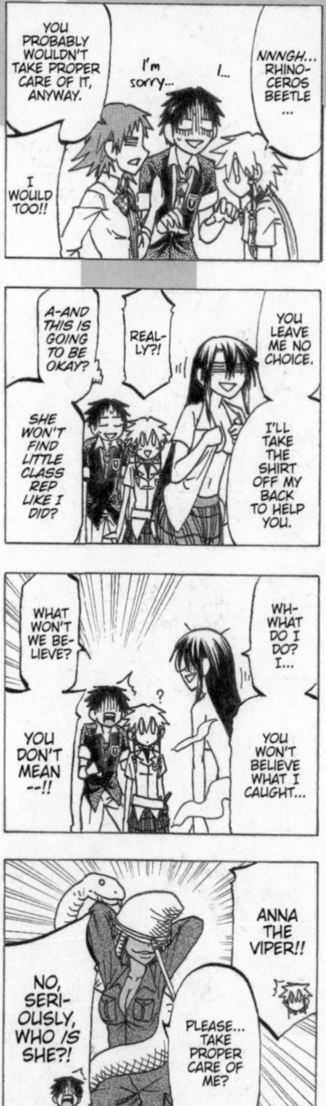
NNNGH... RHINOCEROS BEETLE...
I...
I'm sorry...
YOU PROBABLY WOULDN'T TAKE PROPER CARE OF IT, ANYWAY.
I WOULD TOO!!
YOU LEAVE ME NO CHOICE.
REALLY?!
A-AND THIS IS GOING TO BE OKAY?
I'LL TAKE THE SHIRT OFF MY BACK TO HELP YOU.
SHE WON'T FIND LITTLE CLASS REP LIKE I DID?
WH-WHAT DO I DO? I...
WHAT WON'T WE BELIEVE?
YOU WON'T BELIEVE WHAT I CAUGHT...
YOU DON'T MEAN--!!
ANNA THE VIPER!!
PLEASE... TAKE PROPER CARE OF ME?
NO, SERIOUSLY, WHO *IS* SHE?!

STAFF!

- Garage Okada-san
- Shuumeigiku-san
- Suzuki Seijun-san
- Nakamura Yuji-san
- Hayashi Rie-san
- Mana Haruki-san
- Minemura Hiroki-san
- Mori Keiko-san
  (in syllabary order)

SPECIAL THANKS!!

- Adachi-san
- Araki Nozomu-san
- Katou Shinichi-san
- Kishida Akari-san
- Daifuku Mochiko-san
- Yuoka Youko-san

Editor: Mukawa-san,
         Otsuka-san

I give my thanks to you, the one
holding this book right now,
everyone who watched the anime,
and everyone who let me and my
work be a part of their lives.

Eiji Masuda